Data Mining Tools for Malware Detection

IT MANAGEMENT TITLES
FROM AUERBACH PUBLICATIONS AND CRC PRESS

Data Mining Tools for Malware Detection

Mehedy Masud, Latifur Khan, and Bhavani Thuraisingham

CRC Press
Taylor & Francis Group
Boca Raton   London   New York

CRC Press is an imprint of the
Taylor & Francis Group, an **informa** business
AN AUERBACH BOOK

CRC Press
Taylor & Francis Group
6000 Broken Sound Parkway NW, Suite 300
Boca Raton, FL 33487-2742

© 2012 by Taylor & Francis Group, LLC
CRC Press is an imprint of Taylor & Francis Group, an Informa business

No claim to original U.S. Government works

Printed in the United States of America on acid-free paper
Version Date: 20111020

International Standard Book Number: 978-1-4398-5454-9 (Hardback)

Library of Congress Cataloging-in-Publication Data

Masud, Mehedy.
    Data mining tools for malware detection / Mehedy Masud, Latifur Khan, Bhavani Thuraisingham.
        p. cm.
    Includes bibliographical references and index.
    ISBN 978-1-4398-5454-9 (hardcover : alk. paper)
    1. Data mining. 2. Computer security. 3. Computer networks--Security measures. I. Khan, Latifur. II. Thuraisingham, Bhavani M. III. Title.

QA76.9.D343M385 2012
005.8--dc23   2011039383

Visit the Taylor & Francis Web site at
http://www.taylorandfrancis.com

and the CRC Press Web site at
http://www.crcpress.com

Dedication

We dedicate this book to our respective families for their support that enabled us to write this book.

Contents

Preface

Introductory Remarks

Data mining is the process of posing queries to large quantities of data and extracting information, often previously unknown, using mathematical, statistical, and machine learning techniques. Data mining has many applications in a number of areas, including marketing and sales, web and e-commerce, medicine, law, manufacturing, and, more recently, national and cyber security. For example, using data mining, one can uncover hidden dependencies between terrorist groups, as well as possibly predict terrorist events based on past experience. Furthermore, one can apply data mining techniques for targeted markets to improve e-commerce. Data mining can be applied to multimedia, including video analysis and image classification. Finally, data mining can be used in security applications, such as suspicious event detection and malicious software detection. Our previous book focused on data mining tools for applications in intrusion detection, image classification, and web surfing. In this book, we focus entirely on the data mining tools we have developed for cyber security applications. In particular, it extends the work we presented in our previous book on data mining for intrusion detection. The cyber security applications we discuss are email worm detection, malicious code detection, remote exploit detection, and botnet detection. In addition, some other tools for stream mining, insider threat detection, adaptable malware detection, real-time data mining, and firewall policy analysis are discussed.

We are writing two series of books related to data management, data mining, and data security. This book is the second in our second series of books, which describes techniques and tools in detail and is co-authored with faculty and students at the University of Texas at Dallas. It has evolved from the first series of books (by single author Bhavani Thuraisingham), which currently consists of ten books. These ten books are the following: Book 1 (*Data Management Systems Evolution and Interoperation*) discussed data management systems and interoperability. Book 2 (*Data Mining*) provided an overview of data mining concepts. Book 3 (*Web Data Management and E-Commerce*) discussed concepts in web databases and e-commerce. Book 4 (*Managing and Mining Multimedia Databases*) discussed concepts in multimedia data management as well as text, image, and video mining. Book 5 (*XML Databases and the Semantic Web*) discussed high-level concepts relating to the semantic web. Book 6 (*Web Data Mining and Applications in Counter-Terrorism*) discussed how data mining may be applied to national security. Book 7 (*Database and Applications Security*), which is a textbook, discussed details of data security. Book 8 (*Building Trustworthy Semantic Webs*), also a textbook, discussed how semantic webs may be made secure. Book 9 (*Secure Semantic Service-Oriented Systems*) is on secure web services. Book 10, to be published in early 2012, is titled *Building and Securing the Cloud*. Our first book in Series 2 is *Design and Implementation of Data Mining Tools*. Our current book (which is the second book of Series 2) has evolved from Books 3, 4, 6, and 7 of Series 1 and book 1 of Series 2. It is mainly based on the research work carried out at The University of Texas at Dallas by Dr. Mehedy Masud for his PhD thesis with his advisor Professor Latifur Khan and supported by the Air Force Office of Scientific Research from 2005 until now.

Background on Data Mining

Data mining is the process of posing various queries and extracting useful information, patterns, and trends, often previously unknown, from large quantities of data possibly stored in databases. Essentially, for many organizations, the goals of data mining include improving marketing capabilities, detecting abnormal patterns, and predicting the future based on past experiences and current trends. There is clearly a need for this technology. There are large amounts of current and historical data being stored. Therefore, as databases become larger, it becomes increasingly difficult to support decision making. In addition, the data could be from multiple sources and multiple domains. There is a clear need to analyze the data to support planning and other functions of an enterprise.

Some of the data mining techniques include those based on statistical reasoning techniques, inductive logic programming, machine learning, fuzzy sets, and neural networks, among others. The data mining problems include classification (finding rules to partition data into groups), association (finding rules to make associations between data), and sequencing (finding rules to order data). Essentially one arrives at some hypothesis, which is the information extracted from examples and patterns observed. These patterns are observed from posing a series of queries; each query may depend on the responses obtained from the previous queries posed.

Data mining is an integration of multiple technologies. These include data management such as database management, data warehousing, statistics, machine learning, decision support, and others, such as visualization and parallel computing. There is a series of steps involved in data mining. These include getting the data organized for mining, determining the desired outcomes to mining, selecting tools for mining, carrying out the mining process, pruning the results so that only the useful ones are considered further, taking actions from the mining, and evaluating the actions to determine benefits. There are various types of data mining. By this we do not mean the actual techniques used to mine the data but what the outcomes will be. These outcomes have also been referred to as data mining tasks. These include clustering, classification, anomaly detection, and forming associations.

Although several developments have been made, there are many challenges that remain. For example, because of the large volumes of data, how can the algorithms determine which technique to select and what type of data mining to do? Furthermore, the data may be incomplete, inaccurate, or both. At times there may be redundant information, and at times there may not be sufficient information. It is also desirable to have data mining tools that can switch to multiple techniques and support multiple outcomes. Some of the current trends in data mining include mining web data, mining distributed and heterogeneous databases, and privacy-preserving data mining where one ensures that one can get useful results from mining and at the same time maintain the privacy of the individuals.

Data Mining for Cyber Security

Data mining has applications in cyber security, which involves protecting the data in computers and networks. The most prominent application is in intrusion detection. For example, our computers and networks are being intruded on by unauthorized individuals. Data mining techniques, such as those for classification and anomaly detection, are being used extensively to detect such unauthorized intrusions. For example, data about normal behavior is gathered and when something occurs out of the ordinary, it is flagged as an unauthorized intrusion. Normal behavior could be John's computer is never used between 2 am and 5 am in the morning. When John's computer is in use, say, at 3 am, this is flagged as an unusual pattern.

Data mining is also being applied for other applications in cyber security, such as auditing, email worm detection, botnet detection, and malware detection. Here again, data on normal database access is gathered and when something unusual happens, then this is flagged as a possible access violation. Data mining is also being used for biometrics. Here, pattern recognition and other machine learning techniques are being used to learn the features of a person and then to authenticate the person based on the features.

However, one of the limitations of using data mining for malware detection is that the malware may change patterns. Therefore, we need tools that can detect adaptable malware. We also discuss this aspect in our book.

Organization of This Book

This book is divided into seven parts. Part I, which consists of four chapters, provides some background information on data mining techniques and applications that has influenced our tools; these chapters also provide an overview of malware. Parts II, III, IV, and V describe our tools for email worm detection, malicious code detection, remote exploit detection, and botnet detection, respectively. Part VI describes our tools for stream data mining. In Part VII, we discuss data mining for emerging applications, including adaptable malware detection, insider threat detection, and firewall policy analysis, as well as real-time data mining. We have four appendices that provide some of the background knowledge in data management, secure systems, and semantic web.

Concluding Remarks

Data mining applications are exploding. Yet many books, including some of the authors' own books, have discussed concepts at the high level. Some books have made the topic very theoretical. However, data mining approaches depend on nondeterministic reasoning as well as heuristics approaches. Our first book on the design and implementation of data mining tools provided step-by-step information on how data mining tools are developed. This book continues with this approach in describing our data mining tools.

For each of the tools we have developed, we describe the system architecture, the algorithms, and the performance results, as well as the limitations of the tools. We believe that this is one of the few books that will help tool developers as well as technologists and managers. It describes algorithms as well as the practical aspects. For example, technologists can decide on the tools to select for a particular application. Developers can focus on alternative designs if an approach is not suitable. Managers can decide whether to proceed with a data mining project. This book will be a very valuable reference guide to those in industry, government, and academia, as it focuses on both concepts and practical techniques. Experimental results are also given. The book will also be used as a textbook at The University of Texas at Dallas on courses in data mining and data security.

Acknowledgments

We are especially grateful to the Air Force Office of Scientific Research for funding our research on malware detection. In particular, we would like to thank Dr. Robert Herklotz for his encouragement and support for our work. Without his support for our research this book would not have been possible.

We are also grateful to the National Aeronautics and Space Administration for funding our research on stream mining. In particular, we would like to thank Dr. Ashok Agrawal for his encouragement and support.

We thank our colleagues and collaborators who have worked with us on *Data Mining Tools for Malware Detection*. Our special thanks are to the following colleagues.

> Prof. Peng Liu and his team at Penn State University for collaborating with us on Data Mining for Remote Exploits (Part III).
>
> Prof. Jiawei Han and his team at the University of Illinois for collaborating with us on Stream Data Mining (Part VI).
>
> Prof. Kevin Hamlen at the University of Texas at Dallas for collaborating with us on Data Mining for Active Defense (Chapter 21).
>
> Our student, Dr. M. Farhan Husain, for collaborating with us on Insider Threat Detection (Chapter 22).

Our colleagues, Prof. Chris Clifton (Purdue University), Dr. Marion Ceruti (Department of the Navy), and Mr. John Maurer (MITRE), for collaborating with us on Real-Time Data Mining (Chapter 23).

Our students, Muhammad Abedin and Syeda Nessa, for collaborating with us on Firewall Policy Analysis (Chapter 24).

The Authors

Mehedy Masud is a postdoctoral fellow at The University of Texas at Dallas (UTD), where he earned his PhD in computer science in December 2009. He has published in premier journals and conferences, including *IEEE Transactions on Knowledge and Data Engineering* and the IEEE International Conference on Data Mining. He will be appointed as a research assistant professor at UTD in Fall 2012. Masud's research projects include reactively adaptive malware, data mining for detecting malicious executables, botnet, and remote exploits, and cloud data mining. He has a patent pending on stream mining for novel class detection.

Latifur Khan is an associate professor in the computer science department at The University of Texas at Dallas, where he has been teaching and conducting research since September 2000. He received his PhD and MS degrees in computer science from the University of Southern California in August 2000 and December 1996, respectively. Khan is (or has been) supported by grants from NASA, the National Science Foundation (NSF), Air Force Office of Scientific Research (AFOSR), Raytheon, NGA, IARPA, Tektronix, Nokia Research Center, Alcatel, and the SUN academic equipment grant program. In addition, Khan is the director of the state-of-the-art DML@UTD, UTD Data Mining/Database Laboratory, which is the primary center of research related to data mining, semantic web, and image/video annotation at The University of Texas at Dallas. Khan has published more than 100 papers, including articles in several IEEE Transactions journals, the *Journal of Web Semantics,* and the *VLDB Journal* and conference proceedings such as *IEEE ICDM* and *PKDD.* He is a senior member of IEEE.

Bhavani Thuraisingham joined The University of Texas at Dallas (UTD) in October 2004 as a professor of computer science and director of the Cyber Security Research Center in the Erik Jonsson School of Engineering and Computer Science and is currently the Louis Beecherl, Jr., Distinguished Professor. She is an elected Fellow of three professional organizations: the IEEE (Institute for Electrical and Electronics Engineers), the AAAS (American Association for the Advancement of Science), and the BCS (British Computer Society) for her work in data security. She received the IEEE Computer Society's prestigious 1997 Technical Achievement Award for "outstanding and innovative contributions to secure data management." Prior to joining UTD, Thuraisingham worked for the MITRE Corporation for 16 years, which included an IPA (Intergovernmental Personnel Act) at the National Science Foundation as Program Director for Data and Applications Security. Her work in information security and information management has resulted in more than 100 journal articles, more than 200 refereed conference papers, more than 90 keynote addresses, and 3 U.S. patents. She is the author of ten books in data management, data mining, and data security.

Copyright Permissions

Figure 21.2; Figure 21.3
B. Thuraisingham, K. Hamlen, V. Mohan, M. Masud, L. Khan, Exploiting an antivirus interface; in *Computer Standards & Interface*s, Vol. 31, No. 6, p. 1182-1189, 2009, with permission from Elsevier.

Figure 7.4; Table 8.1; Table 8.2; Table 8.3; Table 8.4; Figure 8.2; Table 8.5; Table 8.6; Table 8.7, Table 8.8
B. Thuraisingham, M. Masud, L. Khan, Email worm detection using data mining, *International Journal of Information Security and Privacy*, 1:4, 47-61, Copyright 2007, IGI Global, www.igi-global.com.

Figure 23.2; Figure 23.3; Figure 23.4; Figure 23.5; Figure 23.6; Figure 23.7
L. Khan, C. Clifton, J. Maurer, M. Ceruti, Dependable real-time data mining, *Proceedings ISORC 2005*, p. 158-165, © 2005 IEEE.

Figure 22.3
M. Farhan Husain, L. Khan, M. Kantarcioglu, Data intensive query processing for large RDF graphs using cloud computing tools, *IEEE Cloud Computing*, Miami, FL, July 2010, p. 1-10, © 2005 IEEE.

1

INTRODUCTION

1.1 Trends

Data mining is the process of posing various queries and extracting useful and often previously unknown and unexpected information, patterns, and trends from large quantities of data, generally stored in databases. These data could be accumulated over a long period of time, or they could be large datasets accumulated simultaneously from heterogeneous sources such as different sensor types. The goals of data mining include improving marketing capabilities, detecting abnormal patterns, and predicting the future based on past experiences and current trends. There is clearly a need for this technology for many applications in government and industry. For example, a marketing organization may need to determine who their potential customers are. There are large amounts of current and historical data being stored. Therefore, as databases become larger, it becomes increasingly difficult to support decision-making. In addition, the data could be from multiple sources and multiple domains. There is a clear need to analyze the data to support planning and other functions of an enterprise.

Data mining has evolved from multiple technologies, including data management, data warehousing, machine learning, and statistical reasoning; one of the major challenges in the development of data mining tools is to eliminate false positives and false negatives. Much progress has also been made on building data mining tools based on a variety of techniques for numerous applications. These applications include those for marketing and sales, healthcare, medical, financial, e-commerce, multimedia, and more recently, security.

Our previous books have discussed various data mining technologies, techniques, tools, and trends. In a recent book, our main focus was on the design and development as well as to discuss the results obtained for the three tools that we developed between 2004 and 2006. These tools include one for intrusion detection, one for web page surfing prediction, and one for image classification. In this book, we continue with the descriptions of data mining tools we have developed over the past five years for cyber security. In particular, we discuss our tools for malware detection.

Malware, also known as malicious software, is developed by hackers to steal data and identity, causes harm to computers and denies legitimate services to users, among others. Malware has plagued the society and the software industry for almost four decades. Malware includes viruses, worms, Trojan horses, time and logic bombs, botnets, and spyware. In this book we describe our data mining tools for malware detection.

The organization of this chapter is as follows. Supporting technologies are discussed in Section 1.2. These supporting technologies are elaborated in Part II. The tools that we discuss in this book are summarized in Sections 1.3 through 1.8. These tools include data mining for email worm detection, remote exploits detection, malicious code detection, and botnet detection. In addition, we discuss our stream data mining tool as well as our approaches for inside threat detection, adaptable malware detection, real-time data mining for suspicious event detection, and firewall policy management. Each of these tools and approaches are discussed in Parts II through VII. The contents of this book are summarized in Section 1.9 of this chapter, and next steps are discussed in Section 1.10.

1.2 Data Mining and Security Technologies

Data mining techniques have exploded over the past decade, and we now have tools and products for a variety of applications. In Part I, we discuss the data mining techniques that we describe in this book, as well as provide an overview of the applications we discuss. Data mining techniques include those based on machine learning, statistical reasoning, and mathematics. Some of the popular techniques include association rule mining, decision trees, and K-means clustering. Figure 1.1 illustrates the data mining techniques.

Data mining has been used for numerous applications in several fields including in healthcare, e-commerce, and security. We focus on data mining for cyber security applications.

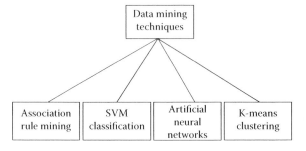

Figure 1.1   Data mining techniques.

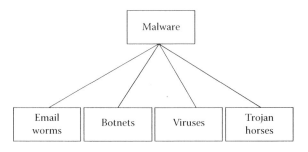

Figure 1.2   Malware.

While data mining technologies have exploded over the past two decades, the developments in information technologies have resulted in an increasing need for security. As a result, there is now an urgent need to develop secure systems. However, as systems are being secured, malware technologies have also exploded. Therefore, it is critical that we develop tools for detecting and preventing malware. Various types of malware are illustrated in Figure 1.2.

In this book we discuss data mining for malware detection. In particular, we discuss techniques such as support vector machines, clustering, and classification for cyber security applications. The tools we have developed are illustrated in Figure 1.3.

1.3 Data Mining for Email Worm Detection

An email worm spreads through infected email messages. The worm may be carried by an attachment, or the email may contain links to an infected website. When the user opens the attachment, or clicks the link, the host gets infected immediately. The worm exploits the vulnerable email software in the host machine to send infected emails

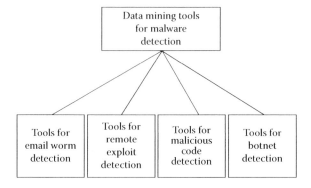

Figure 1.3 Data mining tools for malware detection.

to addresses stored in the address book. Thus, new machines get infected. Worms bring damage to computers and people in various ways. They may clog the network traffic, cause damage to the system, and make the system unstable or even unusable.

We have developed tools on applying data mining techniques for intrusion email worm detection. We use both Support Vector Machine (SVM) and Naïve Bayes (NB) data mining techniques. Our tools are described in Part III of the book.

1.4 Data Mining for Malicious Code Detection

Malicious code is a great threat to computers and computer society. Numerous kinds of malicious codes wander in the wild. Some of them are mobile, such as worms, and spread through the Internet causing damage to millions of computers worldwide. Other kinds of malicious codes are static, such as viruses, but sometimes deadlier than their mobile counterpart.

One popular technique followed by the antivirus community to detect malicious code is "signature detection." This technique matches the executables against a unique telltale string or byte pattern called signature, which is used as an identifier for a particular malicious code. However, such techniques are not effective against "zero-day" attacks. A zero-day attack is an attack whose pattern is previously unknown. We are developing a number of data mining tools for malicious code detection that do not depend on the signature of the malware. Our hybrid feature retrieval model is described in Part IV of this book.

1.5 Data Mining for Detecting Remote Exploits

Remote exploits are a popular means for attackers to gain control of hosts that run vulnerable services or software. Typically, a remote exploit is provided as an input to a remote vulnerable service to hijack the control-flow of machine-instruction execution. Sometimes the attackers inject executable code in the exploit that is executed after a successful hijacking attempt. We refer to these code-carrying remote exploits as *exploit code*.

We are developing a number of data mining tools for detecting remote exploits. Our tools use different classification models, such as Support Vector Machine (SVM), Naïve Bayes (NB), and decision trees. These tools are described in Part V of this book.

1.6 Data Mining for Botnet Detection

Botnets are a serious threat because of their volume and power. Botnets containing thousands of *bots* (compromised hosts) are controlled from a *Command and Control* (C&C) center, operated by a human *botmaster* or *botherder*. The botmaster can instruct these bots to recruit new bots, launch coordinated distributed denial of service (DDoS) attacks against specific hosts, steal sensitive information from infected machines, send mass spam emails, and so on.

We have developed data mining tools for botnet detection. Our tools use Support Vector Machine (SVM), Bayes Net, decision tree (J48), Naïve Bayes, and Boosted decision tree (Boosted J48) for the classification task. These tools are described in Part VI of this book.

1.7 Stream Data Mining

Stream data are quite common. They include video data, surveillance data, and financial data that arrive continuously. There are some problems related to stream data classification. First, it is impractical to store and use all the historical data for training, because it would require infinite storage and running time. Second, there may be concept-drift in the data, meaning the underlying concept of the data may change over time. Third, novel classes may evolve in the stream.

We have developed stream mining techniques for detecting novel cases. We believe that these techniques could be used for detecting novel malware. Our tools for stream mining are described in Part VI of this book.

1.8 Emerging Data Mining Tools for Cyber Security Applications

In addition to the tools described in Sections 1.3 through 1.7, we are also exploring techniques for (a) detecting malware that reacts and adapts to the environment, (b) insider threat detection, (c) real-time data mining, and (d) firewall policy management.

For malware that adapts, we are exploring the stream mining techniques. For insider threat detection, we are applying graph mining techniques. We are exploring real-time data mining to detect malware in real time. Finally, we are exploring the use of association rule mining techniques for ensuring that the numerous firewall policies are consistent. These techniques are described in Part VII of this book.

1.9 Organization of This Book

This book is divided into seven parts. Part I consists of this introductory chapter and four additional chapters. Chapter 2 provides some background information in the data mining techniques and applications that have influenced our research and tools. Chapter 3 describes types of malware. In Chapter 4, we provide an overview of data mining for security applications. The tools we have described in our previous book are discussed in Chapter 5. We discuss the three tools, as many of the tools we discuss in this current book have been influenced by our early tools.

Part II consists of three chapters, 6, 7, and 8, which describe our tool for email worm detection. An overview of email worm detection is discussed in Chapter 6. Our tool is discussed in Chapter 7. Evaluation and results are discussed in Chapter 8. Part III consists of three chapters, 9, 10, and 11, and describes our tool for malicious code detection. An overview of malicious code detection is discussed in Chapter 9. Our tool is discussed in Chapter 10. Evaluation and results are discussed in Chapter 11. Part IV consists of three chapters, 12, 13, and 14, and describes our tool for detecting remote exploits. An overview of detecting remote exploits is discussed in Chapter 12. Our tool is discussed in Chapter 13. Evaluation and results are discussed in Chapter 14. Part V consists of three chapters, 15, 16, and 17, and describes our tool for botnet detection. An overview of botnet detection is discussed in Chapter 15. Our tool is discussed in Chapter 16. Evaluation and results are discussed in Chapter 17. Part VI consists of three chapters, 18, 19, and 20, and describes our tool for stream mining. An overview of stream mining is discussed in Chapter 18. Our tool is discussed in Chapter 19. Evaluation and results are discussed in Chapter 20. Part VII consists of four chapters, 21, 22, 23, and 24, and describes our tools for emerging applications. Our approach to detecting adaptive malware is discussed in Chapter 21. Our approach for insider threat detection is discussed in Chapter 22. Real-time data mining is discussed in Chapter 23. Firewall policy management tool is discussed in Chapter 24.

The book is concluded in Chapter 25. Appendix A provides an overview of data management and describes the relationship between our books. Appendix B describes trustworthy systems. Appendix C describes secure data, information, and knowledge management, and Appendix D describes semantic web technologies. The appendices, together with the supporting technologies described in Part I, provide the necessary background to understand the content of this book.

We have essentially developed a three-layer framework to explain the concepts in this book. This framework is illustrated in Figure 1.4. Layer 1 is the data mining techniques layer. Layer 2 is our tools layer. Layer 3 is the applications layer. Figure 1.5 illustrates how Chapters 2 through 24 in this book are placed in the framework.

1.10 Next Steps

This book provides the information for a reader to get familiar with data mining concepts and understand how the techniques are applied step-by-step to some real-world applications in malware detection. One of the main contributions of this book is raising the awareness of the importance of data mining for a variety of applications in cyber security. This book could be used as a guide to build data mining tools for cyber security applications.

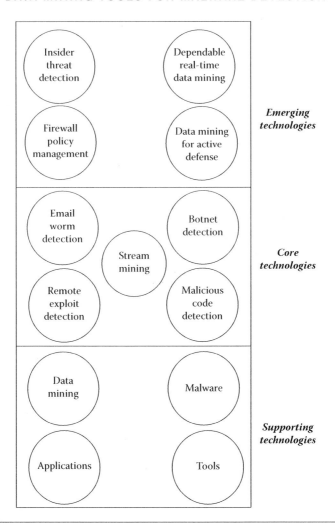

Figure 1.4   Framework for data mining tools.

We provide many references that can help the reader in understanding the details of the problem we are investigating. Our advice to the reader is to keep up with the developments in data mining and get familiar with the tools and products and apply them for a variety of applications. Then the reader will have a better understanding of the limitation of the tools and be able to determine when new tools have to be developed.

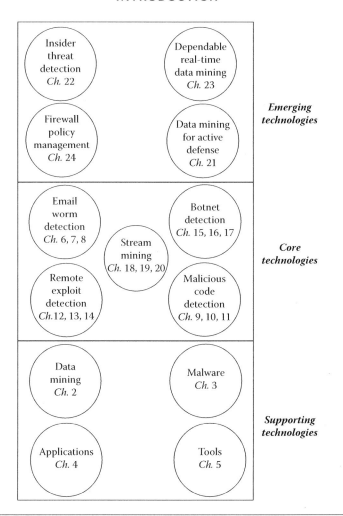

Figure 1.5 Contents of the book with respect to the framework.

PART I

DATA MINING
AND SECURITY

Introduction to Part I: Data Mining and Security

Supporting technologies for data mining for malware detection include data mining and malware technologies. Data mining is the process of analyzing the data and uncovering hidden dependencies. The outcomes of data mining include classification, clustering, forming associations, as well as detecting anomalies. Malware technologies are being developed at a rapid speed. These include worms, viruses, and Trojan horses.

Part I, consisting of five chapters, discusses supporting technologies for data mining for malware detection. Chapter 1 provides a brief overview of data mining and malware. In Chapter 2, we discuss the data mining techniques we have utilized in our tools. Specifically, we present the Markov model, support vector machines, artificial neural networks, and association rule mining. In Chapter 3, we discuss various types of malware, including worms, viruses, and Trojan horses. In Chapter 4, we discuss data mining for security applications. In particular, we discuss the threats to the computers and networks and describe the applications of data mining to detect such threats and attacks. Some of our current research at The University of Texas at Dallas also is discussed. In Chapter 5, we discuss the three applications we have considered in our previous book on the design and implementation of data mining tools. These tools have influenced the work discussed in this book a great deal. In particular, we discuss intrusion detection, web surfing prediction, and image classification tools.

2
DATA MINING TECHNIQUES

2.1 Introduction

Data mining outcomes (also called tasks) include classification, clustering, forming associations, as well as detecting anomalies. Our tools have mainly focused on classification as the outcome, and we have developed classification tools. The classification problem is also referred to as Supervised Learning, in which a set of labeled examples is learned by a model, and then a new example with an unknown label is presented to the model for prediction.

There are many prediction models that have been used, such as the Markov model, decision trees, artificial neural networks, support vector machines, association rule mining, and many others. Each of these models has strengths and weaknesses. However, there is a common weakness among all of these techniques, which is the inability to suit all applications. The reason that there is no such ideal or perfect classifier is that each of these techniques is initially designed to solve specific problems under certain assumptions.

In this chapter, we discuss the data mining techniques we have utilized in our tools. Specifically, we present the Markov model, support vector machines, artificial neural networks, association rule mining, and the problem of multi-classification, as well as image classification, which is an aspect of image mining. These techniques are also used in developing and comparing results in Parts II, III, and IV. In our research and development, we propose hybrid models to improve the prediction accuracy of data mining algorithms in various applications, namely, intrusion detection, WWW prediction, and image classification.

The organization of this chapter is as follows. In Section 2.2, we provide an overview of various data mining tasks and techniques. The techniques that are relevant to the contents of this book are discussed in Sections 2.2 through 2.7. In particular, neural networks, support vector machines, Markov models, and association rule mining, as well as some other classification techniques are described. The chapter is summarized in Section 2.8.

2.2 Overview of Data Mining Tasks and Techniques

Before we discuss data mining techniques, we provide an overview of some of the data mining tasks (also known as data mining outcomes). Then we discuss the techniques. In general, data mining tasks can be grouped into two categories: predictive and descriptive. Predictive tasks essentially predict whether an item belongs to a class or not. Descriptive tasks, in general, extract patterns from the examples. One of the most prominent predictive tasks is classification. In some cases, other tasks, such as anomaly detection, can be reduced to a predictive task such as whether a particular situation is an anomaly or not. Descriptive tasks, in general, include making associations and forming clusters. Therefore, classification, anomaly detection, making associations, and forming clusters are also thought to be data mining tasks.

Next, the data mining techniques can be either predictive, descriptive, or both. For example, neural networks can perform classification as well as clustering. Classification techniques include decision trees, support vector machines, as well as memory-based reasoning. Association rule mining techniques are used, in general, to make associations. Link analysis that analyzes links can also make associations between links and predict new links. Clustering techniques include K-means clustering. An overview of the data mining tasks (i.e., the outcomes of data mining) is illustrated in Figure 2.1. The techniques discussed in this book (e.g., neural networks, support vector machines) are illustrated in Figure 2.2.

2.3 Artificial Neural Network

Artificial neural network (ANN) is a very well-known, powerful, and robust classification technique that has been used to approximate real-valued, discrete-valued, and vector-valued functions from examples. ANNs have been used in many areas such as interpreting visual scenes,

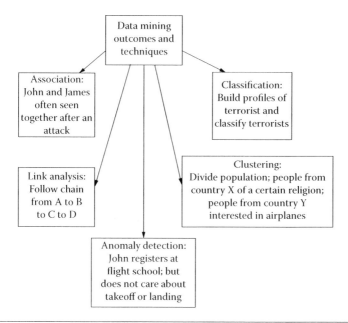

Figure 2.1 Data mining tasks.

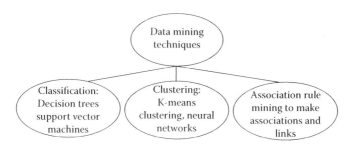

Figure 2.2 Data mining techniques.

speech recognition, and learning robot control strategies. An artificial neural network (ANN) simulates the biological nervous system in the human brain. Such a nervous system is composed of a large number of highly interconnected processing units (neurons) working together to produce our feelings and reactions. ANNs, like people, learn by example. The learning process in a human brain involves adjustments to the synaptic connections between neurons. Similarly, the learning process of ANN involves adjustments to the node weights. Figure 2.3 presents a simple neuron unit, which is called perceptron. The perceptron input, x, is a vector or real-valued input, and w is the weight vector, in which its value is determined after training. The perceptron

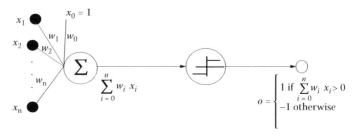

Figure 2.3 The perceptron.

computes a linear combination of an input vector x as follows (Eq. 2.1).

$$o(x_1,...,x_n) = \begin{cases} 1 \text{ if } w_0 + w_1x_1 + ... + w_nx_n > 0 \\ -1 \text{ otherwise} \end{cases} \tag{2.1}$$

Notice that w_i corresponds to the contribution of the input vector component x_i of the perceptron output. Also, in order for the perceptron to output a 1, the weighted combination of the inputs

$$\left(\sum_{i=1}^{n} w_i x_i \right)$$

must be greater than the threshold w_0.

Learning the perceptron involves choosing values for the weights $w_0 + w_1x_1 + ... + w_nx_n$. Initially, random weight values are given to the perceptron. Then the perceptron is applied to each training example updating the weights of the perceptron whenever an example is misclassified. This process is repeated many times until all training examples are correctly classified. The weights are updated according to the following rule (Eq. 2.2):

$$\begin{cases} w_i = w_i + \delta w_i \\ \delta w_i = \eta(t - o)x_i \end{cases} \tag{2.2}$$

where η is a learning constant, o is the output computed by the perceptron, and t is the target output for the current training example.

The computation power of a single perceptron is limited to linear decisions. However, the perceptron can be used as a building block

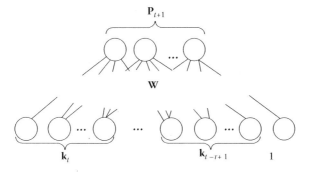

Figure 2.4 Artificial neural network.

to compose powerful multi-layer networks. In this case, a more complicated updating rule is needed to train the network weights. In this work, we employ an artificial neural network of two layers and each layer is composed of three building blocks (see Figure 2.4). We use the back propagation algorithm for learning the weights. The back propagation algorithm attempts to minimize the squared error function.

A typical training example in WWW prediction is $\langle [k_{t-\tau+1}, ..., k_{t-1}, k_t]^T, d \rangle$, where $[k_{t-\tau+1}, ..., k_{t-1}, k_t]^T$ is the input to the ANN and d is the target web page. Notice that the input units of the ANN in Figure 2.5 are τ previous pages that the user has recently visited, where k is a web page id. The output of the network is a boolean value, not a probability. We will see later how to approximate the probability of the output by fitting a sigmoid function after ANN output. The

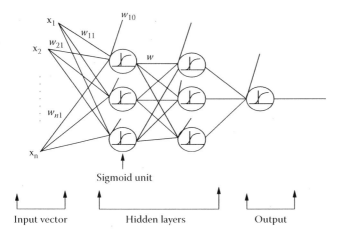

Figure 2.5 The design of ANN used in our implementation.

approximated probabilistic output becomes $o' = f(o(I) = p_{t+1}$, where I is an input session and $p_{t+1} = p(d|k_{t-\tau+1}, ..., k_t)$. We choose the sigmoid function (Eq. 2.3) as a transfer function so that the ANN can handle a non-linearly separable dataset [Mitchell, 1997]. Notice that in our ANN design (Figure 2.5), we use a sigmoid transfer function, Eq. 2.3, in each building block. In Eq. 2.3, I is the input to the network, O is the output of the network, W is the matrix of weights, and σ is the sigmoid function.

$$\begin{cases} O = \sigma(W.I) \\ \sigma(y) = \dfrac{1}{1+e^{-y}} \end{cases} \tag{2.3}$$

$$E(W) = \frac{1}{2} \sum_{k \in D} \sum_{i \in outputs} (t_{ik} - o_{ik})^2 \tag{2.4}$$

$$\begin{cases} w_{ji} = w_{ji} + \delta w_{ji} \\ \delta w_{ji} = -\eta \dfrac{\partial E_d}{\partial w_{ji}} \end{cases} \tag{2.5}$$

$$\delta w_{ji}(n) = -\eta \frac{\partial E_d}{\partial w_{ji}} + \alpha \delta w_{ji}(n-1) \tag{2.6}$$

We implement the back propagation algorithm for training the weights. The back propagation algorithm employs gradient descent to attempt to minimize the squared error between the network output values and the target values of these outputs. The sum of the error over all of the network output units is defined in Eq. 2.4. In Eq. 2.4, the *outputs* is the set of output units in the network, D is the training set, and t_{ik} and o_{ik} are the target and the output values associated with the ith output unit and training example k. For a specific weight w_{ji} in the network, it is updated for each training example as in Eq. 2.5, where η is the learning rate and w_{ji} is the weight associated with the ith input to the network unit j (for details see [Mitchell, 1997]). As we can see from Eq. 2.5, the search direction δw is computed using the gradient descent, which guarantees convergence toward a local minimum. To mitigate that, we add a momentum to the weight update rule such that the weight update direction $\delta w_{ji}(n)$ depends partially on the update direction in the previous iteration $\delta w_{ji}(n-1)$. The new weight update direction is shown in Eq. 2.6, where n is the current iteration, and α is the momentum constant. Notice that in Eq. 2.6, the step size is slightly larger than in Eq. 2.5. This contributes to a smooth convergence of the search in regions where the gradient is unchanging [Mitchell, 1997].

In our implementation, we set the step size η dynamically based on the distribution of the classes in the dataset. Specifically, we set the step size to large values when updating the training examples that belong to low distribution classes and vice versa. This is because when the distribution of the classes in the dataset varies widely (e.g., a dataset might have 5% positive examples and 95% negative examples), the network weights converge toward the examples from the class of larger distribution, which causes a slow convergence. Furthermore, we adjust the learning rates slightly by applying the momentum constant, Eq. 2.6, to speed up the convergence of the network [Mitchell, 1997].

2.4 Support Vector Machines

Support vector machines (SVMs) are learning systems that use a hypothesis space of linear functions in a high dimensional feature space, trained with a learning algorithm from optimization theory. This learning strategy, introduced by Vapnik [1995, 1998, 1999; see also Cristianini and Shawe-Taylor, 2000], is a very powerful method that has been applied in a wide variety of applications. The basic concept in SVM is the hyper-plane classifier, or linear separability. To achieve linear separability, SVM applies two basic ideas: margin maximization and kernels, that is, mapping input space to a higher dimension space, feature space.

For binary classification, the SVM problem can be formalized as in Eq. 2.7. Suppose we have N training data points $\{(x_1,y_1), (x_2,y_2), \ldots, (x_N,y_N)\}$, where $x_i \in R^d$ and $y_i \in \{+1,-1\}$. We would like to find a linear separating hyper-plane classifier as in Eq. 2.8. Furthermore, we want this hyper-plane to have the maximum separating margin with respect to the two classes (see Figure 2.6). The functional margin, or the margin for short, is defined geometrically as the Euclidean distance of the closest point from the decision boundary to the input space.

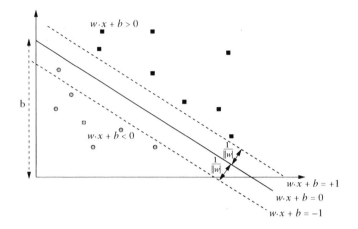

Figure 2.6   Linear separation in SVM.

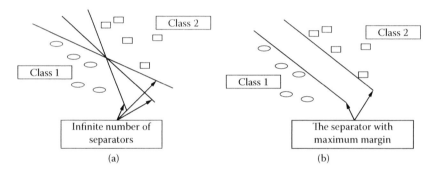

Figure 2.7   The SVM separator that causes the maximum margin.

Figure 2.7 gives an intuitive explanation of why margin maximization gives the best solution of separation. In part (a) of Figure 2.7, we can find an infinite number of separators for a specific dataset. There is no specific or clear reason to favor one separator over another. In part (b), we see that maximizing the margin provides only one thick separator. Such a solution achieves the best generalization accuracy, that is, prediction for the unseen [Vapnik, 1995, 1998, 1999].

$$\begin{cases} \text{minimize}_{(w,b)} \dfrac{1}{2} w^T w \\ \text{subject to } y_i(w \cdot x_i - b) \geq 1 \end{cases} \tag{2.7}$$

$$f(x) = sign(w \cdot x - b) \tag{2.8}$$

$$\text{maximize } L(w,b,\alpha) = \frac{1}{2} w^T w - \sum_{i=1}^{N} \alpha_i y_i (w \cdot x_i - b) + \sum_{i=1}^{N} \alpha_i \quad (2.9)$$

$$f(x) = sign(wx - b) = sign\left(\sum_{i=1}^{N} \alpha_i y_i (x \cdot x_i - b) \right) \quad (2.10)$$

Notice that Eq. 2.8 computes the sign of the functional margin of point x in addition to the prediction label of x, that is, functional margin of x equals $wx - b$.

The SVM optimization problem is a convex quadratic programming problem (in w, b) in a convex set Eq. 2.7. We can solve the Wolfe dual instead, as in Eq. 2.9, with respect to α, subject to the constraints that the gradient of $L(w,b,\alpha)$ with respect to the primal variables w and b vanish and $\alpha_i \geq 0$. The primal variables are eliminated from $L(w,b,\alpha)$ (see [Cristianini and Shawe-Taylor, 1999] for more details). When we solve α_i we can get

$$w = \sum_{i=1}^{N} \alpha_i y_i x_i$$

and we can classify a new object x using Eq. 2.10. Note that the training vectors occur only in the form of a dot product and that there is a Lagrangian multiplier α_i for each training point, which reflects the importance of the data point. When the maximal margin hyper-plane is found, only points that lie closest to the hyper-plane will have $\alpha_i > 0$ and these points are called *support vectors*. All other points will have $\alpha_i = 0$ (see Figure 2.8a). This means that only those points that lie closest to the hyper-plane give the representation of the hypothesis/classifier. These most important data points serve as support vectors. Their values can also be used to give an independent boundary with regard to the reliability of the hypothesis/classifier [Bartlett and Shawe-Taylor, 1999].

Figure 2.8a shows two classes and their boundaries, that is, margins. The support vectors are represented by solid objects, while the empty objects are non-support vectors. Notice that the margins are only affected by the support vectors; that is, if we remove or add empty

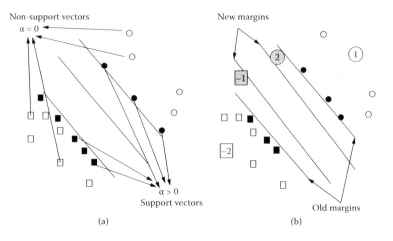

Figure 2.8   (a) The α values of support vectors and non-support vectors. (b) The effect of adding new data points on the margins.

objects, the margins will not change. Meanwhile, any change in the solid objects, either adding or removing objects, could change the margins. Figure 2.8b shows the effects of adding objects in the margin area. As we can see, adding or removing objects far from the margins, for example, data point 1 or –2, does not change the margins. However, adding and/or removing objects near the margins, for example, data point 2 and/or –1, has created new margins.

2.5 Markov Model

Some recent and advanced predictive methods for web surfing are developed using Markov models [Pirolli et al., 1996], [Yang et al., 2001]. For these predictive models, the sequences of web pages visited by surfers are typically considered as Markov chains, which are then fed as input. The basic concept of the Markov model is that it predicts the next action depending on the result of previous action or actions. Actions can mean different things for different applications. For the purpose of illustration, we will consider actions specific for the WWW prediction application. In WWW prediction, the next action corresponds to prediction of the next page to be traversed. The previous actions correspond to the previous web pages to be considered. Based on the number of previous actions considered, the Markov model can have different orders.

$$pr(P_k) = pr(S_k) \tag{2.11}$$

$$pr(P_2 \mid P_1) = pr(S_2 = P_2 \mid S_1 = P_1) \tag{2.12}$$

$$pr(P_N \mid P_{N-1}, \ldots, P_{N-k}) =$$
$$pr(S_N = P_N \mid S_{N-1} = P_{N-1}, \ldots, S_{N-k} = P_{N-k}) \tag{2.13}$$

The zeroth-order Markov model is the unconditional probability of the state (or web page), Eq. 2.11. In Eq. 2.11, P_k is a web page and S_k is the corresponding state. The first-order Markov model, Eq. 2.12, can be computed by taking page-to-page transitional probabilities or the n-gram probabilities of $\{ P_1, P_2 \}, \{ P_2, P_3 \}, \ldots, \{ P_{k-1}, P_k \}$.

In the following, we present an illustrative example of different orders of the Markov model and how it can predict.

Example Imagine a web site of six web pages: P1, P2, P3, P4, P5, and P6. Suppose we have user sessions as in Table 2.1. Table 2.1 depicts the navigation of many users of that web site. Figure 2.9 shows the *first-order Markov model*, where the next action is predicted based only on the last action performed, i.e., last page traversed, by the user. States S and F correspond to the initial and final states, respectively. The probability of each transition is estimated by the ratio of the number of times the sequence of states was traversed and the number of times the anchor state was visited. Next to each arch in Figure 2.8, the first number is the frequency of that transition, and the second number is the transition probability. For example, the transition probability of the transition (P2 to P3) is 0.2 because the number of times users traverse from page 2 to page 3 is 3, and the number of times page 2 is visited is 15 (i.e., 0.2 = 3/15).

Notice that the transition probability is used to resolve prediction. For example, given that a user has already visited P2, the most probable page she visits next is P6. That is because the transition probability from P2 to P6 is the highest.

Table 2.1 Collection of User Sessions and Their Frequencies

SESSION	FREQUENCY
P1,P2,P4	5
P1,P2,P6	1
P5,P2,P6	6
P5,P2,P3	3

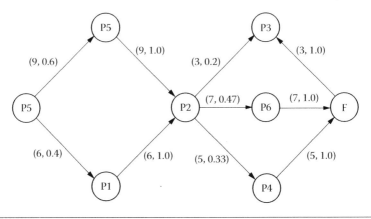

Figure 2.9   First-order Markov model.

Notice that that transition probability might not be available for some pages. For example, the transition probability from P2 to P5 is not available because no user has visited P5 after P2. Hence, these transition probabilities are set to zeros. Similarly, the Kth-order Markov model is where the prediction is computed after considering the last K^{th} action performed by the users, Eq. 2.13. In WWW prediction, the Kth-order Markov model is the probability of user visit to P_k^{th} page given its previous k-1 page visits.

Figure 2.10 shows the second-order Markov model that corresponds to Table 2.1. In the second-order model we consider the last two pages. The transition probability is computed in a similar fashion. For example, the transition probability of the transition (P1,P2) to (P2, P6) is 0.16 = 1 × 1/6 because the number of times users traverse

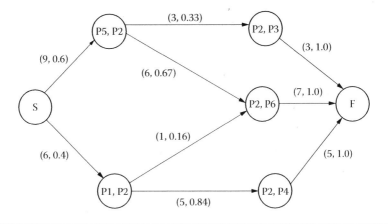

Figure 2.10   Second-order Markov model.

from state (P1,P2) to state (P2,P6) is 1 and the number of times pages (P1,P2) is visited is 6 (i.e., 0.16 = 1/6). The transition probability is used for prediction. For example, given that a user has visited P1 and P2, she most probably visits P4 because the transition probability from state (P1,P2) to state (P2,P4) is greater than the transition probability from state (P1,P2) to state (P2,P6).

The order of Markov model is related to the sliding window. The Kth-order Markov model corresponds to a sliding window of size K-1.

Notice that there is another concept that is similar to the sliding window concept, which is *number of hops*. In this book we use *number of hops* and *sliding window* interchangeably.

In WWW prediction, Markov models are built based on the concept of *n*-gram. The *n*-gram can be represented as a tuple of the form $\langle x_1, x_2, ..., x_n \rangle$ to depict sequences of page clicks by a population of users surfing a web site. Each component of the *n*-gram takes a specific page id value that reflects the surfing path of a specific user surfing a web page. For example, the *n*-gram $\langle P_{10}, P_{21}, P_4, P_{12} \rangle$ for some user U states that the user U has visited the pages 10, 21, 4, and finally page 12 in a sequence.

2.6 Association Rule Mining (ARM)

Association rule is a data mining technique that has been applied successfully to discover related transactions. The association rule technique finds the relationships among itemsets based on their co-occurrence in the transactions. Specifically, association rule mining discovers the frequent patterns (regularities) among those itemsets, for example, what the items purchased together in a super store are. In the following, we briefly introduce association rule mining. For more details, see [Agrawal et al., 1993], [Agrawal and Srikant, 1994].

Assume we have m items in our database; define $I = \{i_1, i_2, ..., i_m\}$ as the set of all items. A transaction T is a set of items such that $T \subseteq I$. Let D be the set of all transactions in the database. A transaction T contains X if $X \subseteq T$ and $X \subseteq I$. An association rule is an implication of the form $X \rightarrow Y$, where $X \subset I$, $Y \subset I$, and $X \cap Y = \phi$. There are two parameters to consider a rule: confidence and support. A rule $R = X \rightarrow Y$ holds with confidence c if $c\%$ of the transactions of D that contain X also contain Y (i.e., $c = pr(Y|X)$). The rule R holds with support

s if s% of the transactions in D contain X and Y (i.e., $s = pr(X,Y)$). The problem of mining association rules is defined as the following: given a set of transactions D, we would like to generate all rules that satisfy a confidence and a support greater than a minimum confidence (σ), *minconf*, and minimum support (ϑ), *minsup*. There are several efficient algorithms proposed to find association rules, for example, the AIS algorithm [Agrawal et al., 1993], [Agrawal and Srikant, 1994], SETM algorithm [Houstma and Swanu, 1995], and AprioriTid [Agrawal and Srikant, 1994].

In the case of web transactions, we use association rules to discover navigational patterns among users. This would help to cache a page in advance and reduce the loading time of a page. Also, discovering a pattern of navigation helps in personalization. Transactions are captured from the clickstream data captured in web server logs.

In many applications, there is one main problem in using association rule mining. First, a problem with using global minimum support (*minsup*), because rare hits (i.e., web pages that are rarely visited) will not be included in the frequent sets because it will not achieve enough support. One solution is to have a very small support threshold; however, we will end up with a very large frequent itemset, which is computationally hard to handle. [Liu et al., 1999] propose a mining technique that uses different support thresholds for different items. Specifying multiple thresholds allow rare transactions, which might be very important, to be included in the frequent itemsets. Other issues might arise depending on the application itself. For example, in the case of WWW prediction, a session is recorded for each user. The session might have tens of clickstreams (and sometimes hundreds depending on the duration of the session). Using each session as a transaction will not work because it is rare to find two sessions that are frequently repeated (i.e., identical); hence it will not achieve even a very high support threshold, *minsup*. There is a need to break each session into many subsequences. One common method is to use a sliding window of size w. For example, suppose we use a sliding window $w = 3$ to break the session $S = \langle A, B, C, D, E, E, F \rangle$, then we will end up with the subsequences $S' = \{\langle A,B,C \rangle, \langle B,C,D \rangle, \langle C,D,E \rangle, \langle D,E,F \rangle\}$. The total number of subsequences of a session S using window w is $length(S) - w$. To predict the next page in an active user session, we use a sliding window of the active session and ignore the previous pages. For example, if the current session is $\langle A,B,C \rangle$, and the user references page D, then the new active session becomes $\langle B,C,D \rangle$, using a sliding window 3. Notice that page A is dropped, and $\langle B,C,D \rangle$ will be used for prediction. The rationale behind this is that most users go back and forth while surfing the web trying to find the desired information, and it may be most appropriate to use the recent portions of the user history to generate recommendations/predictions [Mobasher et al., 2001].

[Mobasher et al., 2001] propose a recommendation engine that matches an active user session with the frequent itemsets in the database and predicts the next page the user most probably visits. The engine works as follows. Given an active session of size w, the engine finds all the frequent itemsets of length $w + 1$ satisfying some minimum support *minsup* and containing the current active session. Prediction for the active session A is based on the confidence (ψ) of the corresponding association rule. The confidence (ψ) of an association rule $X \to z$ is defined as $\psi(X \to z) = \sigma(X \cup z)/\sigma(X)$, where the length of z is 1. Page p is recommended/predicted for an active session A, if

$$\forall V, R \text{ in the frequent itemsets,}$$

$$length(R) = length(V) = length(A) + 1 \wedge$$

$$R = A \cup \{p\} \wedge$$

$$V = A \cup \{q\} \wedge$$

$$\psi(A \to p) > \psi(A \to q)$$

The engine uses a cyclic graph called the Frequent Itemset Graph. The graph is an extension of the lexicographic tree used in the tree projection algorithm of [Agrawal et al., 2001]. The graph is organized in levels. The nodes in level l have itemsets of size l. For example, the sizes of the nodes (i.e., the size of the itemsets corresponding to these nodes) in level 1 and 2 are 1 and 2, respectively. The root of the graph, level 0, is an empty node corresponding to an empty itemset. A node X in level l is linked to a node Y in level $l + 1$ if $X \subset Y$. To further explain the process, suppose we have the following sample

Table 2.2 Sample Web Transaction

TRANSACTION ID	ITEMS
T1	1,2,4,5
T2	1,2,5,3,4
T3	1,2,5,3
T4	2,5,2,1,3
T5	4,1,2,5,3
T6	1,2,3,4
T7	4,5
T8	4,5,3,1

Table 2.3 Frequent Itemsets Generated by the Apriori Algorithm

SIZE 1	SIZE 2	SIZE 3	SIZE 4
{2}(6)	{2,3}(5)	{2,3,1}(5)	{2,3,1,5}(4)
{3}(6)	{2,4}(4)	{2,3,5}(4)	
{4}(6)	{2,1}(6)	{2,4,1}(4)	
{1}(7)	{2,5}(5)	{2,1,5}(5)	
{5}(7)	{3,4}(4)	{3,4,1}(4)	
	{3,1}(6)	{3,1,5}(5)	
	{3,5}(5)	{4,1,5}(4)	
	{4,1}(5)		
	{4,5}(5)		
	{1,5}(6)		

web transactions involving pages 1, 2, 3, 4, and 5 as in Table 2.2. The Apriori algorithm produces the itemsets as in Table 2.3, using a *min-sup* = 0.49. The frequent itemset graph is shown in Figure 2.11.

Suppose we are using a sliding window of size 2, and the current active session A = ⟨2,3⟩. To predict/recommend the next page, we first start at level 2 in the frequent itemset graph and extract all the itemsets in level 3 linked to A. From Figure 2.11, the node {2,3} is linked to {1,2,3} and {2,3,5} nodes with confidence:

$$\psi(\{2,3\} \to 1) = \sigma(\{1,2,3\}/\sigma(\{2,3\}) = 5/5 = 1.0$$

$$\psi(\{2,3\} \to 5) = \sigma(\{2,3,5\}/\sigma(\{2,3\}) = 4/5 = 0.8$$

and the recommended page is 1 because its confidence is larger. Notice that, in Recommendation Engines, the order of the clickstream is not

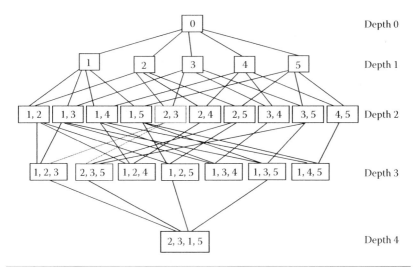

Figure 2.11   Frequent Itemset Graph.

considered; that is, there is no distinction between a session ⟨1,2,4⟩ and ⟨1,4,2⟩. This is a disadvantage of such systems because the order of pages visited might bear important information about the navigation patterns of users.

2.7 Multi-Class Problem

Most classification techniques solve the binary classification problem. Binary classifiers are accumulated to generalize for the multi-class problem. There are two basic schemes for this generalization, namely, one-vs-one, and one-vs-all. To avoid redundancy, we will present this generalization only for SVM.

2.7.1 One-vs-One

The one-vs-one approach creates a classifier for each pair of classes. The training set for each pair classifier (i,j) includes only those instances that belong to either class i or j. A new instance x belongs to the class upon which most pair classifiers agree. The prediction decision is quoted from the majority vote technique. There are $n(n - 1)/2$ classifiers to be computed, where n is the number of classes in the dataset. It is evident that the disadvantage of this scheme is that we need to generate a large number of classifiers, especially if there are a large number of classes in the training set. For example, if we have a training set of 1,000 classes, we need 499,500 classifiers. On the other hand, the size of training set for each classifier is small because we exclude all instances that do not belong to that pair of classes.

2.7.2 One-vs-All

One-vs-all creates a classifier for each class in the dataset. The training set is pre-processed such that for a classifier j, instances that belong to class j are marked as class (+1) and instances that do not belong to class j are marked as class (−1). In the one-vs-all scheme, we compute n classifiers, where n is the number of pages that users have visited (at the end of each session). A new instance x is predicted by assigning it to the class that its classifier outputs the largest positive value (i.e., maximal marginal), as in Eq. 2.15. We can compute the margin of point x as in Eq. 2.14. Notice that the recommended/predicted page is the sign of the margin value of that page (see Eq. 2.10).

$$f(x) = wx - b = \sum_{i}^{N} \alpha_i \, y_i \, (x.x_i - b) \tag{2.14}$$

$$prediction(x) = \arg\max_{1 \le c \le M} f_c(x) \tag{2.15}$$

In Eq. 2.15, M is the number of classes, $x = \langle x_1, x_2, \ldots, x_n \rangle$ is the user session, and f_i is the classifier that separates class i from the rest of the classes. The prediction decision in Eq. 2.15 resolves to the classifier f_c that is the most distant from the testing example x. This might be explained as f_c has the most separating power, among all other classifiers, of separating x from the rest of the classes.

The advantage of this scheme (one-vs-all), compared to the one-VS-one scheme, is that it has fewer classifiers. On the other hand, the size of the training set is larger for one-vs-all than for a one-vs-one scheme because we use the whole original training set to compute each classifier.

2.8 Image Mining

Along with the development of digital images and computer storage technologies, huge amounts of digital images are generated and saved every day. Applications of digital image have rapidly penetrated many domains and markets, including commercial and news media photo libraries, scientific and non-photographic image databases, and medical image databases. As a consequence, we face a daunting problem of organizing and accessing these huge amounts of available images. An efficient image retrieval system is highly desired to find images of specific entities from a database. The system is expected to manage a huge collection of images efficiently, respond to users' queries with high speed, and deliver a minimum of irrelevant information (high precision), as well as ensure that relevant information is not overlooked (high recall).

To generate such kinds of systems, people tried many different approaches. In the early 1990s, because of the emergence of large image collections, content-based image retrieval (CBIR) was proposed. CBIR computes relevance based on the similarity of visual content/low-level image features such as color histograms, textures, shapes, and spatial layout. However, the problem is that visual similarity is not semantic similarity. There is a gap between low-level visual features and semantic meanings. The so-called semantic gap is the major problem that needs to be solved for most CBIR approaches. For example, a CBIR system may answer a query request for a "red ball" with an image of a "red rose." If we undertake the annotation of images with keywords, a typical way to publish an image data repository is to create a keyword-based query interface addressed to an image database. If all images came with a detailed and accurate description, image retrieval would be convenient based on current powerful pure text search techniques. These search techniques would retrieve the images if their descriptions/annotations contained some combination of the keywords specified by the user. However, the major problem is that most of images are not annotated. It is a laborious, error-prone, and subjective process to manually annotate a large collection of images. Many images contain the desired semantic information, even though they do not contain the user-specified keywords. Furthermore, keyword-based search is useful especially to a user who knows what keywords are used to index the images and who can therefore easily formulate queries. This approach is problematic, however, when the user does not have a clear goal in mind, does not know what is in the database, and does not know what kind of semantic concepts are involved in the domain.

Image mining is a more challenging research problem than retrieving relevant images in CBIR systems. The goal of image mining is to find an image pattern that is significant for a given set of images and helpful to understand the relationships between high-level semantic concepts/descriptions and low-level visual features. Our focus is on aspects such as feature selection and image classification.

2.8.1 Feature Selection

Usually, data saved in databases is with well-defined semantics such as numbers or structured data entries. In comparison, data with ill-defined semantics is unstructured data. For example, images, audio, and video are data with ill-defined semantics. In the domain of image processing, images are represented by derived data or features such as color, texture, and shape. Many of these features have multiple values (e.g., color histogram, moment description). When people generate these derived data or features, they generally generate as many features as possible, since they are not aware which feature is more relevant. Therefore, the dimensionality of derived image data is usually very high. Some of the selected features might be duplicated or may not even be relevant to the problem. Including irrelevant or duplicated information is referred to as "noise." Such problems are referred to as the "curse of dimensionality." Feature selection is the research topic for finding an optimal subset of features. In this section, we will discuss this curse and feature selection in detail.

We developed a wrapper-based simultaneous feature weighing and clustering algorithm. The clustering algorithm will bundle similar image segments together and generate a finite set of visual symbols (i.e., blob-token). Based on histogram analysis and chi-square value, we assign features of image segments different weights instead of removing some of them. Feature weight evaluation is wrapped in a clustering algorithm. In each iteration of the algorithm, feature weights of image segments are reevaluated based on the clustering result. The reevaluated feature weights will affect the clustering results in the next iteration.

2.8.2 *Automatic Image Annotation*

Automatic image annotation is research concerned with object recognition, where the effort is concerned with trying to recognize objects in an image and generate descriptions for the image according to semantics of the objects. If it is possible to produce accurate and complete semantic descriptions for an image, we can store descriptions in an image database. Based on a textual description, more functionality (e.g., browse, search, and query) of an Image DBMS could be implemented easily and efficiently by applying many existing text-based search techniques. Unfortunately, the automatic image annotation problem has not been solved in general, and perhaps this problem is impossible to solve.

However, in certain subdomains, it is still possible to obtain some interesting results. Many statistical models have been published for image annotation. Some of these models took feature dimensionality into account and applied singular value decomposition (SVD) or principle component analysis (PCA) to reduce dimension. But none of them considered feature selection or feature weight. We proposed a new framework for image annotation based on a translation model (TM). In our approach, we applied our weighted feature selection algorithm and embedded it in image annotation framework. Our weighted feature selection algorithm improves the quality of visual tokens and generates better image annotations.

2.8.3 *Image Classification*

Image classification is an important area, especially in the medical domain, because it helps manage large medical image databases and has great potential as a diagnostic aid in a real-world clinical setting. We describe our experiments for the image CLEF medical image retrieval task. Sizes of classes of CLEF medical image datasets are not balanced, and this is a really serious problem for all classification algorithms. To solve this problem, we re-sample data by generating subwindows. k nearest neighbor (kNN) algorithm, distance weighted kNN, fuzzy kNN, nearest prototype classifier, and evidence theory-based kNN are implemented and studied. Results show that evidence-based kNN has the best performance based on classification accuracy.

2.9 Summary

In this chapter, we first provided an overview of the various data mining tasks and techniques and then discussed some of the techniques that we will utilize in this book. These include neural networks, support vector machines, and association rule mining.

Numerous data mining techniques have been designed and developed, and many of them are being utilized in commercial tools. Several of these techniques are variations of some of the basic classification, clustering, and association rule mining techniques. One of the major challenges today is to determine the appropriate techniques for various applications. We still need more benchmarks and performance studies. In addition, the techniques should result in fewer false positives and negatives. Although there is still much to be done, the progress over the past decade is extremely promising.

References

[Agrawal et al., 1993] Agrawal, R., T. Imielinski, A. Swami, Mining Association Rules between Sets of Items in Large Databases, in *Proceedings of the ACM SIGMOD Conference on Management of Data*, Washington, DC, May 1993, pp. 207–216.

[Agrawal et al., 2001] Agrawal, R., C. Aggarwal, V. Prasad, A Tree Projection Algorithm for Generation of Frequent Item Sets, *Journal of Parallel and Distributed Computing Archive*, Vol. 61, No. 3, 2001, pp. 350–371.

[Agrawal and Srikant, 1994] Agrawal, R., and R. Srikant, Fast Algorithms for Mining Association Rules in Large Database, in *Proceedings of the 20th International Conference on Very Large Data Bases*, San Francisco, CA, 1994, pp. 487–499.

[Bartlett and Shawe-Taylor, 1999] Bartlett, P., and J. Shawe-Taylor, Generalization Performance of Support Vector Machines and Other Pattern Classifiers, *Advances in Kernel Methods—Support Vector Learning*, MIT Press, Cambridge, MA, 1999, pp. 43–54.

[Cristianini and Shawe-Taylor, 2000] Cristianini, N., and J. Shawe-Taylor, *Introduction to Support Vector Machines*, Cambridge University Press, 2000, pp. 93–122.

[Houstma and Swanu, 1995] Houtsma, M., and A. Swanu, Set-Oriented Mining of Association Rules in Relational Databases, in *Proceedings of the Eleventh International Conference on Data Engineering*, Washington, DC, 1995, pp. 25–33.

[Liu et al., 1999] Liu, B., W. Hsu, Y. Ma, Association Rules with Multiple Minimum Supports, in *Proceedings of the Fifth ACM SIGKDD International Conference on Knowledge Discovery and Data Mining*, San Diego, CA, 1999, pp. 337–341.

[Mitchell, 1997] Mitchell, T. M., *Machine Learning*, McGraw-Hill, 1997, chap. 4.

[Mobasher et al., 2001] Mobasher, B., H. Dai, T. Luo, M. Nakagawa, Effective Personalization Based on Association Rule Discovery from Web Usage Data, in *Proceedings of the ACM Workshop on Web Information and Data Management (WIDM01)*, 2001, pp. 9–15.

[Pirolli et al., 1996] Pirolli, P., J. Pitkow, R. Rao, Silk from a Sow's Ear: Extracting Usable Structures from the Web, in *Proceedings of 1996 Conference on Human Factors in Computing Systems (CHI-96)*, Vancouver, British Columbia, Canada, 1996, pp. 118–125.

[Vapnik, 1995] Vapnik, V.N., *The Nature of Statistical Learning Theory*, Springer, 1995.

[Vapnik, 1998] Vapnik, V.N., *Statistical Learning Theory*, Wiley, 1998.

[Vapnik, 1999] Vapnik, V.N., *The Nature of Statistical Learning Theory*, 2nd Ed., Springer, 1999.

[Yang et al., 2001] Yang, Q., H. Zhang, T. Li, Mining Web Logs for Prediction Models in WWW Caching and Prefetching, in *The 7th ACM SIGKDD International Conference on Knowledge Discovery and Data Mining KDD*, August 26–29, 2001, pp. 473–478.

3

MALWARE

3.1 Introduction

Malware is the term used for malicious software. Malicious software is developed by hackers to steal data identities, cause harm to computers, and deny legitimate services to users, among others. Malware has plagued society and the software industry for almost four decades. Some of the early malware includes Creeper virus of 1970 and the Morris worm of 1988.

As computers became interconnected, the number of malwares developed increased at an alarming rate in the 1990s. Today, with the World Wide Web and so many transactions and acuities being carried out on the Internet, the malware problem is causing chaos among the computer and network users.

There are various types of malware, including viruses, worms, time and logic bombs, Trojan horses, and spyware. Preliminary results from Symantec published in 2008 suggest that "the release rate of malicious code and other unwanted programs may be exceeding that of legitimate software applications" [Malware, 2011]. CME (Common Malware Enumeration) was "created to provide single, common identifiers to new virus threats and to the most prevalent virus threats in the wild to reduce public confusion during malware incidents" [CME, 2011].

In this chapter we discuss various types of malware. In this book we describe the data mining tools we have developed to handle some types of malware. The organization of this chapter is as follows. In Section 3.2, we discuss viruses. In Section 3.3, we discuss worms. Trojan horses are discussed in Section 3.4. Time and logic bombs are discussed in Section 3.5. Botnets are discussed in Section 3.6. Spyware is discussed in Section 3.7. The chapter is summarized in Section 3.8. Figure 3.1 illustrates the concepts discussed in this chapter.

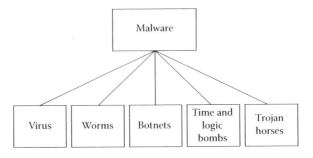

Figure 3.1   Concepts discussed in this chapter.

3.2 Viruses

Computer viruses are malware that piggyback onto other executables and are capable of replicating. Viruses can exhibit a wide range of malicious behaviors ranging from simple annoyance (such as displaying messages) to widespread destruction such as wiping all the data in the hard drive (e.g., CIH virus). Viruses are not independent programs. Rather, they are code fragments that exist on other binary files. A virus can infect a host machine by replicating itself when it is brought in contact with that machine, such as via a shared network drive, removable media, or email attachment. The replication is done when the virus code is executed and it is permitted to write in the memory.

There are two types of viruses based on their replication strategy: nonresident and resident. The nonresident virus does not store itself on the hard drive of the infected computer. It is only attached to an executable file that infects a computer. The virus is activated each time the infected executable is accessed and run. When activated, the virus looks for other victims (e.g., other executables) and infects them. On the contrary, resident viruses allocate memory in the computer hard drive, such as the boot sector. These viruses become active every time the infected machine starts.

The earliest computer virus dates back to 1970 with the advent of Creeper virus, detected on ARPANET [SecureList, 2011]. Since then, hundreds of thousands of different viruses have been written and corresponding antiviruses have also been devised to detect and eliminate the viruses from computer systems. Most commercial antivirus products apply a signature matching technique to detect a virus. A virus signature is a unique bit pattern in the virus binary that can accurately identify the virus [Signature, 2011]. Traditionally, virus signatures are generated manually. However, automated signature generation techniques based on data mining have been proposed recently [Masud et al., 2007, 2008].

3.3 Worms

Computer worms are malware but, unlike viruses, they need not attach themselves to other binaries. Worms are capable of propagating themselves to other hosts through network connections. Worms also exhibit a wide range of malicious behavior, such as spamming, phishing, harvesting and sending sensitive information to the worm writer, jamming or slowing down network connections, deleting data from hard drive, and so on. Worms are independent programs, and they reside in the infected machine by camouflage. Some of the worms open a backdoor in the infected machine, allowing the worm writer to control the machine and making it a zombie (or bot) for his malicious activities (see Section 3.6).

The earliest computer worm dates back to 1988, programmed by Robert Morris, who unleashed the Morris worm. It infected 10% of the then Internet, and his act resulted in the first conviction in the United States under the Computer Fraud and Abuse Act [Dressler, 2007]. One of the three authors of this book was working in computer security at Honeywell Inc. in Minneapolis at that time and vividly remembers what happened that November day.

Other infamous worms since then include the Melissa worm, unleashed in 1999, which crashed servers; the Mydoom worm released in 2004, which was the fastest spreading email worm; and the SQL Slammer worm, founded in 2003, which caused a global Internet slowdown.

Commercial antivirus products also detect worms by scanning worm signature against the signature database. However, although this technique is very effective against regular worms, it is usually not effective against zero-day attacks [Frei et al., 2008], polymorphic, and metamorphic worms. However, recent techniques for worm detection address these problems by automatic signature generation techniques [Kim and Karp, 2004], [Newsome et al., 2005]. Several data mining techniques also exist for detecting different types of worms [Masud et al., 2007, 2008].

3.4 Trojan Horses

Trojan horses have been studied within the context of multi-level databases. They covertly pass information from a high-level process to a low-level process. A good example of a Trojan horse is the manipulation of file locks. Now, according to the Bell and La Padula Security Policy (discussed in Appendix B), a secret process cannot directly send data to an unclassified process, as this will constitute a write down. However, a malicious secret process can covertly pass data to an unclassified process by manipulating the file locks as follows. Suppose both processes want to access an unclassified file. The Secret process wants to read from the file while the unclassified process can write into the file. However, both processes cannot obtain the read and write locks at the same time. Therefore, at time T1, let's assume that the Secret process has the read lock while the unclassified process attempts to get a write lock. The unclassified process cannot obtain this lock. This means a one bit information say, 0, is passed to the unclassified process. At time T2, let's assume the situation does not change. This means one bit information of 0 is passed. However, at time T3, let's assume the Secret process does not have the read lock, in which case the unclassified process can obtain the write lock. This time one bit information of 1 is passed. Over time a classified string of 0011000011101 could be passed from the Secret process to the unclassified process.

As stated in [Trojan Horse, 2011], a Trojan horse is software that appears to perform a desirable function for the user but actually carries out a malicious activity. In the previous example, the Trojan horse does have read access to the data object. It is reading from the object on behalf of the user. However, it also carries out malicious activity by manipulating the locks and sending data covertly to the unclassified user.

3.5 Time and Logic Bombs

In the software paradigm, *time bomb* refers to a computer program that stops functioning after a prespecified time or date has reached. This is usually imposed by software companies in beta versions of software so that the software stops functioning after a certain date. An example is the Windows Vista Beta 2, which stopped functioning on May 31, 2007 [Vista, 2007].

A *logic bomb* is a computer program that is intended to perform malicious activities when certain predefined conditions are met. This technique is sometimes injected into viruses or worms to increase the chances of survival and spreading before getting caught.

An example of a logic bomb is the Fannie Mae bomb in 2008 [Claburn, 2009]. A logic bomb was discovered at the mortgage company Fannie Mae on October 2008. An Indian citizen and IT contractor, Rajendrasinh Babubhai Makwana, who worked in Fannie Mae's Urbana, Maryland, facility, allegedly planted it, and it was set to activate on January 31, 2009, to wipe all of Fannie Mae's 4,000 servers. As stated in [Claburn, 2009], Makwana had been terminated around 1:00 pm on October 24, 2008, and planted the bomb while he still had network access. He was indicted in a Maryland court on January 27, 2009, for unauthorized computer access.

3.6 Botnet

Botnet is a network of compromised hosts, or bots, under the control of a human attacker known as the botmaster. The botmaster can issue commands to the bots to perform malicious actions, such as recruiting new bots, launching coordinated DDoS attacks against some hosts, stealing sensitive information from the bot machine, sending mass spam emails, and so on. Thus, botnets have emerged as an enormous threat to the Internet community.

According to [Messmer, 2009], more than 12 million computers in the United States are compromised and controlled by the top 10 notorious botnets. Among them, the highest number of compromised machines is due to the Zeus botnet. Zeus is a kind of Trojan (a malware), whose main purpose is to apply key-logging techniques to steal sensitive data such as login information (passwords, etc.), bank account numbers, and credit card numbers. One of its key-logging techniques is to inject fake HTML forms into online banking login pages to steal login information.

The most prevailing botnets are the IRC-botnets [Saha and Gairola, 2005], which have a centralized architecture. These botnets are usually very large and powerful, consisting of thousands of bots [Rajab et al., 2006]. However, their enormous size and centralized architecture also make them vulnerable to detection and demolition. Many approaches for detecting IRC botnets have been proposed recently ([Goebel and Holz, 2007], [Karasaridis et al., 2007], [Livadas et al., 2006], [Rajab et al., 2006]). Another type of botnet is the peer-to-peer (P2P) botnet. These botnets are distributed and much smaller than IRC botnets. So, they are more difficult to locate and destroy. Many recent works in P2P botnet analyzes their characteristics ([Grizzard et al., 2007], [Group, 2004], [Lemos, 2006]).

3.7 Spyware

As stated in [Spyware, 2011], spyware is a type of malware that can be installed on computers, which collects information about users without their knowledge. For example, spyware observes the web sites visited by the user, the emails sent by the user, and, in general, the activities carried out by the user in his or her computer. Spyware is usually hidden from the user. However, sometimes employers can install spyware to find out the computer activities of the employees.

An example of spyware is keylogger (also called keystroke logging) software. As stated in [Keylogger, 2011], keylogging is the action of tracking the keys struck on a keyboard, usually in a covert manner so that the person using the keyboard is unaware that their actions are being monitored. Another example of spyware is adware, when advertisement pops up on the computer when the person is doing some usually unrelated activity. In this case, the spyware monitors the web sites surfed by the user and carries out targeted marketing using adware.

3.8 Summary

In this chapter, we have provided an overview of malware (also known as malicious software). We discussed various types of malware, such as viruses, worms, time and logic bombs, Trojan horses, botnets, and spyware. As we have stated, malware is causing chaos in society and in the software industry. Malware technology is getting more and more sophisticated. Developers of malware are continuously changing patterns so as not to get caught. Therefore, developing solutions to detect and/or prevent malware has become an urgent need.

In this book, we discuss the tools we have developed to detect malware. In particular, we discuss tools for email worm detection, remote exploits detection, and botnet detection. We also discuss our stream mining tool that could potentially detect changing malware. These tools are discussed in Parts III through VII of this book. In Chapter 4, we will summarize the data mining tools we discussed in our previous book [Awad et al., 2009]. Our tools discussed in our current book have been influenced by the tools discussed in [Awad et al., 2009].

References

[Awad et al., 2009] Awad, M., L. Khan, B. Thuraisingham, L. Wang, *Design and Implementation of Data Mining Tools*, CRC Press, 2009.

[CME, 2011] http://cme.mitre.org

[Claburn, 2009] Claburn, T., Fannie Mae Contractor Indicted for Logic Bomb, *InformationWeek*, http://www.informationweek.com/news/security/management/showArticle.jhtml?articleID=212903521

[Dressler, 2007] Dressler, J. *"United States v. Morris": Cases and Materials on Criminal Law*, St. Paul, MN, Thomson/West, 2007.

[Frei et al., 2008] Frei, S., B. Tellenbach, B. Plattner, 0-Day Patch—Exposing Vendors(In)security Performance, *techzoom.net Publications*, http://www.techzoom.net/publications/0-day-patch/index.en

[Goebel and Holz, 2007] Goebel, J., and T. Holz, *Rishi: Identify Bot Contaminated Hosts by IRC Nickname Evaluation*, in USENIX/Hotbots '07 Workshop, 2007.

[Grizzard et al., 2007] Grizzard, J. B., V. Sharma, C. Nunnery, B. B. Kang, D. Dagon, *Peer-to-Peer Botnets: Overview and Case Study*, in USENIX/Hotbots '07 Workshop, 2007.

[Group, 2004] LURHQ Threat Intelligence Group, Sinit p2p Trojan Analysis, LURHQ, http://www.lurhq.com/sinit.html

[Karasaridis et al., 2007] Karasaridis, A., B. Rexroad, D. Hoeflin, *Wide-Scale Botnet Detection and Characterization*, in USENIX/Hotbots '07 Workshop, 2007.

[Keylogger, 2011] http://en.wikipedia.org/wiki/Keystroke_logging

[Kim and Karp, 2004] Kim, H. A., and Karp, B. (2004). Autograph: Toward Automated, Distributed Worm Signature Detection, in *Proceedings of the 13th USENIX Security Symposium (Security 2004)*, pp. 271–286.

[Lemos, 2006] Lemos, R. Bot Software Looks to Improve Peerage, http://www.securityfocus.com/news/11390

[Livadas et al., 2006] Livadas, C., B. Walsh, D. Lapsley, T. Strayer, Using Machine Learning Techniques to Identify Botnet Traffic, in *2nd IEEE LCN Workshop on Network Security (WoNS'2006)*, November 2006.

[Malware, 2011] http://en.wikipedia.org/wiki/Malware

[Masud et al., 2007] Masud, M., L. Khan, B. Thuraisingham, E-mail Worm Detection Using Data Mining, *International Journal of Information Security and Privacy*, Vol. 1, No. 4, 2007, pp. 47–61.

[Masud et al., 2008] Masud, M., L. Khan, B. Thuraisingham, A Scalable Multi-level Feature Extraction Technique to Detect Malicious Executables, *Information System Frontiers*, Vol. 10, No. 1, 2008, pp. 33–45.

[Messmer, 2009] Messmer, E., America's 10 Most Wanted Botnets, *Network World*, July 22, 2009, http://www.networkworld.com/news/2009/072209-botnets.html

[Newsome et al., 2005] Newsome, J., B. Karp, D. Song, Polygraph: Automatically Generating Signatures for Polymorphic Worms, in *Proceedings of the IEEE Symposium on Security and Privacy*, 2005, pp. 226–241.

[Rajab et al., 2006] Rajab, M. A., J. Zarfoss, F. Monrose, A. Terzis, A Multifaceted Approach to Understanding the Botnet Phenomenon, in *Proceedings of the 6th ACM SIGCOMM on Internet Measurement Conference (IMC)*, 2006, pp. 41–52.

[Saha and Gairola, 2005] Saha, B., and A. Gairola, *Botnet: An Overview*, CERT-In White Paper CIWP-2005-05, 2005.

[SecureList, 2011] Securelist.com Threat Analysis and Information, Kaspersky Labs, http://www.securelist.com/en/threats/detect

[Signature, 2011] Virus Signature, *PC Magazine Encyclopedia*, http://www.pcmag.com/encyclopedia_term/0,2542,t=virus+signature&i=53969,00.asp

[Spyware, 2011] http://en.wikipedia.org/wiki/Spyware

[Trojan Horse, 2011] http://en.wikipedia.org/wiki/Trojan_horse_(computing)

[Vista, 2007] Windows Vista, http://windows.microsoft.com/en-us/windows-vista/products/home

4

DATA MINING FOR SECURITY APPLICATIONS

4.1 Introduction

Ensuring the integrity of computer networks, both in relation to security and with regard to the institutional life of the nation in general, is a growing concern. Security and defense networks, proprietary research, intellectual property, and data-based market mechanisms that depend on unimpeded and undistorted access can all be severely compromised by malicious intrusions. We need to find the best way to protect these systems. In addition, we need techniques to detect security breaches.

Data mining has many applications in security, including in national security (e.g., surveillance) as well as in cyber security (e.g., virus detection). The threats to national security include attacking buildings and destroying critical infrastructures, such as power grids and telecommunication systems [Bolz et al., 2005]. Data mining techniques are being investigated to find out who the suspicious people are and who is capable of carrying out terrorist activities. Cyber security is involved with protecting the computer and network systems against corruption due to Trojan horses and viruses. Data mining is also being applied to provide solutions such as intrusion detection and auditing. In this chapter, we will focus mainly on data mining for cyber security applications.

To understand the mechanisms to be applied to safeguard the nation and the computers and networks, we need to understand the types of threats. In [Thuraisingham, 2003] we described real-time threats as well as non-real-time threats. A real-time threat is a threat that must be acted upon within a certain time to prevent some catastrophic situation. Note that a non-real-time threat could become

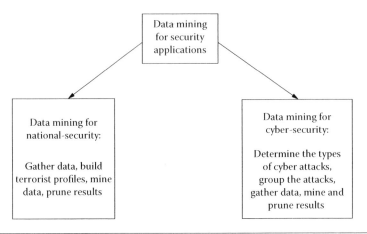

Figure 4.1   Data mining applications in security.

a real-time threat over time. For example, one could suspect that a group of terrorists will eventually perform some act of terrorism. However, when we set time bounds, such as that a threat will likely occur, say, before July 1, 2004, then it becomes a real-time threat and we have to take actions immediately. If the time bounds are tighter, such as "a threat will occur within two days," then we cannot afford to make any mistakes in our response.

There has been a lot of work on applying data mining for both national security and cyber security. Much of the focus of our previous book was on applying data mining for national security [Thuraisingham, 2003]. In this part of the book, we discuss data mining for cyber security. In Section 4.2, we discuss data mining for cyber security applications. In particular, we discuss the threats to the computers and networks and describe the applications of data mining to detect such threats and attacks. Some of our current research at the University of Texas at Dallas is discussed in Section 4.3. The chapter is summarized in Section 4.4. Figure 4.1 illustrates data mining applications in security.

4.2 Data Mining for Cyber Security

4.2.1 Overview

This section discusses information-related terrorism. By information-related terrorism, we mean cyber-terrorism as well as security violations through access control and other means. Trojan horses as well

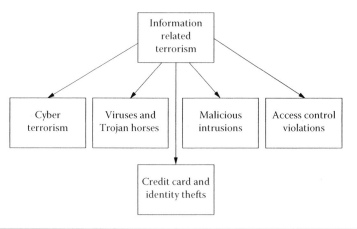

Figure 4.2 Cyber security threats.

as viruses are also information-related security violations, which we group into information-related terrorism activities.

In the next few subsections, we discuss various information-related terrorist attacks. In Section 4.2.2 we give an overview of cyber-terrorism and then discuss insider threats and external attacks. Malicious intrusions are the subject of Section 4.2.3. Credit card and identity theft are discussed in Section 4.2.4. Attacks on critical infrastructures are discussed in Section 4.2.5, and data mining for cyber security is discussed in Section 4.2.6. Figure 4.2 illustrates cyber security threats.

4.2.2 Cyber-Terrorism, Insider Threats, and External Attacks

Cyber-terrorism is one of the major terrorist threats posed to our nation today. As we have mentioned earlier, there is now so much information available electronically and on the web. Attack on our computers, as well as networks, databases, and the Internet, could be devastating to businesses. It is estimated that cyber-terrorism could cost billions of dollars to businesses. For example, consider a banking information system. If terrorists attack such a system and deplete accounts of the funds, then the bank could lose millions and perhaps billions of dollars. By crippling the computer system, millions of hours of productivity could be lost, and that also equates to money in the end. Even a simple power outage at work through some accident could cause several hours of productivity loss and, as a result, a major financial loss. Therefore, it is critical that our information systems be secure. We discuss various types of cyber-terrorist attacks. One is spreading viruses and Trojan horses that can wipe away files and other important documents; another is intruding the computer networks.

Note that threats can occur from outside or from the inside of an organization. Outside attacks are attacks on computers from someone outside the organization. We hear of hackers breaking into computer systems and causing havoc within an organization. There are hackers who start spreading viruses, and these viruses cause great damage to the files in various computer systems. But a more sinister problem is the insider threat. Just like non-information-related attacks, there is the insider threat with information-related attacks. There are people inside an organization who have studied the business practices and develop schemes to cripple the organization's information assets. These people could be regular employees or even those working at computer centers. The problem is quite serious, as someone may be masquerading as someone else and causing all kinds of damage. In the next few sections, we examine how data mining could detect and perhaps prevent such attacks.

4.2.3 Malicious Intrusions

Malicious intrusions may include intruding the networks, the web clients, the servers, the databases, and the operating systems. Many of the cyber-terrorism attacks are due to malicious intrusions. We hear much about network intrusions. What happens here is that intruders try to tap into the networks and get the information that is being transmitted. These intruders may be human intruders or Trojan horses set up by humans. Intrusions can also happen on files. For example, one can masquerade as someone else and log into someone else's computer system and access the files. Intrusions can also occur on databases. Intruders posing as legitimate users can pose queries such as SQL queries and access data that they are not authorized to know.

Essentially cyber-terrorism includes malicious intrusions as well as sabotage through malicious intrusions or otherwise. Cyber security consists of security mechanisms that attempt to provide solutions to cyber attacks or cyber-terrorism. When we discuss malicious intrusions or cyber attacks, we may need to think about the non-cyber world—that is, non-information-related terrorism—and then translate those attacks to attacks on computers and networks. For example, a thief could enter a building through a trap door. In the same way, a computer intruder could enter the computer or network through some sort of a trap door that has been intentionally built by a malicious insider and left unattended through perhaps careless design. Another example is a thief entering the bank with a mask and stealing the money. The analogy here is an intruder masquerades as someone else, legitimately enters the system, and takes all of the information assets. Money in the real world would translate to information assets in the cyber world. That is, there are many parallels between non-information-related attacks and information-related attacks. We can proceed to develop counter-measures for both types of attacks.

4.2.4 Credit Card Fraud and Identity Theft

We are hearing a lot these days about credit card fraud and identity theft. In the case of credit card fraud, others get hold of a person's credit card and make purchases; by the time the owner of the card finds out, it may be too late. The thief may have left the country by then. A similar problem occurs with telephone calling cards. In fact, this type of attack has happened to one of the authors once. Perhaps phone calls were being made using her calling card at airports, someone must have noticed, say, the dial tones and used the calling card, which was a company calling card. Fortunately, the telephone company detected the problem and informed the company. The problem was dealt with immediately.

A more serious theft is identity theft. Here one assumes the identity of another person, for example, by getting hold of the social security number and essentially carries out all the transactions under the other person's name. This could even be selling houses and depositing the income in a fraudulent bank account. By the time the owner finds out, it will be too late. The owner may have lost millions of dollars due to the identity theft.

We need to explore the use of data mining both for credit card fraud detection and identity theft. There have been some efforts on detecting credit card fraud [Chan, 1999]. We need to start working actively on detecting and preventing identity theft.

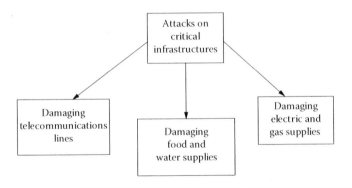

Figure 4.3   Attacks on critical infrastructures.

4.2.5 Attacks on Critical Infrastructures

Attacks on critical infrastructures could cripple a nation and its economy. Infrastructure attacks include attacks on the telecommunication lines; the electronic, power, and gas reservoirs; and water supplies, food supplies, and other basic entities that are critical for the operation of a nation.

Attacks on critical infrastructures could occur during any type of attack whether they are non-information-related, information-related, or bio-terrorist attacks. For example, one could attack the software that runs the telecommunications industry and close down all the telecommunications lines. Similarly, software that runs the power and gas supplies could be attacked. Attacks could also occur through bombs and explosives; for example, telecommunication lines could be attacked through bombs. Attacking transportation lines such as highways and railway tracks are also attacks on infrastructures.

Infrastructures could also be attacked by natural disasters, such as hurricanes and earthquakes. Our main interest here is the attacks on infrastructures through malicious attacks, both information-related and non-information-related. Our goal is to examine data mining and related data management technologies to detect and prevent such infrastructure attacks. Figure 4.3 illustrates attacks on critical infrastructures.

4.2.6 Data Mining for Cyber Security

Data mining is being applied for problems such as intrusion detection and auditing. For example, anomaly detection techniques could be used to detect unusual patterns and behaviors. Link analysis may be used to trace the viruses to the perpetrators. Classification may be used to group various cyber attacks and then use the profiles to detect an attack when it occurs. Prediction may be used to determine potential future attacks depending on information learned about terrorists through email and phone conversations. Also, for some threats, non-real-time data mining may suffice, whereas for certain other threats such as for network intrusions, we may need real-time data mining. Many researchers are investigating the use of data mining for intrusion detection. Although we need some form of real-time data mining—that is, the results have to be generated in real time—we also need to build models in real time. For example, credit card fraud detection is a form of real-time processing. However, here, models are usually built ahead of time. Building models in real time remains a challenge. Data mining can also be used for analyzing web logs as well as analyzing the audit trails. Based on the results of the data mining tool, one can then determine whether any unauthorized intrusions have occurred and/or whether any unauthorized queries have been posed.

Other applications of data mining for cyber security include analyzing the audit data. One could build a repository or a warehouse containing the audit data and then conduct an analysis using various data mining tools to see if there are potential anomalies. For example, there could be a situation where a certain user group may access the database between 3 am and 5 am. It could be that this group is working the night shift, in which case there may be a valid explanation. However, if this group is working between 9 am and 5 pm, then this may be an unusual occurrence. Another example is when a person accesses the databases always between 1 pm and 2 pm, but for the past two days he has been accessing the database between 1 am and 2 am. This could then be flagged as an unusual pattern that would require further investigation.

Insider threat analysis is also a problem from a national security, as well as a cyber security, perspective. That is, those working in a corporation who are considered to be trusted could commit espionage. Similarly, those with proper access to the computer system could plant Trojan horses and viruses. Catching such terrorists is far more difficult than catching terrorists outside of an organization. One may need to monitor the access patterns of all the individuals of a corporation

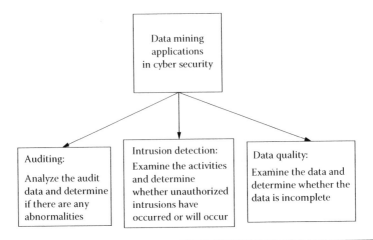

Figure 4.4   Data mining for cyber security.

even if they are system administrators, to see whether they are carrying out cyber-terrorism activities. There is some research now on applying data mining for such applications by various groups.

Although data mining can be used to detect and prevent cyber attacks, data mining also exacerbates some security problems, such as the inference and privacy problems. With data mining techniques one could infer sensitive associations from the legitimate responses. Figure 4.4 illustrates data mining for cyber security. For more details on a high-level overview, we refer the reader to [Thuraisingham, 2005a] and [Thuraisingham, 2005b].

4.3 Current Research and Development

We are developing a number of tools on data mining for cyber security applications at The University of Texas at Dallas. In our previous book we discussed one such tool for intrusion detection [Awad et al., 2009]. An intrusion can be defined as any set of actions that attempt to compromise the integrity, confidentiality, or availability of a resource. As systems become more complex, there are always exploitable weaknesses as a result of design and programming errors, or through the use of various "socially engineered" penetration techniques. Computer attacks are split into two categories: host-based attacks and network-based attacks. Host-based attacks target a machine and try to gain access to privileged services or resources on that machine. Host-based detection usually uses routines that obtain system call data from an audit process that tracks all system calls made on behalf of each user.

Network-based attacks make it difficult for legitimate users to access various network services by purposely occupying or sabotaging network resources and services. This can be done by sending large amounts of network traffic, exploiting well-known faults in networking services, overloading network hosts, and so forth. Network-based attack detection uses network traffic data (i.e., tcpdump) to look at traffic addressed to the machines being monitored. Intrusion detection systems are split into two groups: anomaly detection systems and misuse detection systems.

Anomaly detection is the attempt to identify malicious traffic based on deviations from established normal network traffic patterns. Misuse detection is the ability to identify intrusions based on a known pattern for the malicious activity. These known patterns are referred to as signatures. Anomaly detection is capable of catching new attacks. However, new legitimate behavior can also be falsely identified as an attack, resulting in a false positive. The focus with the current state of the art is to reduce false negative and false positive rates.

Our current tools, discussed in this book, include those for email worm detection, malicious code detection, buffer overflow detection, and botnet detection, as well as analyzing firewall policy rules. Figure 4.5 illustrates the various tools we have developed. Some of these tools are discussed in Parts II through VII of this book. For example, for email worm detection, we examine emails and extract features such as "number of attachments" and then train data mining tools with techniques such as SVM (support vector machine) or Naïve Bayesian classifiers and develop a model. Then we test the model and determine whether the email has a virus/worm or not.

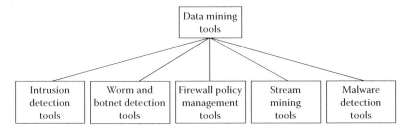

Figure 4.5   Data mining tools at UT Dallas.

We use training and testing datasets posted on various web sites. Similarly, for malicious code detection, we extract *n*-gram features with both assembly code and binary code. We first train the data mining tool using the SVM technique and then test the model. The classifier will determine whether the code is malicious or not. For buffer overflow detection, we assume that malicious messages contain code whereas normal messages contain data. We train SVM and then test to see if the message contains code or data.

4.4 Summary

This chapter has discussed data mining for security applications. We first started with a discussion of data mining for cyber security applications and then provided a brief overview of the tools we are developing. We describe some of these tools in Parts II through VII of this book. Note that we will focus mainly on malware detection. However, in Part VII, we also discuss tools for insider threat detection, active defense, and real-time data mining.

Data mining for national security as well as for cyber security is a very active research area. Various data mining techniques, including link analysis and association rule mining, are being explored to detect abnormal patterns. Because of data mining, users can now make all kinds of correlations. This also raises privacy concerns. More details on privacy can be obtained in [Thuraisingham, 2002].

References

[Awad et al., 2009] Awad, M., L. Khan, B. Thuraisingham, L. Wang, *Design and Implementation of Data Mining Tools*, CRC Press, 2009.

[Bolz et al., 2005] Bolz, F., K. Dudonis, D. Schulz, *The Counterterrorism Handbook: Tactics, Procedures, and Techniques,* Third Edition, CRC Press, 2005.

[Chan, 1999] Chan, P., W. Fan, A. Prodromidis, S. Stolfo, Distributed Data Mining in Credit Card Fraud Detection, *IEEE Intelligent Systems,* Vol. 14, No. 6, 1999, pp. 67–74.

[Thuraisingham, 2002] Thuraisingham, B., Data Mining, National Security, Privacy and Civil Liberties, *SIGKDD Explorations,* 2002, 4:2, 1–5.

[Thuraisingham, 2003] Thuraisingham, B., *Web Data Mining Technologies and Their Applications in Business Intelligence and Counter-Terrorism,* CRC Press, 2003.

[Thuraisingham, 2005a] Thuraisingham, B., *Managing Threats to Web Databases and Cyber Systems: Issues, Solutions and Challenges,* Kluwer, 2004 (Editors: V. Kumar, J. Srivastava, A. Lazarevic).

[Thuraisingham, 2005b] Thuraisingham, B., *Database and Applications Security,* CRC Press, 2005.

5

DESIGN AND IMPLEMENTATION OF DATA MINING TOOLS

5.1 Introduction

Data mining is an important process that has been integrated in many industrial, governmental, and academic applications. It is defined as the process of analyzing and summarizing data to uncover new knowledge. Data mining maturity depends on other areas, such as data management, artificial intelligence, statistics, and machine learning.

In our previous book [Awad et al., 2009], we concentrated mainly on the classification problem. We applied classification in three critical applications, namely, intrusion detection, WWW prediction, and image classification. Specifically, we strove to improve performance (time and accuracy) by incorporating multiple (two or more) learning models. In intrusion detection, we tried to improve the training time, whereas in WWW prediction, we studied hybrid models to improve the prediction accuracy. The classification problem is also sometimes referred to as "supervised learning," in which a set of labeled examples is learned by a model, and then a new example with an unknown label is presented to the model for prediction.

There are many prediction models that have been used, such as Markov models, decision trees, artificial neural networks, support vector machines, association rule mining, and many others. Each of these models has strengths and weaknesses. However, there is a common weakness among all of these techniques, which is the inability to suit all applications. The reason that there is no such ideal or perfect classifier is that each of these techniques is initially designed to solve specific problems under certain assumptions.

There are two directions in designing data mining techniques: model complexity and performance. In model complexity, new data structures, training set reduction techniques, and/or small numbers of adaptable parameters are proposed to simplify computations during learning without compromising the prediction accuracy. In model performance, the goal is to improve the prediction accuracy with some complication of the design or model. It is evident that there is a tradeoff between the performance complexity and the model complexity. In this book, we present studies of hybrid models to improve the prediction accuracy of data mining algorithms in two important applications, namely, intrusion detection and WWW prediction.

Intrusion detection involves processing and learning a large number of examples to detect intrusions. Such a process becomes computationally costly and impractical when the number of records to train against grows dramatically. Eventually, this limits our choice of the data mining technique to apply. Powerful techniques, such as support vector machines (SVMs), will be avoided because of the algorithm complexity. We propose a hybrid model, which is based on SVMs and clustering analysis, to overcome this problem. The idea is to apply a reduction technique using clustering analysis to approximate support vectors to speed up the training process of SVMs. We propose a method; namely, clustering trees-based SVM (CT-SVM), to reduce the training set and approximate support vectors. We exploit clustering analysis to generate support vectors to improve the accuracy of the classifier.

Surfing prediction is another important research area upon which many application improvements depend. Applications such as latency reduction, web search, and recommendation systems utilize surfing prediction to improve their performance. There are several challenges present in this area. These challenges include low accuracy rate [Pitkow and Pirolli, 1999]; sparsity of the data [Burke, 2002], [Grcar et al., 2005]; and large number of labels, which makes it a complex multiclass problem [Chung et al., 2004], not fully utilizing the domain knowledge. Our goal is to improve the predictive accuracy by combining several powerful classification techniques, namely, SVMs, artificial neural networks (ANNs), and the Markov model. The Markov model is a powerful technique for predicting seen data; however, it cannot predict the unseen data. On the other hand, techniques such as SVM and ANN are powerful predictors and can predict not only for the seen data but also for the unseen data. However, when dealing with large numbers of classes/labels, or when there is a possibility that one

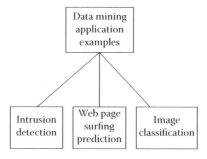

Figure 5.1 Data mining applications.

instance may belong to many classes, predictive power may decrease. We use Dempster's rule to fuse the prediction outcomes of these models. Such fusion combines the best of different models because it has achieved the best accuracy over the individual models.

In this chapter, we discuss the three applications we have considered in our previous book, *Design and Implementation of Data Mining Tools* [Awad et al., 2009]. This previous book is a useful reference and provides some background information for our current book. The applications are illustrated in Figure 5.1. In Section 5.2, we discuss intrusion detection. WWW surfing prediction is discussed in Section 5.3. Image classification is discussed in Section 5.4. More details in broader applications of data mining, such as data mining for security applications, web data mining, and image/multimedia data mining, can be found in [Awad et al., 2009].

5.2 Intrusion Detection

Security and defense networks, proprietary research, intellectual property, and data-based market mechanisms, which depend on unimpeded and undistorted access, can all be severely compromised by intrusions. We need to find the best way to protect these systems.

An intrusion can be defined as "any set of actions that attempts to compromise the integrity, confidentiality, or availability of a resource" [Heady et al., 1990], [Axelsson, 1999], [Debar et al., 2000]. User authentication (e.g., using passwords or biometrics), avoiding programming errors, and information protection (e.g., encryption) have all been used to protect computer systems. As systems become more complex, there are always exploitable weaknesses due to design and programming errors, or through the use of various "socially engineered" penetration techniques. For example, exploitable "buffer overflow" still exists in some recent system software as a result of programming errors. Elements central to intrusion detection are resources to be protected in a target system, i.e., user accounts, file systems, and system kernels; models that characterize the "normal" or "legitimate" behavior of these resources; and techniques that compare the actual system activities with the established models, identifying those that are "abnormal" or "intrusive." In pursuit of a secure system, different measures of system behavior have been proposed, based on an ad hoc presumption that normalcy and anomaly (or illegitimacy) will be accurately manifested in the chosen set of system features.

Intrusion detection attempts to detect computer attacks by examining various data records observed through processes on the same network. These attacks are split into two categories: host-based attacks [Anderson et al., 1995], [Axelsson, 1999], [Freeman et al., 2002] and network-based attacks [Ilgun et al., 1995], [Marchette, 1999]. Host-based attacks target a machine and try to gain access to privileged services or resources on that machine. Host-based detection usually uses routines that obtain system call data from an audit process, which tracks all system calls made on behalf of each user.

Network-based attacks make it difficult for legitimate users to access various network services by purposely occupying or sabotaging network resources and services. This can be done by sending large amounts of network traffic, exploiting well-known faults in networking services, and overloading network hosts. Network-based attack detection uses network traffic data (i.e., tcpdump) to look at traffic addressed to the machines being monitored. Intrusion detection systems are split into two groups: anomaly detection systems and misuse detection systems. Anomaly detection is the attempt to identify malicious traffic based on deviations from established normal network traffic patterns [McCanne et al., 1989], [Mukkamala et al., 2002]. Misuse detection is the ability to identify intrusions based on a known pattern for the malicious activity [Ilgun et al., 1995], [Marchette, 1999]. These known patterns are referred to as signatures. Anomaly detection is capable of catching new attacks. However, new legitimate behavior can also be falsely identified as an attack, resulting in a false positive. Our research will focus on network-level systems. A significant challenge in data mining is to reduce false negative and false positive rates. However, we also need to develop a realistic intrusion detection system.

SVM is one of the most successful classification algorithms in the data mining area, but its *long training time limits its use*. Many applications, such as data mining for bioinformatics and geoinformatics, require the processing of huge datasets. The training time of SVM is a serious obstacle in the processing of such datasets. According to [Yu et al., 2003], it would take years to train SVM on a dataset consisting of one million records. Many proposals have been submitted to enhance SVM to increase its training performance [Agarwal, 2002], [Cauwenberghs and Poggio, 2000], either through random selection or approximation of the marginal classifier [Feng and Mangasarian, 2001]. However, such approaches are still not feasible with large datasets where even multiple scans of an entire dataset are too expensive to perform or result in the loss, through oversimplification, of any benefit to be gained through the use of SVM [Yu et al., 2003].

In Part II of this book we propose a new approach for enhancing the training process of SVM when dealing with large training datasets. It is based on the combination of SVM and clustering analysis. The idea is as follows: SVM computes the maximal margin separating data points; hence, only those patterns closest to the margin can affect the computations of that margin, while other points can be discarded without affecting the final result. Those points lying close to the margin are called support vectors. We try to approximate these points by applying clustering analysis.

In general, using hierarchical clustering analysis based on a dynamically growing self-organizing tree (DGSOT) involves expensive computations, especially if the set of training data is large. However, in our approach, we control the growth of the hierarchical tree by allowing tree nodes (support vector nodes) close to the marginal area to grow, while halting distant ones. Therefore, the computations of SVM and further clustering analysis will be reduced dramatically. Also, to avoid the cost of computations involved in clustering analysis, we train SVM on the nodes of the tree after each phase or iteration, in which few nodes are added to the tree. Each iteration involves growing the hierarchical tree by adding new children nodes to the tree. This could cause a degradation of the accuracy of the resulting classifier. However, we use the support vector set as a priori knowledge to instruct the clustering algorithm to grow support vector nodes and to stop growing non-support vector nodes. By applying this procedure, the accuracy of the classifier improves and the size of the training set is kept to a minimum.

We report results here with one benchmark dataset, the 1998 DARPA dataset [Lippmann et al., 1998]. Also, we compare our approach with the Rocchio bundling algorithm, proposed for classifying documents by reducing the number of data points [Shih et al., 2003]. Note that the Rocchio bundling method reduces the number of data points before feeding those data points as support vectors to SVM for training. On the other hand, our clustering approach is intertwined with SVM. We have observed that our approach outperforms pure SVM and the Rocchio bundling technique in terms of accuracy, false positive (FP) rate, false negative (FN) rate, and processing time.

The contribution of our work to intrusion detection is as follows:

1. We propose a new support vector selection technique using clustering analysis to reduce the training time of SVM. Here, we combine clustering analysis and SVM training phases.
2. We show analytically the degree to which our approach is asymptotically quicker than pure SVM, and we validate this claim with experimental results.
3. We compare our approach with random selection and Rocchio bundling on a benchmark dataset and demonstrate impressive results in terms of training time, FP (false positive) rate, FN (false negative) rate, and accuracy.

5.3 Web Page Surfing Prediction

Surfing prediction is an important research area upon which many application improvements depend. Applications such as latency reduction, web search, and personalization systems utilize surfing prediction to improve their performance.

Latency of viewing with regard to web documents is an early application of surfing prediction. Web caching and pre-fetching methods are developed to pre-fetch multiple pages for improving the performance of World Wide Web systems. The fundamental concept behind all these caching algorithms is the ordering of various web documents using some ranking factors such as the popularity and the size of the document according to existing knowledge. Pre-fetching the highest ranking documents results in a significant reduction of latency during document viewing [Chinen and Yamaguchi, 1997], [Duchamp, 1999], [Griffioen and Appleton, 1994], [Teng et al., 2005], [Yang et al., 2001].

Improvements in web search engines can also be achieved using predictive models. Surfers can be viewed as having walked over the entire WWW link structure. The distribution of visits over all WWW pages is computed and used for re-weighting and re-ranking results. Surfer path information is considered more important than the text keywords entered by the surfers; hence, the more accurate the predictive models are, the better the search results will be [Brin and Page, 1998].

In Recommendation systems, collaborative filtering (CF) has been applied successfully to find the k top users having the same tastes or interests based on a given target user's records [Yu et al., 2003]. The k Nearest-Neighbor (kNN) approach is used to compare a user's historical profile and records with profiles of other users to find the top k similar users. Using Association Rule Mining (ARM), [Mobasher, et al., 2001] propose a method that matches an active user session with frequent itemsets and predicts the next page the user is likely to visit. These CF-based techniques suffer from well-known limitations, including scalability and efficiency [Mobasher et al., 2001], [Sarwar et al., 2000]. [Pitkow and Pirolli, 1999] explore pattern extraction and pattern matching based on a Markov model that predicts future surfing paths. Longest Repeating Subsequences (LRS) is proposed to reduce the model complexity (not predictive accuracy) by focusing on significant surfing patterns.

There are several problems with the current state-of-the-art solutions. First, the predictive accuracy using a proposed solution such as a Markov model is low; for example, the maximum training accuracy is 41% [Pitkow and Pirolli, 1999]. Second, prediction using Association Rule Mining and LRS pattern extraction is done based on choosing the path with the highest probability in the training set; hence, any new surfing path is misclassified because the probability of such a path occurring in the training set is zero. Third, the sparsity nature of the user sessions, which are used in training, can result in unreliable predictors [Burke, 2002], [Grcar et al., 2005]. Finally, many of the previous methods have ignored domain knowledge as a means for improving prediction. Domain knowledge plays a key role in improving the predictive accuracy because it can be used to eliminate irrelevant classifiers during prediction or reduce their effectiveness by assigning them lower weights.

WWW prediction is a multi-class problem, and prediction can resolve into many classes. Most multi-class techniques, such as one-VS-one and one-VS-all, are based on binary classification. Prediction is required to check any new instance against all classes. In WWW prediction, the number of classes is very large (11,700 classes in our experiments). Hence, prediction accuracy is very low [Chung et al., 2004] because it fails to choose the right class. For a given instance, domain knowledge can be used to eliminate irrelevant classes.

We use several classification techniques, namely, Support Vector Machines (SVMs), Artificial Neural Networks (ANNs), Association Rule Mining (ARM), and Markov model in WWW prediction. We propose a hybrid prediction model by combining two or more of them using Dempster's rule. Markov model is a powerful technique for predicting seen data; however, it cannot predict unseen data. On the other hand, SVM is a powerful technique, which can predict not only for the seen data but also for the unseen data. However, when dealing with too many classes or when there is a possibility that one instance may belong to many classes (e.g., a user after visiting the web pages 1, 2, 3, might go to page 10, while another might go to page 100), SVM predictive power may decrease because such examples confuse the training process. To overcome these drawbacks with SVM, we extract domain knowledge from the training set and incorporate this knowledge in the testing set to improve prediction accuracy of SVM by reducing the number of classifiers during prediction.

ANN is also a powerful technique, which can predict not only for the seen data but also for the unseen data. Nonetheless, ANN has similar shortcomings as SVM when dealing with too many classes or when there is a possibility that one instance may belong to many classes. Furthermore, the design of ANN becomes complex with a large number of input and output nodes. To overcome these drawbacks with ANN, we employ domain knowledge from the training set and incorporate this knowledge in the testing set by reducing the number of classifiers to consult during prediction. This improves the prediction accuracy and reduces the prediction time.

Our contributions to WWW prediction are as follows:

1. We overcome the drawbacks of SVM and ANN in WWW prediction by extracting and incorporating domain knowledge in prediction to improve accuracy and prediction time.
2. We propose a hybrid approach for prediction in WWW. Our approach fuses different combinations of prediction techniques, namely, SVM, ANN, and Markov, using Dempster's rule [Lalmas, 1997] to improve the accuracy.
3. We compare our hybrid model with different approaches, namely, Markov model, Association Rule Mining (ARM), Artificial Neural Networks (ANNs), and Support Vector Machines (SVMs) on a standard benchmark dataset and demonstrate the superiority of our method.

5.4 Image Classification

Image classification is about determining the class in which the image belongs to. It is an aspect of image data mining. Other image data mining outcomes include determining anomalies in images in the form of change detection as well as clustering images. In some situations, making links between images may also be useful. One key aspect of image classification is image annotation. Here the system understands raw images and automatically annotates them. The annotation is essentially a description of the images.

Our contributions to image classification include the following:

- We present a new framework of automatic image annotation.
- We propose a dynamic feature weighing algorithm based on histogram analysis and Chi-square.
- We present an image re-sampling method to solve the imbalanced data problem.
- We present a modified kNN algorithm based on evidence theory.

In our approach, we first annotate images automatically. In particular, we utilize K-means clustering algorithms to cluster image blobs and then make a correlation between the blobs and words. This will result in annotating images. Our research has also focused on classifying images using ontologies for geospatial data. Here we classify images using a region growing algorithm and then use high-level concepts in the form of homologies to classify the regions. Our research on image classification is given in [Awad et al., 2009].

5.5 Summary

In this chapter, we have discussed three applications that were described in [Awad et al., 2009]. We have developed data mining tools for these three applications. They are intrusion detection, web page surfing prediction, and image classification. They are part of the broader class of applications: cyber security, web information management, and multimedia/image information management, respectively. In this book, we have taken one topic discussed in our prior book and elaborated on it. In particular, we have described data mining for cyber security and have focused on malware detection.

Future directions will focus on two aspects. One is enhancing the data mining algorithms to address the limitations, such as false positives and false negatives, as well as reason with uncertainty. The other is to expand on applying data mining to the broader classes of applications, such as cyber security, multimedia information management, and web information management.

References

[Agarwal, 2002] Agarwal, D. K., Shrinkage Estimator Generalizations of Proximal Support Vector Machines, in *Proceedings of the 8th International Conference Knowledge Discovery and Data Mining*, Edmonton, Canada, 2002, pp. 173–182.

[Anderson et al., 1995] Anderson, D., T. Frivold, A. Valdes, *Next-Generation Intrusion Detection Expert System (NIDES): A Summary*, Technical Report SRI-CSL-95-07, Computer Science Laboratory, SRI International, Menlo Park, California, May 1995.

[Awad et al., 2009]), Awad M., L. Khan, B. Thuraisingham, L. Wang, *Design and Implementation of Data Mining Tools*, CRC Press, 2009.

[Axelsson, 1999] Axelsson, S., *Research in Intrusion Detection Systems: A Survey*, Technical Report TR 98-17 (revised in 1999), Chalmers University of Technology, Goteborg, Sweden, 1999.

[Brin and Page, 1998] Brin, S., and L. Page, The Anatomy of a Large-Scale Hypertextual Web Search Engine, in *Proceedings of the 7th International WWW Conference*, Brisbane, Australia, 1998, pp. 107–117.

[Burke, 2002] Burke, R., Hybrid Recommender Systems: Survey and Experiments, *User Modeling and User-Adapted Interaction*, Vol. 12, No. 4, 2002, pp. 331–370.

[Cauwenberghs and Poggio, 2000] Cauwenberghs, G., and T. Poggio, Incremental and Decremental Support Vector Machine Learning, *Advances in Neural Information Processing Systems 13, Papers from Neural Information Processing Systems (NIPS) 2000*, Denver, CO. MIT Press 2001, T. K. Leen, T. G. Dietterich, V. Tresp (Eds.).

[Chinen and Yamaguchi, 1997] Chinen, K., and S. Yamaguchi, An Interactive Prefetching Proxy Server for Improvement of WWW Latency, in *Proceedings of the Seventh Annual Conference of the Internet Society (INET'97)*, Kuala Lumpur, June 1997.

[Chung et al., 2004] Chung, V., C. H. Li, J. Kwok, Dissimilarity Learning for Nominal Data, *Pattern Recognition*, Vol. 37, No. 7, 2004, pp. 1471–1477.

[Debar et al., 2000] Debar, H., M. Dacier, A. Wespi, A Revised Taxonomy for Intrusion Detection Systems, *Annales des Telecommunications*, Vol. 55, No. 7–8, 2000, pp. 361–378.

[Duchamp, 1999] Duchamp, D., Prefetching Hyperlinks, in *Proceedings of the Second USENIX Symposium on Internet Technologies and Systems (USITS)*, Boulder, CO, 1999, pp. 127–138.

[Feng and Mangasarian, 2001] Feng, G., and O. L. Mangasarian, Semi-supervised Support Vector Machines for Unlabeled Data Classification, *Optimization Methods and Software*, 2001, Vol. 15, pp. 29–44.

[Freeman et al., 2002] Freeman, S., A. Bivens, J. Branch, B. Szymanski, Host-Based Intrusion Detection Using User Signatures, in *Proceedings of Research Conference*, RPI, Troy, NY, October 2002.

[Grcar et al., 2005] Grcar, M., B. Fortuna, D. Mladenic, *k*NN versus SVM in the Collaborative Filtering Framework, *WebKDD '05*, August 21, 2005, Chicago, Illinois.

[Griffioen and Appleton, 1994] Griffioen, J., and R. Appleton, Reducing File System Latency Using a Predictive Approach, in *Proceedings of the 1994 Summer USENIX Technical Conference*, Cambridge, MA.

[Heady et al., 1990] Heady, R., Luger, G., Maccabe, A., Servilla, M., The Architecture of a Network Level Intrusion Detection System, University of New Mexico Technical Report TR-CS-1990-20, 1990.

[Ilgun et al., 1995] Ilgun, K., R. A., Kemmerer, P. A. Porras, State Transition Analysis: A Rule-Based Intrusion Detection Approach, *IEEE Transactions on Software Engineering*, Vol. 21, No. 3, 1995, pp. 181–199.

[Lalmas, 1997] Lalmas, M., Dempster-Shafer's Theory of Evidence Applied to Structured Documents: Modelling Uncertainty, in *Proceedings of the 20th Annual International ACM SIGIR*, Philadelphia, PA, 1997, pp. 110–118.

[Lippmann et al., 1998] Lippmann, R. P., I. Graf, D. Wyschogrod, S. E. Webster, D. J. Weber, S. Gorton, The 1998 DARPA/AFRL Off-Line Intrusion Detection Evaluation, *First International Workshop on Recent Advances in Intrusion Detection (RAID)*, Louvain-la-Neuve, Belgium, 1998.

[Marchette, 1999] Marchette, D., A Statistical Method for Profiling Network Traffic, *First USENIX Workshop on Intrusion Detection and Network Monitoring*, Santa Clara, CA, 1999, pp. 119–128.

[Mobasher et al., 2001] Mobasher, B., H. Dai, T. Luo, M. Nakagawa, Effective Personalization Based on Association Rule Discovery from Web Usage Data, in *Proceedings of the ACM Workshop on Web Information and Data Management (WIDM01)*, 2001, pp. 9–15.

[Mukkamala et al., 2002] Mukkamala, S., G. Janoski, A. Sung, Intrusion Detection: Support Vector Machines and Neural Networks, in *Proceedings of IEEE International Joint Conference on Neural Networks (IJCNN)*, Honolulu, HI, 2002, pp. 1702–1707.

[Pitkow and Pirolli, 1999] Pitkow, J., and P. Pirolli, Mining Longest Repeating Subsequences to Predict World Wide Web Surfing, in *Proceedings of 2nd USENIX Symposium on Internet Technologies and Systems (USITS'99)*, Boulder, CO, October 1999, pp. 139–150.

[Sarwar et al., 2000] Sarwar, B. M., G. Karypis, J. Konstan, J. Riedl, Analysis of Recommender Algorithms for E-Commerce, in *Proceedings of the 2nd ACM E-Commerce Conference (EC'00)*, October 2000, Minneapolis, Minnesota, pp. 158–167.

[Shih et al., 2003] Shih, L., Y. D. M. Rennie, Y. Chang, D. R. Karger, Text Bundling: Statistics-Based Data Reduction, *Proceedings of the Twentieth International Conference on Machine Learning (ICML)*, 2003, Washington, DC, pp. 696-703.

[Teng et al., 2005] Teng, W.-G., C.-Y. Chang, M.-S. Chen, Integrating Web Caching and Web Prefetching in Client-Side Proxies, *IEEE Transaction on Parallel and Distributed Systems*, Vol. 16, No. 5, May 2005, pp. 444–455.

[Yang et al., 2001] Yang, Q., H. Zhang, T. Li, Mining Web Logs for Prediction Models in WWW Caching and Prefetching, in *The 7th ACM SIGKDD International Conference on Knowledge Discovery and Data Mining KDD*, August 26–29, 2001, pp. 475–478.

[Yu et al., 2003] Yu, H., J. Yang, J. Han, Classifying Large Data Sets Using SVM with Hierarchical Clusters, *SIGKDD 2003*, August 24–27, 2003, Washington, DC, pp. 306–315.

Conclusion to Part I

We have presented various supporting technologies for data mining for malware detection. These include data mining technologies, malware technologies, as well as data mining applications. First, we provided an overview of data mining techniques. Next, we discussed various types of malware. This was followed by a discussion of data mining for security applications. Finally we provided a summary of the data mining tools we discussed in our previous book, *Design and Implementation of Data Mining Tools.*

Now that we have provided an overview of supporting technologies, we can discuss the various types of data mining tools we have developed for malware detection. In Part II, we discuss email worm detection tools. In Part III, we discuss data mining tools for detecting malicious executables. In Part IV, we discuss data mining for detecting remote exploits. In Part V, we discuss data mining for botnet detection. In Part VI, we discuss stream mining tools. Finally, in Part VII we discuss some of the emerging tools, including data mining for insider threat detection and firewall policy analysis.

PART II

DATA MINING
FOR EMAIL
WORM DETECTION

Introduction to Part II

In this part, we will discuss data mining techniques to detect email worms. Email messages contain a number of different features such as the total number of words in the message body/subject, presence/absence of binary attachments, type of attachments, and so on. The goal is to obtain an efficient classification model based on these features. The solution consists of several steps. First, the number of features is reduced using two different approaches: *feature selection* and *dimension reduction*. This step is necessary to reduce noise and redundancy from the data. The feature selection technique is called *Two-Phase Selection* (TPS), which is a novel combination of decision tree and greedy selection algorithm. The dimension reduction is performed by *Principal Component Analysis*. Second, the reduced data are used to train a classifier. Different classification techniques have been used, such as Support Vector Machine (SVM), Naïve Bayes, and their combination. Finally, the trained classifiers are tested on a dataset containing both known and unknown types of worms. These results have been compared with published results. It is found that the proposed TPS selection along with SVM classification achieves the best accuracy in detecting both known and unknown types of worms.

Part II consists of three chapters: 6, 7, and 8. In Chapter 6, we provide an overview of email worm detection, including a discussion of related work. In Chapter 7, we discuss our tool for email worm detection. In Chapter 8, we analyze the results we have obtained by using our tool.

6

EMAIL WORM DETECTION

6.1 Introduction

An email worm spreads through infected email messages. The worm may be carried by an attachment, or the email may contain links to an infected web site. When the user opens the attachment or clicks the link, the host gets infected immediately. The worm exploits the vulnerable email software in the host machine to send infected emails to addresses stored in the address book. Thus, new machines get infected. Worms bring damage to computers and people in various ways. They may clog the network traffic, cause damage to the system, and make the system unstable or even unusable.

The traditional method of worm detection is signature based. A signature is a unique pattern in the worm body that can identify it as a particular type of worm. Thus, a worm can be detected from its signature. But the problem with this approach is that it involves a significant amount of human intervention and may take a long time (from days to weeks) to discover the signature. Thus, this approach is not useful against "zero-day" attacks of computer worms. Also, signature matching is not effective against polymorphism.

Thus, there is a growing need for a fast and effective detection mechanism that requires no manual intervention. Our work is directed toward automatic and efficient detection of email worms. In our approach, we have developed a two-phase feature selection technique for email worm detection. In this approach, we apply TPS to select the best features using decision tree and greedy algorithm. We compare our approach with two baseline techniques. The first baseline approach does not apply any feature reduction. It trains a classifier with the unreduced dataset. The second baseline approach reduces data dimension using principal component analysis (PCA) and trains

Figure 6.1 Concepts in this chapter. (This figure appears in Email Work Detection Using Data Mining, *International Journal of Information Security and Privacy,* Vol. 1, No. 4, pp. 47–61, 2007, authored by M. Masud, L. Kahn, and B. Thuraisingham. Copyright 2010, IGI Global, www.igi-global. com. Posted by permission of the publisher.)

a classifier with the reduced dataset. It is shown empirically that our TPS approach outperforms the baseline techniques. We also report the feature set that achieves this performance. For the base learning algorithm (i.e., classifier), we use both support vector machine (SVM) and Naïve Bayes (NB). We observe relatively better performance with SVM. Thus, we strongly recommend applying SVM with our TPS process for detecting novel email worms in a feature-based paradigm.

The organization of this chapter is as follows. Section 6.2 describes our architecture. Section 6.3 describes related work in automatic email worm detection. Our approach is briefly discussed in Section 6.3. The chapter is summarized in section 6.4. Figure 6.1 illustrates the concepts in this chapter.

6.2 Architecture

Figure 6.2 illustrates our architecture at a high level. At first we build a classifier from training data containing both benign and infected

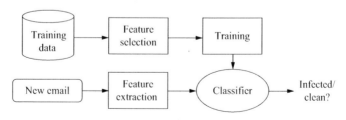

Figure 6.2 Architecture for email worm detection. (This figure appears in Email Work Detection Using Data Mining, *International Journal of Information Security and Privacy,* Vol. 1, No. 4, pp. 47–61, 2007, authored by M. Masud, L. Kahn, and B. Thuraisingham. Copyright 2010, IGI Global, www.igi-global.com. Posted by permission of the publisher.)

emails. Then, unknown emails are tested with the classifier to predict whether it is infected or clean.

The training data consist of both benign and malicious (infected) emails. These emails are called training instances. The training instances go through the *feature selection* module, where features are extracted and best features are selected (see Sections 7.3, 7.4). The output of the feature selection module is a feature vector for each training instance. These feature vectors are then sent to the *training* module to train a classification model (*classifier* module). We use different classification models such as support vector machine (SVM), Naïve Bayes (NB), and their combination (see Section 7.5). A new email arriving in the host machine first undergoes the *feature extraction* module, where the same features, selected in the feature selection module, are extracted and a feature vector is produced. This feature vector is given as input to the classifier, and the classifier predicts the *class* (i.e., benign/infected) of the email.

6.3 Related Work

There are different approaches to automating the detection of worms. These approaches are mainly of two types: *behavioral* and *content based*. Behavioral approaches analyze the behavior of messages like source-destination addresses, attachment types, message frequency, and so forth. Content-based approaches look into the content of the message and try to detect the signature automatically. There are also combined methods that take advantage of both techniques.

An example of behavioral detection is social network analysis [Golbeck and Hendler, 2004], [Newman et al., 2002]. It detects worm-infected emails by creating graphs of a network, where users are represented as nodes, and communications between users are represented as edges. A social network is a group of nodes among which there exists edges. Emails that propagate beyond the group boundary are considered to be infected. The drawback of this system is that worms can easily bypass social networks by intelligently choosing recipient lists by looking at recent emails in the user's outbox.

Another example of behavioral approach is the application of the Email Mining Toolkit (EMT) [Stolfo et al., 2006]. The EMT computes *behavior profiles* of user email accounts by analyzing email logs. They use some modeling techniques to achieve high detection rates with very low false positive rates. Statistical analysis of outgoing emails is another behavioral approach [Schultz et al., 2001], [Symantec, 2005]. Statistics collected from frequency of communication between clients and their mail server, byte sequences in the attachment, and so on, are used to predict anomalies in emails and thus worms are detected.

An example of the content-based approach is the EarlyBird System [Singh et al., 2003]. In this system, statistics on highly repetitive packet contents are gathered. These statistics are analyzed to detect possible infection of host or server machines. This method generates the content signature of a worm without any human intervention. Results reported by this system indicated a very low false positive rate of detection. Other examples are the Autograph [Kim and Karp, 2004] and the Polygraph [Newsome et al., 2005], developed at Carnegie Mellon University.

There are other approaches to detect early spreading of worms, such as employing "honeypot." A honeypot [Honeypot, 2006] is a closely monitored decoy computer that attracts attacks for early detection and in-depth adversary analysis. The honeypots are designed to not send out email in normal situations. If a honeypot begins to send out emails after running the attachment of an email, it is determined that this email is an email worm.

Another approach, by [Sidiroglou et al., 2005], employs behavior-based anomaly detection, which is different from signature-based or statistical approaches. Their approach is to open all suspicious attachments inside an instrumented virtual machine looking for dangerous actions, such as writing to the Windows registry, and flag suspicious messages.

Our work is related to [Martin et al., 2005-a]. They report an experiment with email data, where they apply a statistical approach to find an optimum subset of a large set of features to facilitate the classification of outgoing emails and, eventually, detect novel email worms. However, our approach is different from their approach in that we apply PCA and TPS to reduce noise and redundancy from data.

6.4 Overview of Our Approach

We apply a feature-based approach to worm detection. A number of features of email messages have been identified in [Martin et al.,

2005-a) and discussed in this chapter. The total number of features is large, some of which may be redundant or noisy. So we apply two different feature-reduction techniques: a *dimension-reduction* technique called PCA and our novel *feature-selection* technique called TPS, which applies decision tree and greedy elimination. These features are used to train a classifier to obtain a classification model. We use three different classifiers for this task: SVM, NB, and a combination of SVM and NB, mentioned henceforth as the *Series* classifier. The Series approach was first proposed by [Martin et al., 2005-b].

We use the dataset of [Martin et al., 2005-a] for evaluation purpose. The original data distribution was unbalanced, so we balance it by rearranging. We divide the dataset into two disjoint subsets: the *known worms set* or K-Set and the *novel worms set* or N-Set. The K-Set contains some clean emails and emails infected by five different types of worms. The K-Set contains emails infected by a sixth type worm but no clean email. We run a threefold cross validation on the K-Set. At each iteration of the cross validation, we test the accuracy of the trained classifiers on the N-Set. Thus, we obtain two different measures of accuracy, namely, the accuracy of the threefold cross validation on K-Set, and the average accuracy of novel worm detection on N-Set.

Our contributions to this work are as follows. First, we apply two special feature-reduction techniques to remove redundancy and noise from data. One technique is PCA, and the other is our novel TPS algorithm. PCA is commonly used to extract patterns from high-dimensional data, especially when the data are noisy. It is a simple and nonparametric method. TPS applies decision tree C4.5 [Quinlan, 1993] for initial selection, and thereafter it applies greedy elimination technique (see Section 7.4.2, "Two-Phase Feature Selection (TPS)"). Second, we create a balanced dataset as explained earlier. Finally, we compare the individual performances among NB, SVM, and Series and show empirically that the Series approach proposed by [Martin et al., 2005-b] performs worse than either NB or SVM. Our approach is illustrated in Figure 6.3.

6.5 Summary

In this chapter we have argued that feature-based approaches for worm detection are superior to the traditional signature-based approaches.

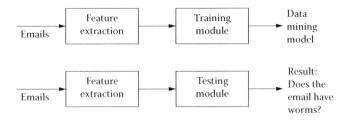

Figure 6.3 Email worm detection using data mining. (This figure appears in Email Work Detection Using Data Mining, *International Journal of Information Security and Privacy,* Vol. 1, No. 4, pp. 47–61, 2007, authored by M. Masud, L. Kahn, and B. Thuraisingham. Copyright 2010, IGI Global, www.igi-global.com. Posted by permission of the publisher.)

Next, we described some related work on email worm detection and then briefly discussed our approach, which uses feature reduction and classification using PCA, SVM, and NB.

In the future, we are planning to detect worms by combining the feature-based approach with the content-based approach to make it more robust and efficient. We are also focusing on the statistical property of the contents of the messages for possible contamination of worms. Our approach is discussed in Chapter 7. Analysis of the results of our approach is given in Chapter 8.

References

[Golbeck and Hendler, 2004] Golbeck, J., and J. Hendler, Reputation Network Analysis for Email Filtering, in *Proceedings of CEAS 2004 First Conference on Email and Anti-Spam.*

[Honeypot, 2006] Intrusion Detection, Honeypots, and Incident Handling Resources, *Honeypots.net,* http://www.honeypots.net

[Kim and Karp, 2004] Kim, H.-A., and B. Karp, Autograph: Toward Automated, Distributed Worm Signature Detection, in *Proceedings of the 13th USENIX Security Symposium (Security 2004),* San Diego, CA, August 2004, pp. 271–286.

[Martin et al., 2005-a] Martin, S., A. Sewani, B. Nelson, K. Chen, A. D. Joseph, Analyzing Behavioral Features for Email Classification, in *Proceedings of the IEEE Second Conference on Email and Anti-Spam (CEAS 2005),* July 21 & 22, Stanford University, CA.

[Martin et al., 2005-b] Martin, S., A. Sewani, B. Nelson, K. Chen, A. D. Joseph, *A Two-Layer Approach for Novel Email Worm Detection.* Submitted to USENIX Steps on Reducing Unwanted Traffic on the Internet (SRUTI).

[Newman et al., 2002] Newman, M. E. J., S. Forrest, J. Balthrop, Email Networks and the Spread of Computer Viruses, *Physical Review* E 66, 035101, 2002.

[Newsome et al., 2005] Newsome, J., B. Karp, D. Song, Polygraph: Automatically Generating Signatures for Polymorphic Worms, in *Proceedings of the IEEE Symposium on Security and Privacy*, May 2005.

[Quinlan, 1993] Quinlan, J. R. *C4.5: Programs for Machine Learning*, Morgan Kaufmann Publishers, 1993.

[Schultz et al., 2001] Schultz, M., E. Eskin, E. Zadok, MEF: Malicious Email Filter: A UNIX Mail Filter That Detects Malicious Windows Executables, in *USENIX Annual Technical Conference—FREENIX Track*, June 2001.

[Sidiroglou et al., 2005] Sidiroglou, S., J. Ioannidis, A. D. Keromytis, S. J. Stolfo, An Email Worm Vaccine Architecture, in *Proceedings of the First International Conference on Information Security Practice and Experience (ISPEC 2005)*, Singapore, April 11–14, 2005, pp. 97–108.

[Singh et al., 2003] Singh, S., C. Estan, G. Varghese, S. Savage, *The EarlyBird System for Real-Time Detection of Unknown Worms*, Technical Report CS2003-0761, University of California, San Diego, August 4, 2003.

[Stolfo et al., 2006] Stolfo, S. J., S. Hershkop, C. W. Hu, W. Li, O. Nimeskern, K. Wang, Behavior-Based Modeling and Its Application to Email Analysis, *ACM Transactions on Internet Technology (TOIT)*, February 2006.

[Symantec, 2005] *W32.Beagle.BG@mm*, http://www.sarc.com/avcenter/venc/data/w32.beagle.bg@mm.html

7

DESIGN OF THE DATA MINING TOOL

7.1 Introduction

As we have discussed in Chapter 6, feature-based approaches for worm detection are superior to the traditional signature-based approaches. Our approach for worm detection carries out feature reduction and classification using principal component analysis (PCA), support vector machine (SVM), and Naïve Bayes (NB). In this chapter, we first discuss the features that are used to train classifiers for detecting email worms. Second, we describe our dimension reduction and feature selection techniques. Our proposed two-phase feature selection technique utilizes information gain and decision tree induction algorithm for feature selection. In the first phase, we build a decision tree using the training data on the whole feature set. The decision tree selects a subset of features, which we call the minimal subset of features. In the second phase, we greedily select additional features and add to the minimal subset. Finally, we describe the classification techniques, namely, Naïve Bayes (NB), support vector machine (SVM), and a combination of NB and SVM.

The organization of this chapter is as follows. Our architecture is discussed in Section 7.2. Feature descriptions are discussed in Section 7.3. Section 7.4 describes feature reduction techniques. Classification techniques are described in Section 7.5. In particular, we provide an overview of the feature selection, dimension reduction, and classification techniques we have used in our tool. The chapter is summarized in Section 7.6. Figure 7.1 illustrates the concepts in this chapter.

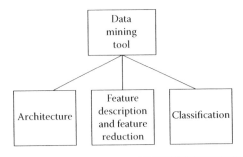

Figure 7.1   Concepts in this chapter.

7.2 Architecture

Figure 7.2 illustrates our system architecture, which includes components for feature reduction and classification. There are two stages of the process: training and classification. Training is performed with collected samples of benign and infected emails, that is, the *training data*. The training samples are first analyzed and a set of features are identified (Section 7.3). To reduce the number of features, we apply a *feature selection* technique called "two-phase feature selection" (Section 7.4). Using the selected set of features, we generate feature vectors for each training sample, and the feature vectors are used to train a *classifier* (Section 7.5). When a new email needs to be tested, it first goes through a feature extraction module that generates a feature vector. This feature vector is used by the classifier to *predict* the class of the email, that is, to predict whether the email is clean or infected.

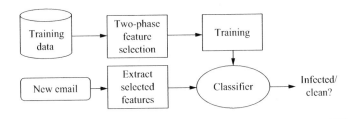

Figure 7.2   Architecture.

7.3 Feature Description

The features are extracted from a repository of outgoing emails collected over a period of two years [Martin et al., 2005-a]. These features are categorized into two different groups: per-email feature and per-window feature. Per-email features are features of a single email, whereas per-window features are features of a collection of emails sent/received within a window of time.

For a detailed description of the features, please refer to [Martin et al., 2005-a]. Each of these features is either continuous valued or binary. The value of a binary feature is either 0 or 1, depending on the presence or absence of this feature in a data point. There are a total of 94 features. Here we describe some of them.

7.3.1 Per-Email Features

HTML in body: Whether there is HTML in the email body. This feature is used because a bug in the HTML parser of the email client is a vulnerability that may be exploited by worm writers. It is a binary feature.

Embedded image: Whether there is any embedded image. This is used because a buggy image processor of the email client is also vulnerable to attacks.

Hyperlinks: Whether there are hyperlinks in the email body. Clicking an infected link causes the host to be infected. It is also a binary feature.

Binary attachment: Whether there are any binary attachments. Worms are mainly propagated by binary attachments. This is also a binary feature.

Multipurpose Internet Mail Extension (MIME) type of attachments: There are different MIME types, for example. "application/msword," "application/pdf," "image/gif," "text/plain," and others. Each of these types is used as a binary feature (total 27).

UNIX "magic number" of file attachments: Sometimes a different MIME type is assigned by the worm writers to evade detection. Magic numbers can accurately detect the MIME type. Each of these types is used as a binary feature (total 43).

Number of attachments: It is a continuous feature.

Number of words/characters in subject/body: These features are continuous. Most worms choose random text, whereas a user may have certain writing characteristics. Thus, these features are sometimes useful to detect infected emails.

7.3.2 Per-Window Features

Number of emails sent in window: An infected host is supposed to send emails at a faster rate. This is a continuous feature.

Number of unique email recipients, senders: These are also important criteria to distinguish between normal and infected host. This is a continuous feature too.

Average number of words/characters per subject, body, average word length: These features are also useful in distinguishing between normal and viral activity.

Variance in number of words/characters per subject, body, variance in word length: These are also useful properties of email worms.

Ratio of emails to attachments: Usually, normal emails do not contain attachments, whereas most infected emails do contain them.

7.4 Feature Reduction Techniques

7.4.1 Dimension Reduction

The high dimensionality of data always appears to be a major problem for classification tasks because (a) it increases the running time of the classification algorithms, (b) it increases chance of overfitting, and (c) a large number of instances is required for learning tasks. We apply PCA (Principal Components Analysis) to obtain a reduced dimensionality of data in an attempt to eliminate these problems.

PCA finds a reduced set of attributes by projecting the original dimension into a lower dimension. PCA is also capable of discovering hidden patterns in data, thereby increasing classification accuracy. As high-dimensional data contain redundancies and noise, it is much harder for the learning algorithms to find a hypothesis consistent with the training instances. The learned hypothesis is likely to be too complex and susceptible to overfitting. PCA reduces the dimension, without losing much information, and thus allows the learning algorithms to find a simpler hypothesis that is consistent with the training examples, and thereby reduces the chance of overfitting. But it should be noted that PCA projects data into a lower dimension in the direction of maximum dispersion. Maximum dispersion of data does not necessarily imply maximum separation of between-class data and/or maximum concentration of within-class data. If this is the case, then PCA reduction may result in poor performance.

7.4.2 Two-Phase Feature Selection (TPS)

Feature selection is different from dimension reduction because it selects a subset of the feature set, rather than projecting a combination of features onto a lower dimension. We apply a two-phase feature selection (TPS) process. In phase I, we build a decision tree from the training data. We select the features found at the internal nodes of the tree. In phase II, we apply a greedy selection algorithm. We combine these two selection processes because of the following reasons. The decision tree selection is fast, but the selected features may not be a good choice for the novel dataset. That is, the selected features may not perform well on the novel data, because the novel data may have a different set of important features. We observe this fact when we apply a decision tree on the Mydoom.M and VBS.BubbleBoy dataset. That is why we apply another phase of selection, the greedy selection, on top of decision tree selection. Our goal is to determine if there is a more general feature set that covers all important features. In our experiments, we are able to find such a feature set using greedy selection. There are two reasons why we do not apply only greedy selection: First, it is very slow compared to decision tree selection because, at each iteration, we have to modify the data to keep only the selected features and run the classifiers to compute the accuracy. Second, the greedy elimination process may lead to a set of features that are inferior to the decision tree-selected set of features. That is why we keep the decision tree-selected features as the minimal features set.

7.4.2.1 Phase I We apply decision tree as a feature selection tool in phase I. The main reason behind applying decision tree is that it

selects the best attributes according to information gain. Information gain is a very effective metric in selecting features. Information gain can be defined as a measure of the effectiveness of an attribute (i.e., feature) in classifying the training data [Mitchell, 1997]. If we split the training data on these attribute values, then information gain gives the measurement of the expected reduction in entropy after the split. The more an attribute can reduce entropy in the training data, the better the attribute in classifying the data. Information gain of a binary attribute A on a collection of examples S is given by (Eq. 7.1):

$$Gain(S, A) \equiv Entropy(S) - \sum_{v \in Values(A)} \frac{|S_v|}{|S|} Entropy(S_v) \qquad (7.1)$$

where Values(A) is the set of all possible values for attribute A, and S_v is the subset of S for which attribute A has value v. In our case, each binary attribute has only two possible values (0, 1). Entropy of subset S is computed using the following equation:

$$Entropy(S) = -\frac{p(s)}{n(s) + p(s)} \log_2 \left(\frac{p(s)}{n(s) + p(s)} \right)$$
$$-\frac{n(s)}{n(s) + p(s)} \log_2 \left(\frac{n(s)}{n(s) + p(s)} \right) \qquad (7.2)$$

where $p(S)$ is the number of positive examples in S and $n(S)$ is the total number of negative examples in S. Computation of information gain of a continuous attribute is a little tricky, because it has an infinite number of possible values. One approach followed by [Quinlan, 1993] is to find an optimal threshold and split the data into two halves. The optimal threshold is found by searching a threshold value with the highest information gain within the range of values of this attribute in the dataset.

We use J48 for building decision tree, which is an implementation of C4.5. Decision tree algorithms choose the best attribute based on information gain criteria at each level of recursion. Thus, the final tree actually consists of the most important attributes that can distinguish between the positive and negative instances. The tree is further pruned to reduce chances of overfitting. Thus, we are able to identify the features that are necessary and the features that are redundant, and use only the necessary features. Surprisingly enough, in our experiments we find that on average, only 4.5 features are selected by the decision tree algorithm, and the total number of nodes in the tree is only 11. It indicates that only a few features are important. We have six different datasets for six different worm types. Each dataset is again divided into two subsets: the *known worms set* or K-Set and the *novel worm set* or N-Set. We apply threefold cross validation on the K-Set.

7.4.2.2 Phase II   In the second phase, we apply a greedy algorithm to select the best subset of features. We use the feature subset selected in phase I as the *minimal subset* (MS). At the beginning of the algorithm, we select all the features from the original set and call it the *potential feature set* (PFS). At each iteration of the algorithm, we compute the average novel detection accuracy of six datasets, using PFS as the feature set. Then we pick up a feature at random from the PFS, which is not in MS, and eliminate it from the PFS if the elimination does not reduce the accuracy of novel detection of any classifier (NB, SVM, Series). If the accuracy drops after elimination, then we do not eliminate the feature, and we add it to MS. In this way, we reduce PFS and continue until no further elimination is possible. Now the PFS contains the most effective subset of features. Although this process is time consuming, we finally come up with a subset of features that can outperform the original set.

Algorithm 7.1 sketches the two-phase feature selection process. At line 2, the decision tree is built using original feature set *FS* and unreduced dataset D_{FS}. At line 3, the set of features selected by the decision tree is stored in the minimal subset, *MS*. Then the potential subset, *PFS*, is initialized to the original set *FS*. Line 5 computes the average novel detection accuracy of three classifiers. The functions NB-Acc(*PFS*, D_{PFS}), SVM-Acc(*PFS*, D_{PFS}), and Series-Acc(*PFS*, D_{PFS}) return the average novel detection accuracy of NB, SVM, and Series, respectively, using *PFS* as the feature set.

Algorithm 7.1   Two-Phase Feature Selection

1. Two-Phase-Selection (FS, D_{FS}) returns $FeatureSet$
   // FS : original set of features
   // D_{FS} : original dataset with FS as the feature set
2. $T \leftarrow$ Build-Decision-Tree (FS, D_{FS})
3. $MS \leftarrow$ Feature-Set (T)   //minimal subset of features
4. $PFS \leftarrow FS$ //potential subset of features
   //compute novel detection accuracy of FS
5. $p_{avg} \leftarrow$ (NB-Acc(PFS, D_{PFS}) + SVM-Acc(PFS, D_{PFS})
         + Series-Acc(PFS, D_{PFS})) /3
6. **while** $PFS <> MS$ **do**
7. $X \leftarrow$ a randomly chosen feature from PFS that is not in MS
8. $PFS \leftarrow PFS - X$
   //compute novel detection accuracy of PFS
9. $C_{avg} \leftarrow$ (NB-Acc(PFS, D_{PFS}) + SVM-Acc(PFS, D_{PFS})
         + Series-Acc(PFS, D_{PFS})) /3
10. **if** $C_{avg} \geq p_{avg}$
11. $\quad p_{avg} \leftarrow C_{avg}$
12. **else**
13. $\quad PFS \leftarrow PFS \cup \{X\}$
14. $\quad MS \leftarrow MS \cup \{X\}$
15. **end if**
16. **end while**
17. **return** PFS

In the while loop, we randomly choose a feature X, such that $X \in PFS$ but $X \notin MS$, and delete it from PFS. The accuracy of the new PFS is calculated. If, after deletion, the accuracy increases or remains the same, then X is redundant. So we remove this feature permanently. Otherwise, if the accuracy drops after deletion, then this feature is essential, so we add it to the minimal set, MS (lines 13 and 14). In this way, we either delete a redundant feature or add it to the minimal selection. It is repeated until we have nothing more to select (i.e., MS equals PFS). We return the PFS as the best feature set.

7.5 Classification Techniques

Classification is a supervised data mining technique in which a data mining model is first trained with some "ground truth," that is, training data. Each instance (or data point) in the training data is represented as a vector of features, and each training instance is associated with a "class label." The data mining model trained from the training data is called a "classification model," which can be represented as a function $f(x)$: *feature vector* → *class label*. This function approximates the feature vector-class label mapping from the training data. When a test instance with an unknown class label is passed to the classification model, it predicts (i.e., outputs) a class label for the test instance. The accuracy of a classifier is determined by how many unknown instances (instances that were not in the training data) it can classify correctly.

We apply the NB [John and Langley, 1995], SVM [Boser et al., 1992], and C4.5 decision tree [Quinlan, 1993] classifiers in our experiments. We also apply our implementation of the Series classifier [Martin et al., 2005-b] to compare its performance with other classifiers. We briefly describe the Series approach here for the purpose of self-containment.

NB assumes that features are independent of each other. With this assumption, the probability that an instance $x = (x_1, x_2, ...,x_n)$ is in class c ($c \in \{1, ..., C\}$) is

$$P(c \mid X_1 = x_1, X_2 = x_2, ..., X_n = x_n) = P(c)\prod_{j=1}^{n} P(X_j = x_j \mid c)$$

where x_i is the value of the i-th feature of the instance x, $P(c)$ is the prior probability of class C, and $P(X_j = x_j \mid c)$ is the conditional probability that the j-th attribute has the value x_j given class c.

So the NB classifier outputs the following class:

$$c_{NB} = \arg\max_{c \in \{1,...,C\}} P(c)\prod_{j=1}^{n} P(X_j = x_j \mid c)$$

NB treats discrete and continuous attributes differently. For each discrete attribute, $p(X = x|c)$ is modeled by a single real number between 0 and 1 which represents the probability that the attribute X will take on the particular value x when the class is c. In contrast, each numeric (or real) attribute is modeled by some continuous probability distribution over the range of that attribute's values. A common assumption not intrinsic to the NB approach but often made nevertheless is that within each class the values of numeric attributes are normally distributed. One can represent such a distribution in terms of its mean and standard deviation, and one can efficiently compute the probability of an observed value from such estimates. For continuous attributes we can write

$$P(X = x \mid c) = g(x; \mu_c, \sigma_c)$$

where

$$g(x; \mu_c, \sigma_c) = \frac{1}{\sqrt{2\pi}\sigma} e^{-\frac{(x-\mu)^2}{2\sigma^2}} .$$

Smoothing (m-estimate) is used in NB. We have used the value $m = 100$ and $p = 0.5$ while calculating the probability

$$\frac{n_c + mp}{n + m}$$

where n_c = total number of instances for which $X = x$ given Class c and n = total number of instances for which $X = x$.

SVM can perform either linear or non-linear classification. The linear classifier proposed by [Boser et al., 1992] creates a hyperplane that separates the data into two classes with the maximum margin. Given positive and negative training examples, a maximum-margin hyperplane is identified, which splits the training examples such that the distance between the hyperplane and the closest examples is maximized. The non-linear SVM is implemented by applying kernel trick to maximum-margin hyperplanes. The feature space is transformed into a higher dimensional space, where the maximum-margin hyperplane is found. This hyperplane may be non-linear in the original feature space. A linear SVM is illustrated in Figure 7.3. The circles are negative instances and the squares are positive instances. A

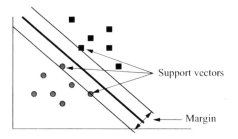

Figure 7.3 Illustration of support vectors and margin of a linear SVM.

hyperplane (the bold line) separates the positive instances from negative ones. All of the instances are at least at a minimal distance (margin) from the hyperplane. The points that are at a distance exactly equal to the hyperplane are called the support vectors. As mentioned earlier, the SVM finds the hyperplane that has the maximum margin among all hyperplanes that can separate the instances.

In our experiments, we have used the SVM implementation provided at [Chang and Lin, 2006]. We also implement the Series or "two-layer approach" proposed by [Martin et al., 2005-b] as a baseline technique. The Series approach works as follows: In the first layer, SVM is applied as a novelty detector. The parameters of SVM are chosen such that it produces almost zero false positive. This means, if SVM classifies an email as infected, then with probability (almost) 100%, it is an infected email. If, otherwise, SVM classifies an email as clean, then it is sent to the second layer for further verification. This is because, with the previously mentioned parameter settings, while SVM reduces false positive rate, it also increases the false negative rate. So, any email classified as negative must be further verified. In the second layer, NB classifier is applied to confirm whether the suspected emails are really infected. If NB classifies it as infected, then it is marked as infected; otherwise, it is marked as clean. Figure 7.4 illustrates the Series approach.

7.6 Summary

In this chapter, we have described the design and implementation of the data mining tools for email worm detection. As we have stated, feature-based methods are superior to the signature-based methods for worm detection. Our approach is based on feature extraction. We

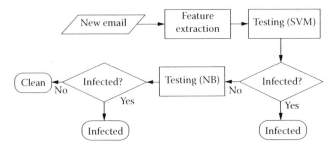

Figure 7.4 Series combination of SVM and NB classifiers for email worm detection. (This figure appears in Email Work Detection Using Data Mining, *International Journal of Information Security and Privacy*, Vol. 1, No. 4, pp. 47–61, 2007, authored by M. Masud, L. Kahn, and B. Thuraisingham. Copyright 2010, IGI Global, www.igi-global.com. Posted by permission of the publisher.)

reduce the dimension of the features by using PCA and then use classification techniques based on SVM and NB for detecting worms. In Chapter 8, we discuss the experiments we carried out and analyze the results obtained.

As stated in Chapter 6, as future work, we are planning to detect worms by combining the feature-based approach with the content-based approach to make it more robust and efficient. We will also focus on the statistical property of the contents of the messages for possible contamination of worms. In addition, we will apply other classification techniques and compare the performance and accuracy of the results.

References

[Boser et al., 1992] Boser, B. E., I. M. Guyon, V. N. Vapnik, *A Training Algorithm for Optimal Margin Classifiers*, in D. Haussler, editor, *5th Annual ACM Workshop on COLT*, Pittsburgh, PA, ACM Press, 1992, pp. 144–152.

[Chang and Lin, 2006] Chang, C.-C., and C.-J. Lin, *LIBSVM: A Library for Support Vector Machines*, http://www.csie.ntu.edu.tw/~cjlin/libsvm

[John and Langley, 1995] John, G. H., and P. Langley, Estimating Continuous Distributions in Bayesian Classifiers, in *Proceedings of the Eleventh Conference on Uncertainty in Artificial Intelligence*, Morgan Kaufmann Publishers, San Mateo, CA, 1995, pp. 338–345.

[Martin et al., 2005-a] Martin, S., A. Sewani, B. Nelson, K. Chen, A. D. Joseph, Analyzing Behavioral Features for Email Classification, in *Proceedings of the IEEE Second Conference on Email and Anti-Spam (CEAS 2005)*, July 21 & 22, Stanford University, CA.

[Martin et al., 2005-b] Martin, S., A. Sewani, B. Nelson, K. Chen, A. D. Joseph, *A Two-Layer Approach for Novel Email Worm Detection*, Submitted to USENIX Steps on Reducing Unwanted Traffic on the Internet (SRUTI).

[Mitchell, 1997] Mitchell, T. *Machine Learning*, McGraw-Hill, 1997.

[Quinlan, 1993] Quinlan, J. R. *C4.5: Programs for Machine Learning*, Morgan Kaufmann Publishers, 1993.

8

EVALUATION AND RESULTS

8.1 Introduction

In Chapter 6 we described email worm detection, and in Chapter 7 we described our data mining tool for email worm detection. In this chapter, we describe the datasets, experimental setup, and the results of our proposed approach and other baseline techniques.

The dataset contains a collection of 1,600 clean and 1,200 viral emails, which are divided into six different evaluation sets (Section 8.2). The original feature set contains 94 features. The evaluation compares our two-phase feature selection technique with two other approaches, namely, dimension reduction using PCA, and no feature selection or reduction. Performance of three different classifiers has been evaluated on these feature spaces, namely, NB, SVM, and Series approach (see Table 8.8 for summary). Therefore, there are nine different combinations of feature set–classifier pairs, such as two-phase feature selection + NB, no feature selection + NB, two-phase feature selection + SVM, and so on. In addition, we compute three different metrics on these datasets for each feature set–classifier pair: classification accuracy, false positive rate, and accuracy in detecting a new type of worm.

The organization of this chapter is as follows. In Section 8.2, we describe the distribution of the datasets used. In Section 8.3, we discuss the experimental setup, including hardware, software, and system parameters. In Section 8.4, we discuss results obtained from the experiments. The chapter is summarized in Section 8.5. Concepts in this chapter are illustrated in Figure 8.1.

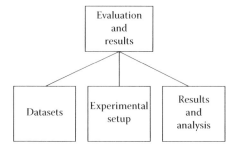

Figure 8.1 Concepts in this chapter.

8.2 Dataset

We have collected the worm dataset used in the experiment by [Martin et al., 2005]. They have accumulated several hundreds of clean and worm emails over a period of two years. All of these emails are outgoing emails. Several features are extracted from these emails, as explained in Section 7.3 ("Feature Description").

There are six types of worms contained in the dataset: VBS. BubbleBoy, W32.Mydoom.M, W32.Sobig.F, W32.Netsky.D, W32. Mydoom.U, and W32.Bagle.F. But the classification task is binary: {clean, infected}. The original dataset contains six training and six test sets. Each training set is made up of 400 clean emails and 1,000 infected emails, consisting of 200 samples from each of the five different worms. The sixth virus is then included in the test set, which contains 1,200 clean emails and 200 infected messages. Table 8.1 clarifies this distribution. For ease of representation, we abbreviate the worm names as follows:

B: VBS.BubbleBoy
F: W32.Bagle.F
M: W32.Mydoom.M
N: W32.Netsky.D
S: W32.Sobig.F
U: W32.Mydoom.U

NB, SVM, and the Series classifiers are applied to the original data, the PCA-reduced data, and the TPS-selected data. The decision tree is applied on the original data only.

Table 8.1 Data Distribution from the Original Dataset

	TRAINING SET		TEST SET	
SET	TOTAL CLEAN EMAILS	TOTAL INFECTED EMAILS	TOTAL CLEAN EMAILS	TOTAL INFECTED EMAILS
B	400	1000 (= 200 × 5), 200 from each different type except B	1000	200 (only B)
M	400	1000 (= 200 × 5), 200 from each different type except M	1000	200 (only M)
S	400	1000 (= 200 × 5), 200 from each different type except S	1000	200 (only S)
N	400	1000 (= 200 × 5), 200 from each different type except N	1000	200 (only N)
U	400	1000 (= 200 × 5), 200 from each different type except U	1000	200 (only U)
F	400	1000 (= 200 × 5), 200 from each different type except F	1000	200 (only F)

Source: This table appears in Email Work Detection Using Data Mining, *International Journal of Information Security and Privacy,* Vol. 1, No. 4, pp. 47–61, 2007, authored by M. Masud, L. Kahn, and B. Thuraisingham. Copyright 2010, IGI Global, www.igi-global.com. Posted by permission of the publisher.

We can easily notice that the original dataset is unbalanced, because the ratio of clean emails to infected emails is 2:5 in the training set, whereas it is 5:1 in the test set. So, the results obtained from this dataset may not be reliable. We make it balanced by redistributing the examples. In our distribution, each balanced set contains two subsets. The *Known-worms set* or K-Set contains 1,600 clean email messages, which are the combination of all the clean messages in the original dataset (400 from training set, 1,200 from test set). The K-Set also contains 1,000 infected messages, with five types of worms marked as the "known worms." The N-Set contains 200 infected messages of a sixth type of worm, marked as the "novel worm." Then we apply cross validation on K-Set. The cross validation is done as follows: We randomly divide the set of 2,600 (1,600 clean + 1,000 viral) messages into three equal-sized subsets, such that the ratio of clean messages to viral messages remains the same in all subsets. We take two subsets as the training set and the remaining set as the test set. This is done three times by rotating the testing and training sets. We take the average accuracy of these three runs. This accuracy is shown under the column "Acc" in Tables 8.3, 8.5, and 8.6. In addition to testing the

Table 8.2 Data Distribution from the Redistributed Dataset

	CROSS VALIDATION SET		NOVEL WORM SET	
SET	TOTAL CLEAN EMAILS	TOTAL INFECTED EMAILS	TOTAL CLEAN EMAILS	TOTAL INFECTED EMAILS
B	1600	1000 (= 200 × 5), 200 from each different type except B	0	200 (only B)
M	1600	1000 (= 200 × 5), 200 from each different type except M	0	200 (only M)
S	1600	1000 (= 200 × 5), 200 from each different type except S	0	200 (only S)
N	1600	1000 (= 200 × 5), 200 from each different type except N	0	200 (only N)
U	1600	1000 (= 200 × 5), 200 from each different type except U	0	200 (only U)
F	1600	1000 (= 200 × 5), 200 from each different type except F	0	200 (only F)

Source: This table appears in Email Work Detection Using Data Mining, *International Journal of Information Security and Privacy,* Vol. 1, No. 4, pp. 47–61, 2007, authored by M. Masud, L. Kahn, and B. Thuraisingham. Copyright 2010, IGI Global, www.igi-global.com. Posted by permission of the publisher.

accuracy of the test set, we also test the detection accuracy of each of the three learned classifiers on the N-Set, and take the average. This accuracy is also averaged over all runs and shown as *novel detection accuracy.* Table 8.2 displays the data distribution of our dataset.

8.3 Experimental Setup

In this section, we describe the experimental setup including a discussion of the hardware and software utilized. We run all our experiments on a Windows XP machine with Java version 1.5 installed. For running SVM, we use the LIBSVM package [Chang and Lin, 2006].

We use our own C++ implementation of NB. We implement PCA with MATLAB. We use the WEKA machine learning tool [Weka, 2006] for decision tree, with pruning applied.

Parameter settings: Parameter settings for LIBSVM are as follows: classifier type is C-Support Vector Classification (C-SVC); the kernel is chosen to be the radial basis function (RBF); the values of "*gamma*" = 0.2 and "C" = 1 are chosen.

Baseline techniques: We compare our TPS technique with two different feature selection/reduction techniques. Therefore, the competing techniques are the following:

TPS. This is our two-phase feature selection technique.

PCA. Here we reduce the dimension using PCA. With PCA, we reduce the dimension size to 5, 10, 15, ..., 90, 94. That is, we vary the target dimension from 5 to 94 with step 5 increments.

No reduction (unreduced). Here the full feature set is used.

Each of these feature vectors are used to train three different classifiers, namely, NB, SVM, and Series. Decision tree is also trained with the unreduced feature set.

8.4 Results

We discuss the results in three separate subsections. In subsection 8.4.1, we discuss the results found from unreduced data; that is, data before any reduction or selection is applied. In subsection 8.4.2, we discuss the results found from PCA-reduced data, and in subsection 8.4.3, we discuss the results obtained using TPS-reduced data.

8.4.1 Results from Unreduced Data

Table 8.3 reports the accuracy of the cross validation accuracy and false positive for each set. The cross validation accuracy is shown under the column *Acc* and the false positive rate is shown under the column *FP*. The set names at the row headings are the abbreviated names, as explained in "Dataset" section. From the results reported in Table 8.3, we see that SVM observes the best accuracy among all classifiers, although the difference with other classifiers is small.

Table 8.4 reports the accuracy of detecting novel worms. We see that SVM is very consistent over all sets, but NB, Series, and decision tree perform significantly worse in the Mydoom.M dataset.

8.4.2 Results from PCA-Reduced Data

Figure 8.2 shows the results of applying PCA on the original data. The X axis denotes dimension of the reduced dimensional data, which

Table 8.3   Comparison of Accuracy (%) and False Positive (%) of Different Classifiers on the Worm Dataset

SET	NB ACC	NB FP	SVM ACC	SVM FP	SERIES ACC	SERIES FP	DECISION TREE ACC	DECISION TREE FP
M	99.3	0.6	99.5	0.6	99.4	0.5	99.3	0.6
S	99.1	0.6	99.5	0.6	99.2	0.5	99.4	0.6
N	99.2	0.5	99.5	0.6	99.2	0.4	99.2	1.1
U	99.1	0.6	99.5	0.6	99.2	0.5	99.2	0.8
F	99.2	0.6	99.5	0.7	99.3	0.4	99.4	0.4
B	99.2	0.6	99.3	0.8	99.2	0.6	99.6	0.4
Avg	99.19	0.58	99.47	0.64	99.24	0.49	99.35	0.65

Source: This table appears in Email Work Detection Using Data Mining, *International Journal of Information Security and Privacy,* Vol. 1, No. 4, pp. 47–61, 2007, authored by M. Masud, L. Kahn, and B. Thuraisingham. Copyright 2010, IGI Global, www.igi-global.com. Posted by permission of the publisher.

Table 8.4   Comparison of Novel Detection Accuracy (%) of Different Classifiers on the Worm Dataset

SET NAME	NB	SVM	SERIES	DECISION TREE
M	17.4	92.4	16.6	32.0
S	97.0	95.0	95.0	97.5
N	97.0	97.0	97.0	99.0
U	97.0	97.2	97.0	97.0
F	97.0	97.0	97.0	99.5
B	96.0	96.0	96.0	0.5
Avg	83.58	95.77	83.11	70.92

Source: This table appears in Email Work Detection Using Data Mining, *International Journal of Information Security and Privacy,* Vol. 1, No. 4, pp. 47–61, 2007, authored by M. Masud, L. Kahn, and B. Thuraisingham. Copyright 2010, IGI Global, www.igi-global.com. Posted by permission of the publisher.

has been varied from 5 to 90, with step 5 increments. The last point on the X axis is the unreduced or original dimension. Figure 8.2 shows the cross validation accuracy for different dimensions. The data from the chart should be read as follows: a point (x, y) on a given line, say the line for SVM, indicates the cross validation accuracy y of SVM, averaged over all six datasets, where each dataset has been reduced to x dimension using PCA.

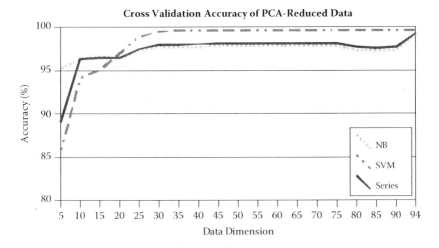

Figure 8.2 Average cross validation accuracy of the three classifiers on lower dimensional data, reduced by PCA. (This figure appears in Email Work Detection Using Data Mining, *International Journal of Information Security and Privacy,* Vol. 1, No. 4, pp. 47–61, 2007, authored by M. Masud, L. Kahn, and B. Thuraisingham. Copyright 2010, IGI Global, www.igi-global.com. Posted by permission of the publisher.)

Figure 8.2 indicates that at lower dimensions, cross validation accuracy is lower, for each of the three classifiers. But SVM achieves its near maximum accuracy at dimension 30. NB and Series reaches within 2% of maximum accuracy at dimension 30 and onward. All classifiers attain their maximum at the highest dimension 94, which is actually the unreduced data. So, from this observation, we may conclude that PCA is not effective on this dataset, in terms of cross validation accuracy. The reason behind this poorer performance on the reduced dimensional data is possibly the one that we have mentioned earlier in subsection "Dimension Reduction." The reduction by PCA is not producing a lower dimensional data where dissimilar class instances are maximally dispersed and similar class instances are maximally concentrated. So, the classification accuracy is lower at lower dimensions.

We now present the results, at dimension 25, similar to the results presented in the previous subsection. Table 8.5 compares the novel detection accuracy and cross validation accuracy of different classifiers. The choice of this particular dimension is that, at this dimension, all the classifiers seem to be the most balanced in all aspects: cross validation accuracy, false positive and false negative rate, and novel

Table 8.5   Comparison of Cross Validation Accuracy (Acc) and Novel Detection Accuracy (NAcc) among Different Classifiers on the PCA-Reduced Worm Dataset at Dimension 25

	NB		SVM		SERIES	
SET	ACC (%)	NACC (%)	ACC (%)	NACC (%)	ACC (%)	NACC (%)
M	99.08	0.0	99.46	30.02	99.15	24.7
S	97.31	97.01	99.19	97.01	97.77	97.01
N	96.61	97.51	98.62	97.01	96.73	97.01
U	96.92	97.51	98.46	97.34	97.15	97.34
F	96.92	97.51	98.93	97.01	97.07	97.01
B	96.96	97.68	98.88	97.51	97.08	97.51
Avg	97.3	81.2	98.92	85.98	97.49	85.1

Source: This table appears in Email Work Detection Using Data Mining, *International Journal of Information Security and Privacy,* Vol. 1, No. 4, pp. 47–61, 2007, authored by M. Masud, L. Kahn, and B. Thuraisingham. Copyright 2010, IGI Global, www.igi-global.com. Posted by permission of the publisher.

detection accuracy. We conclude that this dimension is the optimal dimension for projection by PCA. From Table 8.5, it is evident that accuracies of all three classifiers on PCA-reduced data are lower than the accuracy of the unreduced data. It is possible that some information that is useful for classification might have been lost during projection onto a lower dimension.

We see in Table 8.5 that both the accuracy and novel detection accuracy of NB has dropped significantly from the original dataset. The novel detection accuracy of NB on the Mydoom.M dataset has become 0%, compared to 17% in the original set. The novel detection accuracy of SVM on the same dataset has dropped to 30%, compared to 92.4% in the original dataset. So, we can conclude that PCA reduction does not help in novel detection.

8.4.3 Results from Two-Phase Selection

Our TPS selects the following features (in no particular order):

Attachment type *binary*
MIME (magic) type of attachment *application/msdownload*
MIME (magic) type of attachment *application/x-ms-dos-executable*
Frequency of email sent in window
Mean words in body

Mean characters in subject
Number of attachments
Number of From Address in Window
Ratio of emails with attachment
Variance of attachment size
Variance of words in body
Number of HTML in email
Number of links in email
Number of To Address in Window
Variance of characters in subject

The first three features actually reflect important characteristics of an infected email. Usually, infected emails have binary attachment, which is a dos/windows executable. Mean/variance of *words in body* and *characters in subject* are also considered as important symptoms, because usually infected emails contain random subject or body, thus having irregular size of body or subject. *Number of attachments*, and *ratio of emails with attachments*, and *number of links in email* are usually higher for infected emails. *Frequency of emails sent in window*, and *number of To Address in window* are higher for an infected host, as a compromised host sends infected emails to many addresses and more frequently. Thus, most of the features selected by our algorithm are really practical and useful.

Table 8.6 reports the cross validation accuracy (%) and false positive rate (%) of the three classifiers on the TPS-reduced dataset. We see that both the accuracy and false positive rates are almost the same as the unreduced dataset. The accuracy of Mydoom.M dataset (shown at row M) is 99.3% for NB, 99.5% for SVM, and 99.4% for Series. Table 8.7 reports the novel detection accuracy (%) of the three classifiers on the TPS-reduced dataset. We find that the average novel detection accuracy of the TPS-reduced dataset is higher than that of the unreduced dataset. The main reason behind this improvement is the higher accuracy on the Mydoom.M set by NB and Series. The accuracy of NB on this dataset is 37.1% (row M), compared to 17.4% in the unreduced dataset (see Table 8.4, row M). Also, the accuracy of Series on the same is 36.0%, compared to 16.6% on the unreduced dataset (as show in Table 8.4, row M). However, accuracy of SVM remains almost the same, 91.7%, compared to 92.4% in the unreduced dataset.

Table 8.6   Cross Validation Accuracy (%) and False Positive (%) of Three Different Classifiers on the TPS-Reduced Dataset

SET NAME	NB		SVM		SERIES	
	ACC	FP	ACC	FP	ACC	FP
M	99.3	0.6	99.5	0.6	99.4	0.5
S	99.1	0.7	99.5	0.6	99.2	0.5
N	99.1	0.6	99.5	0.6	99.2	0.4
U	99.1	0.7	99.5	0.6	99.2	0.5
F	99.2	0.6	99.5	0.6	99.3	0.4
B	99.2	0.6	99.3	0.8	99.2	0.6
Avg	99.16	0.58	99.49	0.6	99.25	0.49

Source: This table appears in Email Work Detection Using Data Mining, *International Journal of Information Security and Privacy,* Vol. 1, No. 4, pp. 47–61, 2007, authored by M. Masud, L. Kahn, and B. Thuraisingham. Copyright 2010, IGI Global, www.igi-global.com. Posted by permission of the publisher.

Table 8.7   Comparison of Novel Detection Accuracy (%) of Different Classifiers on the TPS-Reduced Dataset

SET NAME	NB	SVM	SERIES
M	37.1	91.7	36.0
S	97.0	95.0	95.0
N	97.0	97.0	97.0
U	97.0	97.2	97.0
F	97.0	97.0	97.0
B	96.0	96.0	96.0
Avg	86.87	95.66	86.34

Source: This table appears in Email Work Detection Using Data Mining, *International Journal of Information Security and Privacy,* Vol. 1, No. 4, pp. 47–61, 2007, authored by M. Masud, L. Kahn, and B. Thuraisingham. Copyright 2010, IGI Global, www.igi-global.com. Posted by permission of the publisher.

In Table 8.8, we summarize the averages from Tables 8.3 through Table 8.7.

The first three rows (after the header row) report the cross validation accuracy of all four classifiers that we have used in our experiments. Each row reports the average accuracy on a particular dataset. The first row reports the average accuracy for the unreduced dataset; the second

Table 8.8 Summary of Results (Averages) Obtained from Different Feature-Based Approaches

	DATASET	NB	SVM	SERIES	DECISION TREE
Cross Validation Accuracy	Unreduced	99.2	99.5	99.2	99.4
	PCA-reduced	97.3	98.9	97.5	—
	TPS-selected	99.2	99.5	99.3	—
False Positive	Unreduced	0.6	0.6	0.5	0.7
	PCA-reduced	0.9	1.5	0.6	—
	TPS-selected	0.6	0.6	0.5	—
Novel Detection Accuracy	Unreduced	83.6	95.8	83.1	70.9
	PCA-reduced	81.2	86.0	81.0	—
	TPS-selected	86.7	95.7	86.3	—

Source: This table appears in Email Work Detection Using Data Mining, *International Journal of Information Security and Privacy,* Vol. 1, No. 4, pp. 47–61, 2007, authored by M. Masud, L. Kahn, and B. Thuraisingham. Copyright 2010, IGI Global, www.igi-global.com. Posted by permission of the publisher.

row reports the same for PCA-reduced dataset and the third row for TPS-reduced dataset. We see that the average accuracies are almost the same for the TPS-reduced and the unreduced set. For example, average accuracy of NB (shown under column NB) is the same for both, which is 99.2%; the accuracy of SVM (shown under column SVM) is also the same, 99.5%. The average accuracies of these classifiers on the PCA-reduced dataset are 1% to 2% lower. There is no entry under the decision tree column for the PCA-reduced and TPS-reduced dataset because we only test the decision tree on the unreduced dataset.

The middle three rows report the average false positive values and the last three rows report the average novel detection accuracies. We see that the average novel detection accuracy on the TPS-reduced dataset is the highest among all. The average novel detection accuracy of NB on this dataset is 86.7%, compared to 83.6% on the unreduced dataset, which is a 3.1% improvement on average. Also, Series has a novel detection accuracy of 86.3% on the TPS-reduced dataset, compared to that of the unreduced dataset, which is 83.1%. Again, it is a 3.2% improvement on average. However, average accuracy of SVM remains almost the same (only 0.1% difference) on these two datasets. Thus, on average, we have an improvement in novel detection accuracy across different classifiers on the TPS-reduced dataset. While TPS-reduced dataset is the best among the three, the best classifier among the four is SVM. It has the highest average accuracy and novel detection accuracy on all datasets, and also very low average false positive rates.

8.5 Summary

In this chapter, we have discussed the results obtained from testing our data mining tool for email worm detection. We first discussed the datasets we used and the experimental setup. Then we described the results we obtained. We have two important findings from our experiments. First, SVM has the best performance among all four different classifiers: NB, SVM, Series, and decision tree. Second, feature selection using our TPS algorithm achieves the best accuracy, especially in detecting novel worms. Combining these two findings, we conclude that SVM with TPS reduction should work as the best novel worm detection tool on a feature-based dataset.

In the future, we would like to extend our work to content-based detection of the email worm by extracting binary level features from the emails. We would also like to apply other classifiers for the detection task.

References

[Chang and Lin, 2006] Chang, C.-C., and C.-J. Lin, *LIBSVM: A Library for Support Vector Machines*, http://www.csie.ntu.edu.tw/~cjlin/libsvm

[Martin et al., 2005] Martin, S., A. Sewani, B. Nelson, K. Chen, and A. D. Joseph, Analyzing Behavioral Features for Email Classification, in *Proceedings of the IEEE Second Conference on Email and Anti-Spam (CEAS 2005)*, July 21 & 22, Stanford University, CA.

[Weka, 2006] Weka 3: *Data Mining Software in Java*, http://www.cs.waikato.ac.nz/~ml/weka

Conclusion to Part II

In this part, we discussed our proposed data mining technique to detect email worms. Different features, such as total number of words in message body/subject, presence/absence of binary attachments, types of attachments, and others, are extracted from the emails. Then the number of features is reduced using a *Two-phase Selection* (TPS) technique, which is a novel combination of decision tree and greedy selection algorithm. We have used different classification techniques, such as Support Vector Machine (SVM), Naïve Bayes, and their combination. Finally, the trained classifiers are tested on a dataset containing both known and unknown types of worms. Compared to the baseline approaches, our proposed TPS selection along with SVM classification achieves the best accuracy in detecting both known and unknown types of worms.

In the future, we would like to apply our technique on a larger corpus of emails and optimize the feature extraction selection techniques to make them more scalable to large datasets.

PART III

Data Mining for Detecting Malicious Executables

Introduction to Part III

We present a scalable and multi-level feature extraction technique to detect malicious executables. We propose a novel combination of three different kinds of features at different levels of abstraction. These are binary *n*-grams, assembly instruction sequences, and dynamic link library (DLL) function calls, extracted from binary executables, disassembled executables, and executable headers, respectively. We also propose an efficient and scalable feature extraction technique and apply this technique on a large corpus of real benign and malicious executables. The previously mentioned features are extracted from the corpus data and a classifier is trained, which achieves high accuracy and low false positive rate in detecting malicious executables. Our approach is knowledge based for several reasons. First, we apply the knowledge obtained from the binary *n*-gram features to extract assembly instruction sequences using our Assembly Feature Retrieval algorithm. Second, we apply the statistical knowledge obtained during feature extraction to select the best features and to build a classification model. Our model is compared against other feature-based approaches for malicious code detection, and found to be more efficient in terms of detection accuracy and false alarm rate.

Part III consists of three chapters: 9, 10, and 11. Chapter 9 describes our approach to detecting malicious executables. Chapter 10 describes the design and implementation of our data mining tools. Chapter 11 describes our evaluation and results.

9
MALICIOUS EXECUTABLES

9.1 Introduction

Malicious code is a great threat to computers and computer society. Numerous kinds of malicious codes wander in the wild. Some of them are mobile, such as worms, and spread through the Internet, causing damage to millions of computers worldwide. Other kinds of malicious codes are static, such as viruses, but sometimes deadlier than their mobile counterpart. Malicious code writers usually exploit software vulnerabilities to attack host machines. A number of techniques have been devised by researchers to counter these attacks. Unfortunately, the more successful the researchers become in detecting and preventing the attacks, the more sophisticated the malicious code in the wild appears. Thus, the battle between malicious code writers and researchers is virtually never ending.

One popular technique followed by the antivirus community to detect malicious code is "signature detection." This technique matches the executables against a unique telltale string or byte pattern called *signature*, which is used as an identifier for a particular malicious code. Although signature detection techniques are being used widely, they are not effective against zero-day attacks (new malicious code), polymorphic attacks (different encryptions of the same binary), or metamorphic attacks (different code for the same functionality). So there has been a growing need for fast, automated, and efficient detection techniques that are robust to these attacks. As a result, many automated systems [Golbeck and Hendler, 2004], [Kolter and Maloof, 2004], [Newman et al., 2002], [Newsome et al., 2005], have been developed.

In this chapter we describe our novel *hybrid feature retrieval* (HFR) model that can detect malicious executables efficiently [Masud et al.,

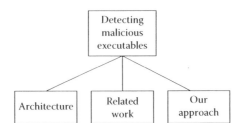

Figure 9.1 Concepts in this chapter.

2007-a], [Masud et al., 2007-b]. The organization of this chapter is as follows. Our architecture is discussed in Section 9.2. Related work is given in Section 9.3. Our approach is discussed in Section 9.4. The chapter is summarized in Section 9.5. Figure 9.1 illustrates the concepts in this chapter.

9.2 Architecture

Figure 9.2 illustrates our architecture for detecting malicious executables. The training data consist of a collection of benign and malicious executables. We extract three different kinds of features (to be explained shortly) from each executable. These extracted features are then analyzed and only the best discriminative features are selected. Feature vectors are generated from each training instance using the selected feature set. The feature vectors are used to train a classifier. When a new executable needs to be tested, at first the features selected during training are extracted from the executable, and a feature vector is generated. This feature vector is classified using the classifier to predict whether it is a benign or malicious executable.

In our approach, we extract three different kinds of features from the executables at different levels of abstraction and combine them

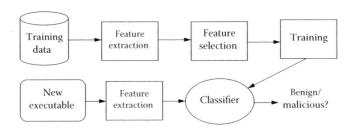

Figure 9.2 Architecture.

into one feature set, called the *hybrid feature set* (HFS). These features are used to train a classifier (e.g., support vector machine [SVM], decision tree, etc.), which is applied to detect malicious executables. These features are (a) binary n-gram features, (b) derived assembly features (DAFs), and (c) dynamic link library (DLL) call features. Each binary n-gram feature is actually a sequence of n consecutive bytes in a binary executable, extracted using a technique explained in Chapter 10. Binary n-grams reveal the distinguishing byte patterns between the benign and malicious executables. Each DAF is a sequence of assembly instructions in an executable, and corresponds to one binary n-gram feature. DAFs reveal the distinctive instruction usage patterns between the benign and malicious executables. They are extracted from the disassembled executables using our assembly feature retrieval (AFR) algorithm. It should be noted that DAF is different from assembly n-gram features, mentioned in Chapter 10. Assembly n-gram features are not used in HFS because of our findings that DAF performs better than them. Each DLL call feature actually corresponds to a DLL function call in an executable, extracted from the executable header. These features reveal the distinguishing DLL call patterns between the benign and malicious executables. We show empirically that the combination of these three features is always better than any single feature in terms of classification accuracy.

Our work focuses on expanding features at different levels of abstraction rather than using more features at a single level of abstraction. There are two main reasons behind this. First, the number of features at a given level of abstraction (e.g., binary) is overwhelmingly large. For example, in our larger dataset, we obtain 200 million binary n-gram features. Training with this large number of features is way beyond the capabilities of any practical classifier. That is why we limit the number of features at a given level of abstraction to an applicable range. Second, we empirically observe the benefit of adding more levels of abstraction to the combined feature set (i.e., HFS). HFS combines features at three levels of abstraction, namely, binary executables, assembly programs, and system API calls. We show that this combination has higher detection accuracy and lower false alarm rate than the features at any single level of abstraction.

Our technique is related to knowledge management because of several reasons. First, we apply our knowledge of binary n-gram features to obtain DAFs. Second, we apply the knowledge obtained from the feature extraction process to select the best features. This is accomplished by extracting all possible binary n-grams from the training data, applying the statistical knowledge corresponding to each n-gram (i.e., its frequency in malicious and benign executables) to compute its *information gain* [Mitchell 1997], and selecting the best S of them. Finally, we apply another statistical knowledge (presence/absence of a feature in an executable) obtained from the feature extraction process to train classifiers.

Our research contributions are as follows. First, we propose and implement our HFR model, which combines the three kinds of features previously mentioned. Second, we apply a novel idea to extract assembly instruction features using binary n-gram features, implemented with the AFR algorithm. Third, we propose and implement a scalable solution to the n-gram feature extraction and selection problem in general. Our solution works well with limited memory and significantly reduces running time by applying efficient and powerful data structures and algorithms. Thus, it is scalable to a large collection of executables (in the order of thousands), even with limited main memory and processor speed. Finally, we compare our results against the results of [Kolter and Maloof, 2004], who used only the binary n-gram feature, and show that our method achieves better accuracy. We also report the performance/cost trade-off of our method against the method of [Kolter and Maloof, 2004]. It should be pointed out here that our main contribution is an efficient feature extraction technique, not a classification technique. We empirically prove that the combined feature set (i.e., HFS) extracted using our algorithm performs better than other individual feature sets (such as binary n-grams) regardless of the classifier (e.g., SVM or decision tree) used.

9.3 Related Work

There has been significant research in recent years to detect malicious executables. There are two mainstream techniques to automate the detection process: behavioral and content based. The behavioral approach is primarily applied to detect mobile malicious code. This technique is applied to analyze network traffic characteristics such as source-destination ports/IP addresses, various packet-level/flow-level statistics, and application-level characteristics such as email attachment type and attachment size. Examples of behavioral approaches include social network analysis [Golbeck and Hendler, 2004], [Newman et al., 2002] and statistical analysis [Schultz et al., 2001-a]. A data mining-based behavioral approach for detecting email worms has been proposed by [Masud et al., 2007-a]. [Garg et al., 2006] apply the feature extraction technique along with machine learning for *masquerade detection*. They extract features from user behavior in GUI-based systems, such as mouse speed, number of clicks per session, and so on. Then the problem is modeled as a binary classification problem, and trained and tested with SVM. Our approach is content based, rather than behavioral.

The content-based approach analyzes the content of the executable. Some of them try to automatically generate signatures from network packet payloads. Examples are EarlyBird [Singh et al., 2003], Autograph [Kim and Karp, 2004], and Polygraph [Newsome et al., 2005]. In contrast, our method does not require signature generation or signature matching. Some other content-based techniques extract features from the executables and apply machine learning to detect malicious executables. Examples are given in [Schultz et al., 2001b] and [Kolter and Maloof, 2004]. The work in [Schultz et al., 2001-b] extracts DLL call information using GNU Bin-Utils and character strings using GNU strings from the header of Windows PE executables [Cygnus, 1999]. Also, they use byte sequences as features. We also use byte sequences and DLL call information, but we also apply disassembly and use assembly instructions as features. We also extract byte patterns of various lengths (from 2 to 10 bytes), whereas they extract only 2-byte length patterns. A similar work is done by [Kolter and Maloof, 2004]. They extract binary n-gram features from the binary executables, apply them to different classification methods, and report accuracy. Our model is different from [Kolter and Maloof, 2004] in that we extract not only the binary n-grams but also assembly instruction sequences from the disassembled executables, and gather DLL call information from the program headers. We compare our model's performance only with [Kolter and Maloof, 2004], because they report higher accuracy than that given in [Schultz et al., 2001b].

9.4 Hybrid Feature Retrieval (HFR) Model

Our HFR model is a novel idea in malicious code detection. It extracts useful features from disassembled executables using the information obtained from binary executables. It then combines the assembly features with other features like DLL function calls and binary n-gram features. We have addressed a number of difficult implementation issues and provided efficient, scalable, and practical solutions. The difficulties that we face during implementation are related to memory limitations and long running times. By using efficient data structures, algorithms, and disk I/O, we are able to implement a fast, scalable, and robust system for malicious code detection. We run our experiments on two datasets with different class distribution and show that a more realistic distribution improves the performance of our model.

Our model also has a few limitations. First, it does not directly handle obfuscated DLL calls or encrypted/packed binaries. There are techniques available for detecting obfuscated DLL calls in the binary [Lakhotia et al., 2005] and to unpack the packed binaries automatically. We may apply these tools for de-obfuscation/decryption and use their output to our model. Although this is not implemented yet, we look forward to integrating these tools with our model in our future versions. Second, the current implementation is an offline detection mechanism, which means it cannot be directly deployed on a network to detect malicious code. However, it can detect malicious codes in near real time.

We address these issues in our future work and vow to solve these problems. We also propose several modifications to our model. For example, we would like to combine our features with run-time characteristics of the executables. We also propose building a feature database that would store all the features and be updated incrementally. This would save a large amount of training time and memory. Our approach is illustrated in Figure 9.3.

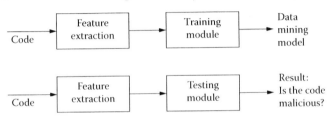

Figure 9.3   Our approach to detecting malicious executables.

9.5 Summary

In this work, we have proposed a data mining-based model for malicious code detection. Our technique extracts three different levels of features from executables, namely, binary level, assembly level, and API function call level. These features then go through a feature selection phase for reducing noise and redundancy in the feature set and generate a manageable-sized set of features. These feature sets are then used to build feature vectors for each training data. Then a classification model is trained using the training data point. This classification model classifies future instances (i.e., executables) to detect whether they are benign or malicious.

In the future, we would like to extend our work in two directions. First, we would like to extract and utilize behavioral features for malware detection. This is because obfuscation against binary patterns may be achieved by polymorphism and metamorphism, but it will be difficult for the malware to obfuscate its behavioral pattern. Second, we would like to make the feature extraction and classification more scalable to applying the cloud computing framework.

References

[Cygnus, 1999]. *GNU Binutils Cygwin,* http://sourceware.cygnus.com/cygwin

[Freund and Schapire, 1996] Freund, Y., and R. Schapire, Experiments with a New Boosting Algorithm, in *Proceedings of the Thirteenth International Conference on Machine Learning,* Morgan Kaufmann, 1996, pp. 148–156.

[Garg et al., 2006] Garg, A., R. Rahalkar, S. Upadhyaya, K. Kwiat, Profiling Users in GUI Based Systems for Masquerade Detection, in *Proceedings of the 7th IEEE Information Assurance Workshop (IAWorkshop 2006),* IEEE, 2006, pp. 48–54.

[Golbeck and Hendler, 2004] Golbeck, J., and J. Hendler, Reputation Network Analysis for Email Filtering, in *Proceedings of CEAS 2004, First Conference on Email and Anti-Spam.*

[Kim and Karp, 2004] Kim, H. A., B. Karp, Autograph: Toward Automated, Distributed Worm Signature Detection, in *Proceedings of the 13th USENIX Security Symposium (Security 2004),* San Diego, CA, August 2004, pp. 271–286.

[Kolter and Maloof, 2004] Kolter, J. Z., and M. A. Maloof, Learning to Detect Malicious Executables in the Wild, *Proceedings of the Tenth ACM SIGKDD International Conference on Knowledge Discovery and Data Mining,* ACM, 2004, pp. 470–478.

[Lakhotia et al., 2005] Lakhotia, A., E. U. Kumar, M. Venable, A Method for Detecting Obfuscated Calls in Malicious Binaries, *IEEE Transactions on Software Engineering*, 31(11), 955–968.

[Masud et al, 2007a] Masud, M. M., L. Khan, and B. Thuraisingham, Feature-Based Techniques for Auto-Detection of Novel Email Worms, in *Proceedings of the 11th Pacific-Asia Conference on Knowledge Discovery and Data Mining (PAKDD'07)*, Lecture Notes in Computer Science 4426/ Springer 2007, Bangkok, Thailand, pp. 205–216.

[Masud et al., 2007b] Masud, M. M., L. Khan, and B. Thuraisingham, A Hybrid Model to Detect Malicious Executables, in *Proceedings of the IEEE International Conference on Communication (ICC'07)*, pp. 1443–1448.

[Mitchell, 1997] Mitchell, T. *Machine Learning*. McGraw-Hill.

[Newman et al., 2002] Newman, M. E. J., S. Forrest, and J. Balthrop, Email Networks and the Spread of Computer Viruses. *Physical Review A* 66(3), 035101-1–035101-4.

[Newsome et al., 2005] Newsome, J., B. Karp, and D. Song, Polygraph: Automatically Generating Signatures for Polymorphic Worms, in *Proceedings of the IEEE Symposium on Security and Privacy*, May 2005, Oakland, CA, pp. 226–241.

[Schultz et al., 2001a] Schultz, M., E. Eskin, and E. Zadok, MEF Malicious Email Filter, a UNIX Mail Filter That Detects Malicious Windows Executables, in *Proceedings of the FREENIX Track, USENIX Annual Technical Conference*, June 2001, Boston, MA, pp. 245–252.

[Schultz et al., 2001b] Schultz, M., E. Eskin, E. Zadok, and S. Stolfo, Data Mining Methods for Detection of New Malicious Executables, in *Proceedings of the IEEE Symposium on Security and Privacy*, May 2001, Oakland, CA, pp. 38–49.

[Singh et al., 2003] Singh, S., C. Estan, G. Varghese, and S. Savage, The EarlyBird System for Real-Time Detection of Unknown Worms. *Technical Report CS2003-0761*, University of California at San Diego (UCSD), August 2003.

10

DESIGN OF THE DATA MINING TOOL

10.1 Introduction

In this chapter, we describe our data mining tool for detecting malicious executables. It utilizes the feature extraction technique using n-gram analysis. We first discuss how we extract binary n-gram features from the executables and then show how we select the best features using information gain. We also discuss the memory and scalability problem associated with the n-gram extraction and selection and how we solve it. Then we describe how the assembly features and dynamic link library (DLL) call features are extracted. Finally, we describe how we combine these three kinds of features and train a classifier using these features.

The organization of this chapter is as follows. Feature extraction using n-gram analysis is given in Section 10.2. The hybrid feature retrieval model is discussed in Section 10.3. The chapter is summarized in Section 10.4. Figure 10.1 illustrates the concepts in this chapter.

10.2 Feature Extraction Using n-Gram Analysis

Before going into the details of the process, we illustrate a code snippet in Figure 10.2 from the email worm "Win32.Ainjo.e" and use it as a running example throughout the chapter.

Feature extraction using n-gram analysis involves extracting all possible n-grams from the given dataset (*training set*), and selecting the best n-grams among them. Each such n-gram is a feature. We extend the notion of n-gram from bytes to assembly instructions and DLL function calls. That is, an n-gram may be either a sequence of

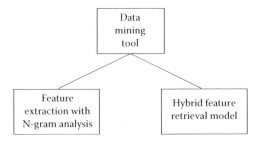

Figure 10.1   Concepts in this chapter.

```
------------------------------------------------------------
CODE SNIPPET:-

Program Entry Point = 00472E70
(Email-Worm.Win32.Ainjo.e File Offset:00000400)

  address   opcode                      assembly
  --------- ------                      -----------------------
:00455000 FF21                          jmp dword[ecx]
:00455002 089000270014                  or byte[eax+14002700], dl
:00455008 00761E                        add byte[esi+1E], dh
:0045500B 45                            inc ebp
:0045500C 00DE                          add dh, bl
:00455010 B4DE                          mov ah, -22


------------------------------------------------------------
DLL FUNCTION CALL INFO FROM THE HEADER

    Module : KERNEL32.DLL

Addr:00073CAE Name: LoadLibraryA
Addr:00073CBC Name: GetProcAddress
Addr:00073CCC Name: ExitProcess
------------------------------------------------------------
```

Figure 10.2   Code snippet and DLL call info from the Email-Worm "Win32.Ainjo.e." (From M. Masud, L. Khan, B. Thuraisingham, *A Scalable Multi-level Feature Extraction Technique to Detect Malicious Executables,* pp. 33–45, Springer. With permission.)

n bytes, *n* assembly instructions, or *n* DLL function calls, depending on whether we are to extract features from binary executables, assembly programs, or DLL call sequences, respectively. Before extracting *n*-grams, we preprocess the binary executables by converting them to *hexdump* files and *assembly program* files, as explained shortly.

10.2.1 Binary n-Gram Feature

Here the granularity level is a *byte*. We apply the UNIX hexdump utility to convert the binary executable files into text files, mentioned henceforth as hexdump files, containing the hexadecimal numbers corresponding to each byte of the binary. This process is performed to ensure safe and easy portability of the binary executables. The feature extraction process consists of two phases: (1) feature collection, and (2) feature selection, both of which are explained in the following subsections.

10.2.2 Feature Collection

We collect binary n-grams from the hexdump files. This is illustrated in Example-I.

Example-I
The 4-grams corresponding to the first 6 bytes sequence (FF2108900027) from the executable in Figure 1 are the 4-byte sliding windows: FF21890, 21089000, and 08900027

The basic feature collection process runs as follows. At first, we initialize a list L of n-grams to empty. Then we scan each hexdump file by sliding an n-byte window. Each such n-byte sequence is an n-gram. Each n-gram g is associated with two values: p_1 and n_1, denoting the total number of positive instances (i.e., malicious executables) and negative instances (i.e., benign executables), respectively, that contain g. If g is not found in L, then g is added to L, and p_1 and n_1 are updated as necessary. If g is already in L, then only p_1 and n_1 are updated. When all hexdump files have been scanned, L contains all the unique n-grams in the dataset along with their frequencies in the positive and negative instances. There are several implementation issues related to this basic approach. First, the total number of n-grams may be very large. For example, the total number of 10-grams in our second dataset is 200 million. It may not be possible to store all of them in the computer's main memory. To solve this problem, we store the n-grams in a disk file F. Second, if L is not sorted, then a linear search is required for each scanned n-gram to test whether it is already in L. If N is the total number of n-grams in the dataset, then the time for collecting all the n-grams would be $O(N^2)$, an impractical amount of time when $N = 200$ million.

To solve the second problem, we use a data structure called Adelson Velsky Landis (AVL) tree [Goodrich and Tamassia, 2006] to store the n-grams in memory. An AVL tree is a height-balanced binary search tree. This tree has a property that the absolute difference between the heights of the left subtree and the right subtree of any node is, at most, 1. If this property is violated during insertion or deletion, a balancing operation is performed, and the tree regains its height-balanced property. It is guaranteed that insertions and deletions are performed in logarithmic time. So, to insert an *n*-gram in memory, we now need only $O(\log_2(N))$ searches. Thus, the total running time is reduced to $O(N\log_2(N))$, making the overall running time about 5 million times faster for N as large as 200 million. Our feature collection algorithm *Extract_Feature* implements these two solutions. It is illustrated in Algorithm 10.1.

Description of the algorithm: the *for* loop at line 3 runs for each hexdump file in the training set. The inner *while* loop at line 4 gathers all the *n*-grams of a file and adds it to the AVL tree if it is not already there. At line 8, a test is performed to see whether the tree size has exceeded the memory limit (a threshold value). If it exceeds and F is empty, then we save the contents of the tree in F (line 9). If F is not empty, then we merge the contents of the tree with F (line 10). Finally, we delete all the nodes from the tree (line 12).

Algorithm 10.1   The *n*-Gram Feature Collection Algorithm

Procedure Extract_Feature (B)

$B = \{ B_1, B_2, \ldots, B_K \}$: all hexdump files

1. $T \leftarrow$ empty tree // Initialize AVL-tree
2. $F \leftarrow$ new file // Initialize disk file
3. **for** each $B_i \in B$ **do**
4.   **while not** $EOF(B_i)$ **do** //while not end of file
5. $g \leftarrow$ next_ngram(B_i) // read next *n*-gram
6. T.insert(g) // insert into tree and/or update frequencies as necessary
7.   **end while**
8.   **if** T.size > *Threshold* **then** //save or merge
9.   **if** F is empty **then** $F \leftarrow T$.inorder() //save tree data in sorted order
10.   **else** $F \leftarrow$ merge(T.inorder(), F) //merge tree data with file data and save

11.   **end if**
12. $T \leftarrow$ empty tree //release memory
13.   **end if**
14. **end for**

The time complexity of Algorithm 10.1 is T = time (n-gram reading and inserting in tree) + time (merging with disk) = O ($B\log_2 K$) + O (N), where B is the total size of the training data in *bytes*, K is the maximum number of nodes of the tree (i.e., threshold), and N is the total number of n-grams collected. The space complexity is O (K), where K is defined as the maximum number of nodes of the tree.

10.2.3 Feature Selection

If the total number of extracted features is very large, it may not be possible to use all of them for training because of several reasons. First, the memory requirement may be impractical. Second, training may be too slow. Third, a classifier may become confused with a large number of features, because most of them would be noisy, redundant, or irrelevant. So, we are to choose a small, relevant, and useful subset of features. We choose *information gain* (IG) as the selection criterion, because it is one of the best criteria used in literature for selecting the best features.

IG can be defined as a measure of effectiveness of an attribute (i.e., feature) in classifying a training data point [Mitchell, 1997]. If we split the training data based on the values of this attribute, then IG gives the measurement of the expected reduction in entropy after the split. The more an attribute can reduce entropy in the training data, the better the attribute is in classifying the data. IG of an attribute A on a collection of instances I is given by Eq. 10.1:

$$Gain(I, A) \equiv Entropy(I) - \sum_{V \in \mathcal{V}alues(A)} \frac{p_v + n_v}{p + n} Entropy(I_v) \quad (10.1)$$

where

values (A) is the set of all possible values for attribute A,

I_v is the subset of I where all instances have the value of $A = v$,

p is the total number of positive instances in I, n is the total number of negative instances in I,

p_v is the total number of positive instances in I_v, and n_v is the total number of negative instances in I_v.

In our case, each attribute has only two possible values, that is, $v \in \{0, 1\}$. If an attribute A (i.e., an n-gram) is present in an instance X, then $X_A = 1$, otherwise it is 0. Entropy of I is computed using the following equation:

$$Entropy(I) = -\frac{p}{p+n} \log_2\left(\frac{p}{p+n}\right) - \frac{n}{p+n} \log_2\left(\frac{n}{p+n}\right) \quad (10.2)$$

where I, p, and n are as defined above. Substituting (2) in (1) and letting $t = n + p$, we get

$$Gain(I, A) \equiv -\frac{p}{t} \log_2\left(\frac{p}{t}\right) - \frac{n}{t} \log_2\left(\frac{n}{t}\right)$$

$$- \sum_{v \in \{0,1\}} \frac{t_v}{t}\left(-\frac{p_v}{t_v} \log_2\left(\frac{p_v}{t_v}\right) - \frac{n_v}{t_v} \log_2\left(\frac{n_v}{t_v}\right)\right) \quad (10.3)$$

The next problem is to select the best S features (i.e., n-grams) according to IG. One naïve approach is to sort the n-grams in non-increasing order of IG and selecting the top S of them, which requires $O(N\log_2 N)$ time and $O(N)$ main memory. But this selection can be more efficiently accomplished using a *heap* that requires $O(N\log_2 S)$ time and $O(S)$ main memory. For $S = 500$ and $N = 200$ million, this approach is more than 3 times faster and requires 400,000 times less main memory. A heap is a balanced binary tree with the property that the root of any subtree contains the minimum (maximum) element in that subtree. We use a *min–heap* that always has the minimum value at its root. Algorithm 10.2 sketches the feature selection algorithm. At first, the heap is initialized to empty. Then the n-grams (along with their frequencies) are read from disk (line 2) and inserted into the heap (line 5) until the heap size becomes S. After the heap size becomes equal to S, we compare the IG of the next n-gram g against the IG of the root. If IG ($root$) $\geq$ IG (g) then g is discarded (line 6) since $root$ has the minimum IG. Otherwise, $root$ is replaced with g

(line 7). Finally, the heap property is *restored* (line 9). The process terminates when there are no more *n*-grams in the disk. After termination, we have the *S* best *n*-grams in the heap.

Algorithm 10.2   The *n*-Gram Feature Selection Algorithm

Procedure Select_Feature (F, H, p, n)

 F: a disk file containing all *n*-grams
 H: empty heap
 p: total number of positive examples
 n: total number of negative examples

 1. **while** not EOF(*F*) **do**
 2. $<g, p_1, n_1> \leftarrow$ next_ngram(*F*) //read *n*-gram with frequency counts
 3. $p_0 = P-p_1, n_0 = N- n_1$ // #of positive and negative examples not containing *g*
 4. $IG \leftarrow$ Gain(p_0, n_0, p_1, n_1, p, n) // using equation (3)
 5.   **if** *H*.size() < *S* **then** *H*.insert(*g*, *IG*)
 6.   **else if** *IG* <= *H.root.IG* **then continue** //discard lower gain *n*-grams
 7.   **else** *H.root* $\leftarrow$ <*g*, *IG*> //replace root
 8.   **end if**
 9.   *H*.restore() //apply restore operation
 10. **end while**

The insertion and restoration takes only $O (\log_2(S))$ time. So, the total time required is $O (N\log_2 S)$, with only $O(S)$ main memory. We denote the best *S* binary features selected using IG criterion as the *binary feature set* (BFS).

10.2.4 Assembly n-Gram Feature

In this case, the level of granularity is an assembly instruction. First, we disassemble all the binary files using a disassembly tool called *PEDisassem*. It is used to disassemble Windows Portable Executable (P.E.) files. Besides generating the assembly instructions with opcode and address information, PEDisassem provides useful information like list of resources (e.g., cursor) used, list of DLL functions called, list of exported functions, and list of strings inside the code block. To extract assembly *n*-gram features, we follow a method similar to the binary *n*-gram feature extraction. First we collect all possible *n*-grams, that is, sequences of *n* consecutive assembly instructions, and select the best *S* of them according to IG. We mention henceforth this selected set of features as the *assembly feature set* (AFS). We face the same difficulties as in binary *n*-gram extraction, such as limited memory and slow running time, and solve them in the same way. Example-II illustrates the assembly *n*-gram features.

> Example-II
> The 2-grams corresponding to the first 4 assemble instructions in Figure 1 are the two-instruction sliding windows:
> jmp dword[ecx]   ;   or byte[eax+14002700], dl
> or byte[eax+14002700], dl   ;   add byte[esi+1E], dl
> add byte[esi+1E], dh   ;   inc ebp

We adopt a standard representation of assembly instructions that has the following format: name.param1.param2. Name is the instruction name (e.g., mov), param1 is the first parameter, and param2 is the second parameter. Again, a parameter may be one of {register, memory, constant}. So, the second instruction above, "or byte [eax+14002700], dl," becomes "or.memory.register" in our representation.

10.2.5 DLL Function Call Feature

Here the granularity level is a DLL function call. An *n*-gram of DLL function call is a sequence of *n* DLL function calls (possibly with other instructions in between two successive calls) in an executable. We extract the information about DLL function calls made by a program from the header of the disassembled file. This is illustrated in Figure 10.2. In our experiments, we use only 1-grams of DLL calls, because the higher grams have poorer performance. We enumerate all the DLL function names that have been used by each of the benign and malicious executables and select the best *S* of them using information gain. We will mention this feature set as *DLL-call feature set* (DFS).

10.3 The Hybrid Feature Retrieval Model

The hybrid feature retrieval (HFR) model extracts and combines three different kinds of features. HFR consists of different phases and components. The feature extraction components have already been discussed in details. This section gives a brief description of the model.

10.3.1 Description of the Model

The HFR model consists of two phases: a training phase and a test phase. The training phase is shown in Figure 10.3a, and the test phase is shown in Figure 10.3b. In the training phase we extract binary *n*-gram features (BFSs) and DLL call features (DFSs) using the approaches explained in this chapter. We then apply AFR algorithm (to be explained shortly) to retrieve the derived assembly features (DAFs) that represent the selected binary *n*-gram features. These three kinds of features are combined into the *hybrid feature set* (HFS). Please note that DAFs are different from assembly *n*-gram features (i.e., AFSs).

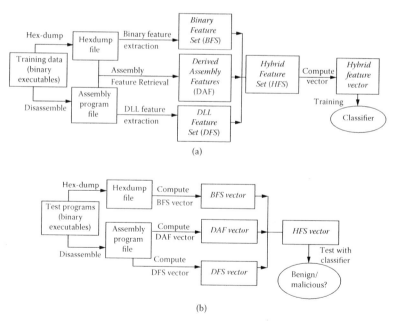

Figure 10.3 The Hybrid Feature Retrieval Model, (a) training phase, (b) test phase. (From M. Masud, L. Khan, B. Thuraisingham, *A Scalable Multi-level Feature Extraction Technique to Detect Malicious Executables*, pp. 33–45, Springer. With permission.)

AFS is not used in HFS because of our findings that DAF performs better. We compute the binary feature vector corresponding to the HFS using the technique explained in this chapter and train a classifier using SVM, boosted decision tree, and other classification methods. In the test phase, we scan each test instance and compute the feature vector corresponding to the HFS. This vector is tested against the classifier. The classifier outputs the class prediction {benign, malicious} of the test file.

10.3.2 *The Assembly Feature Retrieval (AFR) Algorithm*

The AFR algorithm is used to extract assembly instruction sequences (i.e., DAFs) corresponding to the binary *n*-gram features. The main idea is to obtain the complete assembly instruction sequence of a given binary *n*-gram feature. The rationale behind using DAF is as follows. A binary *n*-gram may represent partial information, such as part(s) of one or more assembly instructions or a string inside the code block. We apply AFR algorithm to obtain the complete instruction or instruction sequence (i.e., a DAF) corresponding to the partial one. Thus, DAF represents more complete information, which should be more useful in distinguishing the malicious and benign executables. However, binary *n*-grams are still required because they also contain other information like string data, or important bytes at the program header. AFR algorithm consists of several steps. In the first step, a *linear address matching* technique is applied as follows. The offset address of the *n*-gram in the hexdump file is used to find instructions at the same offset at the corresponding assembly program file. Based on the offset value, one of the three situations may occur:

1. The offset is before program entry point, so there is no corresponding assembly code for the *n*-gram. We refer to this address as *address before entry point* (ABEP).
2. There are some data but no code at that offset. We refer to this address as DATA.
3. There is some code at that offset. We refer to this address as CODE. If this offset is in the middle of an instruction, then we take the whole instruction and consecutive instructions within *n* bytes from the instruction.

In the second step, the best CODE instance is selected from among all CODE instances. We apply a heuristic to find the best sequence, called the *most distinguishing instruction sequence* (MDIS) heuristic. According to this heuristic, we choose the instruction sequence that has the highest IG. The AFR algorithm is sketched in Algorithm 10.3. A comprehensive example of the algorithm is illustrated in Appendix A.

Description of the algorithm: line 1 initializes the lists that would contain the assembly sequences. The *for* loop in line 2 runs for each hexdump file. Each hexdump file is scanned and n-grams are extracted (lines 4 and 5). If any of these n-grams are in the BFS (lines 6 and 7), then we read the instruction sequence from the corresponding assembly program file at the corresponding address (lines 8 through 10). This sequence is added to the appropriate list (line 12). In this way, we collect all the sequences corresponding to each n-gram in the BFS. In phase II, we select the best sequence in each n-gram list using IG (lines 18 through 21). Finally, we return the best sequences, that is, DAFs.

Algorithm 10.3   Assembly Feature Retrieval

Procedure Assembly_Feature_Retrieval(G, A, B)

$G = \{g_1, g_2, ..., g_M\}$: the selected n-gram features (*BFS*)
$A = \{A_1, A_2, ..., A_L\}$: all Assembly files
$B = \{B_1, B_2, ..., B_L\}$: all hexdump files
S = size of *BFS*
L = # of training files
Qi = a list containing the possible instruction sequences for gi
//phase I: sequence collection

1. **for** i = 1 to S **do** $Q_i \leftarrow$ empty   **end for** //initialize sequence
2. **for** each $B_i \in B$ **do**   //phase I: sequence collection
3.   *offset* $\leftarrow$ 0   //current offset in file
4.   **while not** EOF(B_i) **do**   //read the whole file
5. $g \leftarrow$ next_ngram(B_i) //read next n-gram
6.   *<index, found>* $\leftarrow$ BinarySearch(G, g) // *seach g in G*
7.   **if** *found* **then**   // found
8. $q \leftarrow$ an empty sequence

9.   **for** each instruction r in A_i with address$(r) \in [offset,$ $offset + n]$ **do**

10. $q \leftarrow q \cup r$

11.   **end for**

12. $Q_{index} \leftarrow Q_{index} \cup q$ //add to the sequence

13.   **end if**

14. $offset = offset + 1$

15. **end while**

16. **end for**

17. $V \leftarrow$ empty list   //phase II: sequence selection

18. **for** $i = 1$ to S **do**   //for each Q_i

19. $q \leftarrow t \in \{Q_i \mid \forall_{u \in Q_i}\ IG(t) >= IG(u)$ //the sequence with the highest IG

20. $V \leftarrow V \cup q$

21. **end for**

22. **return** V // DAF sequences

Time complexity of this algorithm is $O\ (nB\log_2 S)$, where B is the total size of training set in *bytes*, S is the total number of selected binary n-grams, and n is size of each n-gram in *bytes*. Space complexity is $O\ (SC)$, where S is defined as the total number of selected binary n-grams, and C is the average number of assembly sequences found per binary n-gram. The running time and memory requirements of all three algorithms in this chapter are given in Chapter 11.

10.3.3 Feature Vector Computation and Classification

Each feature in a feature set (e.g., HFS, BFS) is a binary feature, meaning its value is either 1 or 0. If the feature is present in an instance (i.e., an executable), then its value is 1; otherwise, its value is 0. For each training (or testing) instance, we compute a feature vector, which is a bit vector consisting of the feature values of the corresponding feature set. For example, if we want to compute the feature vector V_{BFS} corresponding to BFS of a particular instance I, then for each feature $f \in$ BFS we search f in I. If f is found in I, then we set $V_{BFS}[f]$ (i.e., the bit corresponding to f) to 1; otherwise, we set it to 0. In this way, we set or reset each bit in the feature vector. These feature vectors are used by the classifiers for training and testing.

We apply SVM, Naïve Bayes (NB), boosted decision tree, and other classifiers for the classification task. SVM can perform either linear or non-linear classification. The linear classifier proposed by Vladimir Vapnik creates a hyperplane that separates the data points into two classes with the maximum margin. A maximum-margin hyperplane is the one that splits the training examples into two subsets, such that the distance between the hyperplane and its closest data point(s) is maximized. A non-linear SVM [Boser et al., 2003] is implemented by applying kernel trick to maximum-margin hyperplanes. The feature space is transformed into a higher dimensional space, where the maximum-margin hyperplane is found. A decision tree contains attribute tests at each internal node and a decision at each leaf node. It classifies an instance by performing attribute tests from root to a decision node. Decision tree is a rule-based classifier. Meaning, we can obtain human-readable classification rules from the tree. J48 is the implementation of C4.5 Decision Tree algorithm. C4.5 is an extension to the ID3 algorithm invented by Quinlan. A boosting technique called Adaboost combines multiple classifiers by assigning weights to each of them according to their classification performance. The algorithm starts by assigning equal weights to all training samples, and a model is obtained from these training data. Then each misclassified example's weight is increased, and another model is obtained from these new training data. This is iterated for a specified number of times. During classification, each of these models is applied on the test data, and a weighted voting is performed to determine the class of the test instance. We use the AdaBoost.M1 algorithm [Freund and Schapire, 1996] on NB and J48. We only report SVM and Boosted J48 results because they have the best results. It should be noted that we do not have a preference for one classifier over the other. We report these accuracies in the results in Chapter 11.

10.4 Summary

In this chapter, we have shown how to efficiently extract features from the training data. We also showed how scalability can be achieved using disk access. We have explained the algorithm for feature extraction and feature selection and analyzed their time complexity. Finally, we showed how to combine the feature sets and build the feature vectors. We applied different machine learning techniques such as SVM, J48, and Adaboost for building the classification model. In the next chapter, we will show how our approach performs on different datasets compared to several baseline techniques.

In the future, we would like to enhance the scalability of our approach by applying the cloud computing framework for the feature extraction and selection task. Cloud computing offers a cheap alternative to more CPU power and much larger disk space, which could be utilized for a much faster feature extraction and selection process. We are also interested in extracting behavioral features from the executables to overcome the problem of binary obfuscation by polymorphic malware.

References

[Boser et al., 2003] Boser, B. E., I. M. Guyon, V. N. Vapnik, *A Training Algorithm for Optimal Margin Classifiers,* in D. Haussler, Editor, *5th Annual ACM Workshop on COLT,* ACM Press, 2003, pp. 144–152.

[Freund and Schapire, 1996] Freund, Y., and R. E. Schapire, Experiments with a New Boosting Algorithm, Machine Learning: *Proceedings of the 13th International Conference (ICML),* 1996, Bari, Italy, 148–156.

[Goodrich and Tamassia, 2006] Goodrich, M. T., and R. Tamassia, *Data Structures and Algorithms in Java,* Fourth Edition, John Wiley & Sons, 2006.

[Mitchell, 1997] Mitchell, T. *Machine Learning,* McGraw-Hill, 1997.

11

EVALUATION AND RESULTS

11.1 Introduction

In this chapter, we discuss the experiments and evaluation process in detail. We use two different datasets with different numbers of instances and class distributions. We compare the features extracted with our approach, namely, the hybrid feature set (HFS), with two other baseline approaches: (1) the binary feature set (BFS), and (2) the derived assembly feature set (DAF). For classification, we compare the performance of three different classifiers on each of these feature sets, which are Support Vector Machine (SVM), Naïve Bayes (NB), Bayes Net, decision tree, and boosted decision tree. We show the classification accuracy, false positive and false negative rates for our approach and each of the baseline techniques. We also compare the running times and performance/cost tradeoff of our approach compared to the baselines.

The organization of this chapter is as follows. In Section 11.2, we describe the experiments. Datasets are given in Section 11.3. Experimental setup is discussed in Section 11.4. Results are given in Section 11.5. The example run is given in Section 11.6. The chapter is summarized in Section 11.7. Figure 11.1 illustrates the concepts in this chapter.

11.2 Experiments

We design our experiments to run on two different datasets. Each dataset has a different size and distribution of benign and malicious executables. We generate all kinds of n-gram features (e.g., BFS, AFS, DFS) using the techniques explained in Chapter 10. Notice that the BFS corresponds to the features extracted by the method of [Kolter

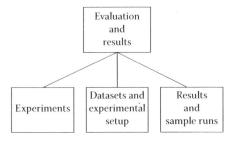

Figure 11.1 Concepts in this chapter.

and Maloof, 2004]. We also generate the DAF and HFS using our model, as explained in Chapter 10. We test the accuracy of each of the feature sets applying a threefold cross validation using classifiers such as SVM, decision tree, Naïve Bayes, Bayes Net, and Boosted decision tree. Among these classifiers, we obtain the best results with SVM and Boosted decision tree, reported in the results section in Chapter 10. We do not report other classifier results because of space limitations. In addition to this, we compute the average accuracy, false positive and false negative rates, and *receiver operating characteristic* (ROC) graphs (using techniques in [Fawcett, 2003]. We also compare the running time and performance/cost tradeoff between HFS and BFS.

11.3 Dataset

We have two non-disjoint datasets. The first dataset (dataset1) contains a collection of 1,435 executables, 597 of which are benign and 838 malicious. The second dataset (dataset2) contains 2,452 executables, having 1,370 benign and 1,082 malicious executables. So, the distribution of dataset1 is benign = 41.6%, malicious = 58.4%, and that of dataset2 is benign = 55.9%, malicious = 44.1%. This distribution was chosen intentionally to evaluate the performance of the feature sets in different scenarios. We collect the benign executables from different Windows XP and Windows 2000 machines, and collect the malicious executables from [VX Heavens], which contains a large collection of malicious executables. The benign executables contain various applications found at the Windows installation folder (e.g., "C:\Windows"), as well as other executables in the default program installation directory (e.g., "C:\Program Files"). Malicious executables contain viruses, worms, Trojan horses, and back-doors. We select only the Win32 Portable Executables in both the cases. We would like to experiment with the ELF executables in the future.

11.4 Experimental Setup

Our implementation is developed in Java with JDK 1.5. We use the LIBSVM library [Chang and Lin, 2006] for running SVM, and Weka ML toolbox [Weka] for running Boosted decision tree and other classifiers. For SVM, we run C-SVC with a Polynomial kernel, using gamma = 0.1, and epsilon = 1.0E-12. For Boosted decision tree we run 10 iterations of the AdaBoost algorithm on the C4.5 decision tree algorithm, called J48.

We set the parameter S (number of selected features) to 500, because it is the best value found in our experiments. Most of our experiments are run on two machines: a Sun Solaris machine with 4GB main memory and 2GHz clock speed, and a LINUX machine with 2GB main memory and 1.8GHz clock speed. The reported running times are based on the latter machine. The disassembly and hex-dump are done only once for all machine executables, and the resulting files are stored. We then run our experiments on the stored files.

11.5 Results

In this subsection, we first report and analyze the results obtained by running SVM on the dataset. Later, we show the accuracies of Boosted J48. Because the results from Boosted J48 are almost the same as SVM, we do not report the analyses based on Boosted J48.

11.5.1 Accuracy

Table 11.1 shows the accuracy of SVM on different feature sets. The columns headed by HFS, BFS, and AFS represent the accuracies of the Hybrid Feature Set (our method), Binary Feature Set (Kolter and Maloof's feature set), and Assembly Feature Set, respectively. Note that the AFS is different from the DAF (i.e., derived assembly

Table 11.1 Classification Accuracy (%) of SVM on Different
Feature Sets

	DATASET1			DATASET2		
n	HFS	BFS	AFS	HFS	BFS	AFS
1	93.4	63.0	88.4	92.1	59.4	88.6
2	96.8	94.1	88.1	96.3	92.1	87.9
4	96.3	95.6	90.9	**97.4**	92.8	89.4
6	**97.4**	95.5	87.2	96.9	93.0	86.7
8	96.9	95.1	87.7	97.2	93.4	85.1
10	97.0	95.7	73.7	97.3	92.8	75.8
Avg	**96.30**	**89.83**	**86.00**	**96.20**	**87.25**	**85.58**
Avg[a]	**96.88**	**95.20**	**85.52**	**97.02**	**92.82**	**84.98**

Source: M. Masud, L. Khan, B. Thuraisingham, *A Scalable Multi-level Feature Extraction Technique to Detect Malicious Executables,* pp. 33–45, Springer. With permission.

[a] Average accuracy excluding 1 gram.

features) that has been used in the HFS (see Section IV-A for details). Table 11.1 reports that the classification accuracy of HFS is always better than other models, on both datasets. It is interesting to note that the accuracies for 1-gram BFS are very low in both datasets. This is because 1 gram is only a 1-byte long pattern, having only 256 different possibilities. Thus, this pattern is not useful at all in distinguishing the malicious executables from the normal, and may not be used in a practical application. So, we exclude the 1-gram accuracies while computing the average accuracies (i.e., the last row).

11.5.1.1 Dataset1 Here the best accuracy of the hybrid model is for $n = 6$, which is 97.4, and is the highest among all feature sets. On average, the accuracy of HFS is 1.68% higher than that of BFS and 11.36% higher than that of AFS. Accuracies of AFS are always the lowest. One possible reason behind this poor performance is that AFS considers only the CODE part of the executables. So, AFS misses any distinguishing pattern carried by the ABEP or DATA parts, and, as a result, the extracted features have poorer performance. Moreover, the accuracy of AFS greatly deteriorates for $n >= 10$. This is because longer sequences of instructions are rarer in either class of executables (malicious/benign), so these sequences have less distinguishing power. On the other hand, BFS considers all parts of the executable, achieving higher accuracy. Finally, HFS considers DLL calls, as well as BFS and DAF. So, HFS has better performance than BFS.

11.5.1.2 Dataset2   Here the differences between the accuracies of HFS and BFS are greater than those of dataset1. The average accuracy of HFS is 4.2% higher than that of BFS. Accuracies of AFS are again the lowest. It is interesting to note that HFS has an improved performance over BFS (and AFS) in dataset2. Two important conclusions may be derived from this observation. First, dataset2 is much larger than dataset1, having a more diverse set of examples. Here HFS performs better than dataset1, whereas BFS performs worse than dataset1. This implies that HFS is more robust than BFS in a diverse and larger set of instances. Thus, HFS is more applicable than BFS in a large, diverse corpus of executables. Second, dataset2 has more benign executables than malicious, whereas dataset1 has fewer benign executables. This distribution of dataset2 is more likely in a real world, where benign executables outnumber malicious executables. This implies that HFS is likely to perform better than BFS in a real-world scenario, having a larger number of benign executables in the dataset.

11.5.1.3 Statistical Significance Test   We also perform a pair-wise two-tailed *t*-test on the HFS and BFS accuracies to test whether the differences between their accuracies are statistically significant. We exclude 1-gram accuracies from this test for the reason previously explained. The result of the *t*-test is summarized in Table 11.2. The *t*-value shown in this table is the value of *t* obtained from the accuracies.

Table 11.2   Pair-Wise Two-Tailed t-Test Results Comparing HFS and BFS

	DATASET1	DATASET2
t-value	8.9	14.6
Degrees of freedom	8	8
Probability	0.9965	1.00
p-value	0.0035	0.0000

Source: M. Masud, L. Khan, B. Thuraisingham, *A Scalable Multi-level Feature Extraction Technique to Detect Malicious Executables*, pp. 33–45, Springer. With permission.

There are $(5 + 5 - 2)$ *degrees of freedom*, since we have five observations in each group, and there are two groups (i.e., HFS and BFS). *Probability* denotes the probability of rejecting the NULL hypothesis (that there is no difference between HFS and BFS accuracies), while *p*-value denotes the probability of accepting the NULL hypothesis. For dataset1, the probability is 99.65%, and for dataset2, it is 100.0%. Thus, we conclude that the average accuracy of HFS is significantly higher than that of BFS.

11.5.1.4 DLL Call Feature Here we report the accuracies of the DLL function call features (DFS). The 1-gram accuracies are 92.8% for dataset1 and 91.9% for dataset2. The accuracies for higher grams are less than 75%, so we do not report them. The reason behind this poor performance is possibly that there are no distinguishing call sequences that can identify the executables as malicious or benign.

11.5.2 ROC Curves

ROC curves plot the true positive rate against the false positive rates of a classifier. Figure 11.2 shows ROC curves of dataset1 for $n = 6$ and dataset2 for $n = 4$ based on SVM testing. ROC curves for other values of n have similar trends, except for $n = 1$, where AFS performs better than BFS. It is evident from the curves that HFS is always dominant (i.e., has a larger area under the curve) over the other two and it

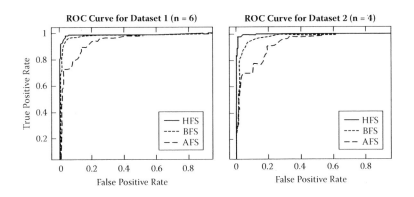

Figure 11.2 ROC curves for different feature sets in dataset1 (left) and dataset2 (right). (From M. Masud, L. Khan, B. Thuraisingham, *A Scalable Multi-level Feature Extraction Technique to Detect Malicious Executables,* pp. 33–45, Springer. With permission.)

Table 11.3 Area under the ROC Curve on Different Feature Sets

	DATASET1			DATASET2		
n	HFS	BFS	AFS	HFS	BFS	AFS
1	0.9767	0.7023	0.9467	0.9666	0.7250	0.9489
2	0.9883	0.9782	0.9403	0.9919	0.9720	0.9373
4	0.9928	0.9825	0.9651	0.9948	0.9708	0.9515
6	0.9949	0.9831	0.9421	0.9951	0.9733	0.9358
8	0.9946	0.9766	0.9398	0.9956	0.9760	0.9254
10	0.9929	0.9777	0.8663	0.9967	0.9700	0.8736
Avg	**0.9900**	**0.9334**	**0.9334**	**0.9901**	**0.9312**	**0.9288**
Avg[a]	**0.9927**	**0.9796**	**0.9307**	**0.9948**	**0.9724**	**0.9247**

Source: M. Masud, L. Khan, B. Thuraisingham, *A Scalable Multi-level Feature Extraction Technique to Detect Malicious Executables,* pp. 33–45, Springer. With permission.

[a] Average value excluding 1-gram

is more dominant in dataset2. Table 11.3 reports the area under the curve (AUC) for the ROC curves of each of the feature sets. A higher value of AUC indicates a higher probability that a classifier will predict correctly. Table 11.3 shows that the AUC for HFS is the highest, and it improves (relative to the other two) in dataset2. This also supports our hypothesis that our model will perform better in a more likely real-world scenario, where benign executables occur more frequently.

11.5.3 False Positive and False Negative

Table 11.4 reports the false positive and false negative rates (in percentage) for each feature set based on SVM output. The last row reports the average. Again, we exclude the 1-gram values from the average. Here we see that in dataset1, the average false positive rate of HFS is 4.9%, which is the lowest. In dataset2, this rate is even lower (3.2%). False positive rate is a measure of false alarm rate. Thus, our model has the lowest false alarm rate. We also observe that this rate decreases as we increase the number of benign examples. This is because the classifier gets more familiar with benign executables and misclassifies fewer of them as malicious. We believe that a large collection of training sets with a larger portion of benign executables would eventually diminish false positive rate toward zero. The false negative rate is also the lowest for HFS, as reported in Table 11.4.

Table 11.4   False Positive and False Negative Rates on Different Feature

	DATASET1			DATASET2		
n	HFS	BFS	AFS	HFS	BFS	AFS
1	8.0/5.6	77.7/7.9	12.4/11.1	7.5/8.3	65.0/9.8	12.8/9.6
2	5.3/1.7	6.0/5.7	22.8/4.2	3.4/4.1	5.6/10.6	15.1/8.3
4	4.9/2.9	6.4/3.0	16.4/3.8	2.5/2.2	7.4/6.9	12.6/8.1
6	3.5/2.0	5.7/3.7	24.5/4.5	3.2/2.9	6.1/8.1	17.8/7.6
8	4.9/1.9	6.0/4.1	26.3/2.3	3.1/2.3	6.0/7.5	19.9/8.6
10	5.5/1.2	5.2/3.6	43.9/1.7	3.4/1.9	6.3/8.4	30.4/16.4
Avg	**5.4/2.6**	**17.8/4.7**	**24.4/3.3**	**3.9/3.6**	**16.1/8.9**	**18.1/9.8**
Avg[a]	**4.9/2.0**	**5.8/4.1**	**26.8/1.7**	**3.2/2.7**	**6.3/8.1**	**19.2/17.8**

Source: M. Masud, L. Khan, B. Thuraisingham, *A Scalable Multi-level Feature Extraction Technique to Detect Malicious Executables,* pp. 33–45, Springer. With permission.

[a] Average value excluding 1-gram

11.5.4 Running Time

We compare in Table 11.5 the running times (feature extraction, training, testing) of different kinds of features (HFS, BFS, AFS) for different values of n. Feature extraction time for HFS and AFS includes the disassembly time, which is 465 seconds (in total) for dataset1 and 865 seconds (in total) for dataset2. Training time is the sum of feature extraction time, feature-vector computation time, and SVM training time. Testing time is the sum of disassembly time (except BFS) feature-vector computation time, and SVM classification time. Training and testing times based on Boosted J48 have almost similar characteristics, so we do not report them. Table 11.5 also reports the cost factor as a ratio of time required for HFS relative to BFS.

The column *Cost Factor* shows this comparison. The average feature extraction times are computed by excluding the 1-gram and 2-grams, because these grams are unlikely to be used in practical applications. The boldface cells in the table are of particular interest to us. From the table we see that the running times for HFS training and testing on dataset1 are 1.17 and 4.87 times higher than those of BFS, respectively. For dataset2, these numbers are 1.08 and 4.5, respectively. The average throughput for HFS is found to be 0.6MB/sec (in both datasets), which may be considered as near real-time performance. Finally, we summarize the cost/performance trade-off in Table 11.6.

Table 11.5 Running Times (in seconds)

	n	DATASET1				DATASET2			
		HFS	BFS	AFS	COST FACTOR[a]	HFS	BFS	AFS	COST FACTOR[a]
Feature Extraction	1	498.41	135.94	553.2	3.67	841.67	166.87	908.42	5.04
	2	751.93	367.46	610.85	2.05	1157.54	443.99	949.7	2.61
	4	1582.21	1189.65	739.51	1.33	3820.71	3103.14	1194.4	1.23
	6	2267.94	1877.6	894.26	1.21	8010.24	7291.4	1519.56	1.1
	8	2971.9	2572.26	1035.06	1.16	11736.99	11011.67	1189.01	1.07
	10	3618.31	3223.21	807.85	1.12	15594.76	14858.68	2957	1.05
	Avg[b]	2610.09	2215.68	869.17	**1.18**	9790.68	9066.22	1714.99	**1.08**
Training	Avg[c]	2654.68	2258.86	910.68	**1.18**	9857.85	9134.36	1782.8	**1.08**
Testing	Avg[c]	195.25	40.09	194.9	**4.87**	377.89	83.91	348.35	**4.5**
Testing/MB									
MB	**1.74**	**0.36**	1.74	4.87	1.57	**0.35**	1.45	4.5	
Throughput(MB/s)	**0.6**	**2.8**	0.6	—	0.64	**2.86**	0.69	—	

Source: M. Masud, L. Khan, B. Thuraisingham, *A Scalable Multi-level Feature Extraction Technique to Detect Malicious Executables,* pp. 33–45, Springer. With permission.

a Ratio of time required for HFS to time required for BFS.
b Average feature extraction times excluding 1-gram and 2-gram.
c Average training/testing times excluding 1-gram and 2-gram.

Table 11.6   Performance/Cost Tradeoff between HFS and BFS

	PERFORMANCE IMPROVEMENT (%) (HFS − BFS)/BFS	TRAINING COST FACTOR (HFS/BFS)	TESTING COST FACTOR (HFS/BFS)
Dataset1	1.73	1.17	4.87
Dataset2	4.52	1.08	4.5

Source: M. Masud, L. Khan, B. Thuraisingham, *A Scalable Multi-level Feature Extraction Technique to Detect Malicious Executables,* pp. 33–45, Springer. With permission.

The column *Performance Improvement* reports the accuracy improvement of HFS over BFS. The cost factors are shown in the next two columns. If we drop the disassembly time from testing time (considering that disassembly is done offline), then the testing cost factor diminishes to 1.0 for both datasets. It is evident from Table 11.6 that the performance/cost tradeoff is better for dataset2 than for dataset1. Again, we may infer that our model is likely to perform better in a larger and more realistic dataset. The main bottleneck of our system is disassembly cost. The testing cost factor is higher because here a larger proportion of time is used up in disassembly. We believe that this factor may be greatly reduced by optimizing the disassembler and considering that disassembly can be done offline.

11.5.5 Training and Testing with Boosted J48

We also train and test with this classifier and report the classification accuracies for different features and different values of n in Table 11.7. The second last row (*Avg*) of Table 11.7 is the average of 2-gram to 10-gram accuracies. Again, for consistency, we exclude 1-gram from the average. We also include the average accuracies of SVM (from the last row of Table 11.1) in the last row of Table 11.7 for ease of comparison. We would like to point out some important observations regarding this comparison. First, the average accuracies of SVM and Boosted J48 are almost the same, being within 0.4% of each other (for HFS). There is no clear winner between these two classifiers. So, we may use any of these classifiers for our model. Second, accuracies of HFS are again the best among all three. HFS has 1.84% and 3.6% better accuracies than BFS in dataset1 and dataset2, respectively. This

Table 11.7 Classification Accuracy (%) of Boosted J48 on Different Feature Sets

n	DATASET1			DATASET2		
	HFS[a]	BFS	AFS	HFS	BFS	AFS
1	93.9	64.1	91.3	93.5	58.8	90.2
2	96.4	93.2	89.4	97.1	92.7	85.1
4	96.3	95.4	92.1	97.2	93.6	87.5
6	96.3	95.3	87.8	97.6	93.6	85.4
8	96.7	94.1	89.1	97.6	94.3	83.7
10	96.6	95.1	77.1	97.8	95.1	82.6
Avg[a] (Boosted J48)	**96.46**	**94.62**	**87.1**	**97.46**	**93.86**	**84.86**
Avg[b] (SVM)	**96.88**	**95.20**	**85.52**	**97.02**	**92.82**	**84.98**

Source: M. Masud, L. Khan, B. Thuraisingham, *A Scalable Multi-level Feature Extraction Technique to Detect Malicious Executables,* pp. 33–45, Springer. With permission.
[a] Average accuracy excluding 1-gram.
[b] Average accuracy for SVM (from Table 11.1).

result also justifies our claim that HFS is a better feature set than BFS, irrespective of the classifier used.

11.6 Example Run

Here we illustrate an example run of the AFR algorithm. The algorithm scans through each hexdump file, sliding a window of n bytes and checking the n-gram against the binary feature set (BFS). If a match is found, then we collect the corresponding (same offset address) assembly instruction sequence in the assembly program file. In this way, we collect all possible instruction sequences of all the features in BFS. Later, we select the best sequence using information gain. *Example-III*: Table 11.8 shows an example of the collection of assembly sequences and their IG values corresponding to the n-gram "00005068." Note that this n-gram has 90 occurrences (in all hexdump files). We have shown only 5 of them for brevity. The bolded portion of the op-code in Table 11.8 represents the n-gram. According to the Most Distinguishing Instruction Sequence (MDIS) heuristic, we find that sequence number 29 attains the highest information gain, which is selected as the DAF of the n-gram. In this way, we select one DAF per binary n-gram and return all DAFs.

Table 11.8   Assembly Code Sequence for Binary 4-Gram "00005068"

SEQUENCE #	OP-CODE	ASSEMBLY CODE	INFORMATION GAIN
1	E8B702**0000**	call 00401818	0.5
	50	push eax	
	6828234000	push 00402328	
2	0FB6800D02**0000**	movzx eax,byte[eax+20]	0.1
	50	push eax	
	68CC000000	push 000000CC	
3	8B805C04**0000**	mov eax, dword[eax+45]	0.2
	50	push eax	
	6801040000	push 00000401	
29	8D8010010**0000**	lea eax, dword[eax+110]	0.7
	50	push eax	
	6807504000	push 00405007	
50	25FFFF**0000**	and eax, 0000FFFF	0.3
	50	push eax	
	68E8164100	push 004116E8	
90	25FFFF**0000**	and eax, 0000FFFF	0.4
	50	push eax	
	68600E4100	push 00410E60	

Source: M. Masud, L. Khan, B. Thuraisingham, *A Scalable Multi-level Feature Extraction Technique to Detect Malicious Executables*, pp. 33–45, Springer. With permission.

Table 11.9   Time and Space Complexities of Different Algorithms

ALGORITHM	TIME COMPLEXITY	SPACE COMPLEXITY
Feature Collection	$O(Blog_2K) + O(N)$	$O(K)$
Feature Selection	$O(Nlog_2S)$	$O(S)$
Assembly Feature Retrieval	$O(nBlog_2S)$	$O(SC)$
Total (worst case)	$\boldsymbol{O(nBlog_2K)}$	$\boldsymbol{O(SC)}$

Source: M. Masud, L. Khan, B. Thuraisingham, *A Scalable Multi-level Feature Extraction Technique to Detect Malicious Executables*, pp. 33–45, Springer. With permission.

Next we summarize the time and space complexities of our algorithms in Table 11.9.

B is the total size of training set in *bytes*, C is the average number of assembly sequences found per binary n-gram, K is the maximum number of nodes of the AVL tree (i.e., threshold), N is the total number of n-grams collected, n is size of each n-gram in *bytes*, and S is the total number of selected n-grams. The worst case assumption: $B > N$ and $SC > K$.

11.7 Summary

In this chapter we have described the experiments done on our approach and several other baseline techniques on two different datasets. We compared both the classification accuracy and running times of each baseline technique. We showed that our approach outperforms other baseline techniques in classification accuracy, without major performance degradation. We also analyzed the variation of results on different classification techniques and different datasets and explained these variations. Overall, our approach is superior to other baselines not only because of higher classification accuracy but also scalability and efficiency.

In the future, we would like to add more features to the feature set, such as behavioral features of the executables. This is because binary features are susceptible to obfuscation by polymorphic and metamorphic malware. But it would be difficult to obfuscate behavioral patterns. We would also extend our work to the cloud computing framework so that the feature extraction and selection process becomes more scalable.

References

[Chang and Lin, 2006] Chang, C.-C., and C.-J. Lin, *LIBSVM: A Library for Support Vector Machine*, http://www.csie.ntu.edu.tw/~cjlin/libsvm

[Faucett, 2003] Fawcett, T. *ROC Graphs: Notes and Practical Considerations for Researchers*, Technical Report HPL-2003-4, HP Laboratories, http://home.comcast.net/~tom.fawcett/public_html/papers/ROC101.pdf

[Freund and Schapire, 1996] Freund, Y., and R. E. Schapire, Experiments with a New Boosting Algorithm, Machine Learning: *Proceedings of the 13th International Conference (ICML)*, 1996, Bari, Italy, pp. 148–156.

[Kolter and Maloof, 2004] Kolter, J. Z., and M. A. Maloof, Learning to Detect Malicious Executables in the Wild, *Proceedings of the Tenth ACM SIGKDD International Conference on Knowledge Discovery and Data Mining*, ACM, 2004, pp. 470–478.

[VX Heavens] VX Heavens, http://vx.netlux.org

[Weka] *Weka 3: Data Mining Software in Java*, http://www.cs.waikato.ac.nz/ml/weka

Conclusion to Part III

We have presented a data mining-based malicious executable detection technique, which is scalable over a large dataset. Here we apply a multi-level feature extraction technique by combining three different kinds of features at different levels of abstraction. These are binary *n*-grams, assembly instruction sequences, and Dynamic Link Library (DLL) function calls, extracted from binary executables, disassembled executables, and executable headers, respectively. We apply this technique on a large corpus of real benign and malicious executables. Our model is compared against other feature-based approaches for malicious code detection and found to be more efficient in terms of detection accuracy and false alarm rate.

In the future, we would like to apply this technique on a much larger corpus of executables and optimize the feature extraction and selection process by applying a cloud computing framework.

PART IV

DATA MINING FOR DETECTING REMOTE EXPLOITS

Introduction to Part IV

In this part we will discuss the design and implementation of *DExtor*, a *D*ata Mining-based *E*xploit code detec*tor*, to protect network services. The main assumption of our work is that normal traffic into the network services contains only data, whereas exploit code contains code. Thus, the "exploit code detection" problem reduces to "code detection" problem. DExtor is an application-layer attack blocker, which is deployed between a web service and its corresponding firewall. The system is first trained with real training data containing both exploit code and normal traffic. Training is performed by applying binary disassembly on the training data, extracting features, and training a classifier. Once trained, DExtor is deployed in the network to detect exploit code and protect the network service. We evaluate DExtor with a large collection of real exploit code and normal data. Our results show that DExtor can detect almost all exploit code with a negligible false alarm rate. We also compare DExtor with other published works and prove its effectiveness.

Part IV consists of three chapters: 12, 13, and 14. Chapter 12 describes the issues involved in remote code exploitation. The design and implementation of our tool DExtor is discussed in Chapter 13. Our results are analyzed in Chapter 14.

12

DETECTING REMOTE EXPLOITS

12.1 Introduction

Remote exploits are a popular means for attackers to gain control of hosts that run vulnerable services/software. Typically, a remote exploit is provided as an input to a remote vulnerable service to hijack the control flow of machine-instruction execution. Sometimes the attackers inject executable code in the exploit that is executed after a successful hijacking attempt. We will refer to these code-carrying remote exploits as *exploit code*.

The problem may be briefly described as follows. Usually, an exploit code consists of three parts: (1) a NOP (no operation) sled at the beginning of the exploit, (2) a payload in the middle, and (3) return addresses at the end. The NOP sled is a sequence of NOP instructions, the payload contains attacker's code, and the return addresses point to the code. Thus, an exploit code always carries some valid executables in the NOP sled and in the payload. Such code is considered as an *attack* input to the corresponding vulnerable service. Inputs to a service that do not exploit its vulnerability are considered as *normal* inputs. For example, with respect to a vulnerable HTTP server, all benign HTTP requests are "normal" inputs, and requests that exploit its vulnerability are "attack" inputs. If we assume that "normal" inputs may contain only data, then the "exploit code detection" problem reduces to a "code detection" problem. To justify this assumption, we refer to [Chinchani and Berg, 2005, p. 286]. They maintain that "the nature of communication to and from network services is predominantly or exclusively data and not executable code." However, there are exploits that do not contain code, such as integer overflow exploits, or return-to-libc exploits. We do not deal with these kinds of exploits. It is also worth mentioning that a code detection problem is fundamentally

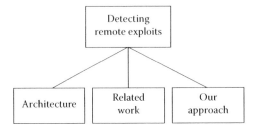

Figure 12.1 Concepts in this chapter.

different from a "malware detection" problem, which tries to identify the presence of malicious content in an executable.

There are several approaches for analyzing network flows to detect exploit code [Bro], [Chinchani and Berg, 2005], [Snort], [Toth and Kruegel, 2002], [Wang et al., 2005], [Wang and Stolfo, 2004]. If an exploit can be detected and intercepted on its way to a server process, then an attack will be prevented. This approach is compatible with legacy code and does not require any change to the underlying computing infrastructure. Our solution, *DExtor*, follows this perspective. It is a data mining approach to the general problem of exploit code detection.

The organization of this chapter is as follows. Our architecture is discussed in Section 12.2. Section 12.3 discusses related work. Section 12.4 briefly describes our approach. The chapter is summarized in Section 12.5. The concepts in this chapter are illustrated in Figure 12.1.

12.2 Architecture

Figure 12.2 illustrates our architecture for detecting remote exploits. A classification model is trained using a training data consisting of a collection of benign non-executable binaries and code-carrying remote

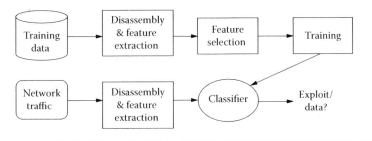

Figure 12.2 Architecture.

exploits. Each training instance first undergoes a feature extraction phase. Here the training instances are first disassembled using techniques described in Section 13.3. Then we extract three different kinds of features, explained in Section 13.4. These extracted features are then used to generate feature vectors and train a classifier (Sections 13.5 and 13.6). We use different classification models, such as Support Vector Machine (SVM), Naïve Bayes (NB), and decision trees.

When new incoming network traffic (such as an HTTP request) is to be tested, at first the test instance undergoes the same disassembly and feature extraction process as done for the training instances. This feature vector is classified using the classifier to predict whether it is a code-carrying exploit or simply a traffic containing only data.

12.3 Related Work

There are many techniques available for detecting exploits in network traffic and protecting network services. Three main categories in this direction are signature matching, anomaly detection, and machine-code analysis.

Signature matching techniques are the most prevailing and popular. Intrusion Detection Systems (IDSs) [Snort] and [Bro] follow this approach. They maintain a signature-database of known exploits. If any traffic matches a signature in the database, the IDS raises an alert. These systems are relatively easy to implement, but they can be defeated by new exploits, as well as polymorphism and metamorphism. On the contrary, DExtor does not depend on signature matching.

Anomaly detection techniques detect anomalies in the traffic pattern and raise alerts when an anomaly is detected. [Wang and Stolfo, 2004] propose a payload-based anomaly detection system called PAYL, which first trains itself with normal network traffic and detects exploit code by computing several byte-level statistical measures. Other anomaly-based detection techniques in the literature are the improved versions of PAYL [Wang et al., 2005] and FLIPS [Locasto et al., 2005]. DExtor is different from anomaly-based intrusion detection systems for two reasons. First, anomaly-based systems train themselves using the "normal" traffic characteristics and detect anomalies based on this characteristic. On the other hand, our method considers both "normal" and "attack" traffic to build a classification model. Second, we consider instruction patterns, rather than raw byte patterns, for building a model.

Machine-code analysis techniques apply binary disassembly and static analysis on network traffic to detect the presence of executables. DExtor falls in this category. [Toth and Kruegel, 2002] use binary disassembly to find long sequences of executable instructions and identify the presence of an NOP sled. DExtor also applies binary disassembly, but it does not need to identify NOP sled. [Chinchani and Berg, 2005] detect exploit code based on the same assumption as DExtor: that normal traffic should contain no code. They apply disassembly and static analysis, and identify several structural patterns and characteristics of code-carrying traffic. Their detection approach is rule based. On the other hand, DExtor does not require generating or following rules. SigFree [Wang et al., 2006] also disassembles inputs to server processes and applies static analysis to detect the presence of code. SigFree applies a code abstraction technique to detect useful instructions in the disassembled byte-stream, and raises an alert if the useful instruction count exceeds a predetermined threshold. DExtor applies the same disassembly technique as SigFree, but it does not detect the presence of code based on a fixed threshold. Rather, it applies data mining to extract several features and learns to distinguish between normal traffic and exploits based on these features.

12.4 Overview of Our Approach

We apply data mining to detect the presence of code in an input. We extract three kinds of features: *Useful Instruction Count* (UIC), *Instruction Usage Frequencies* (IUF), and *Code vs. Data Length* (CDL). These features are explained in detail in Section 13.4. Data mining is applied to differentiate between the characteristics of "attack" inputs from "normal" inputs based on these features. The whole process consists of several steps. First, training data are collected that consist of real examples of "attack" (e.g., exploits) and "normal" (e.g., normal HTTP requests) inputs. The data collection process is explained in Section 14.2. Second, all of the training examples are disassembled, applying the technique explained in Section 13.3. Third, features are extracted from the disassembled examples, and a classifier is trained to obtain a classification model. A number of classifiers are applied, such as *Support Vector Machine* (SVM), *Bayes net, decision tree* (J48), and *boosted J48*, and the best of them is chosen. Finally, DExtor is deployed in a real networking environment. It intercepts all inputs destined to the network service that it protects, and it tests them against the classification model to determine whether they are "normal" or "attack."

The next obvious issue is how we deploy DExtor in a real networking environment and protect network services. DExtor is designed to operate at the application layer and can be deployed between the server and its corresponding firewall. It is completely transparent to the service that it protects; this means no modification at the server is required. It can be deployed as a stand-alone component or coupled with a proxy server as a proxy filter. We have deployed DExtor in a real environment as a proxy, protecting a web server from attack. It successfully blocks "attack" requests in real time. We evaluate our technique in two different ways. First, we apply a fivefold cross validation on the collected data, which contain 9,000 exploits and 12,000 normal inputs, and obtain a 99.96% classification accuracy and 0% false positive rate. Second, we test the efficacy of our method in detecting new kinds of exploits. This also achieves high detection accuracy.

Our contributions are as follows. First, we identify different sets of features and justify their efficacy in distinguishing between "normal" and "attack" inputs. Second, we show how a data mining technique can be efficiently applied in exploit code detection. Finally, we design a system to protect network services from exploit code and implement it in a real environment. In summary, DExtor has several advantages over existing exploit-code detection techniques. First, DExtor is compatible with legacy code and transparent to the service it protects. Second, it is readily deployable in any system. Although currently it is deployed on windows with Intel 32-bit architecture, it can be adapted to any operating system and hardware architecture only by modifying the disassembler. Third, DExtor does not require any signature generation/matching. Finally, DExtor is robust against most attack-side obfuscation techniques, as explained in Section 14.6. Our technique is readily applicable to digital forensics research. For example, after a server crash, we may use our technique to analyze the network traffic that went to the server before the crash. Thus, we may be able to determine whether the crash was caused by any code-carrying exploit attack. We may also be able to determine the source of the attack.

In Chapter 13 we describe DExtor, a data mining approach for detecting exploit code, in more detail. We introduce three different kinds of features, namely, useful instruction count, instruction usage frequencies, and code versus data length, and show how to extract them. These three kinds of features are combined to get a combined feature set. We extract these features from the training data and train a classifier, which is then used for detecting exploits in the network traffic. We evaluate the performance of DExtor on real data and establish its efficacy in detecting new kinds of exploits. Our technique can also be applied to digital forensics research. For example, by analyzing network traffic, we may investigate whether the cause of a server crash was an exploit attack. However, there are several issues related to our technique that are worth mentioning.

First, a popular criticism against data mining is that it is heavily dependent on the training data supplied to it. So, it is possible that it performs poorly on some data and shows excellent performance on another set of data. Thus, it may not be a good solution for exploit code detection, since there is no guarantee that it may catch all exploit codes with 100% accuracy. However, what appears to be the greatest weakness of data mining is also the source of a great power. If the data mining method can be fed with sufficient realistic training data, it is likely to exhibit near-perfect efficiency in classification. Our results justify this fact too. It is one of our future goals to continuously collect real data from networks and feed them into the classification system. Because training is performed "offline," longer training time is not a problem.

Second, we would like to relax our main assumption that "normal traffic carries only data." We propose adding a "malware detector" to our model as follows. We would detect presence of code inside the traffic using our current model. If the traffic contains no code, then it is passed to the server. Otherwise, it is sent to the malware detector for a "secondary inspection." We have already implemented such a detector in one of our previous works. A malware detector detects malicious components inside an executable. If the malware detector outputs a green signal (i.e., benign executable), then we pass the

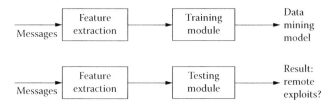

Figure 12.3   Our approach to detecting remote exploits.

executable to the server. Otherwise, we block and discard/quarantine the code. Our approach is illustrated in Figure 12.3.

12.5 Summary

In this chapter, we have argued that we need to consider both binary and assembly language features for detecting remote exploits. We then discussed related approaches in detecting exploits and gave an overview of our data mining tool, called DExtor, which is based on classification. The design and implementation of DExtor is discussed in Chapter 13. Analysis of the results of our approach is given in Chapter 14.

In the future, we are planning to detect remote exploits by examining other data mining techniques including other types of classification algorithms. We will also be examining ways of extracting more useful features.

References

[Bro] Bro Intrusion Detection System, http://bro-ids.org

[Chinchani and Berg, 2005] Chinchani, R., and E.V.D. Berg. A Fast Static Analysis Approach to Detect Exploit Code Inside Network Flows, Recent Advances in Intrusion Detection, 8th International Symposium, RAID 2005, Seattle, WA, September 7–9, 2005, Revised Papers. *Lecture Notes in Computer Science* 3858 Springer 2006, A. Valdes, D. Zamboni (Eds.), pp. 284–308.

[Locasto et al. 2005] Locasto, M. E., K. Wang, A. D. Keromytis, S. J. Stolfo, FLIPS: Hybrid Adaptive Intrusion Prevention, Recent Advances in Intrusion Detection, 8th International Symposium, RAID 2005, Seattle, WA, September 7–9, 2005, Revised Papers. *Lecture Notes in Computer Science* 3858 Springer 2006, A. Valdes, D. Zamboni (Eds.), pp. 82–101.

[Toth and Krügel, 2002] Toth, T., and C. Krügel, Accurate Buffer Overflow Detection via Abstract Payload Execution, Recent Advances in Intrusion Detection, 5th International Symposium, RAID 2002, Zurich, Switzerland, October 16-18, 2002, Proceedings. *Lecture Notes in Computer Science* 2516 Springer 2002, A. Wespi, G. Vigna, L. Deri (Eds.), pp. 274–291.

[Wang et al., 2005] Wang, K., G. Cretu, S. J. Stolfo, Anomalous Payload-Based Network Intrusion Detection and Signature Generation. Recent Advances in Intrusion Detection, 8th International Symposium, RAID 2005, Seattle, WA, September 7-9, 2005, Revised Papers. *Lecture Notes in Computer Science* 3858 Springer 2006, A. Valdes, D. Zamboni (Eds.), pp. 227–246.

[Wang and Stolfo 2004] Wang, K., S. J. Stolfo, Anomalous Payload-Based Network Intrusion Detection, Recent Advances in Intrusion Detection: 7th International Symposium, RAID 2004, Sophia Antipolis, France, September 15-17, 2004. Proceedings. *Lecture Notes in Computer Science* 3224 Springer 2004, E. Jonsson, A. Valdes, M. Almgren (Eds.), pp. 203–222.

[Wang et al., 2006] Wang, X., C. Pan, P. Liu, S. Zhu, SigFree: A Signature-Free Buffer Overflow Attack Blocker, in *USENIX Security,* July 2006.

[Wang and Stolfo, 2004] Wang, K. and S. J. Stolfo, Anomalous payload-based network intrusion detection. In: *Recent Advances In Intrusion Detection (RAID),* 2004.

13

DESIGN OF THE DATA MINING TOOL

13.1 Introduction

In this chapter, we describe the design and implementation of our tool called DExtor for detecting remote exploits. In particular, the architecture of the tool, feature extraction, and classification techniques are discussed.

DExtor can be applied within a network to protect network servers. DExtor can be deployed between the network server that it protects and the firewall that separates the inner network from the outside world. As DExtor is based on data mining, it must be trained with some known training data containing both benign traffic and exploit traffic. An important part of this training is identifying and extracting useful features from the data. Therefore, from the training data we identify several features that can help to distinguish the benign traffic from the remote exploits and extract those features from the training instances to build feature vectors. These feature vectors are then used to train classifiers that can be used to detect future unseen exploits.

The organization of this chapter is as follows. The architecture of DExtor is given in Section 13.2. The modules of DExtor are described in Sections 13.3 through 13.6. In particular, the disassembly, feature extraction, and data mining modules are discussed. The chapter is summarized in Section 13.7. Figure 13.1 illustrates the concepts in this chapter.

13.2 DExtor Architecture

The architecture of DExtor is illustrated in Figure 13.2. DExtor is deployed in a network between the network service and its

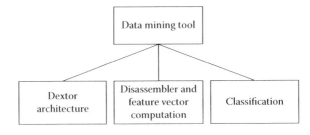

Figure 13.1   Concepts in this chapter.

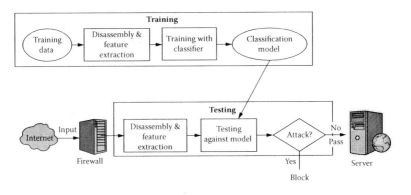

Figure 13.2   DExtor architecture. (From M. Masud, L. Khan, B. Thuraisingham, X. Wang, P. Lie, S. Zhu, *Detecting Remote Exploits Using Data Mining*, pp. 177–189, 2008, Springer. With permission.)

corresponding gateway/firewall. It is first trained offline with real instances of attack (e.g., exploits) and normal (e.g., normal HTTP requests) inputs, and a classification model is obtained. Training consists of three steps: disassembly, feature extraction, and training with a classifier. After training, DExtor is deployed in the network and all incoming inputs to the service are intercepted and analyzed online. Analysis consists of three steps: disassembly, feature extraction, and testing against the model. These processes are explained in detail in this chapter.

The major modules of DExtor are the (1) Disassembly, (2) Feature Extraction, and (3) Classification. The Disassembly module will take the binary code as inputs and output assembly code. The feature extraction module will extract the most useful features. The classification module will carry out data mining and determine whether there are remote exploits. Sections 13.3 through 13.6 describe the various modules of DExtor.

The training data consist of both code-carrying remote exploits and binaries without any valid executables. At first the disassembly and feature extraction modules are applied on the training instances to disassemble them, using the technique discussed in Section 13.3, and then features are extracted from the disassembled binaries using the technique explained in Section 13.4. After feature extraction, feature vectors are generated for each training instance, and the feature vectors are used to train a classification model (Sections 13.5 and 13.6). Once trained, the classification model is used to test new incoming network traffic (such as HTTP get request). The test instance is first passed through the disassembly and feature extraction modules to generate the feature vector, and then the feature vector is tested against the classification model. If the class prediction is "attack" (i.e., "exploit"), the traffic is blocked; otherwise, it is passed to the server.

13.3 Disassembly

The disassembly algorithm is similar to [Wang et al., 2006]. Each input to the server is considered as a byte sequence. There may be more than one valid assembly instruction sequence corresponding to the given byte sequence. The disassembler applies a technique called the "instruction sequence distiller and analyzer" to filter out all redundant and illegal instruction sequences. The main steps of this process are as follows: *Step 1. Generate instruction sequences; Step 2. Prune subsequences; Step 3. Discard smaller sequences; Step 4. Remove illegal sequences;* and *Step 5. Identify useful instructions.*

The main difficulty with the disassembly process lies in the fact that there may be more than one valid assembly instruction sequence corresponding to a given binary sequence. For example, if the input size is n bytes, then starting from byte $k \in \{1, ..., n\}$, we will have a total $O(n)$ different assembly programs (some of the starting positions may not produce any valid assembly program, because they may end up in an illegal instruction). The problem is to identify the most appropriate assembly program among these $O(n)$ programs. The instruction sequence distiller filters out all redundant instruction sequences and outputs a single, most viable assembly sequence (i.e., assembly program). The main steps of this process are briefly discussed here.

Step 1. Generate instruction sequences: The disassembler assigns an address to every byte of a message. Then, it disassembles the message from a certain address until the end of the request is reached or an illegal instruction opcode is encountered. Disassembly is performed using the recursive traversal algorithm [Schwarz et al., 2002].

Step 2. Prune subsequences: If instruction sequence s_a is a subsequence of instruction sequence s_b, the disassembler excludes s_a. The rationale for this is that if s_a satisfies some characteristics of programs, s_b also satisfies these characteristics with a high probability.

Step 3. Discard smaller sequences: If instruction sequence s_a merges to instruction sequence s_b after a few instructions and s_a is no longer than s_b, the disassembler excludes s_a. It is reasonable to expect that s_b will preserve s_a's characteristics. Many distilled instruction sequences are observed to merge into other instruction sequences after a few instructions. This property is called self-repairing [Linn and Debray, 2003] in Intel IA-32 architecture.

Step 4. Remove illegal sequences: Some instruction sequences, when executed, inevitably reach an illegal instruction whatever execution path is being taken. The disassembler excludes the instruction sequences in which illegal instructions are inevitably reachable, because causing the server to execute an illegal instruction (with possible consequence of terminating the web server thread handling this request) is not the purpose of a buffer overflow attack.

Step 5. Identify useful instructions: An instruction sequence obtained after applying the previous four steps filtering may be a sequence of random instructions or a fragment of a program in machine language. This step applies a technique to differentiate these two cases and identifies the useful instructions, that is, instructions that are most likely part of a valid executable. Readers are requested to consult [Wang et al., 2006] for more details.

13.4 Feature Extraction

Feature extraction is the heart of our data mining process. We have identified three important features based on our observation and domain-specific knowledge. These are: *Useful Instruction Count* (IUC), *Instruction Usage Frequencies* (IUF), and *Code vs. Data Lengths* (CDL). These features are described here in detail.

13.4.1 Useful Instruction Count (UIC)

The UIC is the number of useful instructions found in step 5 of the disassembly process. This number is important because a real executable should have a higher number of useful instructions, whereas data should have less or zero useful instructions.

13.4.2 Instruction Usage Frequencies (IUF)

To extract the IUF feature, we just count the frequency of each instruction that appears in an example (normal or attack). Intuitively normal data should not have any bias/preference toward any specific instruction or set of instructions. Thus, the expected distribution of instruction usage frequency in normal data should be random. On the other hand, an exploit code is supposed to perform some malicious activities in the victim machine. So, it must have some bias/ preference toward a specific subset of instructions. Thus, the expected distribution of instruction usage frequencies should follow some pattern. This idea is also supported by our observation of the training data, which is illustrated in Section 14.5.

13.4.3 Code vs. Data Length (CDL)

As explained earlier, an exploit code has three different regions: the NOP sled, the payload, and the return addresses. Following from this knowledge and our observation of the exploit code, we divide each input instance into three regions or "zones": *bzone* or the beginning zone, *czone* or the code zone, and *rzone* or the remainder zone. "bzone" corresponds to the first few bytes in the input that could not

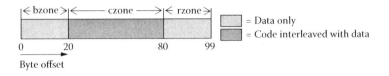

Figure 13.3   Three zones of an input instance. (From M. Masud, L. Khan, B. Thuraisingham, X. Wang, P. Lie, S. Zhu, *Detecting Remote Exploits Using Data Mining*, pp. 177–189, 2008, Springer. With permission.)

be disassembled, and probably contains only data—for example, the first 20 bytes of the exploit in Figure 13.2. "czone" corresponds to the bytes after "bzone" that were successfully disassembled by the disassembler, and probably contains some code (e.g., bytes 20–79 in Figure 13.2). "rzone" corresponds to the remaining bytes in the input after "czone" that could not be disassembled, and probably contains only data (e.g., last 20 bytes in Figure 13.3). We observe that the normalized lengths (in bytes) of these three zones follow a certain distribution for "attack" inputs, which is different from that of the "normal" inputs. These distributions are also illustrated in Section 14.5.

Intuitively, normal inputs should contain code zone at any location with equal probability. Meaning, the expected distribution of "bzone" and "rzone" should be random in normal inputs. Also, normal inputs should have few or no code. Thus, "czone" length should be near zero. On the other hand, exploit code is restricted to follow a certain pattern for the code zone. For example, the exploit code should begin with the NOP sled, necessitating the "bzone" length to be equal to 0. Also, "czone" length for exploit codes should be higher than normal inputs. In summary, the patterns of these three zones should be distinguishable in normal and attack inputs.

13.5 Combining Features and Compute Combined Feature Vector

The feature vectors/values that we have computed for each input sample are (I) UIC—a single integer; (II) IUF—containing K integer numbers representing the frequencies of each instruction, where K is the total number of different instructions found in the training data; and (III) CDL features, containing 3 real values. So, we have a collection of $K+4$ features, of which the first $K+1$ feature values are integer, and the last three are real. These $K+4$ features constitute our combined feature vector for an input instance.

Table 13.1 A Disassembled Exploit (First 16H Bytes)

ADDRESS	OPCODE	INSTRUCTION	USEFUL?
0	6A 50	push 50	Yes
2	59	pop ecx	No
3	D9EE	fldz	No
5	D97424 F4	fstenv [ss:esp-C]	Yes
9	5B	pop ebx	Yes
A	8173 13 36DB85B9	xor [dword ds:ebx+13], B985DB36	Yes
11	83EB FC	sub ebx, -4	No
14	E2 F4	loopd short 0000000A	Yes
16	CA B16E	retf 6EB1	No

We illustrate the feature vector computation with a comprehensive example as follows.

Table 13.1 shows a disassembled exploit with the address and op-code for each instruction. The column "Useful?" describes whether the instruction is useful, which is found during the disassembly step (Section 13.3). The exploit contains 322 bytes total but only the first 16H bytes are shown in the table. Among these 322 bytes, only the first 14H (=20) bytes contain code, and the remaining 302 bytes contain data. Therefore, the three different kinds of features that we extract from this exploit are as follows:

I. UIC = 5, since only five instructions are useful according to the "Useful?" column

II. IUF: push = 1, pop = 2, xor = 1, sub = 1, add = 0, etc... (count of each instruction in the first 20 bytes)

III. CDL:
    bzone = 0 (number of bytes before the first instruction)
    czone = 20 (20 bytes of instructions/code)
    rzone = 302 (number of bytes after the last instruction)

Therefore, the combined feature vector for the exploit would look as follows, assuming the order of features are as shown:

Features = {UIC, IUF(push, pop, add, ..., k-th instruction, CDL(bzone, czone, rzone)}

Vector = {5, 1, 2, 0, ..., *freq of k-th instruction*, 0, 20, 302}

13.6 Classification

We use Support Vector Machine (SVM), Bayes Net, decision tree (J48), and Boosting for the classification task. These classifiers are found to have better performances in our previous work related to malware detection. Each of these classifiers has its own advantages and drawbacks. First, SVM is more robust to noise and high dimensionality. However, it needs to be fine-tuned to perform efficiently on a specific domain. Decision tree has a very good feature selection capability. It is also much faster than many other classifiers, both in training and testing time. On the other hand, it is less stable than SVM, meaning, minor variations in the training data may lead to large changes in the decision tree. This problem can be overcome with Boosting, which applies ensemble methods, because ensemble techniques are more robust than single-model approaches. Bayes Net is capable of finding the inter-dependencies between different attributes. It avoids the unrealistic conditional independence assumption of Naïve Bayes by discovering dependency among attributes. However, it may not perform well when there are too many dimensions (i.e., attributes).

We train a model with each of the four classification techniques discussed earlier. Therefore, we have four different classification models, trained from the same training dataset but built using different base learners. Each of these classification models is evaluated on the evaluation data, and the model with the best accuracy is chosen to be deployed in the system. In our experiments (Chapter 14), we found that Boosted J48 has the best accuracy in detecting existing and new kind of exploits. Therefore, we used Boosted J48 in our tool that we have developed for remote exploit detection.

13.7 Summary

In this chapter, we have described the design and implementation of the data mining tool DExtor for detecting remote exploits. In particular, we discussed the architecture of the tool as well as the major modules of the tool. These modules include Disassembly, Feature Extraction, and Classification. In Chapter 14, we discuss the experiments we carried out and analyze the results obtained.

As stated in Chapter 12, as future work, we are planning to detect remote exploits by examining other types of data mining techniques as well as developing techniques for selecting better features. In addition, we will apply other classification techniques and compare the performance and accuracy of the results.

References

[Linn and Debray, 2003] Linn, C., and S. Debray, Obfuscation of Executable Code to Improve Resistance to Static Disassembly, in *Proceedings of the 10th ACM Conference on Computer and Communications Security (CCS)*, October 2003, pp. 290–299.

[Schwarz et al., 2002] Schwarz, B., S. K. Debray, G. R. Andrews, Disassembly of executable code revisited, in *Proceedings, 9th Working Conference on Reverse Engineering (WCRE)*, October 2002.

[Wang et al., 2006] Wang, X., C. Pan, P. Liu, S. Zhu, SigFree: A Signature-Free Buffer Overflow Attack Blocker, in *Proceedings of USENIX Security*, July 2006.

14

EVALUATION AND RESULTS

14.1 Introduction

In Chapter 12, we described issues in remote exploit detection, and in Chapter 13, we described our data mining tool DExtor for remote exploit detection. In this chapter, we describe the datasets, experimental setup, and the results that we have obtained for DExtor.

We first discuss the datasets that are used to evaluate our techniques. The dataset contains real exploit code generated by different polymorphic engines, as well as benign inputs to web servers. Then we discuss the evaluation process on these datasets. We compare our proposed technique, which combines three different kinds of features, with four baseline techniques. These baseline techniques are SigFree [Wang et al., 2006], and three other techniques that use only one type of feature, that is, only UIC, only IUF, and only CDL. We report the accuracy and running time of each approach. Also, we analyze our results and justify the usefulness of the features we extract. Finally, we discuss some limitations of our approach and explain how these limitations can be overcome.

The organization of this chapter is as follows. In Section 14.2, we describe the datasets used. In Section 14.3, we discuss the experimental setup, such as hardware, software, and system parameters. In Section 14.4, we discuss results obtained from the experiments. Our analysis is given in Section 14.5. The robustness and the limitations of our approach are presented in Section 14.6. Finally, the chapter is summarized in Section 14.7. Figure 14.1 illustrates the concepts in this chapter.

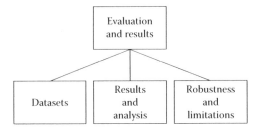

Figure 14.1   Concepts in this chapter.

14.2 Dataset

The dataset contains real exploit code as well as normal inputs to web servers. We obtain the exploit codes as follows. First, we generate 20 unencrypted exploits using the Metasploit framework [Metasploit]. Second, we apply nine polymorphic engines "ADMmutate" [Macaulay], "clet" [Detristan et al.], "Alpha2," "CountDown," "JumpCallAdditive," "Jumpiscodes," "Pex," "PexFnstenvMov," "PexFnstenvSub" on the unencrypted exploits. Each polymorphic engine is applied to generate 1,000 exploits. Thus we obtain a collection of 9,000 exploit codes. We collect the normal inputs from real traces of HTTP request/responses to/from a web server. To collect these traces, we install a client-side proxy that can monitor and collect all incoming and outgoing messages. Thus, the normal inputs consist of a collection of about 12,000 messages containing HTTP requests/responses. HTTP responses consist of texts (.javascript, .html, .xml), applications (.x-javascript, .pdf, .xml), images (.gif, .jpeg, .png), sounds (.wav), and flash. Thus we try to make the dataset as diverse, realistic, and unbiased as possible to get the flavor of a real environment.

We perform two different kinds of evaluation on the data. First, we apply a fivefold cross validation and obtain the accuracy, false positive, and false negative rates. Second, we test the performance of the classifiers on new kinds of exploits. This is done as follows: A classifier is trained using the exploits obtained from eight engines, and tested on the exploits from the ninth engine. This is done nine times by rotating the engine in the test set. Normal examples were distributed in the training and test set with equal proportions. We report the performances of each classifier for all the nine tests.

14.3 Experimental Setup

We run our experiment with a 2.0GHz machine with 1GB RAM on a Windows XP machine. Our algorithms are implemented in java and compiled with jdk version 1.5.0_06.

14.3.1 Parameter Settings

We use the Weka [Weka] Machine Learning tool for the classification tasks. For SVM, the parameter settings are as follows. *Classifier type*: C-Support Vector classifier (C-SVC), *Kernel*: polynomial kernel and *gamma* = 0.01. For Bayes Net, the following parameters are set: *alpha* = 0.5 and *network learning*: hill-climbing search. For decision tree, we use J48 from Weka, *pruning* = true, and *C* = 0.25. For Boosting, we run 10 iterations of the AdaBoost algorithm to generate 10 models (t = 10), and the weak learner for the AdaBoost algorithm is decision tree (J48).

14.2.2 Baseline Techniques

We compare our approach with four different baseline techniques as follows.

   I. *Comb:* The combined feature vector of UIC, IUF, and CDL features. This is our proposed approach.
  II. *UIC:* Here we use only the UIC feature for both training and testing.
 III. *IUF:* Here we use only the IUF features for both training and testing.
  IV. *CDL:* Here we use only the CDL features for both training and testing.
   V. *SigFree:* It is the approach proposed in [Wang et al., 2006].

Note that each of these features sets (I–IV) are used to train four different classifiers, namely, Decision Tree (a.k.a. J48 in weka), Boosted J48, SVM, and Bayes Net.

14.4 Results

We apply three different metrics to evaluate the performance of our method: *Accuracy* (ACC), *False Positive* (FP), and *False Negative* (FN),

Table 14.1   Comparing Performances among Different Features and Classifiers

FEATURE	IUC	IUF	CDL	COMB
METRIC	ACC/FP/FN	ACC/FP/FN	ACC/FP/FN	ACC/FP/FN
SVM	75.0/3.3/53.9	99.7/0.2/0.1	92.7/12.4/0.6	99.8/0.1/0.2
Bayes Net	89.8/7.9/13.4	99.6/0.4/0.4	99.6/0.2/0.6	99.6/0.1/0.9
J48	89.8/7.9/13.4	99.5/0.3/0.2	99.7/0.3/0.3	99.9/0.2/0.1
Boosted J48	89.7/7.8/13.7	99.8/0.1/0.1	99.7/0.3/0.5	99.96/0.0/0.1
SigFree	38.5/0.2/88.5			

Source: M. Masud, L. Khan, B. Thuraisingham, X. Wang, P. Lie, S. Zhu, *Detecting Remote Exploits Using Data Mining*, pp. 177–189, 2008, Springer. With permission.

where ACC is the percentage of correctly classified instances, FP is the percentage of negative instances incorrectly classified as positive, and FN is the percentage of positive instances incorrectly classified as negative.

Table 14.1 shows a comparison among different features of DExtor. We see that accuracy of DExtor's Combined (shown under column *Comb*) feature classified with Boosted J48 is the best, which is 99.96%. Individual features have accuracies less than the combined feature for all classification techniques. Also, the combined feature has the lowest false positive, which is 0.0%, obtained from Boosted J48. The lowest false negative also comes from the combined feature, which is only 0.1%. In summary, the combined feature with Boosted J48 classifier has achieved near perfect detection accuracy. The last row shows the accuracy and false alarm rates of SigFree on the same dataset. SigFree actually uses UIC with a fixed threshold (15). It is evident that SigFree has a low false positive rate (0.2%) but high false negative rate (88.5%), causing the overall accuracy to drop below 39%. Figure 14.2 shows the Receiver Operating Characteristic (ROC) curves of different features for Boosted J48 classifier. ROC curves for other classifiers have similar characteristics, and are not shown because of space limitation. The area under the curve (AUC) is the highest for the combined feature, which is 0.999.

Table 14.2 reports the effectiveness of our approach in detecting new kinds of exploits. Each row reports the detection accuracies and false alarm rates of one particular engine-generated exploit. For example, the row headed by "Admutate" shows the detection accuracy (and false alarm rates) of exploits generated by the Admutate

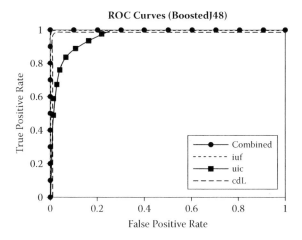

Figure 14.2 ROC curves of different features for BoostedJ48. (From M. Masud, L. Khan, B. Thuraisingham, X. Wang, P. Lie, S. Zhu, *Detecting Remote Exploits Using Data Mining*, pp. 177–189, 2008, Springer. With permission.)

Table 14.2 Effectiveness in Detecting New Kinds of Exploits

CLASSIFIER	SVM	BNET	J48	BJ48
METRIC	ACC/FP/FN	ACC/FP/FN	ACC/FP/FN	ACC/FP/FN
Admutate	86.4/0.2/31.7	57.4/0.0/100	98.2/0.0/4.3	99.7/0.0/0.6
Alpha2	99.9/0.07/ 0.0	56.4/0.0/100	56.4/0.0/100	56.4/0.0/100
Clet	100/0.0/0.0	99.6/0.07/0.8	99.9/0.1/0.0	99.9/0.07/0.0
CountDown	99.8/0.4/0.0	100/0.0/0.0	100/0.0/0.0	99.8/0.3/0.0
JmpCallAdditive	100/0.0/0.0	98.1/0.0/4.6	99.9/0.1/0.0	100/0.0/0.0
JumpisCode	99.4/0.08/1.4	96.2/0.08/8.8	99.9/0.07/0.0	99.9/0.07/0.1
Pex	99.7/0.2/0.4	99.4/0.0/1.4	99.8/0.2/0.2	99.8/0.1/0.3
PexFnStenvMov	99.9/0.0/0.0	99.1/0.0/2.1	99.9/0.07/0.1	99.9/0.0/0.2
PexFnStenvSub	99.7/0.2/0.3	99.3/0.0/1.7	99.8/0.08/0.1	99.9/0.08/0.0

Source: M. Masud, L. Khan, B. Thuraisingham, X. Wang, P. Lie, S. Zhu, *Detecting Remote Exploits Using Data Mining*, pp. 177–189, 2008, Springer. With permission.

engine. In this case, the classifiers have been trained with the exploits from eight other engines. In each case, the training set contains 8,000 exploits and about 10,500 randomly selected normal samples, and the test set contains 1,000 exploits and about 1,500 randomly chosen normal samples. The columns headed by SVM, BNet, J48, and BJ48 show the accuracies (or false positive/false negative rates) of SVM, Bayes Net, J48, and Boosted J48 classifiers, respectively. It is evident from the table that all the classifiers could successfully detect most of the new exploits with 99% or better accuracy.

14.4.1 Running Time

The total training time for the whole dataset is less than 30 minutes. This includes disassembly time, feature extraction time, and classifier training time. This amounts to about 37ms/KB of input. The average testing time/KB of input is 23ms for the combined feature set. This includes the disassembly time, feature value computation time, and classifier prediction time. SigFree, on the other hand, requires 18.5ms to test per KB of input. Considering that training can be done offline, this amounts to only 24% increase in running time compared to SigFree. So the price/performance tradeoff is in favor of DExtor.

14.5 Analysis

As explained earlier, IUF feature observes different frequency distributions for the "normal" and "attack" inputs. This is illustrated in the leftmost chart of Figure 14.3. This graph shows the 30 most frequently used instructions (for both kinds of inputs). It is seen that most of the instructions in this chart are more frequently used by the "attack" inputs than "normal" inputs. The first five of the instructions have high frequencies (>11) in "attack" inputs, whereas they have near zero frequencies in "normal" input. The next 16 instructions in "attack" inputs have frequencies close to 2, whereas "normal" inputs have near zero frequencies for these instructions. To mimic "normal" input, an attacker should avoid using all these instructions. It may be very hard for an attacker to get around more than 20 most frequently used instructions in exploits and craft his code accordingly.

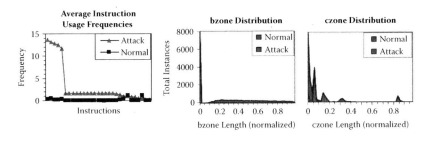

Figure 14.3   Left: average instruction usage frequencies (IUF) of some instructions. Right: distributions of "bzone" and "czone." (From M. Masud, L. Khan, B. Thuraisingham, X. Wang, P. Lie, S. Zhu, *Detecting Remote Exploits Using Data Mining*, pp. 177–189, 2008, Springer. With permission.)

Similarly, we observe specific patterns in the distribution of the CDL feature values. The patterns for "bzone" and "czone" are illustrated in the right two charts of Figure 14.3. These are histograms showing the number of input samples having a particular length (as a fraction of total input size) of "bzone" or "czone." These histograms are generated by dividing the whole range ([0,1]) of "bzone" (or "czone") sizes into 50 equal-sized bins, and counting the total number of inputs instances that fall within the range of a particular bin. By closely observing the histogram for *bzone*, we see that most of the "attack" samples have *bzone* values in the first bin (i.e., [0,0.02]), whereas that of the "normal" samples are spread over the whole range of values starting from 0.1. This means, if the attacker wants to mimic normal traffic, he should leave the first 10% of an exploit without any code. This may increase his chances of failure since the exploit should naturally start with a NOP sled. Again by closely observing the histogram for *czone*, we see that most of the "normal" samples have "czone" values within the range [0,0.05], whereas "attack" samples mostly have "czone" values greater than 0.05. This means that if the attacker wants to mimic normal traffic, he should keep his code length within 5% of the exploit's length. For a 200-byte exploit, this would allot only 10 bytes for code—including the NOP sled. Thus, the attacker would have a hard time figuring out how to craft his exploit.

14.6 Robustness and Limitations

In this section, we discuss different security issues and the robustness and limitations of our system.

14.6.1 Robustness against Obfuscations

Our technique is robust against "Instruction re-ordering" because we do not care about the order of instructions. It is also robust against "junk-instruction insertion," as it increases the frequency of instructions in the exploit. It is robust against instruction replacement as long as all the "most frequently used" instructions are not replaced (as explained in Section 14.5) by other instructions. It is also robust against register-renaming and memory re-ordering, because we do not consider register or memory locations. Junk byte insertion obfuscation is targeted at the disassembler, where junk bytes are inserted at locations that are not reachable at run-time. Our disassembly algorithm applies recursive traversal, which is robust to this obfuscation [Kruegel et al., 2004].

14.6.2 Limitations

DExtor is partially affected by the "branch function" obfuscation. The main goal of this obfuscation is to obscure the control flow in an executable, so that disassembly cannot proceed. Currently, there is no general solution to this problem. In our case, DExtor is likely to produce fragmented "code blocks," missing some of the original code. This will not affect DExtor as long as the "missed" block contains a significant number of instructions.

Another limitation of DExtor is its processing speed. We evaluated the throughput of DExtor in a real environment, which amounts to 42KB/sec. This might seem unrealistic for an intrusion detection system that has to encounter Gigabits of data per second. Fortunately, we intend to protect just one network service, which is likely to process inputs much slower than this rate. We suggest two solutions to get around this limitation: (1) using faster hardware and optimizing all software components (disassembler, feature extraction, classifier), and (2) carefully excluding some incoming traffic from analysis. For example, any bulk input to the server having a size greater than a few hundred KB is too unlikely to be an exploit code because the length of a typical exploit code is within a few KB only. By applying both the solutions, DExtor should be able to operate in a real-time environment.

14.7 Summary

In this chapter, we have discussed the results obtained from testing our data mining tool for detecting remote exploits. We first discussed the datasets we used and the experimental setup. Then we described the results we obtained. These results were subsequently analyzed, and we discussed the robustness and limitations of our approach.

We have shown that code-carrying exploits can be successfully detected using our data mining technique. The data mining technique consists of two processes: training and classification. In the training phase, we take a large number of training instances containing both code-carrying exploits and benign binary files. Each training instance is tagged as either "benign" or "exploit." Each of these training instances is then disassembled and analyzed using an "instruction sequence distiller and analyzer" module. The output of this module is an assembly instruction sequence with appropriate attributes assigned to each instruction (e.g., useful/not useful). From this sequence, we extract three different kinds of features, that is, useful instruction count (IUC), code vs. data length (CDL), and instruction usage frequency (IUF). Using these features, we compute the feature vector for each training instance and train a classification model. This classification model is then used to classify future instances. To classify, each instance (i.e., a binary file transferred through the network) is first disassembled, and its features are extracted using the same approach that was followed during training. The extracted feature values are then supplied to the classification model, and the model outputs the predicted class of the test instance. We have evaluated our approach on a large corpus of exploit and benign data, and obtained very high accuracy and low false alarm rates compared to the previous approach, SigFree [Wang et al., 2006].

In the future, we would like to apply data stream classification techniques to the remote exploit detection problem. Note that network traffic is essentially a data stream, which is both infinite in length and usually evolves over time. Therefore, a data stream mining technique would be a more appropriate and efficient technique for remote exploit detection.

References

[Detristan et al.] Detristan, T., T. Ulenspiegel, Y. Malcom, M. S. Von Underduk, Polymorphic Shellcode Engine Using Spectrum Analysis, *Phrack Magazine*, http://www.phrack.org/issues.html?issue=61&id=9#article

[Kruegal et al., 2004] Kruegel, C., W. Robertson, F. Valeur, G. Vigna, Static Disassembly of Obfuscated Binaries, in *Proceedings of USENIX Security*, August 2004.

[Metasploit] The Metasploit Project, http://www.metasploit.com

[Macaulay] Macaulay, S., Admutate: Polymorphic Shellcode Engine, http://www.ktwo.ca/security.html

[Wang et al., 2006] Wang, X., C. Pan, P. Liu, S. Zhu, SigFree: A Signature-Free Buffer Overflow Attack Blocker, in *Proceedings of USENIX Security*, July 2006.

[Weka] Data Mining Software in Java, http://www.cs.waikato.ac.nz/ml/weka

Conclusion to Part IV

As we have stated, remote exploits are a popular means for attackers to gain control of hosts that run vulnerable services/software. Typically, a remote exploit is provided as an input to a remote vulnerable service to hijack the control flow of machine-instruction execution. Sometimes the attackers inject executable code in the exploit that are executed after a successful hijacking attempt. We refer to these code-carrying remote exploits as *exploit code*. In this part, we discussed the design and implementation of *DExtor*, a *D*ata Mining–based *E*xploit code detec*tor*, to protect network services. In particular, we discussed the system architecture, our approach, and the algorithms we developed, and we reported our performance analysis. We also discussed the strengths and limitations of our approach.

In Parts II, III, and IV we have discussed our data mining tools for email worm detection, detecting malicious executables, and detecting remote exploits. In the next part, we discuss data mining for botnet detection.

PART V
DATA MINING
FOR DETECTING
BOTNETS

Introduction to Part V

Botnet detection and disruption have been a major research topic in recent years. One effective technique for botnet detection is to identify Command and Control (C&C) traffic, which is sent from a C&C center to infected hosts (bots) to control the bots. If this traffic can be detected, both the C&C center and the bots it controls can be detected and the botnet can be disrupted. We propose a multiple log file-based temporal correlation technique for detecting C&C traffic. Our main assumption is that bots respond much faster than humans. By temporally correlating two host-based log files, we are able to detect this property and thereby detect bot activity in a host machine. In our experiments, we apply this technique to log files produced by tcpdump and exedump, which record all incoming and outgoing network packets and the start times of application executions at the host machine, respectively. We apply data mining to extract relevant features from these log files and detect C&C traffic. Our experimental results validate our assumption and show better overall performance when compared to other recently published techniques.

Part V consists of three chapters: 15, 16, and 17. An overview of botnets is provided in Chapter 15. Our data mining tool is described in Chapter 16. Evaluation and results are presented in Chapter 17.

15
DETECTING BOTNETS

15.1 Introduction

Botnets are emerging as "the biggest threat facing the internet today" [Ferguson, 2008] because of their enormous volume and sheer power. Botnets containing thousands of *bots* (compromised hosts) have been tracked by several different researchers [Freiling et al., 2005], [Rajab et al., 2006]. Bots in these botnets are controlled from a *Command and Control* (C&C) center, operated by a human *botmaster* or *botherder*. The botmaster can instruct these bots to recruit new bots, launch coordinated DDoS attacks against specific hosts, steal sensitive information from infected machines, send mass spam emails, and so on.

In this chapter, we discuss our approach to detecting botnets. In particular, we use data mining techniques. There have been some discussions whether data mining techniques are appropriate for detecting botnets as botnets may change patterns. We have developed techniques for detecting novel classes, and such techniques will detect changing patterns. We will describe novel class detection techniques under our work on stream mining in Part VI.

The organization of this chapter is as follows. An architecture for botnets is discussed in Section 15.2. Related work is discussed in Section 15.3. Our approach is discussed in Section 15.4. The chapter is summarized in Section 15.5. Figure 15.1 illustrates the concepts of this chapter.

15.2 Botnet Architecture

Figure 15.2 illustrates a typical botnet architecture. The IRC-based (Internet Relay Chat) botnets are centralized botnets. The IRC

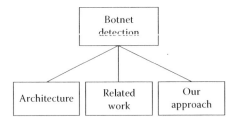

Figure 15.1 Concepts in this chapter.

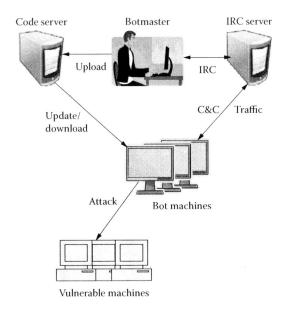

Figure 15.2 A typical IRC-based botnet architecture. (From M. Masud, T. Al-khateeb, L. Khan, B. Thuraisingham, K. Hamlen, *Flow-based Identification of Botnet Traffic by Mining Multiple Log Files*, pp. 200–206, 2008, © IEEE. With permission.)

server is the central server with which all bot machines are connected through an IRC channel. The *botmaster*, a human entity controlling the bots, also connects himself with the IRC server through a channel. The bots are programmed to receive commands from the botmaster through the IRC server. The commands are sent via Command & Control (C&C) traffic. The bots usually recruit other bots by exploiting vulnerable machines. The botmaster may launch a distributed denial of service (DDoS) attack using this bot network. Periodically, the botmaster may want to update the bot software. This is done by placing the updated software in a code server and then sending commands to the bot machines to download the update from the code server.

Numerous researchers are working hard to combat this threat and have proposed various solutions [Grizzard et al., 2007], [Livadas et al., 2006], [Rajab et al., 2006]. One major research direction attempts to detect the C&C center and disable it, preventing the botmaster from controlling the botnet. Locating the C&C center requires identifying the traffic exchanged between it and the bots. Our work adopts this approach by using a data mining-based technique to identify temporal correlations between multiple log files. We maintain two different log files for each host machine: (1) a network packet trace or tcpdump, and (2) an application execution trace or exedump. The tcpdump log file records all network packets that are sent/received by the host, and the exedump log file records the start times of application program executions on the host machine. Our main assumption is that bots respond to commands much faster than humans do. Thus, the command latency (i.e., the time between receiving a command and taking actions) should be much lower, and this should be reflected in the tcpdump and exedump log files.

Bot commands that have an observable effect upon the log files we consider can be grouped into three categories: those that solicit a response from the bot to the botmaster, those that cause the bot to launch an application on the infected host machine, and those that prompt the bot to communicate with some other host (e.g., a victim machine or a code server). This botnet command categorization strategy is explained in more detail in Section 16.5. We apply data mining to learn temporal correlations between an incoming packet and (1) an outgoing packet, (2) a new outgoing connection, or (3) an application startup. Any incoming packet correlated with one of these logged events is considered a possible botnet command packet. Our approach is flow based because rather than classifying a single packet as C&C or normal traffic, we classify an entire flow (or connection) to/from a host as C&C or normal. This makes the detection process more robust and effective. Our system is first trained with log files obtained from clean hosts and hosts infected with a known bot, then tested with logs collected from other hosts. This evaluation methodology is explained in detail in Chapter 17.

Our technique is different from other botnet detection techniques [Goebel and Holz, 2007], [Livadas et al., 2006], [Rajab et al., 2006] in two ways. First, we do not impose any restriction on the communication protocol. Our approach should therefore also work with C&C protocols other than those that use IRC as long as the C&C traffic possesses the observable characteristics previously defined. Second, we do not rely on command string matching. Thus, our method should work even if the C&C payloads are not available.

Our work makes two main contributions to botnet detection research. First, we introduce multiple log correlation for C&C traffic detection. We believe this idea could be successfully extended to additional application-level logs such as those that track process/service execution, memory/CPU utilization, and disk accesses. Second, we have proposed a way to classify botmaster commands into different categories, and we show how to utilize these command characteristics to detect C&C traffic. An empirical comparison of our technique with another recent approach [Livadas et al., 2006] shows that our strategy is more robust in detecting real C&C traffic.

15.3 Related Work

Botnet defenses are being approached from at least three major perspectives: analysis, tracking, and detection. [Barford and Yegneswaran, 2006] present a comprehensive analysis of several botnet codebases and discuss various possible defense strategies that include both reactive and proactive approaches. [Grizzard et al., 2007] analyze botnets that communicate using peer-to-peer networking protocols, concluding that existing defense techniques that assume a single, centralized C&C center are insufficient to counter these decentralized botnets.

[Freiling et al., 2005] summarize a general botnet-tracking methodology for manually identifying and dismantling malicious C&C centers. [Rajab et al., 2006] put this into practice for a specific IRC protocol. They first capture bot malware using a honeynet and related techniques. Captured malware is next executed in a controlled environment to identify the commands that the bot can receive and execute. Finally, *drone machines* are deployed that track botnet activity by mimicking the captured bots to monitor and communicate with the C&C server. [Dagon et al., 2006] tracked botnet activity as related to geographic region and time zone over a six-month period. They concluded that botnet defenses such as those described earlier can be more strategically deployed if they take into account the diurnal cycle of typical botnet propagation patterns.

Our research presented in this chapter is a detection technique. [Cooke et al., 2005] discuss various botnet detection techniques and their relative merits. They conclude that monitoring C&C payloads directly does not typically suffice as a botnet detection strategy because there are no simple characteristics of this content that reliably distinguish C&C traffic from normal traffic. However, [Goebel and Holz, 2007] show that botnets that communicate using IRC can often be identified by their use of unusual IRC channels and IRC user nicknames. [Livadas et al., 2006] use additional features including packet size, flow duration, and bandwidth. Their technique is a two-stage process that first distinguishes IRC flows from non-IRC flows and then distinguishes C&C traffic from normal IRC flows. Although these are effective detection techniques for some botnets, they are specific to IRC-based C&C mechanisms and require access to payload content for accurate analysis and detection. In contrast, our method does not require access to botnet payloads and is not specific to any particular botnet communication infrastructure. [Karasaridis et al., 2007] consider botnet detection from an ISP or network administrator's perspective. They apply statistical properties of C&C traffic to mine large collections of network traffic for botnet activity. Our work focuses on detection from the perspective of individual host machines rather than ISPs.

15.4 Our Approach

We presented the novel idea of correlating multiple log files and applying data mining for detecting botnet C&C traffic. Our idea is to utilize the temporal correlation between two different log files: tcpdump and exedump. The tcpdump file logs all network packets that are sent/received by a host, whereas the exedump file logs the start times of application program executions on the host. We implement a prototype system and evaluate its performance using five different classifiers: Support Vector Machines, decision trees, Bayes Nets, Boosted decision trees, and Naïve Bayes. Figure 15.3 illustrates our approach.

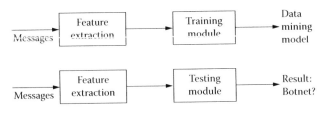

Figure 15.3 Our approach to botnet detection.

Comparison with another technique by [Livadas et al., 2006] for C&C traffic detection shows that our method has overall better performance when used with a Boosted decision tree classifier. The technique used by Livadas et al. first identifies IRC flows and then detects botnet traffic from the IRC flows. Our technique is more general because it does not need to identify IRC traffic and is therefore applicable to non-IRC botnet protocols, as long as certain realistic assumptions about the command-response timing relationships (detailed in Chapter 16) remain valid.

15.5 Summary

Botnets have been a major threat to the global Internet community in the past decade. Although many approaches have been proposed in detecting IRC botnets in recent years, there are very few approaches that apply data mining techniques. We propose a data mining-based technique that combines and correlates two log files in a host machine. The next two chapters discuss the technique and results on botnet traffic generated in a controlled environment.

In the future, we would like to apply more sophisticated data mining techniques, such as the data stream classification techniques for botnet detection. Data stream classification techniques will be particularly suitable for botnet traffic detection, because the botnet traffic itself is a kind of data stream. We would also like to extend our host-based detection technique to a distributed framework.

References

[Barford and Yegneswaran, 2006] Barford, P., and V. Yegneswaran, *An Inside Look at Botnets*, Springer, 2006.

[Cooke et al., 2005] Cooke, E., F. Jahanian, D. McPherson, The Zombie Roundup: Understanding, Detecting, and Disrupting Botnets, in *Proceedings of the Steps to Reducing Unwanted Traffic on the Internet Workshop (SRUTI'05)*, 2005, pp. 39–44.

[Dagon et al., 2008] Dagon, D., C. Zou, W. Lee, Modeling Botnet Propagation Using Time Zones, in *Proceedings of the 13th Network and Distributed System Security Symposium (NDSS '06)*, 2006.

[Ferguson, 2008] Ferguson, T., Botnets Threaten the Internet as We Know It, *ZDNet Australia*, April 2008.

[Freiling et al., 2005] Freiling, F., T. Holz, G. Wicherski, Botnet tracking: Exploring a Root-Cause Methodology to Prevent Distributed Denial-of-Service Attacks, in *Proceedings of the 10th European Symposium on Research in Computer Security (ESORICS)*, September 2005, pp. 319–335.

[Goebel and Holz, 2007] Goebel, J., and T. Holz, Rishi: Identify Bot Contaminated Hosts by IRC Nickname Evaluation, in *Proceedings of the 1st Workshop on Hot Topics in Understanding Botnets*, 2007, p. 8.

[Grizzard et al., 2007] Grizzard, J. B., V. Sharma, C. Nunnery, B. B. Kang, D. Dagon, Peer-to-Peer Botnets: Overview and Case Study, in *Proceedings of the 1st Workshop on Hot Topics in Understanding Botnets*, 2007, p. 1.

[Karasaridis et al., 2007] Karasaridis, A., B. Rexroad, D. Hoeflin, Wide-Scale Botnet Detection and Characterization, in *Proceedings of the 1st Workshop on Hot Topics in Understanding Botnets*, 2007, p. 7.

[Livadas et al., 2006] Livadas, C., B. Walsh, D. Lapsley, W. Strayer, Using Machine Learning Techniques to Identify Botnet Traffic, in *Proceedings of the 31st IEEE Conference on Local Computer Networks (LCN'06)*, November 2006, pp. 967–974.

[Rajab et al., 2006] Rajab, M., J. Zarfoss, F. Monrose, A. Terzis, A Multifaceted Approach to Understanding the Botnet Phenomenon, in *Proceedings of the 6th ACM SIGCOMM Conference on Internet Measurement (IMC'06)*, 2006, pp. 41–52.

16

DESIGN OF THE DATA MINING TOOL

16.1 Introduction

In this chapter we describe our system setup, data collection process, and approach to categorizing bot commands. We build a testbed with an isolated network containing two servers and a three client virtual machine. We execute two different IRC bots and collect packet traces. We also collect packet traces of known benign traffic. We identify several packet-level and flow-level features that can distinguish the botnet traffic from benign traffic. In addition, we find temporal correlations between the system execution log (exedump) and packet trace log (tcpdump) and use these correlations as additional features. Using these features, we then train classifiers with known botnet and benign traffic. This classifier is then used to identify future unseen instances of bot traffic.

The organization of this chapter is as follows. Our implementation architecture is described in Section 16.2. System setup is discussed in Section 16.3. Data collection is discussed in Section 16.4. Bot command categorization is described in Section 16.5. Feature extraction is discussed in Section 16.6. Log file correlation is discussed in Section 16.7. Classification is discussed in Section 16.8. Packet filtering is discussed in Section 16.9. The chapter is summarized in Section 16.10. Figure 16.1 illustrates the concepts in this chapter.

16.2 Architecture

Figure 16.2 illustrates the botnet traffic detection system deployed in each host machine. The host machines are assumed to be connected to the Internet through a firewall. The incoming and outgoing network

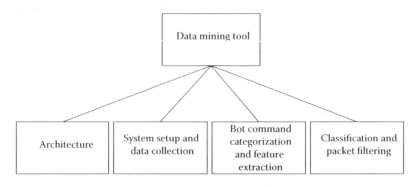

Figure 16.1   Concepts in this chapter.

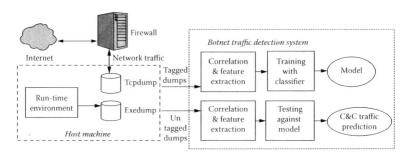

Figure 16.2   System architecture. (From M. Masud, T. Al-khateeb, L. Khan, B. Thuraisingham, K. Hamlen, *Flow-based Identification of Botnet Traffic by Mining Multiple Log Files*, pp. 200–206, 2008, © IEEE. With permission.)

traffic is logged using *tcpdump*, and program executions are logged using *exedump* (see Section 16.4). These dumps are then processed through the feature extraction module (Sections 16.6 and 16.7), and feature vectors are computed for training.

For training, we first label each flow—that is, each (*ip:port,ip':port'*) pair—as a bot flow (conversation between a bot and its C&C center), or a normal flow (all other connections). Then we compute several packet-level features (Section 16.6) for each incoming packet and compute several flow-level features for each flow by aggregating the packet-level features. Finally, these flow-level features are used to train a classifier and obtain a classification model (Section 16.7). For testing, we take an unlabeled flow and compute its flow-level features in the same way. Then we test the feature values against the classification model and label it a normal flow or a bot flow.

16.3 System Setup

We tested our approach on two different IRC-based bots—SDBot (2006) version 05a and RBot (2006) version 0.5.1. The testing platform consisted of five virtual machines running atop a Windows XP host operating system. The host hardware consisted of an Intel Pentium-IV 3.2GHz dual core processor with 2GB RAM and 150GB hard disk. Each virtual machine ran Windows XP with 256 MB virtual RAM and 8GB virtual hard disk space.

The five virtual machines played the role of a botmaster, a bot, an IRC server, a victim, and a code server, respectively. As with a typical IRC-based botnet, the IRC server served as the C&C center through which the botmaster issued commands to control the bot. The IRC server we used was the latest version of [Unreal IRCd, 2007] Daemon, and the botmaster's IRC chat client was MIRC. The code server ran Apache Tomcat and contained different versions of bot malware code and other executables. The victim machine was a normal Windows XP machine. During the experiment the botmaster instructed the bot to target the victim machine with udp and ping attacks. All five machines were interconnected in an isolated network, as illustrated in Figure 16.3.

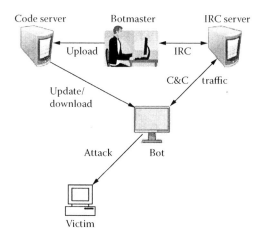

Figure 16.3   System configuration.

16.4 Data Collection

We collect botnet data using our testbed. In each host machine, we collect both the packet traces and program execution traces. Features are extracted from these traces, and the generated feature vectors are used for training classifiers.

Data collection was performed in three steps. First, we implemented a client for the botmaster that automatically sent all possible commands to the bot. Second, we ran [WinDump, 2007] to generate a tcpdump log file, and ran our own implementation of a process tracer to generate a exedump log file. Third, we ran each bot separately on a fresh virtual machine, collected the resulting traces from the log files, and then deleted the infected virtual machine. Traces were also collected from some uninfected machines connected to the Internet. Each trace spanned a 12-hour period. The tcpdump traces amounted to about 3GB in total. Finally, these traces were used for training and testing.

16.5 Bot Command Categorization

Not all bot commands have an observable effect on the log files we consider. We say that a command is *observable* if it matches one or more of the following criteria:

1. **Bot-response:** The command solicits a reply message from the bot to the C&C center. This reply is logged in the tcpdump. For example, the SDbot commands "about" and "sysinfo" are observable according to this criterion.

2. **Bot-app:** The command causes the bot to launch an executable application on the infected host machine. The application start event will be logged in the exedump. The execute command from SDbot is an example of such a command.

3. **Bot-other:** The command causes the bot to contact some host other than the C&C center. For example, the command might instruct the bot to send UDP packets as part of a DoS attack, send spam emails to other hosts, or download new versions of bot malware from a code server. Such events are logged in the tcpdump.

Table 16.1   SDBot and RBot Command Characteristics

OBSERVABLE EFFECTS	COMMANDS					
	ADDALIAS	ABOUT	EXECUTE	UDP	CMD	DOWNLOAD
Bot-app	×	×		×		
Bot-response	×		×			
Bot-other	×	×	×		×	

Source: M. Masud, T. Al-khateeb, L. Khan, B. Thuraisingham, K. Hamlen, *Flow-based Identification of Botnet Traffic by Mining Multiple Log Files,* pp. 200–206, 2008, © IEEE. With permission.

Some of the SDBot and RBot commands are listed in Table 16.1 and categorized using the previously mentioned criteria. For a comprehensive description of these commands, please refer to [RBOT, 2006], [SDBOT, 2006].

16.6 Feature Extraction

First we discuss the packet-level features and then discuss the flow-level features. The intuitive idea behind these features is that human response to a command/request (e.g., a request to send a file or execute an application by his peer) should be much slower than a bot. In what follows, we refer to a packet as *incoming* if its destination is the host being monitored, and as *outgoing* if it originates from the monitored host.

16.6.1 Packet-Level Features

The packet-level features we consider can be summarized as follows:

- **Bot-Response (BR)** (boolean-valued): An incoming packet possesses this feature if it originated from some *ip:port* and there is an outgoing packet to the same *ip:port* within 100 ms of arrival of the incoming packet. This indicates that it is a potential command packet. The 100 ms threshold has been determined by our observation of the bots. We will refer to these incoming packets as *BR packets*.
- **BRtime** (real-valued): This feature records the time difference between a BR packet and its corresponding outgoing packet. This is an important characteristic of a bot.

- **BRsize** (real-valued): This feature records the length (in KB) of a BR packet. We observe that command packets typically have lengths of 1KB or less, whereas normal packets have unbounded size.

- **Bot-Other (BO)** (boolean-valued): An incoming packet possesses this feature if it originated from some *ip:port* and there is an outgoing packet to some *ip':port'* within 200 ms of the arrival of the incoming packet, where *ip'≠ip*. This is also a potential command packet. The 200 ms threshold has also been determined by our observation of the bots. We will refer to these incoming packets as *BO* packets.

- **BODestMatch** (boolean-valued): A BO packet possesses this feature if outgoing destination *ip'* is found in its payload. This indicates that the BO packet is possibly a command packet that tells the bot to establish connection with host *ip'*.

- **BOtime** (real-valued): This feature records the time difference between a BO packet and its corresponding outgoing packet. This is also an important characteristic of a bot.

- **Bot-App (BA)** (boolean-valued): An incoming packet possesses this feature if an application starts on the host machine within 3 seconds of arrival of the incoming packet. This indicates that it is potentially command packet that instructs the bot to run an application. The 3 second threshold has been determined by our observation of the bots. We will refer to these incoming packets as *BA* packets.

- **BAtime** (real-valued): This feature records the time difference between receiving a BA packet and the launching of the corresponding application.

- **BAmatch** (boolean-valued): A BA packet possesses this feature if its payload contains the name of the application that was launched.

16.6.2 Flow-Level Features

As explained earlier, the flow-level features of a flow are the aggregations of packet-level features in that flow. They are summarized in Table 16.2. All flow-level features are real-valued. Also note that we do not use any flow-level feature that requires payload analysis.

Table 16.2 Flow-Level Feature Set

FEATURE	DESCRIPTION
AvgPktLen VarPktLen	Average and variance of length of packets in KB
Bot-App	Number of BA packets as percentage of total packets
AvgBAtime VarBAtime	Average and variance of BAtime of all BA packets
Bot-Reply	Number of BR packets as percentage of total packets
AvgBRtime VarBRtime	Average and variance of BRtime of all BR packets
AvgBRsize VarBRsize	Average and variance of BRsize of all BR packets
Bot-Other	Number of BO packets as percentage of total packets
AvgBOtime VarBOtime	Average and variance of BOtime of all BO packets

Source: M. Masud, T. Al-khateeb, L. Khan, B. Thuraisingham, K. Hamlen,
*Flow-based Identification of Botnet Traffic by Mining Multiple
Log Files,* pp. 200–206, 2008, © IEEE. With permission.

16.7 Log File Correlation

Figure 16.4 shows an example of multiple log file correlation. Portions of the tcpdump (left) and exedump (right) log files are shown in this example, side by side. Each record in the tcpdump file contains the packet number (No), arrival/departure time (Time), source and destination addresses (Src/Dest), and payload or other information (Payload/Info). Each record in the exedump file contains two fields: the process start time (Start Time) and process name (Process). The first packet (#10) shown in the tcpdump is a command packet that instructs the bot to download an executable from the code server and run it.

No	Time	Src	Dst	Proto	Payload/Info	Start Time	Process
10	22:00:01.529	master	bot	IRC	PRIVMSG #testbot ::download http://server:8080/calc2.exe c:\mycalc.exe 1...	21.48.29.953	windump.exe
11	22:00:01.530	bot	master	IRC	PRIVMSG #testbot :downloading http://server:8080/calc2.exe......	21.56.11.203	ping.exe
12	22:00:01.536	bot	server	TCP	SYN	21:58:48.421	notepad.exe
13	22:00:01.543	server	bot	TCP	SYN, ACK		
14	22:00:01.544	bot	server	TCP	ACK		
15	22:00:01.545	bot	server	HTTP	GET /calc2.exe HTTP/1.1	22:0:3.812	mycalc.exe
19	22:00:01.754	server	bot	TCP	ACK		
Other packets during download...........................						22:0:59.156	auifw.exe
33	22:00:02.808	bot	master	IRC	PRIVMSG #testbot :downloaded 112.0 kb to c:\mycalc.exe @ 112.0 kb/sec...	22:3:50.546	notepad.exe
38	22:00:03.924	bot	master	IRC	PRIVMSG #testbot :opened c:\mycalc.exe...		

Figure 16.4 Multiple log file correlation. (From M. Masud, T. Al-khateeb, L. Khan, B. Thuraisingham, K. Hamlen, *Flow-based Identification of Botnet Traffic by Mining Multiple Log Files,* pp. 200–206, 2008, © IEEE. With permission.)

The second packet (#11) is a response from the bot to the botmaster, so the command packet is a BR packet having *BRtime* = 1*ms*. The bot quickly establishes a TCP connection with the code server (other host) in packets 12 through 14. Thus, the command packet is also a BO packet having *BOtime* = 7*ms* (the time difference between the incoming command and the first outgoing packet to another host). After downloading, the bot runs the executable mycalc.exe. Thus, this command packet is also a BA packet having *BAtime* = 2.283s.

16.8 Classification

We use a Support Vector Machine (SVM), Bayes Net, decision tree (J48), Naïve Bayes, and Boosted decision tree (Boosted J48) for the classification task. In our previous work [Masud et al., 2008] we found that each of these classifiers demonstrated good performance for malware detection problems.

Specifically, SVM is robust to noise and high dimensionality and can be fine-tuned to perform efficiently on a specific domain. Decision trees have a very good feature selection capability and are much faster than many other classifiers both in training and testing time. Bayes Nets are capable of finding the inter-dependencies between different attributes. Naïve Bayes is also fast and performs well when the features are independent of one another. Boosting is particularly useful because of its ensemble methods. Thus, each of these classifiers has its own virtue. In a real deployment, we would actually use the best among them.

16.9 Packet Filtering

One major implementation issue related to examining the packet traces is the large volume of traffic that needs to be scanned. We try to reduce unnecessary scanning of packets by filtering out the packets that are not interesting to us, such as the TCP handshaking packets (SYN,ACK,SYNACK) and NetBios session request/response packets. This is because the useful information such as bot commands and bot responses are carried out via TCP protocol.

Packets that do not carry any useful information need not be processed further. To filter a packet, we look into its header and retrieve the protocol for the packet. If it is either TCP or NetBios, we keep it and send it to the feature extraction module. Otherwise, we drop the packet. In this way, we save a lot of execution time that would otherwise be used to extract features from the unimportant packets.

16.10 Summary

In this chapter, we have discussed our log file correlation technique in detail. We also explained what features are extracted from the log files and how the features are used to build a feature vector and train a classification model. We have also shown different characteristics of Bot command and how these characteristics play an important role in detecting the bot traffic. In the next chapter, we discuss the evaluation of our technique on botnet traffic generated in a controlled environment with real IRC bots.

In the future, we would like to add more system-level logs, such as process or service execution logs, memory and CPU utilization logs, disk reads or writes logs, and network read write logs. We believe adding more system-level logs will increase the chances of detecting the botnet traffic to a greater extent.

References

[Masud et al., 2008] Masud, M. M., L. Khan, B. Thuraisingham, A Scalable Multi-level Feature Extraction Technique to Detect Malicious Executables, *Information Systems Frontiers*, Vol. 10, No. 1, pp. 33–45, March 2008.

[RBOT, 2006] RBOT information web page, http://www.f-secure.com/v-descs/rbot.shtml (Accessed December 2006)

[SDBOT, 2006] SDBOT information web page, www.f-secure.com/v-descs/rbot.shtml (Accessed December 2006)

[Unreal IRCd, 2007] The Unreal IRC Daemon, http://www.unrealircd.com

[WinDump, 2007] The WinDump web site, http://www.winpcap.org/windump

17

EVALUATION AND RESULTS

17.1 Introduction

We evaluate our technique on two different datasets. The first dataset is generated by running SDBot, and the second one is generated by running RBot. Benign traffic collected from uninfected machines is mixed with the bot traffic in each dataset to simulate a mixture of benign and bot traffic. From each dataset, we aggregate network *packets* to *flows* (i.e., connections). Each of these flows is considered an event or an instance. Each instance is then tagged as either *bot* flow or *normal* flow depending on whether the flow is between a bot and its C&C center or not.

17.1.1 Baseline Techniques

We compare with another baseline technique discussed here.

1. Temporal: This is our proposed approach. Here we extract feature values for each flow using the technique described in Chapter 16.
2. Livadas: This is the machine-learning technique applied by [Livadas et al., 2006]. They extract several flow-based features, such as a histogram of packet sizes, flow duration, bandwidth, and so forth, but these are different from our feature set. They first identify IRC flows and then detect bot flows in the IRC flows. We don't need to identify IRC flows to detect C&C traffic using our analysis, but to perform a fair comparison, we also filter out non-IRC flows with the temporal approach. The features proposed by [Livadas et al., 2006] are extracted from the filtered data.

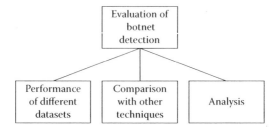

Figure 17.1 Evaluation of botnet detection.

17.1.2 Classifiers

The feature vectors extracted with the Temporal and Livadas methods are used to train classifiers. We explore five different classifiers, namely, SVM, J48, Boosted J48, Naïve Bayes, and Bayes Net.

For evaluation, we apply fivefold cross validation on the data and report the accuracy and false alarm rates. We use the [Weka, 2006] ML toolbox for classification.

The organization of this chapter is as follows. Datasets are discussed in Section 17.2. Comparison with other techniques is given in Section 17.3. Further analysis is given in Section 17.4. Finally, the chapter is summarized in section 17.5. Figure 17.1 illustrates the concepts in this chapter.

17.2 Performance on Different Datasets

We evaluate the proposed technique on two different datasets. The datasets SDBot and RBot correspond to those where the bot flows are generated only from SDBot and RBot, respectively, and normal flows are generated from uninfected machines. For each dataset, we apply fivefold cross validation. This is done for each competing method (i.e., Temporal and Livadas) with each competing classification algorithm (SVM, J48, Boosted J48, Bayes Net, and Naïve Bayes). Evaluation metrics are classification accuracy, false positive, and false negative rates.

Table 17.1 reports the classification accuracies (ACC), false positive rates (FP), and false negative rates (FN) for each of the classifiers for different datasets. Boosted J48 has the best detection accuracy (98.8%) for RBot, whereas Bayes Net has the best detection accuracy (99.0%) for SDBot. However, it is evident that Boosted J48 is less dataset-sensitive since it performs consistently on both datasets, and Bayes

Table 17.1 Performances of Different Classifiers on Flow-Level Features

DATASET	METRIC	BOOSTED J48	BAYES NET	NAÏVE BAYES	J48	SVM
	ACC%	98.9	99.0	98.9	98.8	97.8
SDBot	FP%	1.5	1.3	1.5	1.6	3.0
	FN%	0.0	0.0	0.0	0.0	0.0
	ACC%	98.8	96.4	95.2	96.4	96.4
RBot	FP%	1.5	3.0	3.1	3.2	3.0
	FN%	0.0	4.2	6.5	4.0	4.2

Source: M. Masud, T. Al-khateeb, L. Khan, B. Thuraisingham, K. Hamlen, *Flow-based Identification of Botnet Traffic by Mining Multiple Log Files,* pp. 200–206, 2008, © IEEE. With permission.

Net is only 0.1% better than Boosted J48 for the SDBot dataset. Thus, we conclude that BoostedJ48 has overall better performance than other classifiers. This is also supported by the results presented next.

17.3 Comparison with Other Techniques

The rows labeled "Temporal" and "Livadas" in Table 17.2 report the classification accuracies (ACC), false positive rates (FP), and false negative rates (FN) of our technique and the technique of [Livadas et al., 2006], respectively. The comparison reported is for the combined dataset that consists of bot flows from both SDBot- and RBot-infected machines and all the normal flows from uninfected machines (with non-IRC flows filtered out). We see that Temporal performs

Table 17.2 Comparing Performances between Our Method (Temporal) and the Method of Livadas et al. on the Combined Dataset

METHOD	METRIC	BOOSTED J48	BAYES NET	NAIVE BAYES	J48	SVM
Temporal	ACC%	99.9	99.5	99.1	99.2	99.1
Livadas	ACC%	97.0	99.7	97.1	97.5	99.0
Temporal	FP%	0.0	0.0	0.0	0.0	0.0
Livadas	FP%	0.3	0.0	0.0	0.0	0.0
Temporal	FN%	0.2	0.9	1.9	1.7	1.9
Livadas	FN%	6.5	0.6	6.3	5.9	2.1

Source: M. Masud, T. Al-khateeb, L. Khan, B. Thuraisingham, K. Hamlen, *Flow-based Identification of Botnet Traffic by Mining Multiple Log Files,* pp. 200–206, 2008, © IEEE. With permission.

consistently across all classifiers having an accuracy of greater than 99%, whereas Livadas has less than or equal to 97.5% accuracy in three classifiers and shows slightly better accuracy (0.2% higher) than Temporal only with Bayes Net. Bayes Net tends to perform well on a feature set if there are dependencies among the features. Because it is likely that there are dependencies among the features used by Livadas, we infer that the overall detection accuracy of Livadas is probably sensitive to classifiers, whereas Temporal is robust to all classifiers. Additionally, Temporal outperforms Livadas in false negative rates for all classifiers except Bayes Net. Finally, we again find that Boosted J48 has the best performance among all classifiers, so we conclude that our Temporal method with Boosted J48 has the best overall performance.

Figure. 17.2 presents the *receiver operating characteristic* (ROC) curves corresponding to the combined dataset results. ROC curves plot the true positive rate against the false positive rate. An ROC curve is better if the *area under the curve* (AUC) is higher, which indicates a higher probability that an instance will be correctly classified. In this figure, the ROC curve labeled as "Bayes Net–Livadas" corresponds to the ROC curve of Bayes Net on the combined dataset for the Livadas et al. technique, and so on. We see that all of the ROC curves are almost co-incidental, except Boosted J48–Livadas, which is slightly worse than the others. The AUC of "Boosted J48–Livadas" is 0.993, whereas the AUC of all other curves are greater than or equal to 0.999.

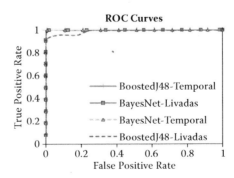

Figure 17.2   ROC curves of Bayes Net and Boosted J48 on the combined data. (From M. Masud, T. Al-khateeb, L. Khan, B. Thuraisingham, K. Hamlen, *Flow-based Identification of Botnet Traffic by Mining Multiple Log Files,* pp. 200–206, 2008, © IEEE. With permission.)

17.4 Further Analysis

We show a couple of analyses to justify the effectiveness of the features chosen for classification. In the first analysis, we show that the average packet lengths of bot traffic maintain a certain range, whereas normal traffic does not have any specific range. In the second analysis, we show that the average BOTime, BATime, and BRTime for bot flows are also distinguishable from benign flows.

Figure. 17.3 shows statistics of several features. The upper chart plots the average packet length (in KB) of each flow that appears in the dataset. Bot flows and normal flows are shown as separate series. A data point (X,Y) represents the average packet length Y of all packets in flow X of a particular series (bot flow or normal). It is clear from the chart that bot flows have a certain packet length ($\leq 0.2KB$), whereas normal flows have rather random packet lengths. Thus, our assumption about packet lengths is validated by this chart. The lower chart plots three different response times: Bot-Response time (*BRtime*), Bot-Other time (*BOtime*), and Bot-App time (*BAtime*) for each bot

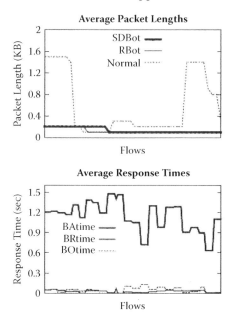

Figure 17.3 Flow summary statistics. Above: Average packet lengths of normal flows and bot flows. Below: Average *BRtime*, *BOtime*, and *BAtime* of bot flows. (From M. Masud, T. Al-khateeb, L. Khan, B. Thuraisingham, K. Hamlen, Flow-based Identification of Botnet Traffic by Mining Multiple Log Files, pp. 200–206, 2008, © IEEE. With permission.)

flow. It is evident that average *BRtime* is less than 0.1 second, average *BOtime* is less than 0.2 seconds, and average *BAtime* is between 0.6 and 1.6 seconds. The threshold values for these response times were chosen according to these observations.

17.5 Summary

In this work we present a data mining-based IRC botnet traffic detection technique. We identify several important features of botnet traffic and demonstrate the importance of correlating the network traces with program execution traces for generating useful features. We apply our technique on real botnet traffic generated using our testbed environment and evaluate the effectiveness of our approach on that traffic. Comparison with another data mining-based botnet detection technique establishes the superiority of our approach.

In future work we intend to apply this temporal correlation technique to more system-level logs such as those that track process/service executions, memory/CPU utilization, disk reads/writes, and so on. We also would like to implement a real-time C&C traffic detection system using our approach.

References

[Livadas et al., 2006] Livadas, C., B. Walsh, D. Lapsley, W. Strayer, "Using Machine Learning Techniques to Identify Botnet Traffic," in *Proceedings of the 31st IEEE Conference on Local Computer Networks (LCN'06)*, November 2006, pp. 967–974.
[Weka, 2008] The Weka Data Mining with Open Source Software, http://www.cs.waikato.ac.nz/ml/weka

Conclusion to Part V

As we have stated, botnets are emerging as "the biggest threat facing the Internet today" because of their enormous volume and sheer power. Botnets containing thousands of *bots* (compromised hosts) have been studied in the literature. In this part, we have described a data mining tool for botnet detection. In particular, we discussed our architecture and algorithms, and we reported our performance analysis. We also discussed the strengths and limitations of our approach.

In Parts II, III, IV, and V, we have described our tools for email worm detection, malicious code detection, remote exploit detection, and malicious code detection. In Part VI, we describe a highly innovative tool for stream mining. In particular, our tool will detect novel classes. This way, it will be able to detect malware that can change patterns.

PART VI
STREAM MINING FOR SECURITY APPLICATIONS

Introduction to Part VI

In a typical data stream classification task, it is assumed that the total number of classes is fixed. This assumption may not be valid in a real streaming environment, where new classes may evolve. Traditional data stream classification techniques are not capable of recognizing novel class instances until the appearance of the novel class is manually identified and labeled instances of that class are presented to the learning algorithm for training. The problem becomes more challenging in the presence of concept-drift, when the underlying data distribution changes over time. We propose a novel and efficient technique that can automatically detect the emergence of a novel class in the presence of concept-drift by quantifying cohesion among unlabeled test instances and separating the test instances from training instances. Our approach is non-parametric, meaning it does not assume any underlying distributions of data. Comparison with the state-of-the-art stream classification techniques proves the superiority of our approach.

Part VI consists of three chapters: 18, 19, and 20. Chapter 18 discusses relevant stream mining approaches and gives an overview of our approach. Chapter 19 describes our approach in detail, and Chapter 20 discusses the application and evaluation of our approach on different synthetic and benchmark data streams.

18

STREAM MINING

18.1 Introduction

It is a major challenge to the data mining community to mine the ever-growing streaming data. There are three major problems related to stream data classification. First, it is impractical to store and use all the historical data for training, because it would require infinite storage and running time. Second, there may be concept-drift in the data, meaning the underlying concept of the data may change over time. Third, novel classes may evolve in the stream. There are many existing solutions in literature that solve the first two problems, such as single-model incremental learning algorithms [Chen et al., 2008], [Hulten et al., 2001], [Yang et al., 2005] and ensemble classifiers [Kolter and Maloof, 2005], [Masud et al., 2008], [Wang et al., 2003]. However, most of the existing techniques are not capable of detecting novel classes in the stream. On the other hand, our approach can handle concept-drift and detect novel classes at the same time.

Traditional classifiers can only correctly classify instances of those classes with which they have been trained. When a new class appears in the stream, all instances belonging to that class will be misclassified until the new class has been manually identified by some experts and a new model is trained with the labeled instances of that class. Our approach provides a solution to this problem by incorporating a novel class detector within a traditional classifier so that the emergence of a novel class can be identified without any manual intervention. The proposed novel class detection technique can benefit many applications in various domains, such as network intrusion detection and credit card fraud detection. For example, in the problem of intrusion detection, when a new kind of intrusion occurs, we should not only be able to detect that it is an intrusion, but also that it is a new kind of

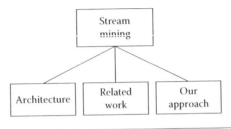

Figure 18.1   Concepts in this chapter.

intrusion. With the intrusion type information, human experts would be able to analyze the intrusion more intensely, find a cure, set an alarm in advance, and make the system more secure.

The organization of this chapter is as follows. In Section 18.2, we describe our architecture; related work is presented in Section 18.3. Our approach is briefly discussed in Section 18.4. The chapter is summarized in Section 18.5. Figure 18.1 illustrates the concepts in this chapter.

18.2 Architecture

We propose an innovative approach to detect novel classes. It is different from traditional novelty (or anomaly/outlier) detection techniques in several ways. First, traditional novelty detection techniques [Markou and Singh, 2003], [Roberts, 2000], [Yeung and Chow, 2002] work by assuming or building a model of normal data and simply identifying data points as outliers/anomalies that deviate from the "normal" points. But our goal is not only to detect whether a single data point deviates from the normality but also to discover whether a group of outliers have any strong bond among themselves. Second, traditional novelty detectors can be considered as a "one-class" model, which simply distinguishes between normal and anomalous data but cannot distinguish between two different kinds of anomalies. Our model is a "multi-class" model, meaning it can distinguish among different classes of data and at the same time detect presence of a novel class data, which is a unique combination of a traditional classifier with a novelty detector.

Our technique handles concept-drift by adapting an ensemble classification approach, which maintains an ensemble of M classifiers for classifying unlabeled data. The data stream is divided into equal-sized chunks, so that each chunk can be accommodated in memory and processed online. We train a classification model from each chunk as soon as it is labeled. The newly trained model replaces one of the existing models in the ensemble, if necessary. Thus, the ensemble evolves, reflecting the most up-to-date concept in the stream.

The central concept of our novel class detection technique is that each class must have an important property: the data points belonging to the same class should be closer to each other (cohesion) and should be far apart from the data points belonging to other classes (separation). Every time a new data chunk appears, we first detect the test instances that are *well separated* from the training data (i.e., outliers). Then filtering is applied to remove the outliers that possibly appear as a result of concept-drift. Finally, if we find strong cohesion among those filtered outliers, we declare a novel class. When the true labels of the novel class(es) arrive and a new model is trained with the labeled instances, the existing ensemble is updated with that model. Therefore, the ensemble of models is continuously enriched with new classes.

Figure 18.2 illustrates the architecture of our novel class detection approach. We assume that the data stream is divided into equal-sized chunks. The heart of this system is an ensemble L of M classifiers:

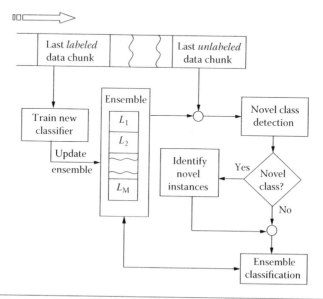

Figure 18.2   Architecture.

$\{L_1, ..., L_M\}$. When a new unlabeled data chunk arrives, the ensemble is used to detect novel class in that chunk. If a novel class is detected, then the instances belonging to the novel class are identified and tagged accordingly. All other instances in the chunk, that is, the instances that are not identified as novel class, are classified using majority voting. As soon as a data chunk is labeled, it is used to train a classifier, which replaces one of the existing classifiers in the ensemble. During training, we create an inventory of the *used* spaces.

We have several contributions. First, we provide a detailed understanding of the characteristic of a novel class and propose a new technique that can detect novel classes in the presence of concept-drift in data streams. Second, we establish a framework for incorporating a novel class detection mechanism into a traditional classifier. Finally, we apply our technique on both synthetic and real-world data and obtain much better results than state-of-the-art stream classification algorithms.

18.3 Related Work

Our work is related to both stream classification and novelty detection. There has been much work on stream data classification. There are two main approaches: single-model classification and ensemble classification. Some single-model techniques have been proposed to accommodate concept-drift [Chen et al., 2008], [Hulten et al., 2001], [Yang et al., 2005]. However, our technique follows the ensemble approach. Several ensemble techniques for stream data mining have been proposed [Kolter and Maloof, 2005], [Masud et al., 2008], [Wang et al., 2003]. These ensemble approaches require simple operations to update the current concept, and they are found to be robust in handling concept-drift. Although these techniques can efficiently handle concept-drift, none of them can detect novel classes in the data stream. On the other hand, our technique is not only capable of handling concept-drift, but it is also able to detect novel classes in data streams. In this light, our technique is also related to novelty detection techniques.

A comprehensive study on novelty detection has been discussed in [Markou and Singh, 2003]. The authors categorize novelty detection techniques into two categories: statistical and neural network based. Our technique is related to the statistical approach. Statistical approaches are of two types: parametric and non-parametric. Parametric approaches assume that data distributions are known (e.g., Gaussian), and they try to estimate the parameters (e.g., mean and variance) of the distribution. If any test data fall outside the normal parameters of the model, it is declared as novel [Roberts, 2000]. Our technique is a non-parametric approach. Non-parametric approaches like parzen window method [Yeung and Chow, 2002] estimate the density of training data and reject patterns whose density is beyond a certain threshold. k-nearest neighbor (kNN) based approaches to novelty detection are also non-parametric [Yang et al., 2002]. All of these techniques for novelty detection consider only whether a test instance is sufficiently close (or far) from the training data based on some appropriate metric (e.g., distance, density etc.). Our approach is different from these approaches in that we not only consider separation from normal data but also cohesion among the outliers. Besides, our model assimilates a novel class into the existing model, which enables it to distinguish future instances of that class from other classes. On the other hand, novelty detection techniques just remember the "normal" trend and do not care about the similarities or dissimilarities among the anomalous instances.

A recent work in the data stream mining domain [Spinosa et al., 2007] describes a clustering approach that can detect both concept-drift and novel class. This approach assumes that there is only one "normal" class and all other classes are novel. Thus, it may not work well if more than one class is to be considered as "normal" or "non-novel." Our approach can handle any number of existing classes. This makes our approach more effective in detecting novel classes than [Spinosa et al., 2007], which is justified by the experimental results.

18.4 Our Approach

We have presented a novel technique to detect new classes in concept-drifting data streams. Most of the novelty detection techniques either assume that there is no concept-drift or build a model for a single "normal" class and consider all other classes as novel. But our approach is capable of detecting novel classes in the presence of concept-drift, even when the model consists of multiple "existing" classes. In addition, our novel class detection technique is non-parametric; that is,

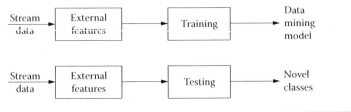

Figure 18.3 Our approach to stream mining.

it does not assume any specific distribution of data. We also show empirically that our approach outperforms the state-of-the-art data stream-based novelty detection techniques in both classification accuracy and processing speed.

It might appear to readers that to detect novel classes, we are in fact examining whether new clusters are being formed, and therefore, the detection process could go on without supervision. But supervision is necessary for classification. Without external supervision, two separate clusters could be regarded as two different classes, although they are not. Conversely, if more than one novel class appears in a chunk, all of them could be regarded as a single novel class if the labels of those instances are never revealed. In future work, we would like to apply our technique in the domain of multiple-label instances. Our approach is illustrated in Figure 18.3.

18.5 Overview of the Novel Class Detection Algorithm

Algorithm 18.1 outlines a summary of our technique. The data stream is divided into equal-sized chunks. The latest chunk, which is unlabeled, is provided to the algorithm as input. At first it detects if there is any novel class in the chunk (line 1). The term *novel class* will be defined shortly. If a novel class is found, we detect the instances that belong to the class(es) (line 2). Then we use the ensemble $L = \{L_1, ..., L_M\}$ to classify the instances that do not belong to the novel class(es). When the data chunk becomes labeled, a new classifier L' is trained using the chunk. Then the existing ensemble is updated by choosing the best M classifiers from the $M + 1$ classifiers $L \cup \{L'\}$ based on their accuracies on the latest labeled data chunk.

Algorithm 18.1 MineClass

Input: D_n: the latest data chunk
L: Current ensemble of best M classifiers
Output: Updated ensemble L

1. found $\leftarrow$ *DetectNovelClass*(D_n,L) (algorithm 19-1)
2. **if** found **then** $Y \leftarrow$ Novel_instances(D_n), $X \leftarrow D_n - Y$ **else** $X \leftarrow D_n$
3. **for** each instance $x \in X$ do *Classify*(L,x)
4. /*Assuming that D_n is now labeled*/
5. L' $\leftarrow$ *Train-and-create-inventory*(D_n) (Section 19.3)
6. L $\leftarrow$ *Update*(L,L',D_n)

Our algorithm will be mentioned henceforth as "MineClass," which stands for Mining novel Classes in data streams. MineClass should be applicable to any base learner. The only operation that is specific to a learning algorithm is *Train-and-create-inventory*. We will illustrate this operation for two base learners.

18.6 Classifiers Used

We apply our novelty detection technique on two different classifiers: decision tree and kNN. We keep M classification models in the ensemble. For the decision tree classifier, each model is a decision tree. For kNN, each model is usually the set of training data itself. However, storing all the raw training data is memory inefficient, and using them to classify unlabeled data is time inefficient. We reduce both the time and memory requirement by building K clusters with the training data, saving the cluster summaries as classification models, and discarding the raw data. This process is explained in detail in [Masud et al., 2008]. The cluster summaries are mentioned henceforth as "pseudopoints." Because we store and use only K pseudopoints, both the time and memory requirements become functions of K (a constant number). The clustering approach followed here is a constraint-based K-means clustering where the constraint is to minimize cluster impurity while minimizing the intra-cluster dispersion. A cluster is considered pure if it contains instances from only one class. The summary of each cluster consists of the centroid and the frequencies of data points of each class in the cluster. Classification is done by finding the nearest cluster centroid from the test point and assigning the class that has the highest frequency to the test point.

18.7 Security Applications

The proposed novel class detection will be useful in several security applications. First, it can be used in detecting novel attacks in network traffic. If there is a completely new kind of attack in the network traffic, existing intrusion detection techniques may fail to detect it. On the contrary, if a completely new kind of attack occurs in the network traffic, our approach should detect it as a "novel class" and would raise an alarm. This would invoke system analysts to quarantine and analyze the characteristics of these unknown kinds of events and tag them accordingly. The classification models would also be updated with these new class instances. Should the same kind of intrusion occur in the future, the classification model would detect it as a known intrusion. Second, our approach can also be used for detecting a new kind of malware. Existing malware detection techniques may fail to detect a completely new kind of malware, but our approach should be able to detect the new malware as a novel class, quarantine it, and raise an alarm. The quarantined binary would be later analyzed and characterized by human experts. In this way, the proposed novel class detection technique can be effectively applied to cyber security.

18.8 Summary

Data stream classification is a challenging task that has been addressed by different researchers in different ways. Most of these approaches ignore the fact that new classes may emerge in the stream. If this phenomenon is considered, the classification problem becomes more challenging. Our approach addresses this challenge in an efficient way. Chapter 19 discusses this approach in detail.

In the future, we would like to extend our approach in two directions. First, we would like to address the real-time data stream classification problem. Real-time data stream mining is more challenging because of the overhead involved in data labeling and training classification models. Second, we would like to utilize the cloud computing framework for data stream mining. The cloud computing framework will be a cheaper alternative to more efficient and powerful computing that is necessary for real-time stream mining.

References

[Chen et al., 2008] Chen, S., H. Wang, S. Zhou, P. Yu, Stop Chasing Trends: Discovering High Order Models in Evolving Data, in *Proceedings ICDE*, 2008, pp. 923–932.

[Hulten et al., 2001] Hulten, G., L. Spencer, P. Domingos, Mining Time-Changing Data Streams, in *Proceedings ACM SIGKDD*, 2001, pp. 97–106.

[Kolter and Maloof, 2005] Kolter, J., and M. Maloof, Using Additive Expert Ensembles to Cope with Concept Drift, in *Proceedings ICML*, 2005, pp. 449–456.

[Markou and Singh, 2003] Markou, M., and S. Singh, Novelty Detection: A Review—Part 1: Statistical Approaches; Part 2: Neural Network-Based Approaches, *Signal Processing*, 83, 2003, pp. 2481–2521.

[Masud et al., 2008] Masud, M., J. Gao, L. Khan, J. Han, B. Thuraisingham, A Practical Approach to Classify Evolving Data Streams: Training with Limited Amount of Labeled Data, in *Proceedings ICDM*, 2008, pp. 929–934.

[Roberts, 2000] Roberts, S. J., Extreme Value Statistics for Novelty Detection in Biomedical Signal Processing, in *Proceedings of the International Conference on Advances in Medical Signal and Information Processing*, 2000, pp. 166–172.

[Spinosa et al., 2007] Spinosa, E. J., A. P. de Leon F. de Carvalho, J. Gama, OLINDDA: A Cluster-Based Approach for Detecting Novelty and Concept Drift in Data Streams, in *Proceedings 2007 ACM Symposium on Applied Computing*, 2007, pp. 448–452.

[Wang et al., 2003] Wang, H., W. Fan, P. Yu, J. Han, Mining Concept-Drifting Data Streams Using Ensemble Classifiers, in *Proceedings ACM SIGKDD*, 2003, pp. 226–235.

[Yeung and Chow, 2002] Yeung, D. Y., and C. Chow, Parzen-Window Network Intrusion Detectors, in *Proceedings International Conference on Pattern Recognition*, 2002, pp. 385–388.

[Yang et al., 2002] Y. Yang, J. Zhang, J. Carbonell, C. Jin, Topic-Conditioned Novelty Detection, in *Proceedings ACM SIGKDD*, 2002, pp. 688–693.

[Yang et al., 2005] Yang, Y., X. Wu, X. Zhu, Combining Proactive and Reactive Predictions for Data Streams, in *Proceedings ACM SIGKDD*, 2005, pp. 710–715.

19

DESIGN OF THE DATA MINING TOOL

19.1 Introduction

In this chapter, we start with the definitions of novel class and existing classes. Then we state the assumptions based on which the novel class detection algorithm works. We illustrate the concept of *novel class* with an example, and introduce several terms such as *used* space and *unused* spaces. We then discuss the three major parts in novel class detection process: (1) saving the inventory of *used* spaces during training, (2) outlier detection and filtering, and (3) computing cohesion among outliers and separating the outliers from the training data. We also show how this technique can be made efficient by raw data reduction using clustering.

The organization of this chapter is as follows. Definitions are given in Section 19.2. Our novel class detection techniques are given in Section 19.3. The chapter is summarized in Section 19.4. The concepts in this chapter are illustrated in Figure 19.1.

19.2 Definitions

We begin with the definition of "novel" and "existing" class.

> **Definition 19.1 (Existing class and Novel class)** Let L be the current ensemble of classification models. A class c is an existing class if at least one of the models $L_i \, \varepsilon \, L$ has been trained with the instances of class c. Otherwise, c is a novel class.

We assume that any class has the following essential property:

> **Property 19.1** A data point should be closer to the data points of its own class (cohesion) and farther apart from the data points of other classes (separation).

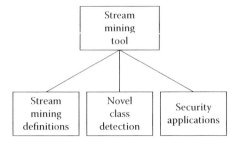

Figure 19.1   Concepts in this chapter.

Our main assumption is that the instances belonging to a class c is generated by an underlying generative model Θ_c, and the instances in each class are independently identically distributed. With this assumption, we can reasonably argue that the instances that are close together are supposed to be generated by the same model, that is, belong to the same class. We now show the basic idea of novel class detection using decision tree in Figure 19.2. We introduce the notion of *used space* to denote a feature space occupied by any instance and *unused space* to denote a feature space unused by an instance.

According to Property 19.1 (separation), a novel class must arrive in the unused spaces. Besides, there must be strong cohesion (e.g., closeness) among the instances of the novel class. Thus, the two basic principles followed by our approach are (1) keeping track of the used

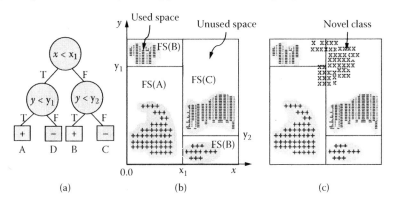

Figure 19.2   (a) A decision tree and (b) corresponding feature space partitioning. FS(X) denotes the feature space defined by a leaf node X. The shaded areas show the used spaces of each partition. (c) A novel class (denoted by x) arrives in the unused space. (From M. Masud, J. Gao, L. Khan, J. Han, B. Thuraisingham, *Integrating Novel Class Detection with Classification for Concept-Drifting Data Streams*, pp. 79–94, 2009, Springer. With permission.)

spaces of each leaf node in a decision tree, and (2) finding strong cohesion among the test instances that fall into the unused spaces.

19.3 Novel Class Detection

We follow two basic steps for novel class detection. First, the classifier is trained such that an inventory of the used spaces (described in Section 19.2) is created and saved. This is done by clustering and saving the cluster summary as "pseudopoint." Second, these pseudopoints are used to detect outliers in the test data and declare a novel class if there is strong cohesion among the outliers.

19.3.1 Saving the Inventory of Used Spaces during Training

The general idea of creating the inventory is to cluster the training data and save the cluster centroids and other useful information as pseudopoints. These pseudopoints keep track of the used spaces. How this clustering is done may be specific to each base learner. For example, for decision tree, clustering is done at each leaf node of the tree, because we need to keep track of the used spaces for each leaf node separately. For the kNN classifier discussed in Section 18.6, already existing pseudopoints are utilized to store the inventory.

It should be noted here that K-means clustering appears to be the best choice for saving the decision boundary and computing the outliers. Density-based clustering could also be used to detect outliers, but it has several problems. First, we would have to save all of the raw data points at the leaf nodes to apply the clustering. Second, the clustering process would take quadratic time, compared to linear time for K-means. Finally, we would have to run the clustering algorithm for every data chunk to be tested. However, the choice of parameter K in K-means algorithm has some impact on the overall outcome, which is discussed in the experimental results.

19.3.1.1 Clustering We build total K clusters per chunk. For kNN, we utilize the existing clusters that were created globally using the approach. For decision tree, clustering is done locally at each leaf node as follows. Suppose S is the chunk size. During decision tree training, when we reach a leaf node l_i, we build $k_i = (t_i/S) * K$ clusters in that leaf, where t_i denotes the number of training instances that ended up in leaf node l_i.

19.3.1.2 Storing the Cluster Summary Information   For each cluster, we store the following summary information in memory: (i) **Weight**, w: defined as the total number of points in the cluster. (ii) **Centroid**, ζ. (iii) **Radius**, R: defined as the maximum distance between the centroid and the data points belonging to the cluster. (iv) **Mean distance**, μ_d: the mean distance from each point to the cluster centroid. The cluster summary of a cluster H_i will be referred to henceforth as a "pseudo-point" ψ_i. So, $w(\psi_i)$ denotes the weight of pseudopoint ψ_i. After computing the cluster summaries, the raw data are discarded. Let Ψ_j be the set of all pseudopoints stored in memory for a classifier L_j.

19.3.2 Outlier Detection and Filtering

Each pseudopoint ψ_i corresponds to a hypersphere in the feature space having center $\zeta(\psi_i)$ and radius $R(\psi_i)$. Thus, the pseudopoints "memorize" the used spaces. Let us denote the portion of feature space covered by a pseudopoint ψ_i as the "region" of ψ_i or $RE(\psi_i)$. So, the union of the regions covered by all the pseudopoints is the union of all the used spaces, which forms a decision boundary $B(L_j) = u_{\psi_i \in \Psi_j} RE(\psi_i)$, for a classifier L_j. Now, we are ready to define outliers.

> **Definition 19.2 (Routlier)** Let x be a test point and ψ_{min} be the pseudopoint whose centroid is nearest to x. Then x is a Routlier (i.e., raw outlier) if it is outside $RE(\psi_{min})$; that is, its distance from $\zeta(\psi_{min})$ is greater than $R(\psi_{min})$.

In other words, any point x outside the decision boundary $B(L_j)$ is a *Routlier* for the classifier L_j. For K-NN, *Routlier*s are detected globally by testing x against all the psuedopoints. For decision tree, x is tested against only the psueodpoints stored at the leaf node where x belongs.

19.3.2.1 Filtering   According to Definition 19.2, a test instance may be erroneously considered as a *Routlier* because of one or more of the following reasons: (1) The test instance belongs to an existing class, but it is a noise. (2) There has been a concept-drift and, as a result, the decision boundary of an existing class has been shifted. (3) The decision tree has been trained with insufficient data. So, the predicted decision boundary is not the same as the actual one.

Due to these reasons, the outliers are filtered to ensure that any outlier that belongs to the existing classes does not end up in being declared as a new class instance. The filtering is done as follows: if a test instance is a *Routlier* to *all* the classifiers in the ensemble, then it is considered as a filtered outlier. All other *Routlier*s are filtered out.

> **Definition 19.3 (Foutlier)** A test instance is a Foutlier (i.e., filtered outlier) if it is a Routlier to all the classifiers L_i in the ensemble L.

Intuitively, being an *Foutlier* is a necessary condition for being in a new class. Because, suppose an instance x is not a *Routlier* to some classifier L_i in the ensemble. Then x must be inside the decision boundary $B(L_j)$. So, it violates Property 19.1 (separation), and therefore, it cannot belong to a new class. Although being a *Foutlier* is a necessary condition, it is not sufficient for being in a new class, because it does not guarantee the Property 19.1 (cohesion). So, we proceed to the next step to verify whether the *Foutlier*s satisfy both cohesion and separation.

19.3.3 Detecting Novel Class

We perform several computations on the *Foutlier*s to detect the arrival of a new class. First, we discuss the general concepts of these computations, and later we describe how these computations are carried out efficiently. For every *Foutlier*, we define a λ_c-neighborhood as follows:

> **Definition 19.4 (λ_c-neighborhood)** The λ_c-neighborhood of an Foutlier x is the set of N-nearest neighbors of x belonging to class c.

Here N is a user-defined parameter. For brevity, we denote the λ_c-neighborhood of a *Foutlier* x as $\lambda_c(x)$. Thus, $\lambda_+(x)$ of a *Foutlier* x is the set of N instances of class c_+ that are closest to the outlier x. Similarly, $\lambda_o(x)$ refers to the set of N *Foutlier*s that are closest to x. This is illustrated in Figure 19.3, where the *Foutlier*s are shown as black dots, and the instances of class c_+ and class c_- are shown with the corresponding symbols. $\lambda_+(x)$ of the *Foutlier* x is the set of $N (= 3)$ instances belonging

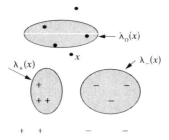

Figure 19.3 λc-neighborhood with $N = 3$. (From M. Masud, J. Gao, L. Khan, J. Han, B. Thuraisingham, *Integrating Novel Class Detection with Classification for Concept-Drifting Data Streams*, pp. 79–94, 2009, Springer. With permission.)

to class c_+ that are nearest to x (inside the circle), and so on. Next, we define the N-neighborhood silhouette coefficient, (N-NSC).

> **Definition 19.5 (N-NSC)** Let $a(x)$ be the average distance from an *Foutlier x* to the instances in $\lambda_o(x)$, and $b_c(x)$ be the average distance from x to the instances in $\lambda_c(x)$ (where c is an existing class). Let $b_{\min}(x)$ be the minimum among all $b_c(x)$. Then N-NSC of x is given by:
>
> $$N - NSC(x) = \frac{b_{\min}(x) - a(x)}{\max(b_{\min}(x), a(x))} \tag{19.1}$$

According to the definition, the value of N-NSC is between −1 and +1. It is actually a unified measure of cohesion and separation. A negative value indicates that x is closer to the other classes (less separation) and farther away from its own class (less cohesion). We declare a *new class* if there are at least N' ($>N$) *Foutlier*s, whose N-NSC is positive.

It should be noted that the larger the value is of N, the greater the confidence we will have in deciding whether a novel class has arrived. However, if N is too large, then we may also fail to detect a new class if the total number of instances belonging to the novel class in the corresponding data chunk is less than or equal to N. We experimentally find an optimal value of N, which is explained in Chapter 20.

19.3.3.1 Computing the Set of Novel Class Instances   Once we detect the presence of a novel class, the next step is to find those instances and separate them from the existing class data. According to the *necessary and sufficient condition*, a set of *Foutlier* instances belong to a novel class if the following three conditions satisfy: (1) all the *Foutliers* in the set have positive N-NSC, (2) all the *Foutliers* in the set have $\lambda_o(x)$ within the set, and (3) cardinality of the set $\geq N$. Let G be such a set. Note that finding the exact set G is computationally expensive, so we follow an approximation. Let G' be the set of all *Foutliers* that have positive N-NSC. If $|G'| \geq N$, then G' is an approximation of G. It is possible that some of the data points in G' may not actually be a novel class instance or vice versa. However, in our experiments, we found that this approximation works well.

19.3.3.2 Speeding up the Computation   Computing N-NSC for every *Foutlier* instance x takes quadratic time in the number of *Foutliers*. To make the computation faster, we also create K_o pseudopoints from *Foutliers* using K-means clustering and perform the computations on the pseudopoints (referred to as *Fpseudopoints*), where $K_o = (N_o/S) * K$. Here S is the chunk size and N_o is the number of *Foutliers*. Thus, the time complexity to compute the N-NSC of all of the *Fpseudopoints* is $O(K_o * (K_o + K))$, which is constant, because both K_o and K are independent of the input size. Note that N-NSC of a *Fpseudopoint* is actually an approximate average of the N-NSC of each *Foutlier* in that *Fpseudopoint*. By using this approximation, although we gain speed, we also lose some precision. However, this drop in precision is negligible when we keep sufficient number of pseudopoints, as shown in the experimental results. The novel class detection process is summarized in Algorithm 19.1 (DetectNovelClass).

Algorithm 19.1   *DetectNovelClass(D,L)*

Input: D: An unlabeled data chunk

L: Current ensemble of best M classifiers

Output: true, if novel class is found; **false**, otherwise

1. **for** each instance $x \in D$ **do**
2.   **if** x is a *Routlier* to all classifiers $L_i \in L$
           then FList $\leftarrow$ FList $\cup$ {x} /* x is a Foutlier*/
3. **end for**
4. Make $K_o = (K * |FList|/|D|)$ clusters with the instances in *FList* using K-means clustering, and create *Fpseudopoints*

5. **for each** classifier $L_i \in L$ **do**
6.   Compute N-NSC(ψ_j) for each Fpseudopoint j
7. $\Psi_p \leftarrow$ the set of Fpseudopoints having positive N-NSC(.).
8. $w(p)$ sum of $w(.)$ of all Fpseudopoints in Ψ_p
9.   **if** $w(p) > N$ then NewClassVote++
10. **end for**
11. return NewClassVote $> M -$ NewClassVote /*Majority voting*/

This algorithm can detect one or more novel classes concurrently (i.e., in the same chunk) as long as each novel class follows Property 19.1 and contains at least N instances. This is true even if the class distributions are skewed. However, if more than one such novel class appears concurrently, our algorithm will identify the instances belonging to those classes as novel, without imposing any distinction among dissimilar novel class instances (i.e., it will treat them simply as "novel"). But the distinction will be learned by our model as soon as those instances are labeled and a classifier is trained with them.

19.3.3.3 Time Complexity Lines 1 through 3 of Algorithm 19.1 require $O(KSL)$ time where S is the chunk size. Line 4 (clustering) requires $O(KS)$ time, and the last for loop (5–10) requires $O(K^2L)$ time. Thus, the overall time complexity of Algorithm 19.1 is $O(KS + KSL + K^2L) = O(K(S + SL + KL))$. Assuming that $S \gg KL$, the complexity becomes $O(KS)$, which is linear in S. Thus, the overall time complexity (per chunk) of MineClass algorithm (Algorithm 18.1) is $O(KS + f_c(LS) + f_t(S))$, where $f_c(n)$ is the time required to classify n instances and $f_t(n)$ is the time required to train a classifier with n training instances.

19.3.3.4 Impact of Evolving Class Labels on Ensemble Classification As the reader might have realized already, arrival of novel classes in the stream causes the classifiers in the ensemble to have different sets of class labels. For example, suppose an older (earlier) classifier L_i in the ensemble has been trained with classes c_0 and c_1, and a newer (later) classifier L_j has been trained with classes c_1, and c_2, where c_2 is a new class that appeared after L_i had been trained. This puts a negative effect on voting decision, since the older classifier misclassifies instances of

c_2. So, rather than counting votes from each classifier, we selectively count their votes as follows: if a newer classifier L_j classifies a test instance x as class c, but an older classifier L_i does not have the class label c in its model, then the vote of L_i will be ignored if x is found to be an outlier for L_i. An opposite scenario occurs when the oldest classifier L_i is trained with some class c', but none of the later classifiers are trained with that class. This means class c' has been outdated, and, in that case, we remove L_i from the ensemble. In this way we ensure that older classifiers have less impact in the voting process. If class c' later reappears in the stream, it will be automatically detected again as a novel class (see Definition 19.1).

19.4 Security Applications

There are several potential security applications of the novel class detection technique, such as intrusion detection in network traffic or malware detection in a host machine. Consider the problem of malware detection. To apply our novel class detection technique, we first need to identify a set of features for each executable. This can be done using n-gram feature extraction and selection [Masud et al., 2008]. As long as the feature set selected using the approach of [Masud et al., 2008] also remains the best set of features for a new kind of malware, the new malware class should be detected as a novel class by our approach. The advantage of our approach with other classification approaches in this regard is twofold. First, it will detect a new kind of malware as a novel class. This detection will lead to further analysis and characterization of the malware. On the contrary, if a new kind of malware emerges, traditional classification techniques would either detect it as benign or simply a "malware." Thus, our approach will be able to provide more information about the new malware by identifying it as a novel type. The second advantage is, if an existing type of malware is tested using the novel class detection system, it will be identified as a malware, and also the "type" of the malware would be predicted.

19.5 Summary

In this chapter, we present the working details of the novel class detection algorithm. Our approach builds a decision boundary around the training data during training. During classification, if any instance falls outside the decision boundary, it is tagged as *outlier* and stored for further analysis. When enough outliers have been found, we compute the cohesion among the outliers and separation of the outliers from the training data. If both the cohesion and separation are significant, the outliers are identified as a novel class. In Chapter 20, we discuss the effectiveness of our approach on several synthetic and benchmark data streams.

As mentioned in Chapter 18, we would like to extend this technique to real-time data stream classification. To achieve this goal, we will have to optimize the training, including the creation of decision boundary. The outlier detection and novel class detection should also be made more efficient. We believe the cloud computing framework can play an important role in increasing the efficiency of these processes.

Reference

[Masud et al., 2008] Masud, M., L. Khan, B. Thuraisingham, A Scalable Multi-level Feature Extraction Technique to Detect Malicious Executables, *Information System Frontiers*, Vol. 10, No. 1, 2008, pp. 33–45.

20

EVALUATION AND RESULTS

20.1 Introduction

We evaluate our proposed method on a number of synthetic and real datasets, and we report results on four datasets. Two of the datasets for which we report the results are synthetic, and the other two are real benchmark datasets. The first synthetic dataset simulates only concept-drift. We use this dataset for evaluation to show that our approach can correctly distinguish between concept-drift and novel classes. The second synthetic dataset simulates both concept-drift and concept-evolution. The two benchmark datasets that we use are the KDD Cup 1999 intrusion detection dataset, and the Forest Cover type dataset, both of which have been widely used in data stream classification literature. Each of the synthetic and real datasets contains more than or equal to 250,000 data points.

We compare our results with two baseline techniques. For each dataset and each baseline technique, we report the overall error rate, percentage of novel instances misclassified as existing class, and percentage of existing class instances misclassified as novel class. We also report the running times of each baseline techniques on each dataset. On all datasets, our approach outperforms the baseline techniques in both classification accuracy and false detection rates. Our approach also outperforms the baseline techniques in running time. The following sections discuss the results in detail.

The organization of this chapter is as follows. Datasets are discussed in Section 20.2. Experimental setup is discussed in Section 20.3. Performance results are given in Section 20.4. The chapter is summarized in Section 20.5. Figure 20.1 illustrates the concepts in this chapter.

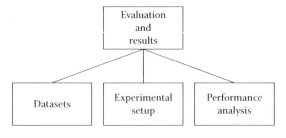

Figure 20.1   Concepts in this chapter.

20.2 Datasets

20.2.1 Synthetic Data with Only Concept-Drift (SynC)

SynC simulates only concept-drift, with no novel classes. This is done to show that concept-drift does not erroneously trigger new class detection in our approach. SynC data are generated with a moving hyperplane. The equation of a hyperplane is as follows: $\sum_{i=1}^{d} a_i x_i = a_0$. If $\sum_{i=1}^{d} a_i x_i <= a_0$, then an example is negative; otherwise, it is positive. Each example is a randomly generated d-dimensional vector $\{x_1, ..., x_d\}$, where $x_i \in [0, 1]$. Weights $\{a_1, ..., a_d\}$ are also randomly initialized with a real number in the range $[0, 1]$. The value of a_0 is adjusted so that roughly the same number of positive and negative examples is generated. This can be done by choosing $a_0 = \sum_{i=1}^{d} a_i$. We also introduce noise randomly by switching the labels of $p\%$ of the examples, where $p = 5$ is set in our experiments. There are several parameters that simulate concept-drift. Parameter m specifies the percentage of total dimensions whose weights are involved in changing, and it is set to 20%. Parameter t specifies the magnitude of the change in every N example. In our experiments, t is set to 0.1, and N is set to 1,000. s_i, $i \in \{1, ..., d\}$ specifies the direction of change for each weight. Weights change continuously; that is, a_i is adjusted by $s_i.t/N$ after each example is generated. There is a possibility of 10% that the change would reverse direction after every N example is generated. We generate a total of 250,000 records.

20.2.2 Synthetic Data with Concept-Drift and Novel Class (SynCN)

These synthetic data simulate both concept-drift and novel class. Data points belonging to each class are generated using Gaussian distribution having different means (–5.0 to +5.0) and variances (0.5 to 6) for different classes. Besides, to simulate the evolving nature of data streams, the probability distributions of different classes are varied with time. This caused some classes to appear and some other classes to disappear at different times. To introduce concept-drift, the mean values of a certain percentage of attributes have been shifted at a constant rate. As done in the SynC dataset, this rate of change is also controlled by the parameters m, t, s, and N in a similar way.

The dataset is normalized so that all attribute values fall within the range [0, 1]. We generate the SynCN dataset with 20 classes, 40 real-valued attributes, having a total of 400K data points.

20.2.3 Real Data—KDD Cup 99 Network Intrusion Detection

We have used the 10% version of the dataset, which is more concentrated, hence more challenging than the full version. It contains around 490,000 instances. Here different classes appear and disappear frequently, making the new class detection challenging. This dataset contains TCP connection records extracted from LAN network traffic at MIT Lincoln Labs over a period of two weeks. Each record refers to either to a normal connection or an attack. There are 22 types of attacks, such as buffer-overflow, portsweep, guess-passwd, neptune, rootkit, smurf, spy, and others. So, there are 23 different classes of data. Most of the data points belong to the normal class. Each record consists of 42 attributes, such as connection duration, the number of bytes transmitted, number of root accesses, and so forth. We use only the 34 continuous attributes and remove the categorical attributes. This dataset is also normalized to keep the attribute values within [0, 1].

20.2.4 Real Data—Forest Cover (UCI Repository)

The dataset contains geospatial descriptions of different types of forests. It contains 7 classes, 54 attributes, and around 581,000 instances.

We normalize the dataset and arrange the data so that in any chunk at most 3 and at least 2 classes co-occur, and new classes appear randomly.

20.3 Experimental Setup

We implement our algorithm in Java. The code for decision tree has been adapted from the Weka machine learning open source repository (http://www.cs.waikato.ac.nz/ml/weka/). The experiments were run on an Intel P-IV machine with 2GB memory and 3GHz dual processor CPU. Our parameter settings are as follows, unless mentioned otherwise: (1) K (number of pseudopoints per chunk) = 50, (2) N = 50, (3) M (ensemble size) = 6, (4) chunk size = 1,000 for synthetic datasets and 4,000 for real datasets. These values of parameters are tuned to achieve an overall satisfactory performance.

20.3.1 Baseline Method

To the best of our knowledge, there is no approach that can classify data streams *and* detect novel class. So, we compare MineClass with a combination of two baseline techniques: *OLINDDA* [Spinosa et al., 2007] and Weighted Classifier Ensemble (*WCE*) [Wang et al., 2003], where the former works as novel class detector, and the latter performs classification. For each chunk, we first detect the novel class instances using *OLINDDA*. All other instances in the chunk are assumed to be in the existing classes, and they are classified using *WCE*. We use *OLINDDA* as the novelty detector, as it is a recently proposed algorithm that is shown to have outperformed other novelty detection techniques in data streams [Spinosa et al., 2007].

However, *OLINDDA* assumes that there is only one "normal" class, and all other classes are "novel." So, it is not directly applicable to the multi-class novelty detection problem, where any combination of classes can be considered as the "existing" classes. We propose two alternative solutions. First, we build parallel *OLINDDA* models, one for each class, which evolve simultaneously. Whenever the instances of a novel class appear, we create a new *OLINDDA* model for that class. A test instance is declared as novel if *all the existing class models* identify this instance as novel. We will refer to this baseline method as WCE-OLINDDA_PARALLEL. Second, we initially build an *OLINDDA* model with all the available classes. Whenever a novel class is found, the class is absorbed into the existing *OLINDDA* model. Thus, only one "normal" model is maintained throughout the stream. This will be referred to as WCE-OLINDDA_SINGLE. In all experiments, the ensemble size and chunk size are kept the same for both these techniques. Besides, the same base learner is used for *WCE* and *MC*. The parameter settings for *OLINDDA* are (1) number of data points per cluster (N_{excl}) = 15, (2) least number of normal instances needed to update the existing model = 100, (3) least number of instances needed to build the initial model = 30. These parameters are chosen either according to the default values used in [Spinosa et al., 2007] or by trial and error to get an overall satisfactory performance. *We will henceforth use the acronyms **MC** for **MineClass**, **W-OP** for **WCE-OLINDDA_PARALLEL**, and **W-OS** for **WCE-OLINDDA_SINGLE**.*

20.4 Performance Study

20.4.1 Evaluation Approach

We use the following performance metrics for evaluation: M_{new} = % of novel class instances Misclassified as existing class, F_{new}= % of existing class instances Falsely identified as novel class, ERR = Total misclassification error (%) (including M_{new} and F_{new}). We build the initial models in each method with the first M chunks. From the M + 1st chunk onward, we first evaluate the performances of each method on that chunk, then use that chunk to update the existing model. The performance metrics for each chunk for each method are saved and averaged for producing the summary result.

20.4.2 Results

Figures 20.2(a) through 20.2(d) show the ERR for decision tree classifier of each approach up to a certain point in the stream in different datasets. kNN classifier also has similar results. For example, at X axis = 100, the Y values show the average ERR of each approach from the beginning of the stream to chunk 100. At this point, the ERR of MC, W-OP, and W-OS are 1.7%, 11.6%, and 8.7%, respectively, for the KDD dataset (Figure 20.2(c)). The arrival of a novel class in

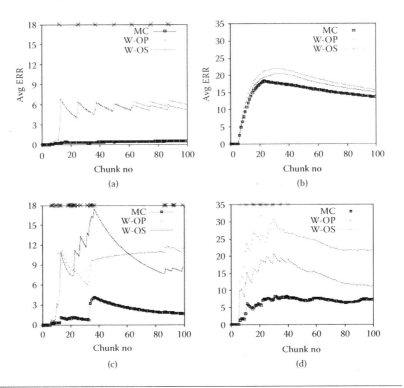

Figure 20.2 Error comparison on (a) SynCN, (b) SynC, (c) KDD, and (d) Forest Cover. (From M. Masud, J. Gao, L. Khan, J. Han, B. Thuraisingham, *Integrating Novel Class Detection with Classification for Concept-Drifting Data Streams,* pp. 79–94, 2009, Springer. With permission.)

each dataset is marked by a cross (x) on the top border in each graph at the corresponding chunk. For example, on the SynCN dataset (Figure 20.2(a)), W-OP and W-OS misses most of the novel class instances, which results in the spikes in their curves at the respective chunks (e.g., at chunks 12, 24, 37, etc.). W-OS misses almost 99% of the novel class instances. Similar spikes are observed for both W-OP and W-OS at the chunks where novel classes appear for KDD and Forest Cover datasets. For example, many novel classes appear between chunks 9 and 14 in KDD, most of which are missed by both W-OP and W-OS. Note that there is no novel class for SynC dataset. MC correctly detects most of these novel classes. Thus, MC outperforms both W-OP and W-OS in all datasets.

Table 20.1 summarizes the error metrics for each of the techniques in each dataset for decision tree and kNN. The columns headed by ERR, M_{new} and F_{new} report the average of the corresponding metric on

Table 20.1 Performance Comparison

CLASSIFIER	DATASET	ERR			M_{NEW}			F_{NEW}		
		MC	W-OP	W-OS	MC	W-OP	W-OS	MC	W-OP	W-OS
Decision tree	SynC	**11.6**	13.0	12.5	0.0	0.0	0.0	**0.0**	1.0	0.6
	SynCN	**0.6**	6.1	5.2	**0.0**	89.4	99.7	0.0	0.6	0.0
	KDD	**1.7**	11.6	8.7	**0.7**	26.7	99.4	1.5	7.0	**0.0**
	Forest Cover	**7.3**	21.8	8.7	**9.8**	18.5	99.4	1.7	15.0	**0.0**
K-NN	SynC	**11.7**	13.1	12.6	0.0	0.0	0.0	**0.0**	1.0	0.6
	SynCN	**0.8**	5.8	5.6	**0**	90.1	99.7	0.9	0.6	**0.0**
	KDD	**2.3**	10.0	7.0	**2.7**	29.0	99.4	2.2	7.1	**0.0**
	Forest Cover	**5.4**	19.2	8.9	**1.0**	18.5	94.0	4.5	15.0	**0.3**

Source: M. Masud, J. Gao, L. Khan, J. Han, B. Thuraisingham, *Integrating Novel Class Detection with Classification for Concept-Drifting Data Streams,* pp. 79–94, 2009, Springer. With permission.

an entire dataset. For example, while using decision tree in the SynC dataset, MC, W-OP, and W-OS have almost the same ERR, which are 11.6%, 13.0%, and 12.5%, respectively. This is because SynC simulates only concept-drift, and both MC and WCE handle concept-drift in a similar manner. In SynCN dataset with decision tree, MC, W-OP, and W-OS have 0%, 89.4%, and 99.7% M_{new}, respectively. Thus, W-OS misses almost all of the novel class instances, whereas W-OP detects only 11% of them. MC correctly detects all of the novel class instances. It is interesting that all approaches have lower error rates in SynCN than SynC. This is because SynCN is generated using Gaussian distribution, which is naturally easier for the classifiers to learn. W-OS mispredicts almost all of the novel class instances in all datasets. The comparatively better ERR rate for W-OS over W-OP can be attributed to the lower false positive rate of W-OS, which occurs because almost all instances are identified as "normal" by W-OS. Again, the overall error (ERR) of MC is much lower than other methods in all datasets and for all classifiers. K-NN also has similar results for all datasets.

Figures 20.3(a) through 20.3(d) illustrate how the error rates of MC change for different parameter settings on KDD dataset and decision tree classifier. These parameters have similar effects on other datasets and K-NN classifier. Figure 20.3(a) shows the effect of chunk size on ERR, F_{new}, and M_{new} rates for default values of other parameters. M_{new} reduces when chunk size is increased. This is desirable, because larger

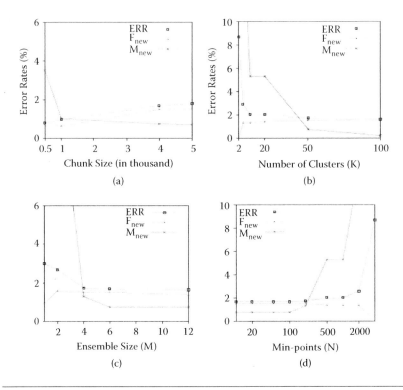

Figure 20.3 Sensitivity to different parameters. (From M. Masud, J. Gao, L. Khan, J. Han, B. Thuraisingham, *Integrating Novel Class Detection with Classification for Concept-Drifting Data Streams*, pp. 79–94, 2009, Springer. With permission.)

chunks reduce the risk of missing a novel class. But F_{new} rate slightly increases because the risk of identifying an existing class instance as novel also rises a little. These changes stabilize from chunk size 4,000 (for Synthetic dataset, it is 1,000). That is why we use these values in our experiments. Figure 20.3(b) shows the effect of number of clusters (K) on error. Increasing K generally reduces error rates, because outliers are more correctly detected, and as a result, M_{new} rate decreases. However, F_{new} rate also starts increasing slowly, as more test instances are becoming outliers (although they are not). The combined effect is that overall error keeps decreasing up to a certain value (e.g., $K = 50$) and then becomes almost flat. This is why we use $K = 50$ in our experiments. Figure 20.3(c) shows the effect of ensemble size (M) on error rates. We observe that the error rates decrease up to a certain size (=6), and become stable since then. This is because when M is increased from a low value (e.g., 2), classification error naturally decreases up to a certain point because of the reduction of error variance [Wang et al., 2003]. Figure 20.3(d) shows the effect of N on error rates. The x-axis in this chart is drawn in a logarithmic scale. Naturally, increasing N up to a certain point (e.g., 20) helps reduce error, because we know that a higher value of N gives us a greater confidence in declaring a new class. But a too large value of N increases M_{new} and ERR rates, as a new class is missed by the algorithm if it has less than N instances in a data chunk. We have found that any value between 20 and 100 is the best choice for N.

20.4.3 Running Time

Table 20.2 compares the running times of MC, W-OP, and W-OS on each dataset for decision tree. kNN also shows similar performances. The columns headed by "Time (sec)/Chunk " show the average running times (train and test) in seconds per chunk, the columns headed by "Points/sec" show how many points have been processed (train and test) per second on average, and the columns headed by "Speed Gain" show the ratio of the speed of MC to that of W-OP and W-OS, respectively. For example, MC is 2,095 and 105 times faster than W-OP on KDD dataset and Forest Cover dataset, respectively. Also, MC is 203 and 27 times faster than W-OP and W-OS, respectively, on the SynCN dataset. W-OP and W-OS are slower on SynCN than on SynC dataset because the SynCN dataset has more attributes (20 vs. 10) and classes (10 vs. 2). W-OP is relatively slower than W-OS because W-OP maintains C parallel models, where C is the number of existing classes, whereas W-OS maintains only one model. Both

Table 20.2   Running Time Comparison in All Datasets

| DATASET | TIME(SEC)/CHUNK | | | POINTS/SEC | | | SPEED GAIN | |
	MC	W-OP	W-OS	MC	W-OP	W-OS	MC OVER W-OP	MC OVER W-OS
SynC	0.18	0.81	0.19	5,446	1,227	5,102	4	1
SynCN	0.27	52.9	7.34	3,656	18	135	203	27
KDD	0.95	1369.5	222.8	4,190	2	17	2,095	246
Forest Cover	2.11	213.1	10.79	1,899	18	370	105	5

Source: M. Masud, J. Gao, L. Khan, J. Han, B. Thuraisingham, *Integrating Novel Class Detection with Classification for Concept-Drifting Data Streams*, pp. 79–94, 2009, Springer. With permission.

W-OP and W-OS are relatively faster on Forest Cover than KDD since Forest Cover has fewer number of classes, and relatively less evolution than KDD. The main reason for this extremely slow processing of W-OP and W-OS is that the number of clusters for each OLINDDA model keeps increasing linearly with the size of the data stream, causing both the memory requirement and the running time to increase linearly. But the running time and memory requirement of MC remain the same over the entire length of the stream.

20.5 Summary

In this chapter, we discussed the datasets, experimental setups, baseline techniques, and evaluation on the datasets. We used four different datasets, two of which are synthetic, and the two others are benchmark data streams. Our approach outperforms other baseline techniques in classification and novel class detection accuracies and running times on all datasets.

In the future, we would like to implement our technique on the cloud computing framework and evaluate the extended version of novel class detection technique on larger and real-world data streams. In addition, we would extend our approach to address the real-time classification and novel class detection problems in data streams.

References

[Spinosa et al., 2007] Spinosa, E. J., A. P. de Leon, F. de Carvalho, J. Gama, OLINDDA: A Cluster-Based Approach for Detecting Novelty and Concept Drift in Data Streams, in *Proceedings of the 2007 ACM Symposium on Applied Computing*, 2007, pp. 448–452.
[Wang et al., 2003] Wang, H., W. Fan, P. Yu, J. Han, Mining Concept-Drifting Data Streams Using Ensemble Classifiers, in *Proceedings of the ACM SIGKDD*, 2003, pp. 226–235.

Conclusion for Part VI

We have presented a novel technique to detect new classes in concept-drifting data streams. Most of the novelty detection techniques either assume that there is no concept-drift or build a model for a single "normal" class and consider all other classes as novel. But our approach is capable of detecting novel classes in the presence of concept-drift, even when the model consists of multiple "existing" classes. In addition, our novel class detection technique is non-parametric, meaning it does not assume any specific distribution of data. We also show empirically that our approach outperforms the state-of-the-art data stream-based novelty detection techniques in both classification accuracy and processing speed. It might appear to readers that to detect novel classes, we are in fact examining whether new clusters are being formed, and therefore, the detection process could go on without supervision. But supervision is necessary for classification. Without external supervision, two separate clusters could be regarded as two different classes, although they are not. Conversely, if more than one novel class appears in a chunk, all of them could be regarded as a single novel class if the labels of those instances are never revealed. In the future, we would like to apply our technique in the domain of multiple-label instances.

PART VII
EMERGING
APPLICATIONS

Introduction to Part VII

In Parts I, II, III, and IV we discussed the various data mining tools we have developed for malware section. These include tools for email worm detection, malicious code detection, remote exploit detection, and botnet detection. In Part V, we discussed stream mining technologies and their applications in security. In this part (i.e., Part VII), we discuss some of the data mining tools we are developing for emerging applications.

Part VII consists of four chapters: 21, 22, 23, and 24. In Chapter 21, we discuss data mining for active defense. The idea here is that the malware will change its patterns continuously, and therefore we need tools that can detect adaptable malware. In Chapter 22, we discuss data mining for insider threat analysis. In particular, we discuss how data mining tools may be used for detecting the suspicious communication represented as large graphs. In Chapter 23, we discuss dependable real-time data mining. In particular, we discuss data mining techniques that have to detect malware in real time. Finally we discuss data mining tools for firewall policy analysis. In particular, there are numerous firewall policy rules that may be outdated. We need a consistent set of firewall policies so that packets arriving from suspicious ports may be discarded.

21

DATA MINING FOR
ACTIVE DEFENSE

21.1 Introduction

Traditional *signature-based* malware detectors identify malware by scanning untrusted binaries for distinguishing byte sequences or *features*. Features unique to malware are maintained in a *signature database*, which must be continually updated as new malware is discovered and analyzed.

Signature-based malware detection generally enforces a static approximation of some desired dynamic (i.e., behavioral) security policy. For example, access control policies, such as those that prohibit code injections into operating system executables, are statically undecidable and can therefore only be approximated by any purely static decision procedure such as signature matching. A signature-based malware detector approximates these policies by identifying syntactic features that tend to appear only in binaries that exhibit policy-violating behavior when executed. This approximation is both unsound and incomplete in that it is susceptible to both false positive and false negative classifications of some binaries. For this reason signature databases are typically kept confidential, because they contain information that an attacker could use to craft malware that the detector would misclassify as benign, defeating the protection system. The effectiveness of signature-based malware detection thus depends on both the comprehensiveness and confidentiality of the signature database.

Traditionally, signature databases have been manually derived, updated, and disseminated by human experts as new malware appears and is analyzed. However, the escalating rate of new malware appearances and the advent of self-mutating, polymorphic malware over the past decade have made manual signature updating less practical. This has led to the development of automated data mining techniques for malware detection (e.g., [Kolter and Maloof, 2004], [Masud et al., 2008], [Schultz et al., 2001]) that are capable of automatically inferring signatures for previously unseen malware.

In this chapter, we show how these data mining techniques can also be applied by an attacker to discover ways to obfuscate malicious binaries so that they will be misclassified as benign by the detector. Our approach hinges on the observation that although malware detectors keep their signature databases confidential, all malware detectors reveal one bit of signature information every time they reveal a classification decision. This information can be harvested particularly efficiently when it is disclosed through a public interface. The classification decisions can then be delivered as input to a data mining malware detection algorithm to infer a model of the confidential signature database. From the inferred model, we derive feature removal and feature insertion obfuscations that preserve the behavior of a given malware binary but cause it to be misclassified as benign. The result is an obfuscation strategy that can defeat any purely static signature-based malware detector.

We demonstrate the effectiveness of this strategy by successfully obfuscating several real malware samples to defeat malware detectors on Windows operating systems. Windows-based antivirus products typically support Microsoft's IOfficeAntiVirus interface [MSDN Digital Library, 2009], which allows applications to invoke any installed antivirus product on a given binary and respond to the classification decision. Our experiments exploit this interface to obtain confidential signature database information from several commercial antivirus products.

This chapter is organized as follows. Section 21.2 describes related work. Section 21.3 provides an overview of our approach, Section 21.4 describes a data mining-based malware detection model, and Section 21.5 discusses methods of deriving binary obfuscations from a detection model. Section 21.6 then describes experiments and evaluation of our technique. Section 21.7 concludes with discussion and suggestions for future work. The contents of this chapter are illustrated in Figure 21.1.

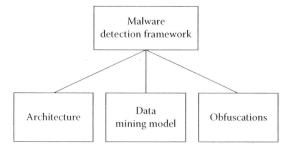

Figure 21.1 Concepts in this chapter.

21.2 Related Work

Both the creation and the detection of malware that self-modifies to defeat signature-based detectors are well-studied problems in the literature [Nachenberg, 1997], [Ször, 2005]. Self-modifying malware has existed at least since the early 1990s and has subsequently become a major obstacle for modern malware protection systems. For example, Kaspersky Labs [Kaspersky, 2009] reported three new major threats in February 2009 that use self-modifying propagation mechanisms to defeat existing malware detection products. Propagation and mutation rates for such malware can be very high. At the height of the *Feebs* virus outbreak in 2007, Commtouch Research Labs [Commtouch, 2007] reported that the malware was producing more than 11,000 unique variants of itself per day.

Most self-modifying malware uses encryption or packing as the primary basis for its modifications. The majority of the binary code in such *polymorphic malware* exists as an encrypted or packed *payload*, which is unencrypted or unpacked at runtime and executed. Signature-based protection systems typically detect polymorphic malware by identifying distinguishing features in the small unencrypted code stub that decrypts the payload (e.g., [Kruegel et al., 2005]). More recently, *metamorphic malware* has appeared, which randomly applies binary transformations to its code segment during propagation to obfuscate features in the unencrypted portion. An example is the MetaPHOR system [cf., Walenstein et al., 2006], which has become the basis for many other metamorphic malware propagation systems. Reversing these obfuscations to obtain reliable feature sets for signature-based detection is the subject of much current research [Brushi et al., 2007], [Kruegel et al., 2005], [Walenstein et al., 2006], but case studies have shown that current antivirus detection schemes remain vulnerable to simple obfuscation attacks until the detector's signature database is updated to respond to the threat [Christodorescu and Jha, 2004].

To our knowledge, all existing self-modifying malware mutates randomly. Our work therefore differs from past approaches in that it proposes an algorithm for choosing obfuscations that target and defeat specific malware defenses. These obfuscations could be inferred and applied fully automatically in the wild, thereby responding to a signature update without requiring re-propagation by the attacker. We argue that simple signature updates are therefore inadequate to defend against such an attack.

Our proposed approach uses technology based on data mining-based malware detectors. Data mining-based approaches analyze the content of an executable and classify it as malware if a certain combination of features is found (or not found) in the executable. These malware detectors are first trained so that they can generalize the distinction between malicious and benign executables and thus detect future instances of malware. The training process involves feature extraction and model building using these features. Data mining-based malware detectors differ mainly on how the features are extracted and which machine learning technique is used to build the model. The performance of these techniques largely depends on the quality of the features that are extracted.

[Schultz et al., 2001] extract DLL call information (using *GNU binutils*) and character strings (using *GNU strings*) from the headers of Windows PE executables, as well as 2-byte sequences from the executable content. The DLL calls, strings, and bytes are used as features to train models. Models are trained using two different machine learning techniques—RIPPER [Cohen, 1996] and Naïve Bayes (NB) [Michie et al., 1994]—to compare their relative performances. [Kolter and Maloof, 2004] extract binary *n*-gram features from executables and apply them to different classification methods, such as *k* nearest neighbor (*k*NN) [Aha et al., 1991], NB, Support Vector Machines (SVMs) [Boser et al., 1992], decision trees [Quinlan, 2003], and boosting [Freund and Schapire, 1996]. Boosting is applied in combination with various other learning algorithms to obtain improved models (e.g., *boosted decision trees*).

Our previous work on data mining-based malware detection [Masud et al., 2008] extracts binary *n*-grams from the executable, assembly instruction sequences from the disassembled executables, and DLL call information from the program headers. The classification models used in this work are SVM, decision tree, NB, boosted decision tree, and boosted NB. In the following sections we show how this technology can also be applied by an attacker to infer and implement effective attacks against malware detectors using information divulged by antivirus interfaces.

21.3 Architecture

The architecture of our binary obfuscation methodology is illustrated in Figure 21.2. We begin by submitting a diverse collection of malicious and benign binaries to the victim signature database via the signature query interface. The interface reveals a classification decision for each query. For our experiments we used the IOfficeAntivirus

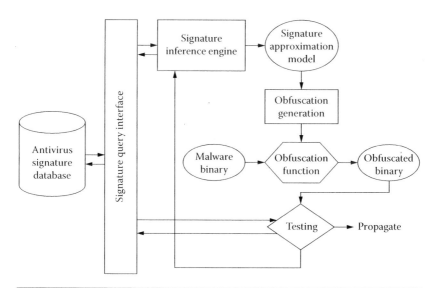

Figure 21.2 Binary obfuscation architecture. (From K. Hamlen, V. Mohan, M. Masud, L. Khan, B. Thuraisingham, *Exploiting an Antivirus Interface*, pp. 1182–1189, 2009, Elsevier. With permission.)

COM interface that is provided by Microsoft Windows operating systems (Windows 95 and later) [MSDN Digital Library, 2009]. The Scan method exported by this interface takes a filename as input and causes the operating system to use the installed antivirus product to scan the file for malware infections. Once the scan is complete, the method returns a success code indicating whether the file was classified as malicious or benign. This allows applications to request virus scans and respond to the resulting classification decisions.

We then use the original inputs and resulting classification decisions as a training set for an inference engine. The inference engine learns an approximating model for the signature database using the training set. In our implementation, this model was expressed as a decision tree in which each node tests for the presence or absence of a specific binary n-gram feature that was inferred to be security-relevant by the data mining algorithm.

This inferred model is then reinterpreted as a recipe for obfuscating malware so as to defeat the model. That is, each path in the decision tree encodes a set of binary features that, when added or removed from a given malware sample, causes the resulting binary to be classified as malicious or benign by the model. The obfuscation problem is thus reduced to finding a binary transformation that, when applied to malware, causes it to match one of the benignly classified feature sets. In addition, the transformation must not significantly alter the behavior of the malware binary being obfuscated. Currently, we identify suitable feature sets by manual inspection, but we believe that future work could automate this process.

Once such a feature set has been identified and applied to the malware sample, the resulting obfuscated sample is submitted as a query to the original signature database. A malicious classification indicates that the inferred signature model was not an adequate approximation for the signature database. In this case, the obfuscated malware is added to the training set and training continues, resulting in an improved model, whereupon the process repeats. A benign classification indicates a successful attack upon the malware detector. In our experiments, we found that repeating the inference process was not necessary; our obfuscations produced misclassified binaries after one round of inference.

21.4 A Data Mining-Based Malware Detection Model

21.4.1 Our Framework

A data mining-based malware detector first trains itself with known instances of malicious and benign executables. Once trained, it can predict the proper classifications of previously unseen executables by testing them against the model. The high-level framework of such a system is illustrated in Figure 21.3.

The predictive accuracy of the model depends on the given training data and the learning algorithm (e.g., SVM, decision tree, Naïve Bayes, etc.) Several data mining-based malware detectors have been proposed in the past [Kolter and Maloof, 2004], [Masud et al., 2008], [Schultz et al., 2001]. The main advantage of these models over the traditional signature-based models is that data mining-based models are more robust to changes in the malware. Signature-based models fail when new malware appears with an unknown signature. On the other hand, data mining-based models generalize the classification process by learning a suitable malware model dynamically over time. Thus, they are capable of detecting malware instances that were not known at the time of training. This makes it more challenging for an attacker to defeat a malware detector based on data mining.

Our previous work on data mining-based malware detection [Masud et al., 2008] has developed an approach that consists of three main steps:

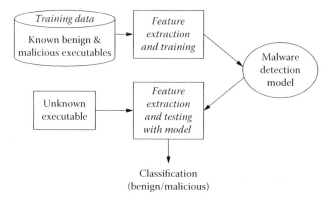

Figure 21.3   A data mining-based malware detection framework. (From K. Hamlen, V. Mohan, M. Masud, L. Khan, B. Thuraisingham, *Exploiting an Antivirus Interface*, pp. 1182–1189, 2009, Elsevier. With permission.)

1. Feature extraction, feature selection, and feature-vector computation from the training data
2. Training a classification model using the computed feature-vector
3. Testing executables with the trained model.

These steps are detailed throughout the remainder of the section.

21.4.2 Feature Extraction

In past work we have extracted three different kinds of features from training instances (i.e., executable binaries):

1. **Binary *n*-gram features:** To extract these features, we consider each executable as a string of bytes and extract all possible *n*-grams from the executables, where *n* ranges from 1 to 10.
2. **Assembly *n*-gram features:** We also disassemble each executable to obtain an assembly language program. We then extract *n*-grams of assembly instructions.
3. **Dynamic link library (DLL) call features:** Library calls are particularly relevant for distinguishing malicious binaries from benign binaries. We extract the library calls from the disassembly and use them as features.

When deriving obfuscations to defeat existing malware detectors, we found that restricting our attention only to binary *n*-gram features sufficed for our experiments, reported in Section 21.6. However, in future work we intend to apply all three feature sets to produce more robust obfuscation algorithms. Next, we describe how these binary features are extracted.

21.4.2.1 Binary n-Gram Feature Extraction First, we apply the UNIX hexdump utility to convert the binary executable files into textual *hexdump files*, which contain the hexadecimal numbers corresponding to each byte of the binary. This process is performed to ensure safe and easy portability of the binary executables. The feature extraction process consists of two phases: (1) feature collection, and (2) feature selection.

The feature collection process proceeds as follows. Let the set of hexdump training files be $H = \{h_1, \ldots, h_b\}$. We first initialize a set L of n-grams to empty. Then we scan each hexdump file h_i by sliding an n-byte window over its binary content. Each recovered n-byte sequence is added to L as an n-gram. For each n-gram $g \in L$ we count the total number of positive instances p_g (i.e., malicious executables) and negative instances n_g (i.e., benign executables) that contain g.

There are several implementation issues related to this basic approach. First, the total number of n-grams may be very large. For example, the total number of 10-grams in our dataset is 200 million. It may not be possible to store all of them in a computer's main memory. Presently we solve this problem by storing the n-grams in a large disk file that is processed via random access. Second, if L is not sorted, then a linear search is required for each scanned n-gram to test whether it is already in L. If N is the total number of n-grams in the dataset, then the time for collecting all the n-grams would be $O(N^2)$, an impractical amount of time when $N = 200$ million. To solve the second problem, we use an Adelson-Velsky-Landis (AVL) tree [Goodrich and Tamassia, 2005] to index the n-grams. An AVL tree is a height-balanced binary search tree. This tree has a property that the absolute difference between the heights of the left subtree and the right subtree of any node is, at most, 1. If this property is violated during insertion or deletion, a balancing operation is performed, and the tree regains its height-balanced property. It is guaranteed that insertions and deletions are performed in logarithmic time. Inserting an n-gram into the database thus requires only $O(\log_2(N))$ searches. This reduces the total running time to $O(\log_2(N))$, making the overall running time about 5 million times faster when N is large as 200 million. Our feature collection algorithm implements these two solutions.

21.4.2.2 Feature Selection   If the total number of extracted features is very large, it may not be possible to use all of them for training. Aside from memory limitations and impractical computing times, a classifier may become confused with a large number of features because most of them would be noisy, redundant, or irrelevant. It is therefore important to choose a small, relevant, and useful subset of features for more efficient and accurate classification. We choose information gain (IG) as the selection criterion because it is recognized in the literature as one of the best criteria isolating relevant features from large feature sets. IG can be defined as a measure of effectiveness of an attribute (i.e., feature) in classifying a training data [Mitchell, 1997]. If we split the training data based on the values of this attribute, then IG gives the measurement of the expected reduction in entropy after the split. The more an attribute can reduce entropy in the training data, the better the attribute is for classifying the data.

The next problem is to select the best S features (i.e., n-grams) according to IG. One naïve approach is to sort the n-grams in non-increasing order of IG and select the top S of them, which requires $O(N\log_2 N)$ time and $O(N)$ main memory. But this selection can be more efficiently accomplished using a heap that requires $O(N\log_2 S)$ time and $O(S)$ main memory. For $S = 500$ and $N = 200$ million, this approach is more than 3 times faster and requires 400,000 times less main memory. A heap is a balanced binary tree with the property that the root of any subtree contains the minimum (maximum) element in that subtree. First, we build a min-heap of size S. The min-heap contains the minimum-IG n-gram at its root. Then each n-gram g is compared with the n-gram at the root r. If $IG(g) \leq IG(r)$ then we discard g. Otherwise, r is replaced with g, and the heap is restored.

21.4.2.3 Feature Vector Computation Suppose the set of features selected in the above step is $F = \{f_1, ..., f_s\}$. For each hexdump file h_i, we build a binary feature vector $h_i(F) = \{h_i(f_1), ..., h_i(f_S)\}$, where $h_i(f_j) = 1$ if h_i contains feature f_j, or 0 otherwise. The training algorithm of a classifier is supplied with a tuple $(h_i(F), l(h_i))$ for each training instance h_i, where $h_i(F)$ is the feature vector and $l(h_i)$ is the class label of the instance h_i (i.e., positive or negative).

21.4.3 Training

We apply SVM, Naïve Bayes (NB), and decision tree (J48) classifiers for the classification task. SVM can perform either linear or non-linear classification. The linear classifier proposed by Vapnik [Boser et al., 1992] creates a hyperplane that separates the data points into two classes with the maximum margin. A maximum-margin hyperplane is the one that splits the training examples into two subsets such that the distance between the hyperplane and its closest data point(s) is maximized. A non-linear SVM [Cortes and Vapnik, 1995] is implemented by applying a kernel trick to maximum-margin hyperplanes. This kernel trick transforms the feature space into a higher dimensional space where the maximum-margin hyperplane is found, through the aid of a kernel function.

A decision tree contains attribute tests at each internal node and a decision at each leaf node. It classifies an instance by performing the attribute tests prescribed by a path from the root to a decision node. Decision trees are rule-based classifiers, allowing us to obtain human-readable classification rules from the tree. J48 is the implementation of the C4.5 Decision Tree algorithm. C4.5 is an extension of the ID3 algorithm invented by [Quinlan, 2003]. To train a classifier, we provide the feature vectors along with the class labels of each training instance that we have computed in the previous step.

21.4.4 Testing

Once a classification model has been trained, we can assess its accuracy by comparing its classification of new instances (i.e., executables) to the original victim malware detector's classifications of the same new instances. To test an executable h, we first compute the feature vector $h(F)$ corresponding to the executable in the manner described earlier. When this feature vector is provided to the classification model, the model outputs (predicts) a class label $l(h)$ for the instance. If we know the true class label of h, then we can compare the prediction with the true label and check the correctness of the learned model. If the model's performance is inadequate, the new instances are added to the training set, resulting in an improved model, and testing resumes.

In the next section, we describe how the model yielded by the previously described process can be used to derive binary obfuscations that defeat the model.

21.5 Model-Reversing Obfuscations

Malware detectors based on static data mining attempt to learn correlations between the syntax of untrusted binaries and the (malicious or benign) behavior that those binaries exhibit when executed. This learning process is necessarily unsound or incomplete because most practically useful definitions of "malicious behavior" are Turing-undecidable. Thus, every purely static algorithm for malware detection is vulnerable to false positives, false negatives, or both. Our obfuscator exploits this weakness by discovering false negatives in the model inferred by a static malware detector.

The decision tree model inferred in the previous section can be used as a basis for deriving binary obfuscations that defeat the model. The obfuscation involves adding or removing features (i.e., binary n-grams) to and from the malware binary so that the model classifies the resulting binary as benign. These binary transformations must be carefully crafted so as to avoid altering the runtime behavior of the malware program lest they result in a policy-adherent or non-executable binary. Details of the obfuscation approach are given in [Hamlen et al., 2009]. We briefly outline the steps in the ensuing paragraphs.

21.5.1 Path Selection

We begin the obfuscation process by searching for a candidate path through the decision tree that ends in a benign leaf node. Our goal will be to add and remove features from the malicious executable so as to cause the detector to follow the chosen decision tree path during classification. Because the path ends in a benign-classifying decision node, this will cause the malware to be misclassified as benign by the detector.

21.5.2 Feature Insertion

Inserting new features into executable binaries without significantly altering their runtime behavior tends to be a fairly straightforward task.

21.5.3 Feature Removal

Removal of a feature from an executable binary is more difficult to implement without changing the program's runtime behavior. Existing malware implement this using one of two techniques: (1) encryption (polymorphic malware), or (2) code mutation (metamorphic malware).

Although polymorphism and metamorphism are powerful existing techniques for obfuscating malware against signature-based detectors, it should be noted that existing polymorphic and metamorphic malware mutates randomly. Our attack therefore differs from these existing approaches in that we choose obfuscations that are derived directly from signature database information leaked by the malware detector being attacked. Our work therefore builds upon this past work by showing how antivirus interfaces can be exploited to choose an effective obfuscation, which can then be implemented using these existing techniques.

21.6 Experiments

To test our approach, we conducted two sets of experiments. In the first experiment, we attempted to collect classification data from several commercial antivirus products by querying their public interfaces automatically. In the second experiment, we obfuscated a malware sample to defeat the data mining-based malware detector we developed in past work [Masud et al., 2008] and that is described in Section 21.4. In future work we intend to combine these two results to test fully automatic obfuscation attacks upon commercial antivirus products.

We have two non-disjoint datasets. The first dataset (dataset1) contains a collection of 1,435 executables, 597 of which are benign and 838 of which are malicious. The second dataset (dataset2) contains 2,452 executables, having 1,370 benign and 1,082 malicious executables. The distribution of dataset1 is hence 41.6% benign and 58.4% malicious, and that of dataset2 is 55.9% benign and 44.1% malicious. This distribution was chosen intentionally to evaluate the performance of the feature sets in different scenarios. We collect the benign executables from different Windows XP and Windows 2000 machines, and collect the malicious executables from [VX Heavens, 2009] which contains a large collection of malicious executables.

We carried out two sets of experiments: the Interface Exploit Experiment and the model-driven obfuscation experiment. These experiments are detailed in [Hamlen et al., 2009]. For example, to test the feasibility of collecting confidential signature database information via the antivirus interface on Windows operating systems, we wrote a small utility that queries the IOfficeAntivirus [MSDN Digital Library, 2009] COM interface on Windows XP and Vista machines. The utility uses this interface to request virus scans of instances in dataset1. We tested our utility on four commercial antivirus products: Norton Antivirus 2009, McAfee VirusScan Plus, AVG 8.0, and Avast Antivirus 2009. In all but Avast Antivirus, we found that we were able to reliably sample the signature database using the interface. In the case of Avast Antivirus 2009, we found that the return code yielded by the interface was not meaningful—it did not distinguish between different classifications. Thus, Avast Antivirus 2009 was not vulnerable to our attack. In the second experiment, the obfuscated malware defeated the detector from which the model was derived.

21.7 Summary

In this chapter, we have outlined a technique whereby antivirus interfaces that reveal classification decisions can be exploited to infer confidential information about the underlying signature database. These classification decisions can be used as training inputs to data mining-based malware detectors. Such detectors will learn an approximating model for the signature database that can be used as a basis for deriving binary obfuscations that defeat the signature database. We conjecture that this technique could be used as the basis for effective, fully automatic, and targeted attacks against signature-based antivirus products.

Our experiments justify this conjecture by demonstrating that classification decisions can be reliably harvested from several commercial antivirus products on Windows operating systems by exploiting the Windows public antivirus interface. We also demonstrated that effective obfuscations can be derived for real malware from an inferred model by successfully obfuscating a real malware sample using our model-reversing obfuscation technique. The obfuscated malware defeated the detector from which the model was derived.

Our signature database inference procedure was not an effective attack against one commercial antivirus product we tested because that product did not fully support the antivirus interface. In particular, it returned the same result code irrespective of its classification decision for the submitted binary file. However, we believe this limitation could be overcome by an attacker in at least two different ways.

First, although the return code did not divulge classification decisions, the product did display observably different responses to malicious binaries, such as opening a quarantine pop-up window. These responses could have been automatically detected by our query engine. Determining classification decisions in this way is a slower but still fully automatic process.

Second, many commercial antivirus products also exist as freely distributed, stand-alone utilities that scan for (but do not necessarily disinfect) malware based on the same signature databases used in the retail product. These lightweight scanners are typically implemented as Java applets or ActiveX controls so that they are web-streamable and executable at low privilege levels. Such applets could be executed in a restricted virtual machine environment to effectively create a suitable query interface for the signature database. The execution environment would provide a limited view of the filesystem to the victim applet and would infer classification decisions by monitoring decision-specific system calls, such as those that display windows and dialogue boxes.

From the work summarized in this chapter, we conclude that effectively concealing antivirus signature database information from an attacker is important but difficult. Current antivirus interfaces, such as the one currently supported by Windows operating systems, invite signature information leaks and subsequent obfuscation attacks. Antivirus products that fail to support these interfaces are less vulnerable to these attacks; however, they still divulge confidential signature database information through covert channels, such as graphical responses and other side effects.

Fully protecting against these confidentiality violations might not be feasible; however, there are some obvious steps that defenders can take to make these attacks more computationally expensive for the attacker. One obvious step is to avoid implementing or supporting interfaces that divulge classification decisions explicitly and on demand through return codes. While this prevents benign applications from detecting and responding to malware quarantines, this reduction in functionality seems reasonable in the (hopefully uncommon) context of a malware attack. Protecting against signature information leaks through covert channels is a more challenging problem. Addressing it effectively might require leveraging antipiracy technologies that examine the current execution environment and refuse to divulge classification decisions in restrictive environments that might be controlled by an attacker. Without such protection, attackers will continue to be able to craft effective, targeted binary obfuscations that defeat existing signature-based malware detection models.

References

[Aha et al., 1991] Aha, D. W., D. Kibler, M. K. Albert, Instance-Based Learning Algorithms, *Machine Learning*, Vol. 6, 1991, pp. 37–66.

[Boser et al., 1992] Boser, B. E., I. M. Guyon, V. N. Vapnik, A Training Algorithm for Optimal Margin Classifiers, in *Proceedings of the 5th ACM Workshop on Computational Learning Theory*, 1992, pp. 144–152.

[Brushi et al., 2007] Brushi, D., L. Martignoni, M. Monga, Code Normalization for Self-Mutating Malware, in *Proceedings of the IEEE Symposium on Security and Privacy*, Vol. 5, No. 2, pp. 46–54, 2007.

[Christodorescu and Jha, 2004] Christodorescu, M., and S. Jha, Testing Malware Detectors, in *Proceedings of the ACM SIGSOFT International Symposium on Software Testing and Analysis (ISSTA)*, 2004, pp. 34–44.

[Cohen, 1996] Cohen, W. W., Learning Rules that Classify E-mail, in *Papers from the AAAI Spring Symposium on Machine Learning in Information Access*, 1996, pp. 18–25.

[Commtouch, 2007] *Q1 Malware Trends Report: Server-Side Malware Explodes across Email*, White Paper, Commtouch Research Labs, Alt-N Technologies, Grapevine, TX, May 2, 2007.

[Cortes and Vapnik, 1995] Cortes, C., and V. Vapnik, Support-Vector Networks, *Machine Learning*, Vol. 20, No. 3, 1995, pp. 273–297.

[Freund and Schapire, 1996] Freund, Y., and R. E. Schapire, Experiments with a New Boosting Algorithm, in *Proceedings of the 13th International Conference on Machine Learning*, 1996, pp. 148–156.

[Goodrich and Tamassia, 2005] Goodrich, M. T., and R. Tamassia, *Data Structures and Algorithms in Java*, Fourth Edition, Wiley, New York, 2005.

[Hamlen et al., 2009] Hamlen, K. W., V. Mohan, M. M. Masud, L. Khan, B. M. Thuraisingham, Exploiting an Antivirus Interface, *Computer Standards & Interfaces*, Vol. 31, No. 6, 2009, pp. 1182–1189.

[Kaspersky, 2009] Kaspersky Labs, Monthly Malware Statistics, http://www.kaspersky.com/news? id=207575761.

[Kolter and Maloof, 2004] Kolter, J. Z., and M. A. Maloof, Learning to Detect Malicious Executables in the Wild, in *Proceedings of the 10th ACM SIGKDD International Conference on Knowledge Discovery and Data Mining*, 2004, pp. 470–478.

[Kruegel et al., 2005] Kruegel, C., E. Kirda, D. Mutz, W. Robertson, G. Vigna, Polymorphic Worm Detection Using Structural Information of Executables, in *Proceedings of the 8th Symposium on Recent Advances in Intrusion Detection (RAID)*, 2005, pp. 207–226.

[Masud et al., 2008] Masud, M., L. Khan, B. M. Thuraisingham, A Scalable Multi-level Feature Extraction Technique to Detect Malicious Executables, *Information System Frontiers*, Vol. 10, No. 1, 2008, pp. 33–35.

[Michie et al., 1994] Michie, D., D. J. Spiegelhalter, C. C. Taylor, Editors, *Machine Learning, Neural and Statistical Classification*, chap. 5: Machine Learning of Rules and Trees, Morgan Kaufmann, 1994, pp. 50–83.

[Mitchell, 1997] Mitchell, T. M., *Machine Learning*, McGraw-Hill, New York, 1997.

[MSDN Digital Library, 2009] IOfficeAntiVirus Interface, http://msdn. microsoft.com/en-us/library/ms537369(VS.85).aspx

[Nachenberg, 1997] Nachenberg, C., Computer Virus-Antivirus Coevolution, *Communications of the ACM*, Vol. 40, No. 1, 1997, pp. 47–51.

[Quinlan, 2003] Quinlan, J. R., *C4.5: Programs for Machine Learning*, Fifth Edition, Morgan Kaufmann, San Francisco, CA, 2003.

[Schultz et al., 2001] Schultz, M. G., E. Eskin, E. Zadok, S. J. Stolfo, Data Mining Methods for Detection of New Malicious Executables, in *Proceedings of the IEEE Symposium on Security and Privacy*, pp. 38–39, 2001.

[Ször, 2005] Ször, P., *The Art of Computer Virus Research and Defense*, Addison-Wesley Professional, 2005.

[VX Heavens, 2009] VX Heavens, http://vx.netlux.org

[Walenstein et al., 2006] Walenstein, A., R. Mathur, M. R. Chouchane, A. Lakhotia, Normalizing Metamorphic Malware Using Term Rewriting, in *Proceedings of the 6th IEEE Workshop on Source Code Analysis and Manipulation (SCAM)*, 2006, pp. 75–84.

22

Data Mining for Insider Threat Detection

22.1 Introduction

Effective detection of insider threats requires monitoring mechanisms that are far more fine-grained than for external threat detection. These monitors must be efficiently and reliably deployable in the software environments where actions endemic to malicious insider missions are caught in a timely manner. Such environments typically include user-level applications, such as word processors, email clients, and web browsers, for which reliable monitoring of internal events by conventional means is difficult.

To monitor the activities of the insiders, tools are needed to capture the communications and relationships between the insiders, store the captured relationships, query the stored relationships, and ultimately analyze the relationships so that patterns can be extracted that would give the analyst better insights into the potential threats. Over time, the number of communications and relationships between the insiders could be in the billions. Using the tools developed under our project, the billions of relationships between the insiders can be captured, stored, queried, and analyzed to detect malicious insiders.

In this chapter, we discuss how data mining technologies may be applied for insider threat detection. First, we discuss how semantic web technologies may be used to represent the communication between insiders. Next, we discuss our approach to insider threat detection. Finally, we provide an overview of our framework for insider threat detection that also incorporated some other techniques.

The organization of this chapter is as follows. In Section 22.2, we discuss the challenges, related work, and our approach to this problem. Our approach is discussed in detail in Section 22.3. Our

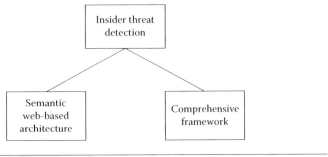

Figure 22.1   Concepts in this chapter.

framework is discussed in Section 22.4. The chapter is concluded in Section 22.5. An overview of semantic web technologies is discussed in Appendix D. Figure 22.1 illustrates the contents of this chapter,

22.2 The Challenges, Related Work, and Our Approach

The insiders and the relationships between the insiders will be presented as nodes and links in a graph. Therefore, the challenge is to represent the information in graphs, develop efficient storage strategies, develop query processing techniques for the graphs, and subsequently develop data mining and analysis techniques to extract information from the graphs. In particular, there are three major challenges:

1. Storing these large graphs in an expressive and unified manner in a secondary storage
2. Devising scalable solutions for querying the large graphs to find relevant data
3. Identifying relevant features for the complex graphs and subsequently detecting insider threats in a dynamic environment that changes over time

The motivation behind our approach is to address the previously mentioned three challenges. We are developing solutions based on cloud computing to (1) characterize graphs containing up to billions of nodes and edges between nodes representing activities (e.g., credit card transactions), email, or text messages. Because the graphs will be massive, we will develop technologies for efficient and persistent storage. (2) To facilitate novel anomaly detection, we require an efficient interface to fetch relevant data in a timely manner from this persistent storage. Therefore, we will develop efficient query techniques on the stored graphs. (3) The fetched relevant data can then be used for further analysis to detect anomalies. To do this, first we have to identify relevant features from the complex graphs and subsequently develop techniques for mining large graphs to extract the nuggets.

As stated earlier, insider threat detection is a difficult problem [Maybury et al., 2005], [Strayer et al., 2009]. The problem becomes increasingly complex with more data originating from heterogeneous sources and sensors. Recently, there is some research that focuses on anomaly-based insider threat detection from graphs [Eberle and Holder, 2009]. This method is based on the minimum description length (MDL) principle. The solution proposed by [Eberle and Holder, 2009] has some limitations. First, with their approach, scalability is an issue. In other words, they have not discussed any issue related to large graphs. Second, the heterogeneity issue has not been addressed. Finally, it is unclear how their algorithm will deal with a dynamic environment.

There are also several graph mining techniques that have been developed especially for social network analysis [Carminati et al., 2009], [Cook and Holder, 2006], [Thuraisingham et al., 2009], [Tong, 2009]. The scalability of these techniques is still an issue. There is some work from the mathematics research community to apply linear programming techniques for graph analysis [Berry et al., 2007]. Whether these techniques will work in a real-world setting is not clear.

For a solution to be viable, it must be highly scalable and support multiple heterogeneous data sources. Current state-of-the-art solutions do not scale well and preserve accuracy. By leveraging Hadoop technology, our solution will be highly scalable. Furthermore, by utilizing the flexible semantic web RDF data model, we are able to easily integrate and align heterogeneous data. Thus, our approach will create a scalable solution in a dynamic environment. No existing threat detection tools offer this level of scalability and interoperability. We will combine these technologies with novel data mining techniques to create a complete insider threat detection solution.

We have exploited the cloud computing framework based on Hadoop/MapReduce technologies. The insiders and their relationships are represented by nodes and links in the form of graphs. In particular, in our approach, the billions of nodes and links will be presented as RDF (Resource Description Framework) graphs. By exploiting RDF representation, we will address heterogeneity. We will develop mechanisms to efficiently store the RDF graphs, query the graphs using SPARQL technologies, and mine the graphs to extract patterns within the cloud computing framework. We will also describe our plans to commercialize the technologies developed under this project.

22.3 Data Mining for Insider Threat Detection

22.3.1 Our Solution Architecture

Figure 22.2 shows the architectural view of our solution. Our solution will pull data from multiple sources and then extract and select features. After feature reduction, the data will be stored in our Hardtop repository. Data will be stored in the Resource Description Framework (RDF) format, so a format conversion may be required if the data is in any other format. RDF is the data format for the semantic web and is very able to represent graph data. The Anomaly Prediction component will submit SPARQL Protocol and RDF Query Language (SPARQL) to the repository to select data. It will then output any detected insider threats. SPARQL is the query language for RDF data. It is similar to SQL in syntax. The details of each of the components are given in the following sections. For choosing RDF representation for graphs

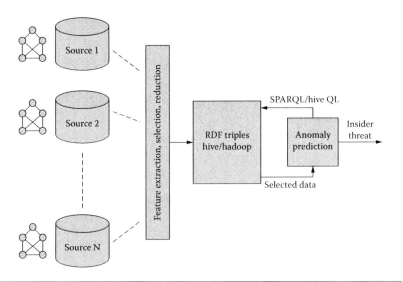

Figure 22.2 Solution architecture.

over relational data models, we will address heterogeneity issues effectively (semi-structured data model). For querying, we will exploit standard query language, SPARQL, instead of starting from scratch. Furthermore, in our proposed framework, inference will be provided.

We are assuming that the large graphs already exist. To facilitate persistent storage and efficient retrieval of these data, we use a distributed framework based on the cloud computing framework Hadoop [Hadoop]. By leveraging the Hadoop technology, our framework is readily fault tolerant and scalable. To support large amounts of data, we can simply add more nodes to the Hadoop cluster. All the nodes of a cluster are commodity class machines; there is no need to buy expensive server machines. To handle large complex graphs, we will exploit Hadoop Distributed File System (HDFS) and MapReduce framework. The former is the storage layer that stores data in multiple nodes with replication. The latter is the execution layer where MapReduce jobs can be run. We use HDFS to store RDF data and the MapReduce framework to answer queries.

22.3.2 Feature Extraction and Compact Representation

In traditional graph analysis, an edge represents a simple number that represents strength. However, we may face additional challenges in representing link values because of the unstructured nature of the content of text and email messages. One possible approach is to keep the whole content as a part of link values, which we call explicit content (EC). EC will not scale well, even for a moderate size graph. This is because content representing a link between two nodes will require a lot of main memory space to process the graph in the memory. We propose a vector representation of the content (VRC) for each message. In RDF triple representation, this will simply be represented as a unique predicate. We will keep track of the feature vector along with physical location or URL of the original raw message in a dictionary encoded table.

VRC: During the preprocessing step for each message, we will extract keywords and phrases (n-grams) as features. Then, if we want to generate vectors for these features, the dimensionality of these vectors will be very high. Here, we will observe the curse of dimensionality (i.e., sparseness and processing time will increase). Therefore, we can apply feature reduction (PCA, SVD, NMF) as well as feature selection. Because feature reduction maps high-dimensional feature spaces to a space of fewer dimensions, and new feature dimension may be the linear combination of old dimensions that may be difficult to interpret, we will exploit feature selection.

With regard to feature selection, we need to use a class label for supervised data. Here, for the message we may not have a class label; however, we know the source/sender and the destination/recipient of a message. Now, we would like to use this knowledge to construct an artificial label. The sender and destination pair will form a unique class label, and all messages sent from this sender to the recipient will serve as data points. Hence, our goal is to find appropriate features that will have discriminating power across all of these class labels based on these messages. There are several methods for feature selection that are widely used in the area of machine learning, such as information gain [Masud et al., 2010-a], [Masud et al., 2010-b], [Mitchell, 1997]; Gini index; chi-square statistics; and subspace clustering [Ahmed and Khan, 2009]. Here, we will present information gain, which is very popular, and for the text domain, we can use subspace clustering for feature selection.

Information gain (IG) can be defined as a measure of the effectiveness of a feature in classifying the training data [Mitchell, 1997]. If we split the training data on these attribute values, then IG provides the measurement of the expected reduction in entropy after the split. The more an attribute can reduce entropy in the training data, the better the attribute will be in classifying the data. IG of an attribute A on a collection of examples S is given by (22.1):

$$Gain(S, A) \equiv Entropy(S) - \sum_{v \in Values(A)} \frac{|S_v|}{|S|} Entropy(S_v) \quad (22.1)$$

where Values (A) is the set of all possible values for attribute A, and S_v is the subset of S for which attribute A has value v. Entropy of S is computed using the following equation (22.2):

$$Entropy(S) = -\sum_{i=1}^{n} p_i(S) \log_2 p_i(S) \quad (22.2)$$

where $p_i(S)$ is the prior probability of class i in the set S.

Subspace clustering: Subspace clustering can be used for feature selection. Subspace clustering is appropriate when the clusters corresponding to a dataset form a subset of the original dimensions. Based on how these subsets are formed, a subspace clustering algorithm can be referred to as soft or hard subspace clustering. In the case of soft subspace clustering, the features are assigned weights according to the contribution each feature or dimension plays during the clustering process for each cluster. In the case of hard subspace clustering, however, a specific subset of features is selected for each cluster and the rest of the features are discarded for that cluster. Therefore, subspace clustering can be utilized for selecting which features are important (and discarding some features if their weights are very small for all clusters). One such soft subspace clustering approach is SISC [Ahmed and Khan, 2009]. The following objective function is used in that subspace clustering algorithm. An E-M formulation is used for the clustering. In every iteration, the feature weights are updated for each cluster and by selecting the features that have higher weights in each cluster, we can select a set of important features for the corresponding dataset.

$$F(W,Z,\Lambda) = \sum_{l=1}^{k}\sum_{j=1}^{n}\sum_{i=1}^{m} w_{lj}^{f}\lambda_{li}^{q}D_{lij} * (1+Imp_l) + \gamma \sum_{l=1}^{k}\sum_{i=1}^{m}\lambda_{li}^{q}\chi_{li}^{2}$$

where

$$D_{lij} = \left(z_{li} - x_{ji}\right)^{2}$$

subject to

$$\sum_{l=1}^{k} w_{lj} = 1, 1 \le j \le n, 1 \le l \le k, 0 \le w_{lj} \le 1$$

$$\sum_{i=1}^{m} \lambda_{li} = 1, 1 \le i \le m, 1 \le l \le k, 0 \le \lambda_{ij} \le 1$$

In this objective function, W, Z, and Λ represent the cluster membership, cluster centroid, and dimension weight matrices. respectively.

Also, the parameter f controls the fuzziness of the membership of each data point, q further modifies the weight of each dimension of each cluster (λ_{ji}), and finally, γ controls the strength of the incentive given to the chi-square component and dimension weights. It is also assumed that there are n documents in the training dataset, m features for each of the data points, and k subspace clusters generated during the clustering process. Imp_j indicates the cluster impurity, whereas χ^2 indicates the chi-square statistic. Details about these notations and how the clustering is done can be found in our prior work, funded by NASA [Ahmed and Khan, 2009]. It should be noted that feature selection using subspace clustering can be considered as an unsupervised approach toward feature selection, as no label information is required during an unsupervised clustering process.

Once we select features, a message between two nodes will be represented as a vector using these features. Each vector's individual value can be binary or weighted. Hence, this will be a compact representation of the original message, and it can be loaded into main memory along with graph structure. In addition, the location or URL of the original message will be kept in the main memory data structure. If needed, we will fetch the message. Over time, the feature vector may be changed as a result of dynamic nature content [Masud et al., 2010-a], and hence, the feature set may evolve. Based on our prior work for evolving streams with dynamic feature sets [Masud et al., 2010-b], we will investigate alternative options.

22.3.3 RDF Repository Architecture

RDF is the data format for semantic web. However, it can be used to represent any linked data in the world. RDF data are actually a collection of triples. Triples consist of three parts: subject, predicate, and object. In RDF, almost everything is a resource and hence the name of the format. Subject and predicate are always resources. Objects may be either resources or literals. Here, RDF data can be viewed as a directed graph where predicates are edges that flow from subjects to objects. Therefore, in our proposed research to model any graph, we will exploit RDF triple format. Here, an edge from the source node to destination node in a graph dataset will be represented as predicate, subject, and object of an RDF triple, respectively. To reduce storage size of RDF triples, we will exploit dictionary encoding, that is, replace each unique string with a unique number and store the RDF data in binary format. Hence, RDF triples will have subject, predicate, and object in an encoded form. We will maintain a separate table/file for keeping track of dictionary encoding information. To address the dynamic nature of the data, we will extend RDF triple to quad by adding a timestamp along with subject, predicate, and object representing information in the network.

Figure 22.3 shows our repository architecture, which consists of two components. The upper part of the figure depicts the data preprocessing component, and the lower part shows the component, which answers a query. We have three subcomponents for data generation and preprocessing. If the data is not in N-Triples, we will convert it to N-Triples serialization format using the N-Triples Converter component. The PS component takes the N-Triples data and splits it into predicate files. The predicate-based files then will be fed into the POS

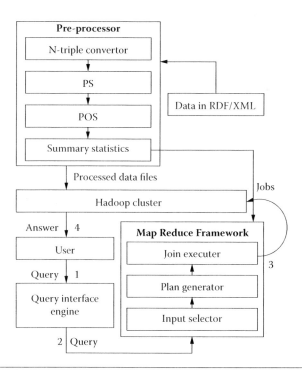

Figure 22.3 RDF repository architecture. (From M. Husain, L. Khan, M. Kantarcioglu, B. Thuraisingham, *Data Intensive Query Processing for Large RDF Graphs Using Cloud Computing Tools*, pp. 1–10, 2010 © IEEE. With permission.)

component, which would split the predicate files into smaller files based on the type of objects.

Our MapReduce framework has three subcomponents in it. It takes the SPARQL query from the user and passes it to the Input Selector and Plan Generator. This component will select the input files and decide how many MapReduce jobs are needed and pass the information to the Join Executer component, which runs the jobs using MapReduce framework. It will then relay the query answer from Hadoop to the user.

22.3.4 Data Storage

We will store the data in N-Triples format because in this format we have a complete RDF triple (Subject, Predicate, and Object) in one line of a file, which is very convenient to use with MapReduce jobs. We will dictionary encode the data for increased efficiency. Dictionary encoding means replacing text strings with a unique binary number. Not only does this reduce disk space required for storage, but also query answering will be fast because handling the primitive data type is much faster than string matching. The processing steps to get the data in our intended format are described next.

22.3.4.1 File Organization   We will not store the data in a single file because, in the Hadoop and MapReduce framework, a file is the smallest unit of input to a MapReduce job and, in absence of caching, a file is always read from the disk. If we have all the data in one file, the whole file will be input to jobs for each query. Instead, we divide the data into multiple smaller files. The splitting will be done in two steps, which we discuss in the following sections.

22.3.4.2 Predicate Split (PS)   In the first step, we will divide the data according to the predicates. In real-world RDF datasets, the number of distinct predicates is no more than 100. This division will immediately enable us to cut down the search space for any SPARQL query that does not have a variable predicate. For such a query, we can just pick a file for each predicate and run the query on those files only. For simplicity, we will name the files with predicates; for example, all the triples containing a predicate p1:pred go into a file named p1-pred.

However, in case we have a variable predicate in a triple pattern and if we cannot determine the type of the object, we have to consider all files. If we can determine the type of the object, then we will consider all files having that type of object.

22.3.4.3 *Predicate Object Split (POS)*   In the next step, we will work with the explicit type information in the rdf_type file. The file will be first divided into as many files as the number of distinct objects the rdf:type predicate has. The object values will no longer be needed to be stored inside the file as they can be easily retrieved from the file name. This will further reduce the amount of space needed to store the data.

Then, we will divide the remaining predicate files according to the type of the objects. Not all the objects are Uniform Resource Identifiers (URIs); some are literals. The literals will remain in the file named by the predicate: no further processing is required for them. The type information of a URI object is not mentioned in these files, but they can be retrieved from the rdf-type_* files. The URI objects will move into their respective file named as predicate_type.

22.3.5 *Answering Queries Using Hadoop MapReduce*

For querying we can utilize HIVE, a SQL-like query language, and SPARQL, the query language for RDF data. When a query is submitted in HiveQL, Hive, which runs on top of the Hadoop installation, can answer that query based on our schema presented earlier. When a SPARQL query is submitted to retrieve relevant data from the graph, first, we will generate a query plan having the minimum number of Hadoop jobs possible.

Next, we will run the jobs and answer the query. Finally, we will convert the numbers used to encode the strings back to the strings when we present the query results to the user. We will focus on minimizing the number of jobs because, in our observation, we have found that setting up Hadoop jobs is very costly, and the dominant factor (time-wise) is query answering. The search space for finding the minimum number of jobs is exponential, so we will try to find a greedy-based solution or, generally speaking, an approximation solution. Our proposed approach will be capable of handling queries involving inference. We can infer on the fly and, if needed, we can materialize the inferred data.

22.3.6 Data Mining Applications

To detect anomaly/insider threat, machine learning and domain knowledge-guided techniques are proposed. Our goal is to create a comparison baseline to assess the effectiveness of chaotic attractors. As a part of this task, rather than modeling normal behavior and detecting changes as anomaly, we will apply a holistic approach based on a semi-supervised model. In particular, first, in our machine learning technique, we will apply a sequence of activities or dimensions as features. Second, domain knowledge (e.g., adversarial behavior) will be a part of semi-supervised learning and will be used for identifying correct features. Finally, our techniques will be able to identify an entirely brand new anomaly. Over time, activities/dimensions may change or deviate. Hence, our classification model needs to be adaptive and identify new types or brand new anomalies. We will develop adaptive and novel class detection techniques so that our insider threat detection can cope with changes and identify or isolate new anomalies from existing ones.

We will apply a classification technique to detect insider threat/anomaly. Each distinct insider mission will be treated as class and dimension and/or activities will be treated as features. Because classification is a supervised task, we require a training set. Given a training set, feature extraction will be a challenge. We will apply n-gram analysis to extract features or generate a number of sequences based on temporal property. Once a new test case comes, first, we test it against our classification model. For classification model, we can apply Support Vector Machine, K-NN, and Markov model.

From a machine learning perspective, it is customary to classify behavior as either anomalous or benign. However, behavior of a malevolent insider (i.e., insider threat) may not be immediately identified as malicious, and it should also have subtle differences from benign behavior. A traditional machine learning-based classification model is likely to classify the behavior of a malevolent insider as benign. It will be interesting to see whether a machine learning-based novel class detection technique [Masud et al., 2010-a] can detect the insider threat as a novel class and therefore trigger a warning.

The novel class detection technique will be applied on the huge amount of data that is being generated from user activities. Because these data have temporal properties and are produced continuously, they are usually referred to as data streams. The novel class detection model will be updated incrementally with the incoming data. This will allow us to keep the memory requirement within a constant limit, as the raw data will be discarded, but the characteristic or pattern of the behaviors will be summarized in the model. This incremental learning will also reduce the training time, as the model need not be built from the scratch with the new incoming data. Therefore, this incremental learning technique will be useful in achieving scalability.

We will examine the techniques that we have developed as well as other relevant techniques to modeling and anomaly detection. In particular, we propose to develop the following:

Tools that will analyze and model benign and anomalous missions
Techniques to identify right dimensions and activities and apply
    pruning to discard irrelevant dimensions
Techniques to cope with changes and novel class/anomaly detection

In a typical data stream classification task, it is assumed that the total number of classes is fixed. This assumption may not be valid in insider threat detection cases, where new classes may evolve. Traditional data stream classification techniques are not capable of recognizing novel class instances until the appearance of the novel class is manually identified, and labeled instances of that class are presented to the learning algorithm for training. The problem becomes more challenging in the presence of concept-drift, when the underlying data distribution changes over time. We have proposed a novel and efficient technique that can automatically detect the emergence of a novel class (i.e., brand new anomaly) by quantifying cohesion among unlabeled test instances and separating the test instances from training instances. Our goal is to use the available data and build this model.

One interesting aspect of this model is that it should capture the dynamic nature of dimensions of the mission, as well as filter out the noisy behaviors. The dimensions (both benign and anomalous) have a dynamic nature because they tend to change over time, which we denote as concept-drift. A major challenge of the novel class detection is to differentiate the novel class from concept-drift and noisy data. We are exploring this challenge in our current work.

22.4 Comprehensive Framework

As we have stated earlier, insider threat detection is an extremely challenging problem. In the previous section, we discussed our approach to handling this problem. Insider threat does not occur only at the application level; rather, it happens at all levels, including the operating system, database system, and the application. Furthermore, due to the fact that the insider will be continually changing patterns, it will be impossible to detect all types of malicious behavior using a purely static algorithm; a dynamic learning approach is required. Essentially we need a comprehensive solution to the insider threat problem. However, to provide a more comprehensive solution, we need a more comprehensive framework. Therefore, we are proposing a framework for insider threat detection. Our framework will implement a number of inter-related solutions to detect malicious insiders. Figure 22.4 illustrates such a framework. We propose four approaches to this problem. At the heart of our framework is the module that implements inline reference monitor-based techniques for feature collection. This feature collection process will be aided by two modules; one uses game theory approach and the other uses the natural language-based approach to determine which features can be collected. The fourth module implements machine learning techniques to analyze the collected features.

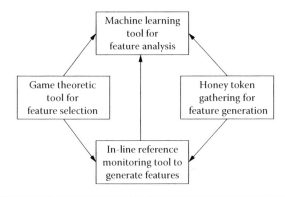

Figure 22.4 Framework for insider threat detection.

In summary, the relationship between the four approaches can be characterized as follows:

Inline Reference Monitors (IRM) perform covert, fine-grained feature collection.

Game-theoretic techniques will identify which features should be collected by the IRMs.

Natural language processing techniques in general and honey token generation in particular will take an active approach to introducing additional useful features (i.e., honey token accesses) that can be collected.

Machine learning techniques will use the collected features to infer and classify the objectives of malicious insiders.

Details of our framework are provided in [Hamlen et al., 2011]. We assume that the inline reference monitor tool, game-theoretic tool, and honey token generation tool will select and refine the features we need. Our data mining tools will analyze the features and determine whether there is a potential for insider threat.

22.5 Summary

In this chapter, we have discussed our approach to insider threat detection. We represent the insiders and their communication as RDF graphs and then query and mine the graphs to extract the nuggets. We also provided a comprehensive framework for insider threat detection.

The insider threat problem is a challenging one. Research is only beginning. The problem is that the insider may change his or her patterns and behaviors. Therefore, we need tools that can be adaptive. For example, our stream mining tools may be used for detecting such threats. We also need real-time data mining solutions. Some of the aspects of real-time data mining are discussed in Chapter 23.

References

[Ahmed and Khan, 2009] Ahmed, M. S., and L. Khan, SISC: A Text Classification Approach Using Semi Supervised Subspace Clustering, DDDM '09: The 3rd International Workshop on Domain Driven Data Mining in conjunction with ICDM 2009, December 6, 2009, Miami, Florida.

[Berry et al., 2007] Berry, M. W., M. Browne, A. Langville, V. P. Pauca, R. J. Plemmons, Algorithms and Applications for Approximate Nonnegative Matrix Factorization, *Computational Statistics & Data Analysis*, Vol. 52, No. 1, 2007, pp. 155–173.

[Carminati et al., 2009] Carminati, B., E. Ferrari, R. Heatherly, M. Kantarcioglu, B. Thuraisingham: A Semantic Web-Based Framework for Social Network Access Control, *Proceedings of the 14th ACM Symposium on Access Control Models and Technologies*. ACM, NY, pp. 177-186, 2009.

[Cook and Holder, 2006] Cook, D., and L. Holder, *Mining Graph Data*, Wiley Interscience, New York, 2006.

[Eberle and Holder, 2009] Eberle, W., and L. Holder, Applying Graph-Based Anomaly Detection Approaches to the Discovery of Insider Threats, *Proceedings of IEEE International Conference on Intelligence and Security Informatics (ISI)*, June 2009, pp. 206–208.

[Guo et al., 2005] Guo, Y., Z. Pan, J. Heflin, LUBM: A Benchmark for OWL Knowledge Base Systems, *Journal of Web Semantics*, Vol. 8, No. 2–3, 2005.

[Hadoop] Apache Hadoop, http://hadoop.apache.org/

[Hamlen et al., 2011] Hamlen, K., L. Khan, M. Kantarcioglu, V. Ng, B. Thuraisingham, Insider Threat Detection, UTD Report, April 2011.

[Masud et al., 2010-a] Masud, M., J. Gao, L. Khan, J. Han, B. Thuraisingham, Classification and Novel Class Detection in Concept-Drifting Data Streams under Time Constraints, *IEEE Transactions on Knowledge & Data Engineering (TKDE)*, April 2010, IEEE Computer Society, Vol. 23, No. 6, pp. 859–874.

[Masud et al., 2010-b] Masud, M., Q. Chen, J. Gao, L. Khan, J. Han, B. Thuraisingham, Classification and Novel Class Detection of Data Streams in a Dynamic Feature Space, in *Proceedings of European Conference on Machine Learning and Knowledge Discovery in Databases (ECML PKDD)*, Barcelona, Spain, September 20–24, 2010, Springer, 2010, pp. 337–352.

[Maybury et al., 2005] Maybury, M., P. Chase, B. Cheikes, D. Brackney, S. Matzner, T. Hetherington, et al., Analysis and Detection of Malicious Insiders, in *2005 International Conference on Intelligence Analysis*, McLean, VA.

[Mitchell, 1997] Mitchell, T., *Machine Learning*, McGraw-Hill, 1997.

[Thuraisingham et al., 2009] Thuraisingham B., M. Kantarcioglu, L. Khan: Building a Geosocial Semantic Web for Military Stabilization and Reconstruction Operations, Intelligence and Security Informatics, Pacific Asia Workshop, PAISI 2009, Bangkok, Thailand, April 27, 2009. Proceedings. *Lecture Notes in Computer Science* 5477 Springer 2009, H. Chen, C. C. Yang, M.Chau, S.-H. Li (Eds.):

[Tong, 2009] Tong, H., *Fast Algorithms for Querying and Mining Large Graphs*, CMU Report No. ML-09-112, September 2009.

23

DEPENDABLE REAL-TIME
DATA MINING

23.1 Introduction

Much of the focus on data mining has been for analytical applications. However, there is a clear need to mine data for applications that have to meet timing constraints. For example, a government agency may need to determine whether a terrorist activity will happen within a certain time or a financial institution may need to give out financial quotes and estimates within a certain time. That is, we need tools and techniques for real-time data mining. Consider, for example, a medical application where the surgeons and radiologists have to work together during an operation. Here, the radiologist has to analyze the images in real time and give inputs to the surgeon. In the case of military applications, images and video may arrive from the war zone. These images have to be analyzed in real time so that advice is given to the soldiers. The challenge is to determine which data to analyze and which data to discard for future analysis in non-real time. In the case of counter-terrorism applications, the system has to analyze the data about the passenger, from the time the passenger gets ticketed until the plane is boarded, and give proper advice to the security agent. For all of these applications, there is an urgent need for real-time data mining.

Thuraisingham et al. introduced the notion of real-time data mining in [Thuraisingham et al., 2001]. In that paper, we focused on mining multimedia data, which is an aspect of real-time data mining. Since then, there have been many developments in sensor data management as well as stream data mining. Furthermore, the need for real-time data mining is more apparent especially due to the need for counter-terrorism applications. In a later paper, we explored

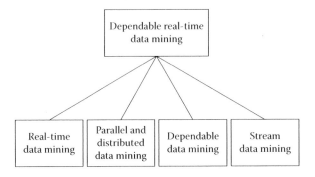

Figure 23.1   Concepts in this chapter.

some issues on real-time data mining [Thuraisingham et al., 2005]. In particular, we discussed the need for real-time data mining and also discussed dependability issues, including incorporating security, integrity, timeliness, and fault tolerance into data mining. In a later paper [Thuraisingham et al., 2009], we discussed real-time data mining for intelligence applications. In this chapter, we summarize the discussions in our prior papers.

The organization of this chapter is as follows. Some issues in real-time data mining, including real-time threats, are discussed in Section 23.2. Adapting data mining techniques to meet real-time constraints is described in Section 23.3. Parallel and distributed real-time data mining is discussed in Section 23.4. Techniques in dependable data mining that integrate security real-time processing and fault tolerance are given in Section 23.5. Stream data mining is discussed in Section 23.6. Summary and directions are provided in Section 23.7. Figure 23.1 illustrates the concepts discussed in this chapter.

23.2 Issues in Real-Time Data Mining

As stated in Section 23.1, data mining has typically been applied to non-real-time analytical applications. Many applications, especially for counter-terrorism and national security, need to handle real-time threats. Timing constraints characterize real-time threats. That is, such threats may occur within a certain time, and therefore we need to respond to them immediately. Examples of such threats include the spread of smallpox virus, chemical attacks, nuclear attacks, network intrusions, and bombing of a building. The question is what types of data mining techniques do we need for real-time threats?

Data mining can be applied to data accumulated over a period of time. The goal is to analyze the data, make deductions, and predict future trends. Ideally it is used as a decision support tool. However, the real-time situation is entirely different. We need to rethink the way we do data mining so that the tools can produce results in real time.

For data mining to work effectively, we need many examples and patterns. We observe known patterns and historical data and then make predictions. Often for real-time data mining, as well as terrorist attacks, we have no prior knowledge. So the question is how do we train the data mining tools based on, say, neural networks without historical data? Here we need to use hypothetical data as well as simulated data. We need to work with counter-terrorism specialists and get as many examples as possible. When we have gathered the examples and start training the neural networks and other data mining tools, the question becomes what sort of models do we build? Often the models for data mining are built beforehand. These models are not dynamic. To handle real-time threats, we need the models to change dynamically. This is a big challenge.

Data gathering is also a challenge for real-time data mining. In the case of non-real-time data mining, we can collect data, clean data, and format the data, build warehouses, and then carry out mining. All these tasks may not be possible for real-time data mining because of time constraints. Therefore, the questions are what tasks are critical and what tasks are not? Do we have time to analyze the data? Which data do we discard? How do we build profiles of terrorists for real-time data mining? How can we increase processing speed and overall efficiency? We need real-time data management capabilities for real-time data mining.

From the previous discussion, it is clear that a lot has to be done before we can perform real-time data mining. Some have argued that there is no such thing as real-time data mining and it will be impossible to build models in real time. Some others have argued that without accurate data, we cannot do effective data mining. These arguments may be true. However, others have predicted the impossibility of technology (e.g., air travel, Internet) that today we take for granted. Our challenge is to then perhaps redefine data mining and figure out ways to handle real-time threats.

As we have stated, there are several situations that have to be managed in real time. Examples are the spread of smallpox, network intrusions, and analyzing data sensor data. For example, surveillance cameras are placed in various places such as shopping centers and in front of embassies and other public places. Often the data from these sensors must be analyzed in real time to detect or prevent attacks. We discuss some of the research directions in the remaining sections. Figure 23.2 illustrates a concept of operation for real-time data management and mining where some data are discarded, other data are analyzed, and a third dataset is stored for future use. Figure 23.3 illustrates the cycle for real-time data mining.

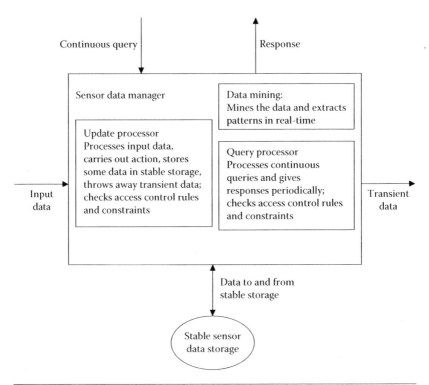

Figure 23.2 Concept of operation for real-time data management and data mining. (From B. Thuraisingham, L. Khan, C. Clifton, J. Mauer, M. Ceruti, *Dependable Real-Time Data Mining*, pp. 158–165, 2005 © IEEE. With permission.)

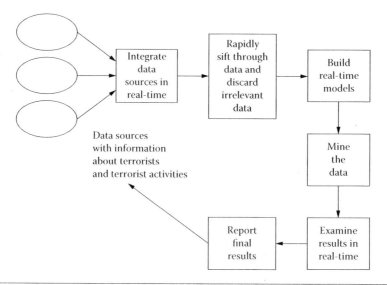

Figure 23.3 Real-time data mining cycle. (From B. Thuraisingham, L. Khan, C. Clifton, J. Mauer, M. Ceruti, *Dependable Real-Time Data Mining*, pp. 158–165, 2005 © IEEE. With permission.)

23.3 Real-Time Data Mining Techniques

In this section, we examine the various data mining outcomes and discuss how they could be applied for real-time applications. The outcomes include making associations, link analysis, cluster formation, classification, and anomaly detection. The techniques that result in these outcomes are based on neural networks, decisions trees, market basket analysis techniques, inductive logic programming, rough sets, link analysis based on the graph theory, and nearest neighbor techniques. As we have stated in [Thuraisingham, 2003], the methods used for data mining are top-down reasoning where we start with a hypothesis and then determine whether the hypothesis is true or bottom-up reasoning where we start with examples and then form a hypothesis.

Let us start with association mining techniques. Examples of these techniques include market basket analysis techniques [Agrawal et al., 1993]. The goal is to find which items go together. For example, we may apply a data mining tool to a dataset and find that John comes from country X and he has associated with James, who has a criminal record. The tool also outputs the result that an unusually large percentage of people from country X have performed some form of terrorist attack. Because of the associations between John and country X, as well as between John and James, and James and criminal records, one may conclude that John has to be under observation. This is an example of an association. Link analysis is closely associated with making associations. Whereas association rule-based techniques are essentially intelligent search techniques, link analysis uses graph-theoretic methods for detecting patterns. With graphs (i.e., nodes and links), one can follow the chain and find links. For example, A is seen with B and B is friends with C and C and D travel a lot together and D has a criminal record. The question is what conclusions can we draw about A? Now, for real-time applications, we need association rule mining and link analysis techniques that output the associations and links in real time.

Relevant research is in progress. Incremental association rule mining techniques were first proposed in [Cheung et al., 1996]. More recently, data stream techniques for mining association have been proposed [Chi et al., 2004]; these will be discussed further in Section 23.6. Whereas they address some of the issues faced by real-time data mining, the key issue of time-critical need for results has not been addressed. The real-time database researchers have developed various techniques, including real-time scheduling and approximate-query processing. We need to examine similar techniques for association rule mining and link analysis and determine the outcomes that can be determined in real time. Are we losing information by imposing real-time constraints? How can we minimize errors when we impose real-time constraints? Are approximate answers accurate enough to base decisions on them?

Next, let us consider clustering techniques. One could analyze the data and form various clusters. For example, people with origins from country X and who belong to a certain religion may be grouped into Cluster I. People with origins from country Y and who are less than 50 years old may form another cluster, Cluster II. These clusters could be formed based on their travel patterns, eating patterns, buying patterns, or behavior patterns. Whereas clustering techniques do not rely on any prespecified condition to divide the population, classification divides the population based on some predefined condition. The condition is found based on examples. For example, we can form a profile of a terrorist. He could have the following characteristics: male less than 30 years of a certain religion and of a certain ethnic origin. This means all males less than 30 years belonging to the same religion and the same ethnic origin will be classified into this group and possibly could be placed under observation. These examples of clustering and classification are for analytical applications. For real-time applications, the challenge is to find the important clusters in real time. Again, data stream techniques may provide a start. Another approach is iterative techniques. Classical clustering methods such as k-means and EM could refine answers based on the time available rather than terminating on distance-based criteria. The question is how much accuracy and precision are we sacrificing by imposing timing constraints?

Another data mining outcome is anomaly detection. A good example here is learning to fly an airplane without wanting to learn to take off or land. The general pattern is that people want to get a complete training course in flying. However, there are now some individuals who want to learn flying but do not care about take-off or landing. This is an anomaly. Another example is John always goes to the grocery store on Saturdays. But on Saturday, October 26, 2002, he goes to a firearms store and buys a rifle. This is an anomaly and may need some further analysis as to why he is going to a firearms store when he has never done so before. Is it because he is nervous after hearing about the sniper shootings, or is it because he has some ulterior motive? If he is living, say, in the Washington, DC, area, then one could understand why he wants to buy a firearm, possibly to protect himself. But if he is living in say Socorro, New Mexico, then his actions may have to be followed up further. Anomaly detection faces many challenges even if time constraints are ignored. Such an example is the approaches for Intrusion Detection (see [Lee and Fan, 2001] and [Axelsson, 1999] for surveys of the problem, and [Wang and Stolfo, 2004] for a recent discussion of anomaly detection approaches.) Adding real-time constraints will only exacerbate the difficulties. In many cases, the anomalies have to be detected in real time both for cyber security as well as for physical security. The technical challenge is to come up with meaningful anomalies as well as meet the timing constraints; however, a larger issue is to define

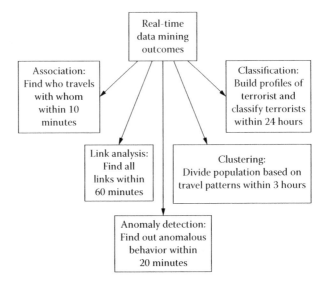

Figure 23.4   Real-time data mining outcomes. (From B. Thuraisingham, L. Khan, C. Clifton, J. Mauer, M. Ceruti, *Dependable Real-Time Data Mining*, pp. 158–165, 2005 © IEEE. With permission.)

the problems and surrounding systems to take advantage of anomaly detection methods in spite of the false positives and false negatives. Figure 23.4 illustrates examples of real-time data mining outcomes.

23.4 Parallel, Distributed, Real-Time Data Mining

For real-time data mining applications, perhaps a combination of techniques may prove most efficient. For example, association rule techniques could be applied either in series or in parallel with clustering techniques, which is illustrated in Figure 23.5. In series, the association rule technique may provide enough information to issue a real-time alert to a decision maker before having to invoke the clustering algorithms.

By using parallel processing software that executes on one or more hardware platforms with multiple processors, several real-time data mining techniques can be explored simultaneously rather than sequentially. Among the many ways to implement this, two basic categories emerge. First, one can execute real-time data mining programs simultaneously but on separate processors and input the results to a control program that compares the results to criteria or threshold values to issue alert reports to a decision maker.

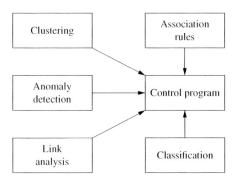

Figure 23.5 Data mining tasks executing in concert on separate platforms with direct link to the control program. (From B. Thuraisingham, L. Khan, C. Clifton, J. Mauer, M. Ceruti, *Dependable Real-Time Data Mining*, pp. 158–165, 2005 © IEEE. With permission.)

The second category is an architecture in which the programs execute in parallel, either on the same hardware platform or over a network, as depicted in Figure 23.6, where a central program would format and parse data inputs to the various processors running the programs to determine the different data mining outcomes. For example, when clusters start to form in the output of the cluster detection processor, these clusters could be compared to the associations found in the association rule processor. Similarly, the patterns formed by the link analysis processor could be input into the anomaly detector for examination to see if the pattern is the same or different from those expected. The various processors could all process the same data in different ways, or they could process data from different sources. The central control program could compare the results to the criteria or thresholds and issue alerts even before the slower algorithms have finished processing. The

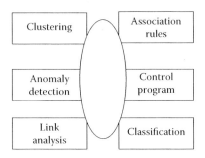

Figure 23.6 Distributed data mining tasks executing on a network. (From B. Thuraisingham, L. Khan, C. Clifton, J. Mauer, M. Ceruti, *Dependable Real-Time Data Mining*, pp. 158–165, 2005 © IEEE. With permission.)

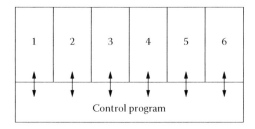

Figure 23.7 Data mining tasks executing on a parallel machine. (From B. Thuraisingham, L. Khan, C. Clifton, J. Mauer, M. Ceruti, *Dependable Real-Time Data Mining*, pp. 158–165, 2005 © IEEE. With permission.)

control program would continue to send newly emerging results to the decision maker while the response to the threat is in progress.

The method of parallel processing depicted in Figure 23.7 is potentially the fastest and most efficient method of real-time data mining because the software that implements every data mining outcome executes on the same hardware platform without any of the delays associated with communications networks, routers, and so forth. It is also the most versatile, challenging, and potentially best implement using artificial intelligence (AI) techniques for pattern recognition and algorithm coordination. These AI techniques could include rule-based reasoning, case-based reasoning, and Bayesian networks.

23.5 Dependable Data Mining

For a system to be dependable, it must be secure and fault tolerant, meet timing deadlines, and manage high-quality data. However, integrating these features into a system means that the system has to meet conflicting requirements determined by the policy makers and the applications specialists. For example, if the systems make all the access control checks, then it may miss some of its deadlines. The challenge in designing dependable systems is to design systems that are flexible. For example, in some situations it may be important to meet all the timing constraints, whereas in other situations it may be critical to satisfy all the security constraints.

The major components of dependable systems include dependable networks, dependable middleware (including infrastructures), dependable operating systems, dependable data managers, and dependable applications. Data mining, which can be regarded as an aspect of information and data management, has to be dependable as well. This means that the data mining algorithms have to have the ability to recover from faults, maintain security, and meet real-time constraints all in the same program.

Sensor data may be available in the form of streams. Special data management systems are needed to process stream data. For example, much of the data may be transient data. Therefore, the system has to analyze the data, discard unneeded data, and store the necessary data all in real time. Special query processing strategies, including query optimization techniques, are needed for data stream management. Many of the queries on stream data are continuous queries.

Aggregating the sensor data and making sense out of it is a major research challenge. The data may be incomplete or sometimes inaccurate. Many data prove to be irrelevant, thus increasing the noise of the detection-in-clutter task. We need the capability to deal with uncertainty and reason with incomplete data. Information management includes extracting knowledge and models from data as well as mining and visualizing the data. Much work has been accomplished in information management in recent years. For example, sensor data must be visualized for a better understanding of the data. We need to develop intelligent, real-time visualization tools for the sensor data. We may also need to aggregate the sensor data and possibly build repositories and warehouses. However, much of the sensor data may be transient. Therefore, we need to determine which data to store and which data to discard. Data may also have to be processed in real time. Some of the data may be stored and possibly warehoused and analyzed for conducting analysis and predicting trends. That is, the sensor data from surveillance cameras must be processed within a certain time. The data may also be warehoused for subsequent analysis.

Sensor and stream data mining are becoming important areas. We need to examine the data mining techniques such as association rule mining, clustering, and link analysis for sensor data and data streams from sensors and other devices. One important consideration is to select the level of granularity at which to mine the data. For example, should we mine raw sensor data or data processed at a higher level of aggregation? For example, patterns found in images are easily detected only when observed in the image context where the relation-ships between image features are preserved. These features are not recognized easily by analyzing a series of pixels from the image.

As we have stressed, we need to manage sensor data in real time. Therefore, we may need to mine the data in real time also. This means not only building models ahead of time, so that we can analyze the data in real time, but also possibly building models in real time. That is, the models have to be flexible and dynamic. Model formation rep-resents the aggregation of information at a very high level. This is a major challenge. As we have stated in Section 23.2, we also need many training examples to build models. For example, we need to mine sensor data to detect and possibly prevent terrorist attacks. This means that we need training examples to train the neural networks, classifiers, and other tools so that they can recognize in real time when a potential anomaly occurs. Sensor data mining is a fairly new research area, and we need a research program for sensor data man-agement and data mining. The mining of data streams is discussed in Section 23.6.

Data mining may be a solution to some dependability issues. Most data mining techniques generate aggregates over large quantities of data, averaging out random errors. Systematic errors pose a greater challenge, but as shown in [Agrawal and Srikant, 2000] and ran-domization approaches to privacy-preserving data mining, knowing something about the source of errors allows high-quality data min-ing even if we cannot reconstruct correct data. Many techniques are non-deterministic; the similarity or dissimilarity of results of repeated runs provides a measure of dependability. (This was used to minimize errors in anomaly detection in [Clifton, 2003].) Data mining has the potential to improve the dependability of decisions based on data, even if each datum taken separately is not dependable.

Data mining has also come under fire, perhaps unfairly, because of perceived impacts on privacy. Researchers are developing techniques for privacy-preserving data mining as well as for handling the infer-ence problem that occurs through data mining [Vaidya and Clifton, 2004]. Many real-time data mining problems involve sensitive data, and privacy will remain an issue. Many privacy-preserving data min-ing approaches come at a significant computational cost. We need to integrate security techniques with real-time data mining so that we can develop algorithms for dependable data mining. In particular, methods that trade security for time constraints may be appropriate for particular problems. A passenger trying to catch a plane may be willing to accept some loss of privacy in return for a faster "anomaly detection" check. However, information about people that is used to develop the data mining model (who have nothing to gain from the faster check) must not be disclosed. Such asymmetric privacy and security requirements raise new challenges.

23.6 Mining Data Streams

In recent years, advances in hardware technology have made it easy to store and record numerous transactions and activities in everyday life in an automated way. Such processes result in data that often grow without limit, referred to as data streams. Stream data could come from sensors, video, and other continuous media, including transactions. Some research has been performed on mining stream data. Several important problems recently have been explored in the data stream domain. Clustering, projected clustering, classification, and frequent pattern mining on data streams are a few examples.

Clustering is a form of data management that must be undertaken with considerable care and attention. The idea behind clustering is that a given set of data points can be organized into groups of similar objects through the use of a distance function. By defining similarity through a distance function, an entire data stream can be partitioned into groups of similar objects. Methods that do this view the problem of partitioning the data stream into object groups as an application of a one-pass clustering algorithm. This has some merit, but a more careful definition of the problem, with far better results, will view the data stream as an infinite process with data continually evolving over time. Consequently, a process is needed which can, *de novo* and continuously, establish dominant clusters apart from distortions introduced by the previous history of the stream. One way to accomplish this is to resize the dataset periodically to include new data sampling and processing from time to time. The operator could set parameters such as how to include old data processed along with the new, at what level of granularity and during what time period. It is important that past discoveries do not bias future searches that could miss newly formed (or rarely formed) clusters.

An interesting proposal for a two-component process for clustering data streams is found in [Aggarwal et al., 2003], where the components are an online micro-clustering process and an off-line macro-clustering process. The first of these, the online micro-clustering component, is based on a procedure for storing appropriate summary statistics in a fast data stream. This must be very efficient. The summary statistics consist of the sum and square of data values, and is a temporal extension of the cluster feature vector shown by BIRCH [Zhang et al., 1996]. With respect to the off-line component, user input is combined with the summary statistics to afford a rapid understanding of the clusters whenever this is required, and because this only utilizes the summary statistics, it is very efficient in practice.

Flexibility to consider the way in which the clusters evolve over time is a feature of this two-phased approach, as is an opportunity for users to develop insight into real applications. The question of how individual clusters are maintained online is discussed in [Aggarwal et al., 2004-b]. Using an iterative approach, the algorithm for high-dimensional clustering is able to determine continuously new cluster structures, while at the same time redefining the set of dimensions included in each cluster. A normalization process, with the aim of equalizing the standard deviation along each dimension, is used for the meaningful comparison of dimensions. As the data stream evolves over time, the values might be expected to change as well, making it necessary to re-compute the clusters and the normalization factor on a periodic basis. A period for this re-computation can be taken as an interval of a certain number of points.

For projected clustering on data streams, [Aggarwal et al., 2004-b] have proposed a method of high-dimensional, projected data stream clustering called "HPStream." HPStream relies upon an exploration of a linear update philosophy in projected clustering, achieving both high scalability and high clustering quality. Through HPStream, consistently high clustering quality can be achieved because of the program's adaptability to the nature of the real dataset, where data reveal their tight clustering behavior only in different subsets of dimension combinations.

For classification of data streams, [Aggarwal et al., 2004-a] propose data stream mining in the context of classification based on one-pass mining. Changes that have occurred in the model since the beginning of the stream construction process are not generally recognized in one-pass mining. However, the authors propose the exploitation of incremental updating of the classification model, which will not be greater than the best sliding window model on a data stream, thus creating micro-clusters for each class in the training stream. Such micro-clusters represent summary statistics of a set of data points from the training data belonging to the same class, similar to the clustering model in the off-line component [Aggarwal et al., 2003]. To classify the test stream in each instance, a nearest neighbor classification process is applied after identifying various time horizons and/or segments. When different time horizons determine different class labels, majority voting is applied.

With regard to frequent pattern mining on data stream, [Han et al., 2002] discuss algorithms at multiple time granularities. They first discuss the landmark model of Motwani and others [Datar et al., 2002] and argue that the landmark model considers a stream from start to finish. As a result, the model is not appropriate for time-sensitive data where the patterns such as video patterns, as well as transactions, may be sensitive to time. Therefore, they focus on data streams over certain intervals, depending on the time sensitivity, and describe algorithms for extracting frequent patterns in stream data. In particular, they consider three types of patterns: frequent patterns, sub-frequent patterns, and infrequent patterns. They argue that due to limited storage space with sensor devices, one cannot handle all kinds of patterns. Therefore, they focus on frequent patterns and sub-frequent patterns as the sub-frequent patterns could become frequent patterns over time. They illustrate tree-building algorithms, which essentially develop a structure that is a pattern tree with a time window. Such a structure is what they call an FP-stream. This technique essentially relies on the FP-streams.

Besides these, [Demers et al., 2004] use the notion of an information sphere that exists within an agency and focus on mining the multiple high-speed data streams within that agency. They also discuss the global information spheres that span across the agencies and focus on joining multiple data streams.

One major difference is noted between what we have called real-time data mining and the data stream mining defined by Han and others. In the case of real-time data mining, the goal is to mine the data and output results in real time. That is, the data mining algorithm must meet timing constraints and observe deadlines. In the case of stream mining, the goal is to find patterns over specified time intervals. That is, the patterns may be time sensitive, but the result may not necessarily lead to an urgent action on the part of a decision maker unless the pattern were to emerge in time to allow appropriate follow-up action. We can also see the similarities between the two notions. That is, while stream mining has to find patterns within a specified time interval, it may also imply that after the interval has passed, the patterns may not be of much value. That is, stream mining also has to meet timing constraints in addition to finding patterns with time-sensitive data. Essentially what we need is a taxonomy for real-time data mining that also includes stream mining. More detail on stream mining was discussed in Part VI.

23.7 Summary

In this chapter, we discussed dependability issues for data mining. Recently, much emphasis has been placed on data mining algorithms meeting timing constraints as well as mining time-sensitive data. For example, how much do we lose by imposing constraints on the data mining algorithms? In some situations, it is critical that analysis be completed and the results reported within a few seconds rather than, say, a few hours.

We first discussed issues of real-time data mining, and then we examined various data mining techniques such as associations and clustering and discussed how they may meet timing constraints. We also discussed issues of using parallel processing techniques and mining data streams. This is because streams come from sensor and video devices, and the patterns hidden in the streams may be time sensitive. We also discussed dependability issues for data mining.

Since we introduced the notion of real-time data mining in [Thuraisingham et al., 2001], much interest has emerged in the field. Many applications, including counter-terrorism and financial analysis, clearly need this type of data mining. This chapter has provided some initial directions. Many opportunities and challenges remain in real-time data mining.

References

[Aggarwal et al., 2003] Aggarwal, C., J. Han, J. Wang, P. S. Yu, A Framework for Clustering Evolving Data Streams, in *Proceedings of the 2003 International Conference on Very Large Data Bases (VLDB'03)*, Berlin, Germany, September 2003, pp. 81–92.

[Aggarwal et al., 2004-a] Aggarwal, C., J. Han, J. Wang, P. S. Yu, On Demand Classification of Data Streams, *Proceedings of the 2004 International Conference on Knowledge Discovery and Data Mining (KDD'04)*, Seattle, WA, August 2004, pp. 503–508.

[Aggarwal et al., 2004-b] Aggarwal, C., J. Han, J. Wang, P. S. Yu, A Framework for Projected Clustering of High Dimensional Data Streams, *Proceedings of the 2004 International Conference on Very Large Data Bases (VLDB'04)*, Toronto, Canada, August 2004, pp. 852–863.

[Agrawal et al., 1993] Agrawal, R., T. Imielinski, A. N. Swami, Mining Association Rules between Sets of Items in Large Databases, *Proceedings of the 1993 ACM SIGMOD International Conference on Management of Data*, Washington, DC, May 1993, pp. 207–216.

[Agrawal and Srikant, 2000] Agrawal, R., and R. Srikant, Privacy-Preserving Data Mining, *Proceedings of the 2000 ACM SIGMOD International Conference on Management of Data*, Dallas, TX, pp. 439–450.

[Axelsson, 1999] Axelsson, S., *Research in Intrusion Detection Systems: A Survey*, Technical Report 98-17 (revised in 1999), Chalmers University of Technology, 1999.

[Cheung et al., 1996] D. W. Cheung, J. Han, V. Ng, C. Y. Wong, Maintenance of Discovered Association Rules in Large Databases: An Incremental Updating Technique, in *Proceedings 1996 International Conference Data Engineering*, New Orleans, LA, February 1996, pp. 106–114.

[Chi et al., 2004] Chi, Y., H. Wang, P. Yu, R. Muntz, Moment: Maintaining Closed Frequent Itemsets over a Stream SlidingWindow, *Proceedings of the 4th IEEE International Conference on Data Mining, ICDM'04*, pp. 59–66.

[Clifton, 2003] Clifton, C., Change Detection in Overhead Imagery using Neural Networks, *International Journal of Applied Intelligence*, Vol. 18, No. 2, March 2003, pp. 215–234.

[Datar et al., 2002] Datar, M., A. Gionis, P. Indyk, R. Motwani, Maintaining Stream Statistics over Sliding Windows, *Proceedings of the 13th SIAM-ACM Symposium on Discrete Algorithms*, 2002.

[Demers, 2004] Demers, A., J. Gehrke, and M. Riedewald, Research Issues in Mining and Monitoring Intelligent Data, *Data Mining: Next Generation Challenges and Future Directions*, AAAI Press, 2004. (H. Kargupta et al. Eds.), pp. 2–46.

[Han et al., 2004] Han, J., J. Pei, Y. Yin, R. Mao, Mining Frequent Patterns without Candidate Generation: A Frequent-Pattern Tree Approach, *Data Mining and Knowledge Discovery*, Vol. 8, No. 1, 2004, pp. 53–87.

[Lee and Fan, 2001] Lee, W., and W. Fan, Mining System Audit Data: Opportunities and Challenges, *SIGMOD* Record, Vol. 30, No. 4, 2001, pp. 33–44.

[Thuraisingham et al., 2001] Thuraisingham, B., C. Clifton, M. Ceruti, J. Maurer, Real-Time Multimedia Data Mining, *Proceedings of the ISORC Conference*, Magdeberg, Germany, 2001.

[Thuraisingham, 2003] Thuraisingham, B., *Data Mining for Business Intelligence and Counter-Terrorism*, CRC Press, 2003.

[Thuraisingham et al., 2005] Thuraisingham B., L. Khan, C. Clifton, J. Maurer, M. Ceruti, Dependable Real-Time Data Mining, *ISORC*, 2005, pp. 158–165.

[Thuraisingham et al., 2009] Thuraisingham, B., L. Khan, M. Kantarcioglu, S. Chib, J. Han, S. Son, Real-Time Knowledge Discovery and Dissemination for Intelligence Analysis, *HICSS*, 2009, pp. 1–12.

[Vaidya and Clifton, 2004] Jaideep, V., and C. Clifton, Privacy-Preserving Data Mining: Why, How, and What For? *IEEE Security & Privacy*, New York, November/December, 2004.

[Wang and Stolfo 2004] Wang, K., S. J. Stolfo, Anomalous Payload-Based Network Intrusion Detection, Recent Advances in Intrusion Detection: 7th International Symposium, RAID 2004, Sophia Antipolis, France, September 15-17, 2004. Proceedings. *Lecture Notes in Computer Science* 3224 Springer 2004, E. Jonsson, A. Valdes, M. Almgren (Eds.), pp. 203–222.

[Zhang et al., 1996] Zhang, T., R. Ramakrishnan, M. Livny, BIRCH: An Efficient Data Clustering Method for Very Large Databases, *Proceedings of the 1996 ACM SIGMOD International Conference on Management of Data*, Montreal, Quebec, Canada, June 4–6, 1996. ACM Press 1996, H. V. Jagadish, I. S. Mumick (Eds.), pp. 103–114.

24

FIREWALL POLICY ANALYSIS

24.1 Introduction

A firewall is a system that acts as an interface of a network to one or more external networks and regulates the network traffic passing through it. The firewall decides which packets to allow through or to drop based on a set of "rules" defined by the administrator. These rules have to be defined and maintained with utmost care, as any slight mistake in defining the rules may allow unwanted traffic to enter or leave the network or may deny passage to legitimate traffic. Unfortunately, the process of manual definition of the rules and trying to detect mistakes in the rule set by inspection is prone to errors and is time consuming. Thus, research in the direction of detecting anomalies in firewall rules has gained momentum recently. Our work focuses on automating the process of detecting and resolving the anomalies in the rule set.

Firewall rules are usually in the form of criteria and an action to take if any packet matches the criteria. Actions are usually "accept" and "reject." A packet arriving at a firewall is tested with each rule sequentially. Whenever it matches with the criteria of a rule, the action specified in the rule is executed, and the rest of the rules are skipped. For this reason, firewall rules are order sensitive. When a packet matches with more than one rule, the first such rule is executed. Thus, if the set of packets matched by two rules are not disjoint, they will create anomalies. For instance, the set of packets matching a rule may be a superset of those matched by a subsequent rule. In this case, all the packets that the second rule could have matched will be matched and handled by the first one, and the second rule will never be executed. More complicated anomalies may arise when the sets of packets matched by two rules are overlapped. If no rule matches the packet,

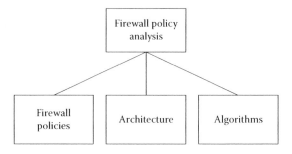

Figure 24.1 Concepts in this chapter.

then the default action of the firewall is taken. Usually such packets are dropped silently, so that nothing unwanted can enter or exit the network. In this chapter, we assume that the default action of the firewall system is to *reject*, and we develop our algorithms accordingly.

In this chapter, we describe our algorithms for resolving anomalies in firewall policy rules. The organization of the chapter is as follows. In Section 24.2, we discuss related work. In Section 24.3, we discuss the basic concepts of firewall systems, representation of rules in firewalls, possible relations between rules, and possible anomalies between rules in a firewall policy definition. In Section 24.4, we first present our algorithm for detecting and resolving anomalies and illustrate the algorithm with an example. Next, we present our algorithm to merge rules and provide an example of its application. The chapter is concluded in Section 24.5. Figure 24.1 illustrates the concepts in this chapter.

24.2 Related Work

Of late, research work on detecting and resolving anomalies in firewall policy rules have gained momentum. [Mayer et al., 2000] presents tools for analyzing firewalls. [Eronen and Zitting, 2001] propose the approach of representing the rules as a knowledge base and present a tool based on *Constraint Logic Programming* to allow the user to write higher level operations and queries. Work focusing on automating the process of detecting anomalies in policy include [Hazelhurst, 1999], in which Hazelhurst describes an algorithm to represent the rules as a *Binary Decision Diagram* and presents a set of algorithms to analyze the rules. [Eppstein and Muthukrishnan, 2001] give an efficient algorithm for determining whether a rule set contains conflicts. Al-Shaer et al. define the possible relations between firewall rules in [Al-Shaer and Hamed, 2002, 2003, 2006], and then define anomalies that can occur in a rule set in terms of these definitions. They also give an algorithm to detect these anomalies and present policy advisor tools using these definitions and algorithm. They extend their work to distributed firewall systems in [Al-Shaer and Hamed, 2004], [Al-Shaer et al., 2005]. A work that focuses on detecting and resolving anomalies in firewall policy rules is [Hari et al., 2000], in which they propose a scheme for resolving conflicts by adding resolve filters. However, this algorithm requires the support of prioritized rules, which is not always available in firewalls. Also their treatment of the criterion values only as prefixes makes their work specific. [Fu et al., 2001] define high-level security requirements and develop mechanisms to detect and resolve conflicts among IPSec policies. [Golnabi et al., 2006] describe a data mining approach to the anomaly resolution.

Most current research focuses on the analysis and detection of anomalies in rules. Those that do address the resolution of anomalies require special features or provisions from the firewall or focus on specific areas. We base our work on the research of [Al-Shaer et al., 2002, 2003, 2004], whose analysis is applicable to all rule-based firewalls in general. However, their work is limited to the detection of anomalies. We also show that one of their definitions is redundant, and the set of definitions do not cover all possibilities. In our work, we remove the redundant definition and modify one definition to cover all the possible relations between rules. We also describe the anomalies in terms of the modified definitions. Then we present a set of algorithms to simultaneously detect and resolve these anomalies to produce an anomaly-free rule set. We also present an algorithm to merge rules whenever possible. Reports are also produced by the algorithms describing the anomalies that were found, how they were resolved, and which rules were merged.

24.3 Firewall Concepts

In this section, we first discuss the basic concepts of firewall systems and their policy definition. We present our modified definitions of

```
1: TCP,INPUT,129.110.96.117,ANY,*.*.*.*,80,DENY
2: TCP,INPUT,*.*.*.*,ANY,*.*.*.*,80,ACCEPT
3: TCP,INPUT,*.*.*.*,ANY,*.*.*.*,443,DENY
4: TCP,INPUT,129.110.96.117,ANY,*.*.*.*,22,DENY
5: TCP,INPUT,*.*.*.*,ANY,*.*.*.*,22,ACCEPT
6: TCP,OUTPUT,129.110.96.80,ANY,*.*.*.*,22,DENY
7: UDP,OUTPUT,*.*.*.*,ANY,*.*.*.*,53,ACCEPT
8: UDP,INPUT,*.*.*.*,53,*.*.*.*,ANY,ACCEPT
9: UDP,OUTPUT,*.*.*.*,ANY,*.*.*.*,ANY,DENY
10: UDP,INPUT,*.*.*.*,ANY,*.*.*.*,ANY,DENY
11: TCP,INPUT,129.110.96.117,ANY,129.110.96.80,22,DENY
12: TCP,INPUT,129.110.96.117,ANY,129.110.96.80,80,DENY
13: UDP,INPUT,*.*.*.*,ANY,129.110.96.80,ANY,DENY
14: UDP,OUTPUT,129.110.96.80,ANY,129.110.10.*,ANY,DENY
15: TCP,INPUT,*.*.*.*,ANY,129.110.96.80,22,ACCEPT
16: TCP,INPUT,*.*.*.*,ANY,129.110.96.80,80,ACCEPT
17: UDP,INPUT,129.110.*.*,53,129.110.96.80,ANY,ACCEPT
18: UDP,OUTPUT,129.110.96.80,ANY,129.110.*.*,53,ACCEPT
```

Rule 1, Rule 2: ==> GENERALIZATION
Rule 1, Rule 16: ==> CORRELATED
Rule 2, Rule 12: ==> SHADOWED
Rule 4, Rule 5: ==> GENERALIZATION
Rule 4, Rule 15: ==> CORRELATED
Rule 5, Rule 11: ==> SHADOWED

Figure 24.2   Firewall policy rules.

the relationships between the rules in a firewall policy, and then present the anomalies as described in [Al-Shaer and Hamed, 2002]. Figure 24.2 illustrates the concepts in this section.

24.3.1 Representation of Rules

A rule is defined as a set of criteria and an action to perform when a packet matches the criteria. The criteria of a rule consist of the elements direction, protocol, source IP, source port, destination IP, and destination port. Therefore, a complete rule may be defined by the ordered tuple _direction, protocol, source IP, source port, destination IP, destination port, action_. Each attribute can be defined as a range of values, which can be represented and analyzed as sets.

24.3.2 Relationship between Two Rules

The relation between two rules essentially means the relation between the set of packets they match. Thus, the action field does not come into play when considering the relation between two rules. Because the values of the other attributes of firewall rules can be represented as sets, we can consider a rule to be a set of sets, and we can compare two rules using the set relations. Two rules can be exactly equal if every criterion in the rules matches exactly; one rule can be the subset of the other if each criterion of one rule is a subset of, or equal to, the other rule's criteria; or they can be overlapped if the rules are not disjoint and at least one of the criteria is overlapped. In the last case, a rule would match a portion of the packets matched by the other but not every packet, and the other rule would also match a portion of packets matched by the first rule, but not all. Al-Shaer et al. discuss these possible relations in [Al-Shaer and Hamed, 2002] and they define the relations *completely disjoint, exactly matched, inclusively matched, partially disjoint* and *correlated*. We propose some modifications to the relations defined in [Al-Shaer and Hamed, 2002]. First, we note that it is not needed to distinguish between *completely disjoint* and *partially disjoint* rules, as two rules will match an entirely different set of packets if they differ, even only in one field. Further, we observe that the formal definition of *correlated* rules does not include the possibility of an overlapped field in which the fields are neither disjoint nor a subset of one or the other. We propose the following modified set of relations between the rules.

Disjoint. Two rules r and s are disjoint, denoted as $r\,R_D\,s$, if they have at least one criterion for which they have completely disjoint values. Formally, $r\,R_D\,s$ if $\exists a \in attr[r.a \cap s.a = \varphi]$.

Exactly Matching. Two rules r and s are exactly matched, denoted by $r\,R_{EM}\,s$, if each criterion of the rules matches exactly. Formally, $r\,R_{EM}\,s$ if $\exists a \in attr[r.a = s.a]$.

Inclusively Matching. A rule r is a subset, or inclusively matched of another rule s, denoted by $r\,R_{EM}\,s$, if there exists at least one criterion for which r's value is a subset of s's value and for the rest of the attributes r's value is equal to s's value. Formally, $r\,R_{EM}\,s$ if $\exists a \subset attr\,[a \neq \varphi \wedge \forall x \in a\,[r.x \subset s.x] \wedge \forall y \in a\,c\,[r.y = s.y]]$.

Correlated. Two rules r and s are correlated, denoted by $r\,R_C\,s$, if r and s are not disjoint, but neither is the subset of the other. Formally, $r\,R_C\,s$ if $(r\,R_D\,s) \wedge (r\,R_{IM}\,s) \wedge (s\,R_{IM}\,r)$.

24.3.3 Possible Anomalies between Two Rules

[Al-Shaer and Hamed, 2002] give formal definitions of the possible anomalies between rules in terms of the relations defined in [Al-Shaer and Hamed, 2002]. Of these anomalies, we consider *generalization* not to be an anomaly, as it is used in practice to handle a specific group of addresses within a larger group, and as such we omit it from our consideration. Here, we define the anomalies in terms of the relations given earlier.

Shadowing Anomaly. A rule r is shadowed by another rule s if s precedes r in the policy, and s can match all the packets matched by r. The effect is that r is never activated. Formally, rule r is shadowed by s if s precedes r, $r\,R_{EM}\,s$, and $r.action \neq s.action$, or s precedes r, $r\,R_{IM}\,s$, and $r.action \neq s.action$.

Correlation Anomaly. Two rules r and s are correlated if they have different filtering actions and the r matches some packets that match s and the s matches some packets that r matches. Formally, rules r and s have a correlation anomaly if $r\,R_C\,s$, $r.action \neq s.action$.

Redundancy Anomaly. A redundant rule r performs the same action on the same packets as another rule s such that if r is removed, the security policy will not be affected. Formally, rule r is redundant of rule s if s precedes r, $r\,R_{EM}\,s$, and $r.action = s.action$, or s precedes r, $r\,R_{IM}\,s$, and $r.action = s.action$; whereas rule s is redundant to rule r if s precedes r, $s\,R_{IM}\,r$, $r.action = s.action$ and $\lceil \exists t$ where s precedes t and t precedes r, $s\{R_{IM}, R_C\}t$, $r.action \neq t.action$.

24.4 Anomaly Resolution Algorithms

This section describes the algorithms to detect and resolve the anomalies present in a set of firewall rules as defined in the previous section. The algorithm is in two parts. The first part analyzes the rules and generates a set of disjoint firewall rules that do not contain any anomaly. The second part analyzes the set of rules and tries to merge the rules in order to reduce the number of rules thus generated without introducing any new anomaly. Figure 24.3 illustrates the flow of firewall policy analysis algorithms discussed in this section.

24.4.1 Algorithms for Finding and Resolving Anomalies

In this section, we present our algorithm to detect and resolve anomalies. In this algorithm, we resolve the anomalies as follows: In case

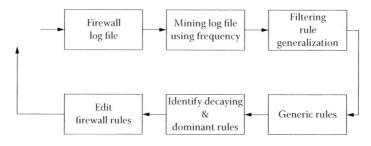

Figure 24.3   Flow of firewall policy analysis algorithms.

of *shadowing anomaly*, when rules are *exactly matched*, we keep the one with the reject action. When the rules are *inclusively matched*, we reorder the rules to bring the subset rule before the superset rule. In case of *correlation anomaly*, we break down the rules into disjoint parts and insert them into the list. Of the part that is common to the correlated rules, we keep the one with the reject action. In case of *redundancy anomaly*, we remove the redundant rule. In our algorithm, we maintain two global lists of firewall rules: an *old rules list* and a *new rules list*. The old rules list will contain the rules as they are in the original firewall configuration, and the new rules list will contain the output of the algorithm, a set of firewall rules without any anomaly. The approach taken here is incremental; we take each rule in the *old rules list* and insert it into the *new rules list* in such a way that the new rules list remains free from anomalies. Algorithm Resolve-Anomalies controls the whole process. After initializing the global lists in lines 1 and 2, it takes each rule from the *old rules list* and invokes algorithm Insert on it in lines 3 to 4. Then, it scans the *new rules list* to resolve any redundancy anomalies that might remain in the list in lines 5 to 10 by looking for and removing any rule that is a subset of a subsequent rule with same action.

Algorithm Insert inserts a rule into the *new rules list* in such a way that the list remains anomaly free. If the list is empty, the rule is unconditionally inserted in line 2. Otherwise, Insert tests the rule with all the rules in *new rules list* using the Resolve algorithm in the "for" loop in line 5. If the rule conflicts with any rule in the list, Resolve will handle it and return *true*, breaking the loop. So, at line 10, if *insert flag* is *true*, it means that Resolve has already handled the rule. Otherwise, the rule is disjoint or superset with all the rules in *new rules list*, and it is inserted at the end of the list in line 11.

Algorithm: Resolve-Anomalies

Resolve anomalies in firewall rules file

1. *old rules list* ← read rules from config file
2. *new rules list* ← empty list
3. **for all** $r \in$ *old rules list* **do**
4. Insert(r, *new rules list*)
5. **for all** $r \in$ *new rules list* **do**
6. **for all** $s \in$ *new rules list* after r **do**
7. **if** $r \subset s$ **then**
8. **if** *r.action* = *s.action* **then**
9. Remove r from *new rules list*
10. **break**

Algorithm: Insert(*r,new rules list*)

Insert the rule r into *new rules list*

1. **if** *new rules list* is empty **then**
2. insert r into *new rules list*
3. **else**
4. *inserted* ← *false*
5. for all $s \in$ *new rules list* **do**
6. **if** r and s are not disjoint **then**
7. *inserted* ← Resolve(r, s)
8. **if** *inserted* = *true* **then**
9. **break**
10. **if** *inserted* = *false* **then**
11. Insert r into *new rules list*

The algorithm Resolve is used to detect and resolve anomalies between two non-disjoint rules. This algorithm is used by the Insert algorithm. The first rule passed to Resolve, r, is the rule being inserted, and the second parameter, s, is a rule already in the *new rules list*. In comparing them, the following are the possibilities:

1. r and s *are equal.* If they are equal, and their actions are same, then any one can be discarded. If the actions are different, then the one with the *reject* action is retained. This case is handled in lines 1 to 6.

2. r *is a subset of* s. In this case, we simply insert r before s regardless of the action. This case is handled in lines 7 to 9.

3. r *is a superset of* s. In this case, r may match with rules further down the list, so it is allowed to be checked further. No operation is performed in this case. This case is handled in lines 10 to 11.

4. r *and* s *are correlated.* In this case, we need to break up the correlated rules into disjoint rules. This case is handled in lines 12 to 19. First the set of attributes in which the two rules differ is determined in line 13, and then Split is invoked for each of the differing attributes in the "for" loop in line 14. After Split returns, r and s contain the common part of the rules, which is then inserted.

Algorithm: Resolve(r, s)

Resolve anomalies between two rules r and s

    1. **if** $r = s$ **then**
    2. **if** r.action $\neq$ $s.action$ **then**
    3. set $s.action$ to REJECT and report anomaly
    4. **else**
    5. report removal of r
    6. **return** *true*
    7. **if** $r \subset s$ **then**
    8. insert r before s into *new rules list* and report reordering
    9. **return** *true*
    10. **if** $s \subset r$ **then**
    11. **return** *false*
    12. Remove s from *new rules list*
    13. Find set of attributes $a = \{x | r.x \neq s.x\}$
    14. **for all** $ai \in a$ **do**
    15. Split(r, s, ai)

16. **if** *r.action* ≠ *s.action* **then**
17. *s.action* ← REJECT
18. Insert(*s, new rules list*)
19. **return** *true*

Algorithm Split is used to split two non-disjoint rules. It is passed through the two rules and the attribute on which the rules differ. It first extracts the parts of the rules that are disjoint to the two rules and invokes the Insert algorithm on them. Then it computes the common part of the two rules. Let *r* and *s* be two rules and let *a* be the attribute for which Split is invoked. The common part will always start with max(r.a.start, s.a.start) and end with min(r.a.end, s.a.end). The disjoint part before the common part begins with min(r.a.start, s.a.start) and ends with max(r.a.start, s.a.start) – 1, and the disjoint part after the common part starts with min(r.a.end, s.a.end) + 1 and ends with max(r.a.end, s.a.end). As these two parts are disjoint with *r* and *s*, but we do not know their relation with the other rules in the new rules list, they are inserted into the new rules list by invoking the Insert procedure. The common part of the two rules is computed in lines 13 and 14. The disjoint part before the common part is computed and inserted in lines 5 to 8. The disjoint part after the common part is computed and inserted in lines 9 to 12.

Algorithm: Split(*r,s,a*)

Split overlapping rules *r* and *s* based on attribute *a*

1. *left* ← min(*r.a.start, s.a.start*)
2. *right* ← max(*r.a.end, s.a.end*)
3. *common start* ← max(*r.a.start, s.a.start*)
4. *common end* ← min(*r.a.end, s.a.end*)
5. **if** *r.a.start* > *s.a.start* **then**
6. Insert(((*left, common start*–1), rest of *s*'s attributes), *new rules list*)
7. **else if** *r.a.start* < *s.a.start* **then**
8. Insert(((*left, common start–1*), rest of *r*'s attributes), *new rules list*)
9. **if** *r.a.end* > *s.a.end* **then**
10. Insert(((*common end*+1, *right*), rest of *r*'s attributes), *new rules list*)

11. **else if** *r.a.end* < *s.a.end* **then**
12. Insert(((*common end*+1, *right*), rest of *s*'s attributes), *new rules list*)
13. *r* ← ((*common start*, *common end*), rest of *r*'s attributes)
14. *s* ← ((*common start*, *common end*), rest of *s*'s attributes)

After completion of the Resolve-Anomalies algorithm, the *new rules list* will contain the list of firewall rules that are free from all the anomalies in consideration.

24.4.1.1 Illustrative Example Let us consider the following set of firewall rules for analysis with the algorithm.

1. (IN, TCP, 129.110.96.117, ANY, ANY, 80, REJECT)
2. (IN, TCP, 129.110.96.*, ANY, ANY, 80, ACCEPT)
3. (IN, TCP, ANY, ANY, 129.110.96.80, 80, ACCEPT)
4. (IN, TCP, 129.110.96.*, ANY, 129.110.96.80, 80, REJECT)
5. (OUT, TCP, 129.110.96.80, 22, ANY, ANY, REJECT)
6. (IN, TCP, 129.110.96.117, ANY, 129.110.96.80, 22, REJECT)
7. (IN, UDP, 129.110.96.117, ANY, 129.110.96.*, 22, REJECT)
8. (IN, UDP, 129.110.96.117, ANY, 129.110.96.80, 22, REJECT)
9. (IN, UDP, 129.110.96.117, ANY, 129.110.96.117, 22, ACCEPT)
10.(IN, UDP, 129.110.96.117, ANY, 129.110.96.117, 22, REJECT)
11. (OUT, UDP, ANY, ANY, ANY, ANY, REJECT)

Step 1. As the *new rules list* is empty, rule 1 is inserted as it is.
Step 2. When rule 2 is inserted, the *new rules list* contains only one rule, the one that was inserted in the previous step. We have, *r* = (IN, TCP, 129.110.96.*, ANY, ANY, 80, ACCEPT) and *s* = (IN, TCP, 129.110.96.117, ANY, ANY, 80, REJECT).

Here, *s* ⊂ *r*, so *r* is inserted into *new rules list* after *s*.

Step 3. In this step, *r* = (IN, TCP, ANY, ANY, 129.110.96.80, 80, ACCEPT). In the first iteration, *s* = (IN,TCP,129.110.96.117, ANY,ANY,80,REJECT).

Clearly these two rules are correlated, with *s.srcip* ⊂ *r.srcip* and *r.destip* ⊂ *s.destip*. Therefore, these rules must be broken down. After splitting the rules into disjoint parts, we have the following rules in the *new rules list*:

1. (IN, TCP, 129.110.96.1-116, ANY, 129.110.96.80, 80, ACCEPT)
2. (IN, TCP, 129.110.96.118-254, ANY, 129.110.96.80, 80, ACCEPT)
3. (IN, TCP, 129.110.96.117, ANY, 129.110.96.1-79, 80, REJECT)
4. (IN, TCP, 129.110.96.117, ANY, 129.110.96.81-254, 80, REJECT)
5. (IN, TCP, 129.110.96.117, ANY, 129.110.96.80, 80, REJECT)
6. (IN, TCP, 129.110.96.*, ANY, ANY, 80, ACCEPT)

After completion of the first "for" loop in line 3 in the algorithm Resolve-Anomalies, the *new rules list* will hold the following rules:

1. (IN, TCP, 129.110.96.1-116, ANY, 129.110.96.80, 80, ACCEPT)
2. (IN, TCP, 129.110.96.118-254, ANY, 129.110.96.80, 80, ACCEPT)
3. (IN, TCP, 129.110.96.117, ANY, 129.110.96.1-79, 80, REJECT)
4. (IN, TCP, 129.110.96.117, ANY, 129.110.96.81-254, 80, REJECT)
5. (IN, TCP, 129.110.96.117, ANY, 129.110.96.80, 80, REJECT)
6. (IN, TCP, 129.110.96.*, ANY, 129.110.96.80, 80, REJECT)
7. (IN, TCP, 129.110.96.*, ANY, ANY, 80, ACCEPT)
8. (OUT, TCP, 129.110.96.80, 22, ANY, ANY, REJECT)
9. (IN, TCP, 129.110.96.117, ANY, 129.110.96.80, 22, REJECT)
10. (IN, UDP, 129.110.96.117, ANY, 129.110.96.80, 22, REJECT)
11. (IN, UDP, 129.110.96.117, ANY, 129.110.96.117, 22, REJECT)
12. (IN, UDP, 129.110.96.117, ANY, 129.110.96.*, 22, REJECT)
13. (OUT, UDP, ANY, ANY, ANY, ANY, REJECT)

The next step is to scan this list to find and resolve the redundancy anomalies. In this list, rule 1 is a subset of rule 6, but as the rules have different action, rule 1 is retained. Similarly, rule 2, which is also a subset of rule 6 with differing action, is also retained. Rules 3 and 4 are subsets of rule 7, but are retained as they have different action than rule 7. Rule 5 is a subset of rule 6, and as they have the same action, rule 5 is removed. After removing these rules, the list is free from all the anomalies.

24.4.2 Algorithms for Merging Rules

After the completion of the anomaly resolution algorithm, there are no correlated rules in the list. In this list, we can merge rules having attributes with consecutive ranges with the same action. To accomplish this, we construct a tree using Algorithm TreeInsert. Each node of the tree represents an attribute. The edges leading out of the nodes represent values of the attribute. Each edge in the tree represents a particular range of value for the attribute of the source node, and it points to a node for the next attribute in the rule represented by the path. For example, the root node of the tree represents the attribute *Direction*, and there can be two edges out of the root representing *IN* and *OUT*. We consider a firewall rule to be represented by the ordered tuple, as mentioned in Section 24.3. So, the edge representing the value *IN* coming out of the root node would point to a node for *Protocol*. The leaf nodes always represent the attribute *Action*. A complete path from the root to a leaf corresponds to one firewall rule in the policy.

Algorithm TreeInsert takes as input a rule and a node of the tree. It checks if the value of the rule for the attribute represented by the node matches any of the values of the edges out of the node. If it matches any edge of the node, then it recursively invokes TreeInsert on the node pointed by the edge with the rule. Otherwise, it creates a new edge and adds it to the list of edges of the node.

Algorithm: TreeInsert(n, r)

Inserts rule r into the node n of the rule tree

    1. **for all** *edge ei* $\in$ *n.edges* **do**
    2. **if** $r.(n.attribute)$ = *ei.range* **then**
    3. TreeInsert(*ei.vertex*, r)
    4. **return**

5. $v \leftarrow$ new Vertex(next attribute after *n.attribute*, NULL)
6. Insert new edge _*r.*(*n.attribute*), *r.*(*n.attribute*), v _ in *n.edges*
7. TreeInsert(v, r)

We use Algorithm Merge on the tree to merge those edges of the tree that have consecutive values of attributes and have exactly matching subtrees. It first calls itself recursively on each of its children in line 2 to ensure that their subtrees are already merged. Then, it takes each edge and matches its range with all the other edges to see if they can be merged. Whether two edges can be merged depends on two criteria. First, their ranges must be contiguous; that is, the range of one starts immediately after the end of the other. Second, the subtrees of the nodes pointed to by the edges must match exactly. This criterion ensures that all the attributes after this attribute are the same for all the rules below this node. If these two criteria are met, they are merged into one edge in place of the original two edges. After merging the possible rules, the number of rules defined in the firewall policy is reduced, and it helps to increase the efficiency of firewall policy management.

Algorithm: Merge(*n*)

Merges edges of node *n* representing a continuous range

1. **for all** *edge e* $\in$ *n.edges* **do**
2. Merge(*e.node*)
3. **for all** *edge e* $\in$ *n.edges* **do**
4. **for all** *edge e'* $\neq$ *e* $\in$ *n.edges* **do**
5. **if** ranges of *e* and *e'* are *contiguous* and Subtree(*e*)=Subtree(*e'*) **then**
6. Merge *e.range* and *e'.range* into *e.range*
7. Remove *e'* from *n.edges*

24.4.2.1 Illustrative Example of the Merge Algorithm   To illustrate the merging algorithm, we start with the following set of non-anomalous rules. We deliberately chose a set of rules with the same action since rules with a different action will never be merged.

1. (IN, TCP, 202.80.169.29-63, 483, 129.110.96.64-127, 100-110, ACCEPT)
2. (IN, TCP, 202.80.169.29-63, 483, 129.110.96.64-127, 111-127, ACCEPT)
3. (IN, TCP, 202.80.169.29-63, 483, 129.110.96.128-164, 100-127, ACCEPT)
4. (IN, TCP, 202.80.169.29-63, 484, 129.110.96.64-99, 100-127, ACCEPT)
5. (IN, TCP, 202.80.169.29-63, 484, 129.110.96.100-164, 100-127, ACCEPT)
6. (IN, TCP, 202.80.169.64-110, 483-484, 129.110.96.64-164, 100-127, ACCEPT)

From this rules list we generate the tree by the TreeInsert algorithm. On this tree, the Merge procedure is run. The Merge algorithm traverses the tree in post order. After the Merge algorithm is complete on the entire tree, we are left with the single rule:

(IN, TCP, 202.80.169.29-110, 483-484, 129.110.96.64-164, 100-127, ACCEPT).

Details of the example are given in [Abedin et al., 2006].

24.5 Summary

Resolution of anomalies from firewall policy rules is vital to the network's security, as anomalies can introduce unwarranted and hard-to-find security holes. Our work presents an automated process for detecting and resolving such anomalies. The anomaly resolution algorithm and the merging algorithm should produce a compact yet anomaly-free rule set that would be easier to understand and maintain. These algorithms can also be integrated into policy advisor and editing tools. This work also establishes the complete definition and analysis of the relations between rules.

In the future, this analysis can be extended to distributed firewalls. Also, we propose to use data mining techniques to analyze the log files of the firewall and discover other kinds of anomalies. These techniques should be applied only after the rules have been made free from anomaly by applying the algorithms in this chapter. That way it would be ensured that not only syntactic but also semantic mistakes in the rules will be captured. Research in this direction has already started.

References

[Abedin et al., 2006] Abedin, M., S. Nessa, L. Khan, B. Thuraisingham, Detection and Resolution of Anomalies in Firewall Policy Rules, *DBSec* 2006, pp. 15–29.

[Al-Shaer and Hamed, 2002] Al-Shaer, E., and H. Hamed, *Design and Implementation of Firewall Policy Advisor Tools*, Technical Report CTI-techrep0801, School of Computer Science Telecommunications and Information Systems, DePaul University, August 2002.

[Al-Shaer and Hamed, 2003] Al-Shaer, E., and H. Hamed, Firewall Policy Advisor for Anomaly Detection and Rule Editing, in *IEEE/IFIP Integrated Management Conference (IM'2003)*, March 2003, pp. 17–30.

[Al-Shaer and Hamed, 2004] Al-Shaer, E., and H. Hamed, Discovery of Policy Anomalies in Distributed Firewalls, in *Proceedings of the 23rd Conference IEEE Communications Society (INFOCOM 2004)*, Vol. 23, No. 1, March 2004, pp. 2605–2616.

[Al-Shaer and Hamed, 2006] Al-Shaer, E., and H. Hamed, Taxonomy of Conflicts in Network Security Policies, *IEEE Communications Magazine*, Vol. 44, No. 3, March 2006, pp. 134–141.

[Al-Shaer et al., 2005] Al-Shaer, E., H. Hamed, R. Boutaba, M. Hasan, Conflict Classification and Analysis of Distributed Firewall Policies, *IEEE Journal on Selected Areas in Communications (JSAC)*, Vol. 23, No. 10, October 2005, pp. 2069–2084.

[Eppstein and Muthukrishnan, 2001] Eppstein, D., and S. Muthukrishnan, Internet Packet Filter Management and Rectangle Geometry, in *Proceedings of the 12th Annual ACM–SIAM Symposium on Discrete Algorithms (SODA 2001)*, January 2001, pp. 827–835.

[Eronen and Zitting, 2001] Eronen, P., and J. Zitting, An Expert System for Analyzing Firewall Rules, in *Proceedings of the 6th Nordic Workshop on Secure IT Systems (NordSec 2001)*, November 2001, pp. 100–107.

[Fu et al., 2001] Fu, Z., S. F. Wu, H. Huang, K. Loh, F. Gong, I. Baldine, C. Xu, IPSec/VPN Security Policy: Correctness, Conflict Detection, and Resolution, *Proceedings of the Policy 2001 Workshop*, January 2001, pp. 39–56.

[Golnabi et al., 2006] Golnabi, K., R. K. Min, L. Khan, E. Al-Shaer, Analysis of Firewall Policy Rules Using Data Mining Techniques, in *IEEE/IFIP Network Operations and Management Symposium (NOMS 2006)*, April 2006, pp. 305–315.

[Hari et al., 2000] Hari, A., S. Suri, G. M. Parulkar, Detecting and Resolving Packet Filter Conflicts, in *INFOCOM*, Vol. 3, March 2000, pp. 1203–1212.

[Hazelhurst, 1999] Hazelhurst, S., *Algorithms for Analysing Firewall and Router Access Lists,* Technical Report TR-WitsCS-1999-5, Department of Computer Science, University of the Witwatersrand, South Africa, July 1999.

[Mayer et al., 2000] Mayer, A., A. Wool, E. Ziskind, Fang: A Firewall Analysis Engine, in *Proceedings of the IEEE Symposium on Security and Privacy,* IEEE Press, May 2000, pp. 177–187.

Conclusion to Part VII

We have presented data mining tools for various emerging security applications. These include data mining tools for active defense and insider threat analysis. In addition, we discussed aspects of real-time data mining as well as data mining for firewall policy rule management. Some of the tools discussed here are in the design stages and need to be developed further. Nevertheless, they provide some ideas on our approach to handling the emerging applications.

This brings us to the end of the discussion of the data mining tools. As we have stated, malware is becoming more and more sophisticated as new technologies emerge. Malware will be continuously changing patterns so that it is not caught. Therefore we need tools that can handle adaptable malware, as well as tools that can detect malware in real time.

25

Summary and Directions

25.1 Introduction

This chapter brings us to the close of *Data Mining Tools for Malware Detection*. We discussed several aspects, including supporting technologies such as data mining, malware, and data mining applications, and we provided a detailed discussion of the tools we have developed for malware detection. The applications we discussed included email worm detection, remote exploited detection, malicious code detection, and botnet detection. This chapter provides a summary of the book and gives directions for data mining for malware detection.

The organization of this chapter is as follows. In Section 25.2 we give a summary of this book. We have taken the summaries from each chapter and formed a summary of this book. In Section 25.3, we discuss directions for data mining for malware detection. In Section 25.4 we give suggestions as to where to go from here.

25.2 Summary of This Book

Chapter 1 provided an introduction to the book. We first provided a brief overview of the data mining techniques and applications and discussed various topics addressed in this book, including the data mining tools we have developed. Our framework is a three-layer framework, and each layer was addressed in one part of this book. This framework was illustrated in Figure 1.10. We replicate this framework in Figure 25.1.

The book is divided into seven parts. Part I consists of four chapters, 2, 3, 4, and 5. Chapter 2 provided an overview of data mining techniques used in this book. Chapter 3 provided some background information on malware. In Chapter 4, we provided an overview of

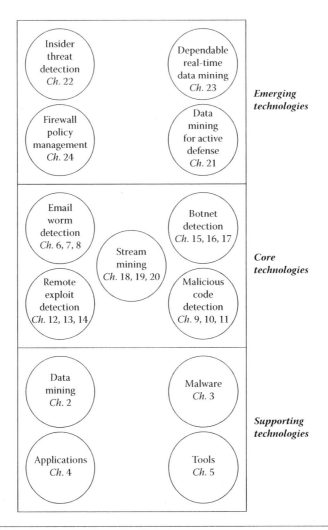

Figure 25.1   Components addressed in this book.

data mining for security applications. The tools we have described in our previous book were discussed in Chapter 5.

Part II consists of three chapters, 6, 7, and 8, and described our tool for email worm detection. An overview of email worm detection was discussed in Chapter 6. Our tool was discussed in Chapter 7. Evaluation and results were discussed in Chapter 8. Part III consists of three chapters, 9, 10, and 11, and described our tool malicious code detection. An overview of malicious code detection was discussed in Chapter 9. Our tool was discussed in Chapter 10. Evaluation and results were discussed in Chapter 11. Part IV consists of three chapters, 12, 13, and 14, and described our tool for detecting remote exploits. An overview of detecting remote exploits was discussed in Chapter 12. Our tool was discussed in Chapter 13. Evaluation and results were discussed in Chapter 14. Part V consists of three chapters, 15, 16, and 17, and described our tool for botnet detection. An overview of botnet detection was discussed in Chapter 15. Our tool was discussed in Chapter 16. Evaluation and results were discussed in Chapter 17. Part VI consists of three chapters, 18, 19, and 20, and described our tool for stream mining. An overview of stream mining was discussed in Chapter 18. Our tool was discussed in Chapter 19. Evaluation and results were discussed in Chapter 20. Part VII consists of four chapters, 21, 22, 23, and 24, and described our tools for emerging applications. Our approach for detecting adaptive malware was discussed in Chapter 21. Our approach for insider threat detection was discussed in Chapter 22. Real-time data mining was discussed in Chapter 23. Firewall policy management tool was discussed in Chapter 24.

Chapter 25, which is this chapter, provides a summary of the book. In addition, we have four appendices that provide supplementary information. Appendix A provides an overview of data management and describes the relationship between our books. Appendix B describes trustworthy systems. Appendix C describes secure data, information, and knowledge management, and Appendix D describes semantic web technologies.

25.3 Directions for Data Mining Tools for Malware Detection

There are many directions for data mining for malware detection. Figure 25.2 illustrates our directions. In the list that follows, we elaborate on the areas that need further work. In particular, we will reiterate the key points raised for each part.

Part I: Data Mining and Security: One of the major challenges is to determine the appropriate techniques for different types of malware. We still need more benchmarks and performance studies. In addition, the techniques should result in fewer false positives and negatives. Furthermore, as we have stated, malware is causing chaos in society and in

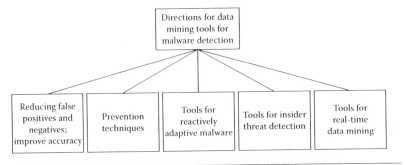

Figure 25.2   Directions for data mining tools for malware detection.

the software industry. Malware technology is getting more and more sophisticated. Malware is continuously changing patterns so as not to get caught. Therefore, developing solutions to detect and/or prevent malware has become an urgent need.

Part II: Data Mining for Email Worm Detection: Future work here will include detecting worms by combining the feature-based approach with content-based approach to make it more robust and efficient. In addition, we need to focus on the statistical property of the contents of the messages for possible contamination of worms.

Part III: Data Mining for Detecting Malicious Executables: In this part, we focused on techniques such as SVM and NB. We need to examine other techniques as well as integrate multiple techniques. We will also work to develop ways of extracting more useful features.

Part IV: Data Mining for Detecting Remote Exploits: As in the case of malicious executables, we need to examine other techniques as well as integrate multiple techniques. We will also work to develop ways of extracting more useful features.

Part V: Data Mining for Detecting Botnets: We need to examine more sophisticated data mining techniques, such as the data stream classification techniques, for botnet detection. Data stream classification techniques will be particularly suitable for botnet traffic detection, because the botnet traffic itself is a kind of data stream. We would need to extend our host-based detection technique to a distributed framework.

Part VI: Stream Mining for Security Application: We need to extend stream mining to real-time data stream classification. For example, we have to optimize the training, including the creation of decision boundary. The outlier detection and novel class detection should also be made more efficient. We believe the cloud computing framework can play an important role in increasing the efficiency of these processes.

Part VII: Emerging Applications: For active defense, we need techniques that can handle adaptable malware. For insider threat detection, we need scalable graph mining techniques. For real-time data mining, we need techniques that can meet timing constraints as well as develop models dynamically. Finally, for firewall policy management, we need scalable association rule mining techniques for mining a very large number of policies.

25.4 Where Do We Go from Here?

This book has discussed a great deal about data mining tools for malware detection. We have stated many challenges in this field in Section 25.3. We need to continue with research and development efforts if we are to make progress in this very important area.

The question is where do we go from here? First of all, those who wish to work in this area must have a good knowledge of the supporting technologies, including data management, statistical reasoning, and machine learning. In addition, knowledge of the application areas, such as malware, security, and web technologies, is needed. Next, because the field is expanding rapidly and there are many developments in the field, the reader has to keep up with the developments, including reading about the commercial products. Finally, we encourage the reader to experiment with the products and also develop security tools. This is the best way to get familiar with a particular field—that is, work on hands-on problems and provide solutions to get a better understanding.

As we have stated, malware is getting more and more sophisticated with the emerging technologies. Therefore, we need to be several steps ahead of the hacker. We have to anticipate the types of malware that would be created and develop solutions. Furthermore, the malware will be changing very rapidly, and therefore we need solutions for adaptive malware.

To develop effective solutions for malware detection, we need research and development support from the government funding agencies. We also need commercial corporations to invest research and development dollars so that progress can be made in industrial research and the research can be transferred to commercial products. We also need to collaborate with the international research community to solve problems and develop useful tools.

Appendix A: Data Management Systems

Developments and Trends

A.1 Introduction

The main purpose of this appendix is to set the context of the series of books we have written in data management, data mining, and data security. Our series started in 1997 with our book, *Data Management Systems Evolution and Interoperation* [Thuraisingham, 1997]. Our subsequent books have evolved from this first book. We have essentially repeated Chapter 1 of our first book in Appendix A of our subsequent books. The purpose of this appendix is to provide an overview of data management systems. We will then discuss the relationships between the books we have written.

As stated in our series of books, the developments in information systems technologies have resulted in computerizing many applications in various business areas. Data have become a critical resource in many organizations, and therefore, efficient access to data, sharing the data, extracting information from the data, and making use of the information have become urgent needs. As a result, there have been several efforts on integrating the various data sources scattered across several sites. These data sources may be databases managed by database management systems, or they could simply be files. To provide the interoperability between the multiple data sources and systems, various tools are being developed. These tools enable users of one system to access other systems in an efficient and transparent manner.

We define data management systems to be systems that manage the data, extract meaningful information from the data, and make use of the information extracted. Therefore, data management systems include database systems, data warehouses, and data mining systems. Data could be structured data, such as that found in relational databases, or it could be unstructured, such as text, voice, imagery, or video. There have been numerous discussions in the past to distinguish between data, information, and knowledge. We do not attempt to clarify these terms. For our purposes, data could be just bits and bytes, or they could convey some meaningful information to the user. We will, however, distinguish between database systems and database management systems. A database management system is that component which manages the database containing persistent data. A database system consists of both the database and the database management system.

A key component to the evolution and interoperation of data management systems is the interoperability of heterogeneous database systems. Efforts on the interoperability between database systems have been reported since the late 1970s. However, it is only recently that we are seeing commercial developments in heterogeneous database systems. Major database system vendors are now providing interoperability between their products and other systems. Furthermore, many of the database system vendors are migrating toward an architecture called the client-server architecture, which facilitates distributed data management capabilities. In addition to efforts on the interoperability between different database systems and client-server environments, work is also directed toward handling autonomous and federated environments.

The organization of this appendix is as follows. Because database systems are a key component of data management systems, we first provide an overview of the developments in database systems. These developments are discussed in Section A.2. Then we provide a vision for data management systems in Section A.3. Our framework for data management systems is discussed in Section A.4. Note that data mining, warehousing, and web data management are components of this framework. Building information systems from our framework with special instantiations is discussed in Section A.5. The relationship between the various texts that we have written (or are writing) for CRC Press is discussed in Section A.6. This appendix is summarized in Section A.7.

A.2 Developments in Database Systems

Figure A.1 provides an overview of the developments in database systems technology. Whereas the early work in the 1960s focused on developing products based on the network and hierarchical data models, much of the developments in database systems took place after the seminal paper by Codd describing the relational model [Codd, 1970] (see also [Date, 1990]). Research and development work on relational database systems was carried out during the early

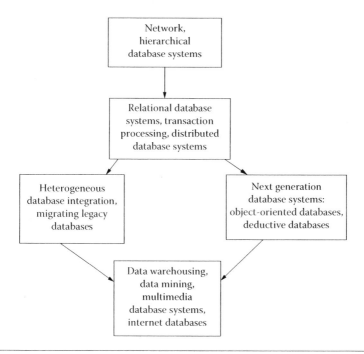

Figure A.1   Developments in database systems technology.

1970s, and several prototypes were developed throughout the 1970s. Notable efforts include IBM's (International Business Machine Corporation's) System R and the University of California at Berkeley's INGRES. During the 1980s, many relational database system products were being marketed (notable among these products are those of Oracle Corporation, Sybase Inc., Informix Corporation, INGRES Corporation, IBM, Digital Equipment Corporation, and Hewlett-Packard Company). During the 1990s, products from other vendors emerged (e.g., Microsoft Corporation). In fact, to date, numerous relational database system products have been marketed. However, Codd stated that many of the systems that are being marketed as relational systems are not really relational (see, e.g., the discussion in [Date, 1990]). He then discussed various criteria that a system must satisfy to be qualified as a relational database system. Whereas the early work focused on issues such as data model, normalization theory, query processing and optimization strategies, query languages, and access strategies and indexes, later the focus shifted toward supporting a multi-user environment. In particular, concurrency control and recovery techniques were developed. Support for transaction processing was also provided.

Research on relational database systems, as well as on transaction management, was followed by research on distributed database systems around the mid-1970s. Several distributed database system prototype development efforts also began around the late 1970s. Notable among these efforts include IBM's System R*, DDTS (Distributed Database Testbed System) by Honeywell Inc., SDD-I and Multibase by CCA (Computer Corporation of America), and Mermaid by SDC (System Development Corporation). Furthermore, many of these systems (e.g., DDTS, Multibase, Mermaid) function in a heterogeneous environment. During the early 1990s, several database system vendors (such as Oracle Corporation, Sybase Inc., Informix Corporation) provided data distribution capabilities for their systems. Most of the distributed relational database system products are based on client-server architectures. The idea is to have the client of vendor A communicate with the server database system of vendor B. In other words, the client-server computing paradigm facilitates a heterogeneous computing environment. Interoperability between relational and non-relational commercial database systems is also possible. The database systems community is also involved in standardization efforts. Notable among the standardization efforts are the ANSI/SPARC 3-level schema architecture, the IRDS (Information Resource Dictionary System) standard for Data Dictionary Systems, the relational query language SQL (Structured Query Language), and the RDA (Remote Database Access) protocol for remote database access.

Another significant development in database technology is the advent of object-oriented database management systems. Active work on developing such systems began in the mid-1980s, and they are now commercially available (notable among them include the products of Object Design Inc., Ontos Inc., Gemstone Systems Inc., and Versant Object Technology). It was felt that new generation applications such as multimedia, office information systems, CAD/CAM, process control, and software engineering have different requirements. Such applications utilize complex data structures. Tighter integration between the programming language and the data model is also desired. Object-oriented database systems satisfy most of the requirements of these new generation applications [Cattell, 1991].

According to the Lagunita report, published as a result of a National Science Foundation (NSF) workshop in 1990 ([Silberschatz et al., 1990]; also see [Kim, 1990]), relational database systems, transaction processing, and distributed (relational) database systems are stated as mature technologies. Furthermore, vendors are marketing object-oriented database systems and demonstrating the interoperability between different database systems. The report goes on to state that as applications are getting increasingly complex, more sophisticated database systems are needed. Furthermore, because many organizations now use database systems, in many cases of different types, the database systems need to be integrated. Although work has begun to address these issues and commercial products are available, several issues still need to be resolved. Therefore, challenges faced by the database systems researchers in the early 1990s were in two areas. One was next generation database systems, and the other was heterogeneous database systems.

Next generation database systems include object-oriented database systems, functional database systems, special parallel architectures to enhance the performance of database system functions, high-performance database systems, real-time database systems, scientific database systems, temporal database systems, database systems that handle incomplete and uncertain information, and intelligent database systems (also sometimes called logic or deductive database systems). Ideally, a database system should provide the support for high-performance transaction processing, model complex applications, represent new kinds of data, and make intelligent deductions. Although significant progress was made during the late 1980s and early 1990s, there is much to be done before such a database system can be developed.

Heterogeneous database systems have been receiving considerable attention during the past decade [March, 1990]. The major issues include handling different data models, different query processing strategies, different transaction processing algorithms, and different query languages. Should a uniform view be provided to the entire system, or should the users of the individual systems maintain their own views of the entire system? These are questions that have yet to be answered satisfactorily. It is also envisaged that a complete solution to heterogeneous database management systems is a generation away. While research should be directed toward finding such a solution, work should also be carried out to handle limited forms of heterogeneity to satisfy the customer needs. Another type of database system that has received some attention lately is a federated database system. Note that some have used the terms *heterogeneous database system* and *federated database system* interchangeably. While heterogeneous database systems can be part of a federation, a federation can also include homogeneous database systems.

The explosion of users on the web, as well as developments in interface technologies, has resulted in even more challenges for data management researchers. A second workshop was sponsored by NSF in 1995, and several emerging technologies have been identified to be important as we go into the twenty-first century [Widom, 1996]. These include digital libraries, large database management, data administration issues, multimedia databases, data warehousing, data mining, data management for collaborative computing environments, and security and privacy. Another significant development in the 1990s is the development of object-relational systems. Such systems combine the advantages of both object-oriented database systems and relational database systems. Also, many corporations are now focusing on integrating their data management products with web technologies. Finally, for many organizations there is an increasing need to migrate some of the legacy databases and applications to newer architectures and systems such as client-server architectures and relational database systems. We believe there is no end to data management systems. As new technologies are developed, there are new opportunities for data management research and development.

A comprehensive view of all data management technologies is illustrated in Figure A.2. As shown, traditional technologies include database design, transaction processing, and benchmarking. Then there are database systems based on data models such as relational and object-oriented. Database systems may depend on features they provide, such as security and real time. These database systems may be relational or object oriented. There are also database systems based on multiple sites or processors, such as distributed and heterogeneous database systems, parallel systems, and systems being migrated. Finally, there are the emerging technologies such as data warehousing and mining, collaboration, and the web. Any comprehensive text

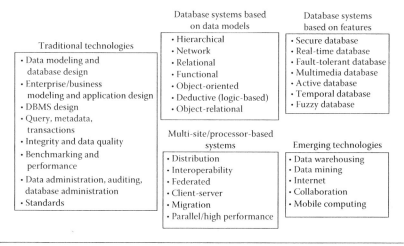

Figure A.2   Comprehensive view of data management systems.

on data management systems should address all of these technologies. We have selected some of the relevant technologies and put them in a framework. This framework is described in Section A.5.

A.3 Status, Vision, and Issues

Significant progress has been made on data management systems. However, many of the technologies are still stand-alone technologies, as illustrated in Figure A.3. For example, multimedia systems have yet to be successfully integrated with warehousing and mining technologies. The ultimate goal is to integrate multiple technologies so that accurate data, as well as information, are produced at the right time and distributed to the user in a timely manner. Our vision for data and information management is illustrated in Figure A.4.

The work discussed in [Thuraisingham, 1997] addressed many of the challenges necessary to accomplish this vision. In particular, integration of heterogeneous databases, as well as the use of distributed object technology for interoperability, was discussed. Although much progress has been made on the system aspects of interoperability, semantic issues still remain a challenge. Different databases have different representations. Furthermore, the same data entity may be interpreted differently at different sites. Addressing these semantic differences and extracting useful information from the heterogeneous and possibly multimedia data sources are major challenges. This book has attempted to address some of the challenges through the use of data mining.

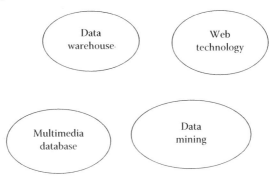

Figure A.3   Stand-alone systems.

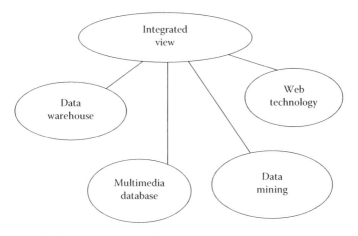

Figure A.4   Vision.

A.4 Data Management Systems Framework

For the successful development of evolvable interoperable data management systems, heterogeneous database systems integration is a major component. However, there are other technologies that have to be successfully integrated to develop techniques for efficient access and sharing of data, as well as for the extraction of information from the data. To facilitate the development of data management systems to meet the requirements of various applications in fields such as medicine, finance, manufacturing, and the military, we have proposed a framework, which can be regarded as a reference model, for data management systems. Various components from this framework have to be integrated to develop data management systems to support the various applications.

Figure A.5 illustrates our framework, which can be regarded as a model, for data management systems. This framework consists of three layers. One can think of the component technologies, which we will also refer to as components, belonging to a particular layer to be more or less built upon the technologies provided by the lower layer. Layer I is the Database Technology and Distribution layer. This layer consists of database systems and distributed database systems technologies. Layer II is the Interoperability and Migration layer. This layer consists of technologies such as heterogeneous database integration, client-server databases, and multimedia database systems to handle heterogeneous data types, and migrating legacy

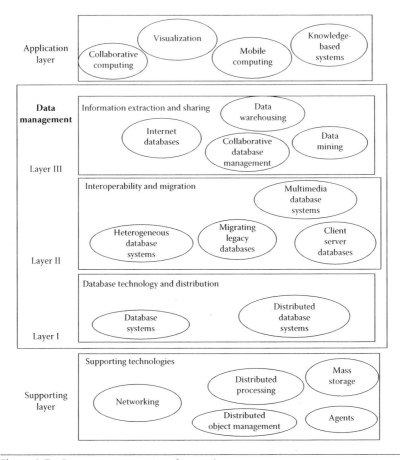

Figure A.5   Data management systems framework.

databases. Layer III is the Information Extraction and Sharing layer. This layer essentially consists of technologies for some of the newer services supported by data management systems. These include data warehousing, data mining [Thuraisingham, 1998], web databases, and database support for collaborative applications. Data management systems may utilize lower-level technologies such as networking, distributed processing, and mass storage. We have grouped these technologies into a layer called the Supporting Technologies layer. This supporting layer does not belong to the data management systems framework. This supporting layer also consists of some higher-level technologies such as distributed object management and agents. Also shown in Figure A.5 is the Application Technologies layer. Systems such as collaborative

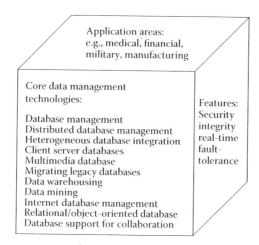

Figure A.6   A three-dimensional view of data management.

computing systems and knowledge-based systems, which belong to the Application Technologies layer, may utilize data management systems. Note that the Application Technologies layer is also outside of the data management systems framework.

The technologies that constitute the data management systems framework can be regarded as some of the core technologies in data management. However, features like security, integrity, real-time processing, fault tolerance, and high performance computing are needed for many applications utilizing data management technologies. Applications utilizing data management technologies may be medical, financial, or military, among others. We illustrate this in Figure A.6, where a three-dimensional view relating data management technologies with features and applications is given. For example, one could develop a secure distributed database management system for medical applications or a fault-tolerant multimedia database management system for financial applications.

Integrating the components belonging to the various layers is important for developing efficient data management systems. In addition, data management technologies have to be integrated with the application technologies to develop successful information systems. However, at present, there is limited integration of these various components. Our previous book *Data Management Systems Evolution and Interoperation* focused mainly on the concepts, developments, and trends belonging to each of the components shown in the framework.

Furthermore, our current book on web data management focuses on the web database component of Layer III of the framework of Figure A.5 [Thuraisingham 2000].

Note that security cuts across all of the layers. Security is needed for the supporting layers such as agents and distributed systems. Security is needed for all of the layers in the framework, including database security, distributed database security, warehousing security, web database security, and collaborative data management security. This is the topic of this book. That is, we have covered all aspects of data and applications security, including database security and information management security.

A.5 Building Information Systems from the Framework

Figure A.5 illustrates a framework for data management systems. As shown in that figure, the technologies for data management include database systems, distributed database systems, heterogeneous database systems, migrating legacy databases, multimedia database systems, data warehousing, data mining, web databases, and database support for collaboration. Furthermore, data management systems take advantage of supporting technologies such as distributed processing and agents. Similarly, application technologies such as collaborative computing, visualization, expert systems, and mobile computing take advantage of data management systems.

Many of us have heard of the term *information systems* on numerous occasions. This term is sometimes used interchangeably with the term *data management systems.* In our terminology, information systems are much broader than data management systems, but they do include data management systems. In fact, a framework for information systems will include not only the data management system layers but also the supporting technologies layer as well as the application technologies layer. That is, information systems encompass all kinds of computing systems. It can be regarded as the finished product that can be used for various applications. That is, whereas hardware is at the lowest end of the spectrum, applications are at the highest end.

We can combine the technologies of Figure A.5 to put together information systems. For example, at the application technology level,

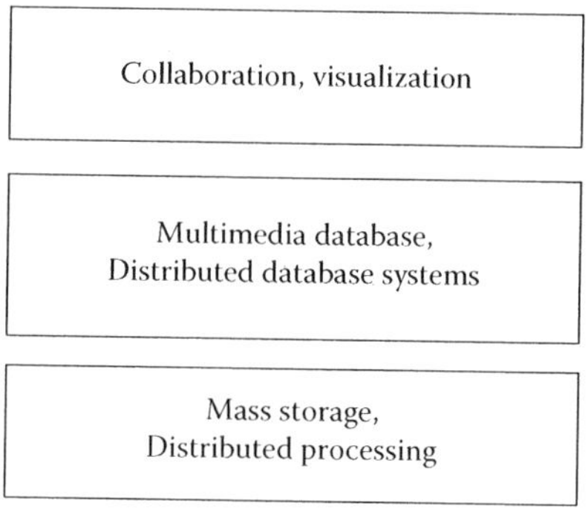

Figure A.7   Framework for multimedia data management for collaboration.

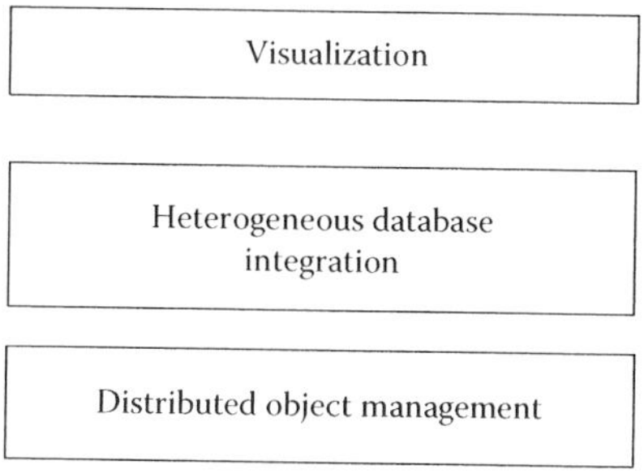

Figure A.8   Framework for heterogeneous database interoperability.

one may need collaboration and visualization technologies so that analysts can collaboratively carry out some tasks. At the data management level, one may need both multimedia and distributed database technologies. At the supporting level, one may need mass storage as well as some distributed processing capability. This special framework is illustrated in Figure A.7. Another example is a special framework for interoperability. One may need some visualization technology to display the integrated information from the heterogeneous databases. At the data management level, we have heterogeneous database systems technology. At the supporting technology level, one may use distributed object management technology to encapsulate the heterogeneous databases. This special framework is illustrated in Figure A.8.

Finally, let us illustrate the concepts that we have described by using a specific example. Suppose a group of physicians or surgeons want a system through which they can collaborate and make decisions about various patients. This could be a medical video

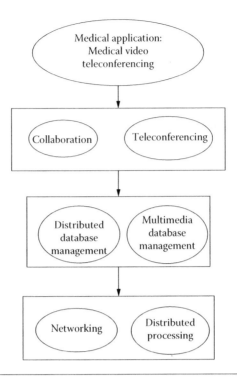

Figure A.9   Specific example.

teleconferencing application. That is, at the highest level, the application is a medical application and, more specifically, a medical video teleconferencing application. At the application technology level, one needs a variety of technologies, including collaboration and teleconferencing. These application technologies will make use of data management technologies such as distributed database systems and multimedia database systems. That is, one may need to support multimedia data such as audio and video. The data management technologies, in turn, draw upon lower-level technologies such as distributed processing and networking. We illustrate this in Figure A.9.

In summary, information systems include data management systems as well as application-layer systems such as collaborative computing systems and supporting-layer systems such as distributed object management systems.

While application technologies make use of data management technologies and data management technologies make use of supporting technologies, the ultimate user of the information system is the application itself. Today numerous applications make use of

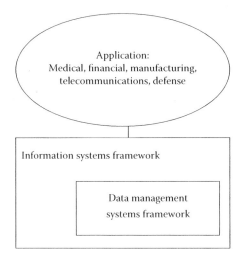

Figure A.10   Application-framework relationship.

information systems. These applications are from multiple domains such as medicine, finance, manufacturing, telecommunications, and defense. Specific applications include signal processing, electronic commerce, patient monitoring, and situation assessment. Figure A.10 illustrates the relationship between the application and the information system.

A.6 Relationship between the Texts

We have published eight books on data management and mining. These books are *Data Management Systems: Evolution and Interoperation* [Thuraisingham, 1997], *Data Mining: Technologies, Techniques, Tools and Trends* [Thuraisingham, 1998], *Web Data Management and Electronic Commerce* [Thuraisingham, 2000], *Managing and Mining Multimedia Databases for the Electronic Enterprise* [Thuraisingham, 2001], *XML Databases and the Semantic Web* [Thuraisingham, 2002], *Web Data Mining and Applications in Business Intelligence and Counter-Terrorism* [Thuraisingham, 2003], and *Database and Applications Security: Integrating Data Management and Information Security* [Thuraisingham, 2005]. Our book on trustworthy semantic webs [Thuraisingham, 2007] has evolved from Chapter 25 of [Thuraisingham, 2005]. Our book on secure web services [Thuraisingham, 2010] has evolved from [Thuraisingham, 2007]. All of these books have evolved from the framework that we illustrated in this appendix and address different

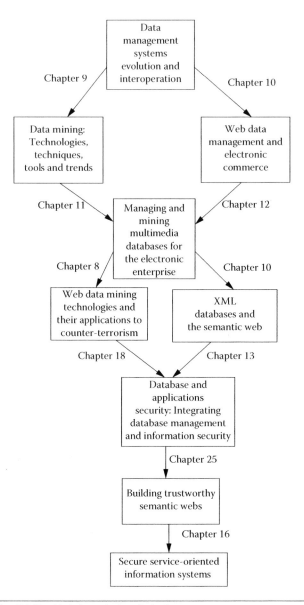

Figure A.11   Relationship between texts—Series I.

parts of the framework. The connection between these texts is illustrated in Figure A.11.

This book is the second in a new series and is illustrated in Figure A.12. This book has evolved from our previous book on the design and implementation of data mining tools [Awad et al., 2009].

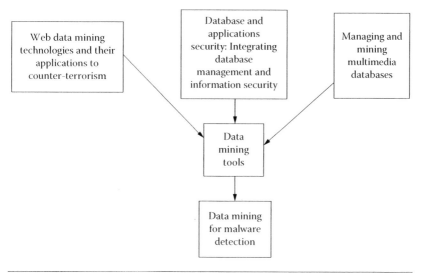

Figure A.12 Relationship between texts—Series II.

A.7 Summary

In this appendix, we have provided an overview of data management. We first discussed the developments in data management and then provided a vision for data management. Then we illustrated a framework for data management. This framework consists of three layers: database systems layer, interoperability layer, and information extraction layer. Web data management belongs to Layer III. Finally, we showed how information systems could be built from the technologies of the framework.

We believe that data management is essential to many information technologies, including data mining, multimedia information processing, interoperability, and collaboration and knowledge management. This appendix focuses on data management. Security is critical for all data management technologies. We will provide background information on trustworthy systems in Appendix B. Background on data, information, and knowledge management, which will provide a better understanding of data mining, will be discussed in Appendix C. Semantic web technologies, which are needed to understand some of the concepts in this book, will be discussed in Appendix D.

References

[Awad et al., 2009] Awad, M., L. Khan, B. Thuraisingham, L. Wang, *Design and Implementation of Data Mining Tools*, CRC Press, 2009.

[Cattell, 1991] Cattell, R., *Object Data Management Systems*, Addison-Wesley, 1991.

[Codd, 1970] Codd, E. F., A Relational Model of Data for Large Shared Data Banks, *Communications of the ACM*, Vol. 13, No. 6, June 1970, pp. 377–387.

[Date, 1990] Date, C. J., *An Introduction to Database Management Systems*, Addison-Wesley, 1990 (6th edition published in 1995 by Addison-Wesley).

[Kim, 1990] Kim, W. (Ed.), Directions for Future Database Research & Development, *ACM SIGMOD Record*, December 1990.

[March, 1990] March, S. T., Editor, Special Issue on Heterogeneous Database Systems, *ACM Computing Surveys*, September 1990.

[Silberschatz et al., 1990] Silberschatz, A., M. Stonebraker, J. D. Ullman, Editors, *Database Systems: Achievements and Opportunities*, The "Lagunita" Report of the NSF Invitational Workshop on the Future of Database Systems Research, February 22–23, Palo Alto, CA (TR-90-22), Department of Computer Sciences, University of Texas at Austin, Austin, TX. (Also in *ACM SIGMOD Record*, December 1990.)

[Thuraisingham, 1997] Thuraisingham, B., *Data Management Systems: Evolution and Interoperation*, CRC Press, 1997.

[Thuraisingham, 1998] Thuraisingham, B., *Data Mining: Technologies, Techniques, Tools and Trends*, CRC Press, 1998.

[Thuraisingham, 2000] Thuraisingham, B., *Web Data Management and Electronic Commerce*, CRC Press, 2000.

[Thuraisingham, 2001] Thuraisingham, B., *Managing and Mining Multimedia Databases for the Electronic Enterprise*, CRC Press, 2001.

[Thuraisingham, 2002] Thuraisingham, B., *XML Databases and the Semantic Web*, CRC Press, 2002.

[Thuraisingham, 2003] Thuraisingham, B., *Web Data Mining Applications in Business Intelligence and Counter-Terrorism*, CRC Press, 2003.

[Thuraisingham, 2005] Thuraisingham, B., *Database and Applications Security: Integrating Data Management and Information Security*, CRC Press, 2005.

[Thuraisingham, 2007] Thuraisingham, B., *Building Trustworthy Semantic Webs*, CRC Press, 2007.

[Thuraisingham, 2010] Thuraisingham, B., *Secure Semantic Service-Oriented Systems*, CRC Press, 2010.

[Widom, 1996] Widom, J., Editor, *Proceedings of the Database Systems Workshop*, Report published by the National Science Foundation, 1995 (also in *ACM SIGMOD Record*, March 1996).

Appendix B: Trustworthy Systems

B.1 Introduction

Trustworthy systems are systems that are secure and dependable. By dependable systems we mean systems that have high integrity, are fault tolerant, and meet real-time constraints. In other words, for a system to be trustworthy, it must be secure and fault tolerant, meet timing deadlines, and manage high-quality data.

This appendix provides an overview of the various developments in trustworthy systems with special emphasis on secure systems. In Section B.2, we discuss secure systems in some detail. In Section B.4, we discuss web security. Building secure systems from entrusted components is discussed in Section B.4. Section B.5 provides an overview of dependable systems that covers trust, privacy, integrity, and data quality. Some other security concerns are discussed in Section B.6. The appendix is summarized in Section B.7.

B.2 Secure Systems

B.2.1 Introduction

Secure systems include secure operating systems, secure data management systems, secure networks, and other types of systems, such as web-based secure systems and secure digital libraries. This section provides an overview of the various developments in information security.

In Section B.2.2, we discuss basic concepts such as access control for information systems. Section B.2.3 provides an overview of the various types of secure systems. Secure operating systems will be discussed in Section B.2.4. Secure database systems will be discussed in Section B.2.5. Network security will be discussed in Section B.2.6. Emerging trends is the subject of section B.2.7. Impact of the web is given in Section B.2.8. An overview of the steps to building secure systems will be provided in Section B.2.9.

B.2.2 *Access Control and Other Security Concepts*

Access control models include those for discretionary security and mandatory security. In this section, we discuss both aspects of access control and also consider other issues. In discretionary access control models, users or groups of users are granted access to data objects. These data objects could be files, relations, objects, or even data items. Access control policies include rules such as User U has read access to Relation R1 and write access to Relation R2. Access control could also include negative access control where user U does not have read access to Relation R.

In mandatory access control, subjects that act on behalf of users are granted access to objects based on some policy. A well-known policy is the Bell and LaPadula policy [Bell and LaPadula, 1973], where subjects are granted clearance levels and objects have sensitivity levels. The set of security levels form a partially ordered lattice where Unclassified < Confidential < Secret < TopSecret. The policy has two properties, which are the following: A subject has read access to an object if its clearance level dominates that of the object. A subject has write access to an object if its level is dominated by that of the object.

Other types of access control include role-based access control. Here access is granted to users depending on their roles and the functions they perform. For example, personnel managers have access to salary data, and project managers have access to project data. The idea here is generally to give access on a need-to-know basis.

Whereas the early access control policies were formulated for operating systems, these policies have been extended to include other

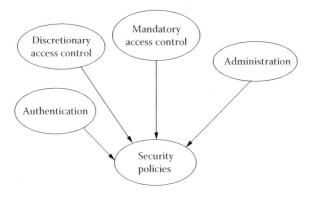

Figure B.1   Security policies.

systems such as database systems, networks, and distributed systems. For example, a policy for networks includes policies for not only reading and writing but also for sending and receiving messages.

Other security policies include administration policies. These policies include those for ownership of data as well as for how to manage and distribute the data. Database administrators as well as system security officers are involved in formulating the administration policies.

Security policies also include policies for identification and authentication. Each user or subject acting on behalf of a user has to be identified and authenticated possibly using some password mechanisms. Identification and authentication becomes more complex for distributed systems. For example, how can a user be authenticated at a global level?

The steps to developing secure systems include developing a security policy, developing a model of the system, designing the system, and verifying and validating the system. The methods used for verification depend on the level of assurance that is expected. Testing and risk analysis are also part of the process. These activities will determine the vulnerabilities and assess the risks involved. Figure B.1 illustrates various types of security policies.

B.2.3 Types of Secure Systems

In the previous section, we discussed various policies for building secure systems. In this section, we elaborate on various types of secure systems. Much of the early research in the 1960s and 1970s was on securing operating systems. Early security policies such as the Bell and LaPadula policy were formulated for operating systems. Subsequently, secure operating systems such as Honeywell's SCOMP and MULTICS were developed (see [IEEE, 1983]). Other policies such as those based on noninterference also emerged in the early 1980s.

Although early research on secure database systems was reported in the 1970s, it was not until the early 1980s that active research began in this area. Much of the focus was on multi-level secure database systems. The security policy for operating systems was modified slightly. For example, the write policy for secure database systems was modified to state that a subject has write access to an object if the subject's level is that of the object. Because database systems enforced relationships between data and focused on semantics, there were additional security concerns. For example, data could be classified based on content, context, and time. The problem of posing multiple queries and inferring sensitive information from the legitimate responses became a concern. This problem is now known as the inference problem. Also, research was carried out not only on securing relational systems but also on object systems and distributed systems, among others.

Research on computer networks began in the late 1970s and throughout the 1980s and beyond. The networking protocols were extended to incorporate security features. The result was secure network protocols. The policies include those for reading, writing, sending, and receiving messages. Research on encryption and cryptography has received much prominence because of networks and the web. Security for stand-alone systems was extended to include distributed systems. These systems included distributed databases and distributed operating systems. Much of the research on distributed systems now focuses on securing the web (known as *web security*), as well as securing systems such as distributed object management systems.

As new systems emerge, such as data warehouses, collaborative computing systems, multimedia systems, and agent systems, security for such systems has to be investigated. With the advent of the World Wide Web, security is being given serious consideration by not only government organizations but also commercial organizations. With e-commerce, it is important to protect the company's intellectual property. Figure B.2 illustrates various types of secure systems.

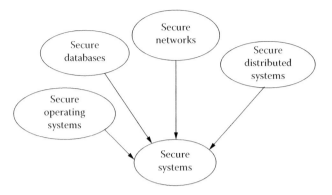

Figure B.2   Secure systems.

B.2.4 Secure Operating Systems

Work on security for operating systems was carried out extensively in the 1960s and 1970s. The research still continues, as new kinds of operating systems such as Windows, Linux, and other products emerge. The early ideas included access control lists and capability-based systems. Access control lists are lists that specify the types of access that processes, which are called subjects, have on files, which are objects. The access is usually read or write access. Capability lists are capabilities that a process must possess to access certain resources in the system. For example, a process with a particular capability can write into certain parts of the memory.

Work on mandatory security for operating systems started with the Bell and La Padula security model, which has two properties.

- The simple security property states that a subject has read access to an object if the subject's security level dominated the level of the object.
- The *-property (pronounced "star property") states that a subject has write access to an object if the subject's security level is dominated by that of the object.

Since then, variations of this model, as well as a popular model called the noninterference model (see [Goguen and Meseguer, 1982]), have been proposed. The non-interference model is essentially about higher-level processes not interfering with lower-level processes.

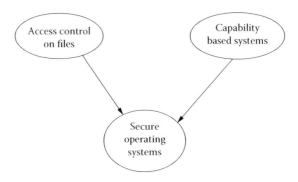

Figure B.3   Secure operating systems.

As stated earlier, security is becoming critical for operating systems. Corporations such as Microsoft are putting in many resources to ensure that their products are secure. Often we hear of vulnerabilities in various operating systems and about hackers trying to break into operating systems especially those with networking capabilities. Therefore, this is an area that will continue to receive much attention for the next several years. Figure B.3 illustrates some key aspects of operating systems security.

B.2.5 Secure Database Systems

Work on discretionary security for databases began in the 1970s, when security aspects were investigated for System R at IBM Almaden Research Center. Essentially, the security properties specified the read and write access that a user may have to relations, attributes, and data elements [Denning, 1982]. In the 1980s and 1990s, security issues were investigated for object systems. Here the security properties specified the access that users had to objects, instance variables, and classes. In addition to read and write access, method execution access was also specified.

Since the early 1980s, much of the focus was on multi-level secure database management systems [AFSB, 1983]. These systems essentially enforce the mandatory policy discussed in Section B.2.2. Since the 1980s, various designs, prototypes, and commercial products of multi-level database systems have been developed. [Ferrari and Thuraisingham, 2000] give a detailed survey of some of the developments. Example efforts include the SeaView effort by SRI

International and the LOCK Data Views effort by Honeywell. These efforts extended relational models with security properties. One challenge was to design a model in which a user sees different values at different security levels. For example, at the Unclassified level an employee's salary may be 20K, and at the secret level it may be 50K. In the standard relational model, such ambiguous values cannot be represented due to integrity properties.

Note that several other significant developments have been made on multi-level security for other types of database systems. These include security for object database systems [Thuraisingham, 1989]. In this effort, security properties specify read, write, and method execution policies. Much work was also carried out on secure concurrency control and recovery. The idea here is to enforce security properties and still meet consistency without having covert channels. Research was also carried out on multi-level security for distributed, heterogeneous, and federated database systems. Another area that received a lot of attention was the inference problem. For details on the inference problem, we refer the reader to [Thuraisingham et al., 1993]. For secure concurrency control, we refer to the numerous algorithms by Atluri, Bertino, Jajodia, et al. (see, e.g., [Alturi et al., 1997]). For information on secure distributed and heterogeneous databases as well as secure federated databases we refer the reader to [Thuraisingham, 1991] and [Thuraisingham, 1994].

As database systems become more sophisticated, securing these systems will become more and more difficult. Some of the current work focuses on securing data warehouses, multimedia databases, and web databases (see, e.g., the Proceedings of the IFIP Database Security Conference Series). Figure B.4 illustrates various types of secure database systems.

B.2.6 Secure Networks

With the advent of the web and the interconnection of different systems and applications, networks have proliferated over the past decade. There are public networks, private networks, classified networks, and unclassified networks. We continually hear about networks being infected with viruses and worms. Furthermore, networks are being intruded by

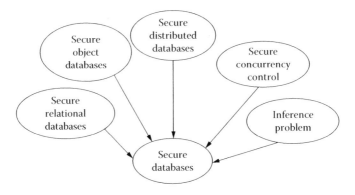

Figure B.4   Secure database systems.

malicious code and unauthorized individuals. Therefore, network security is emerging as one of the major areas in information security.

Various techniques have been proposed for network security. Encryption and cryptography are still dominating much of the research. For a discussion of various encryption techniques, we refer to [Hassler, 2000]. Data mining techniques are being applied for intrusion detection extensively (see [Ning et al., 2004]). There has also been a lot of work on network protocol security, in which security is incorporated into the various layers of, for example, the protocol stack, such as the network layer, transport layer, and session layer (see [Tannenbaum, 1990]). Verification and validation techniques are also being investigated for securing networks. Trusted Network Interpretation (also called the "red book") was developed back in the 1980s to evaluate secure networks. Various books on the topic have also been published (see [Kaufmann et al., 2002]). Figure B.5 illustrates network security techniques.

B.2.7 Emerging Trends

In the mid-1990s, research in secure systems expanded to include emerging systems. These included securing collaborative computing systems, multimedia computing, and data warehouses. Data mining has resulted in new security concerns. Because users now have access to various data mining tools and they can make sensitive associations, it can exacerbate the inference problem. On the other hand, data

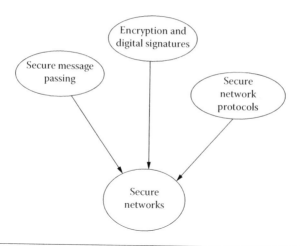

Figure B.5 Secure networks.

mining can also help with security problems, such as intrusion detection and auditing.

The advent of the web resulted in extensive investigations of security for digital libraries and electronic commerce. In addition to developing sophisticated encryption techniques, security research also focused on securing the web clients as well as servers. Programming languages such as Java were designed with security in mind. Much research was also carried out on securing agents.

Secure distributed system research focused on security for distributed object management systems. Organizations such as OMG (Object Management Group) started working groups to investigate security properties [OMG, 2011]. As a result, secure distributed object management systems are commercially available. Figure B.6 illustrates the various emerging secure systems and concepts.

B.2.8 Impact of the Web

The advent of the web has greatly impacted security. Security is now part of mainstream computing. Government organizations and commercial organizations are concerned about security. For example, in a financial transaction, millions of dollars could be lost if security is not maintained. With the web, all sorts of information is available about individuals, and therefore privacy may be compromised.

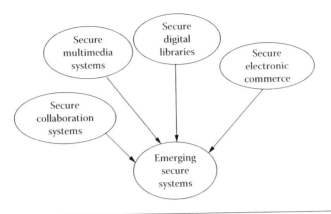

Figure B.6   Emerging trends.

Various security solutions are being proposed to secure the web. In addition to encryption, the focus is on securing clients as well as servers. That is, end-to-end security has to be maintained. Web security also has an impact on electronic commerce. That is, when one carries out transactions on the web, it is critical that security be maintained. Information such as credit card numbers and social security numbers has to be protected.

All of the security issues discussed in the previous sections have to be considered for the web. For example, appropriate security policies have to be formulated. This is a challenge, as no one person owns the web. The various secure systems, including secure operating systems, secure database systems, secure networks, and secure distributed systems, may be integrated in a web environment. Therefore, this integrated system has to be secure. Problems such as the inference and privacy problems may be exacerbated due to the various data mining tools. The various agents on the web have to be secure. In certain cases, tradeoffs need to be made between security and other features. That is, quality of service is an important consideration. In addition to technological solutions, legal aspects also have to be examined. That is, lawyers and engineers have to work together. Although much progress has been made on web security, there is still a lot to be done as progress is made on web technologies. Figure B.7 illustrates aspects of web security. For a discussion of web security, we refer readers to [Ghosh, 1998].

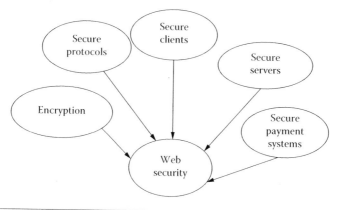

Figure B.7 Web security.

B.2.9 Steps to Building Secure Systems

In this section, we outline the steps to building secure systems. Note that our discussion is general and applicable to any secure system. However, we may need to adapt the steps for individual systems. For example, to build secure distributed database systems, we need secure database systems as well as secure networks. Therefore, the multiple systems have to be composed.

The first step to building a secure system is developing a security policy. The policy can be stated in an informal language and then formalized. The policy essentially specifies the rules that the system must satisfy. Then the security architecture has to be developed. The architecture will include the security-critical components. These are the components that enforce the security policy and therefore should be trusted. The next step is to design the system. For example, if the system is a database system, the query processor, transaction manager, storage manager, and metadata manager modules are designed. The design of the system has to be analyzed for vulnerabilities. The next phase is the development phase. Once the system has been implemented, it has to undergo security testing. This will include designing test cases and making sure that the security policy is not violated. Furthermore, depending on the level of assurance expected of the system, formal verification techniques may be used to verify and validate the system. Finally, the system will be ready for evaluation. Note that systems initially were being evaluated using the Trusted Computer

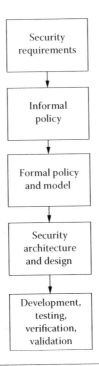

Figure B.8   Steps to building secure systems.

Systems Evaluation Criteria [TCSE, 1985]. There are interpretations of these criteria for networks [TNI, 1987] and for databases [TDI, 1991]. There are also several companion documents for various concepts such as auditing and inference control. Note that more recently, some other criteria have been developed, including the Common Criteria and the Federal Criteria.

Note that before the system is installed in an operational environment, one needs to develop a concept of operation of the environment. Risk assessment has to be carried out. Once the system has been installed, it has to be monitored so that security violations, including unauthorized intrusions, are detected. Figure B.8 illustrates the steps. An overview of building secure systems can be found in [Gasser, 1998].

B.3 Web Security

Because the web is an essential part of our daily activities, it is critical that the web be secure. Some general cyber threats include

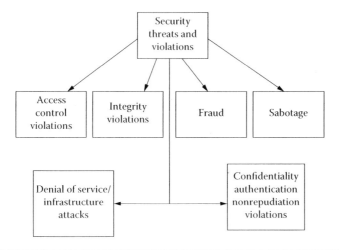

Figure B.9 Attacks on web security.

authentication violations, nonrepudiation, malware, sabotage fraud, and denial of service; infrastructure attacks access control violations, privacy violations, integrity violations, confidentiality violations, inference problem, identity theft, and insider threat [Ghosh, 1998]. Figured B.9 illustrates the various attacks on the web.

The security solutions to the web include securing the components and firewalls and encryption. For example, various components have to be made secure to get a secure web. One desires end-to-end security, and therefore the components include secure clients, secure servers, secure databases, secure operating systems, secure infrastructures, secure networks, secure transactions, and secure protocols. One needs good encryption mechanisms to ensure that the sender and receiver communicate securely. Ultimately, whether it be exchanging messages or carrying out transactions, the communication between sender and receiver or the buyer and the seller has to be secure. Secure client solutions include securing the browser, securing the Java virtual machine, securing Java applets, and incorporating various security features into languages such as Java.

One of the challenges faced by the web managers is implementing security policies. One may have policies for clients, servers, networks, middleware, and databases. The question is how do you integrate these policies? That is, how do you make these policies work together? Who is responsible for implementing these policies? Is there a global administrator, or are there several administrators that have to work together? Security policy integration is an area that is being examined by researchers.

Finally, one of the emerging technologies for ensuring that an organization's assets are protected is firewalls. Various organizations now have web infrastructures for internal and external use. To access the external infrastructure, one has to go through the firewall. These firewalls examine the information that comes into and out of an organization. This way, the internal assets are protected and inappropriate information may be prevented from coming into an organization. We can expect sophisticated firewalls to be developed in the future.

B.4 Building Trusted Systems from Untrusted Components

Much of the discussion in the previous sections has assumed end-to-end security, where the operating system, network, database system, middleware, and the applications all have to be secure. However, in today's environment, where the components may come from different parts of the world, one cannot assume end-to-end security. Therefore, the challenge is to develop secure systems with untrusted components. That is, although the operating system may be compromised, the system must still carry out its missions securely. This is a challenging problem.

We have carried out some preliminary research in this area [Bertino et al., 2010]. Addressing the challenges of protecting applications and data when the underlying platforms cannot be fully trusted dictates a comprehensive defense strategy. Such a strategy requires the ability to address new threats that are smaller and more agile and may arise from the components of the computing platforms. Our strategy, including our tenets and principles, are discussed in [Bertino et al., 2010].

B.5 Dependable Systems

B.5.1 *Introduction*

As we have discussed earlier, by dependability, we mean features such as trust, privacy, integrity, data quality and provenance, and rights management, among others. We have separated confidentiality and

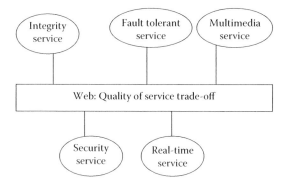

Figure B.10 Aspects of dependability.

included it as part of security. Therefore, essentially trustworthy systems include both secure systems and dependable systems. (Note that this is not a standard definition.)

Whether we are discussing security, integrity, privacy, trust, or rights management, there is always a cost involved. That is, at what cost do we enforce security, privacy, and trust? Is it feasible to implement the sophisticated privacy policies and trust management policies? In addition to bringing lawyers and policy makers together with the technologists, we also need to bring economists into the picture. We need to carry out economic tradeoffs for enforcing security, privacy, trust, and rights management. Essentially, what we need are flexible policies for security, privacy, and trust and rights management.

In this section, we will discuss various aspects of dependability. Trust issues will be discussed in Section B.5.2. Digital rights management is discussed in Section B.5.3. Privacy is discussed in Section B.5.4. Integrity issues, data quality, and data provenance, as well as fault tolerance and real-time processing, are discussed in Section B.5.5. Figure B.10 illustrates the dependability aspects.

B.5.2 Trust Management

Trust management is all about managing the trust that one individual or group has of another. That is, even if a user has access to the data, do I trust the user so that I can release the data? The user may have the clearance or possess the credentials, but he may not be trustworthy. Trust is formed by the user's behavior. The user may have betrayed one's confidence or carried out some act that is inappropriate in nature. Therefore, I may not trust that user. Now, even if I do not trust John, Jane may trust John and she may share her data with John. John may not be trustworthy to Jim, but he may be trustworthy to Jane.

The question is how do we implement trust? Can we trust someone partially? Can we trust say John 50% of the time and Jane 70% of the time? If we trust someone partially, then can we share some of the information? How do we trust the data that we have received from Bill? That is, if we do not trust Bill, then can we trust the data he gives us? There have been many efforts on trusted management systems as well as trust negotiation systems. Winslett et al. have carried out extensive work and developed specification languages for trust as well as designed trust negotiation systems (see [Yu and Winslett, 2003]). The question is how do two parties negotiate trust? A may share data D with B if B shares data C with A. A may share data D with B only if B does not share these data with F. There are many such rules that one can enforce, and the challenge is to develop a system that consistently enforces the trust rules or policies.

B.5.3 Digital Rights Management

Closely related to trust management is digital rights management (DRM). This is especially critical for entertainment applications. Who owns the copyright to a video or an audio recording? How can rights be propagated? What happens if the rights are violated? Can I distribute copyrighted films and music on the web?

We have heard a lot about the controversy surrounding Napster and similar organizations. Is DRM a technical issue, or is it a legal issue? How can we bring technologists, lawyers, and policy makers together so that rights can be managed properly? There have been numerous articles, discussions, and debates about DRM. A useful source is [Iannella, 2001].

B.5.4 Privacy

Privacy is about protecting information about individuals. Furthermore, an individual can specify, say to a web service provider, the information that can be released about him or her. Privacy has been discussed a great deal in the past, especially when it relates to protecting medical information about patients. Social scientists and technologists have been working on privacy issues.

Privacy has received enormous attention during recent years. This is mainly because of the advent of the web, the semantic web, counter-terrorism, and national security. For example, to extract information about various individuals and perhaps prevent or detect potential terrorist attacks, data mining tools are being examined. We have heard much about national security versus privacy in the media. This is mainly due to the fact that people are now realizing that to handle terrorism, the government may need to collect data about individuals and mine the data to extract information. Data may be in relational databases, or it may be text, video, and images. This is causing a major concern with various civil liberties unions (see [Thuraisingham, 2003]). Therefore, technologists, policy makers, social scientists, and lawyers are working together to provide solutions to handle privacy violations.

B.5.5 Integrity, Data Quality, and High Assurance

Integrity is about maintaining the accuracy of the data as well as processes. Accuracy of the data is discussed as part of data quality. Process integrity is about ensuring the processes are not corrupted. For example, we need to ensure that the processes are not malicious processes. Malicious processes may corrupt the data as a result of unauthorized modifications. To ensure integrity, the software has to be tested and verified to develop high assurance systems.

The database community has ensured integrity by ensuring integrity constraints (e.g., the salary value has to be positive) as well as by ensuring the correctness of the data when multiple processes access the data. To achieve correctness, techniques such as concurrency control are enforced. The idea is to enforce appropriate locks so that multiple processes do not access the data at the same time and corrupt the data.

Data quality is about ensuring the accuracy of the data. The accuracy of the data may depend on who touched the data. For example, if the source of the data is not trustworthy, then the quality value of the data may be low. Essentially, some quality value is assigned to each piece of data. When data is composed, quality values are assigned to the data in such a way that the resulting value is a function of the quality values of the original data.

Data provenance techniques also determine the quality of the data. Note that data provenance is about maintaining the history of the data. This will include information such as who accessed the data for read/write purposes. Based on this history, one could then assign quality values of the data as well as determine when the data are misused.

Other closely related topics include real-time processing and fault tolerance. Real-time processing is about the processes meeting the timing constraints. For example, if we are to get stock quotes to purchase stocks, we need to get the information in real time. It does not help if the information arrives after the trading desk is closed for business for the day. Similarly, real-time processing techniques also have to ensure that the data are current. Getting yesterday's stock quotes is not sufficient to make intelligent decisions. Fault tolerance is about ensuring that the processes recover from faults. Faults could be accidental or malicious. In the case of faults, the actions of the processes have to be redone, the processes will then have to be aborted, and, if needed, the processes are re-started.

To build high assurance systems, we need the systems to handle faults, be secure, and handle real-time constraints. Real-time processing and security are conflicting goals, as we have discussed in [Thuraisingham, 2005]. For example, a malicious process could ensure that critical timing constraints are missed. Furthermore, to enforce all the access control checks, some processes may miss the deadlines. Therefore, what we need are flexible policies that will determine which aspects are critical for a particular situation.

B.6 Other Security Concerns

B.6.1 Risk Analysis

As stated in the book by Shon Harris [Harris, 2010], risk is the likelihood that something bad will happen that causes harm to an informational asset (or the loss of the asset). A vulnerability is a weakness that can be used to endanger or cause harm to an informational asset.

A threat is anything (manmade or act of nature) that has the potential to cause harm.

The likelihood that a threat will use a vulnerability to cause harm creates a risk. When a threat uses a vulnerability to inflict harm, it has an impact. In the context of information security, the impact is a loss of availability, integrity, and confidentiality, and possibly other losses (lost income, loss of life, loss of real property). It is not possible to identify all risks, nor is it possible to eliminate all risk. The remaining risk is called residual risk.

The challenges include identifying all the threats that are inherent to a particular situation. For example, consider a banking operation. The bank has to employ security experts and risk analysis experts to conduct a study of all possible threats. Then they have to come up with ways of eliminating the threats. If that is not possible, they have to develop ways of containing the damage so that it is not spread further.

Risk analysis is especially useful for handling malware. For example, once a virus starts spreading, the challenge is how do you stop it? If you cannot stop it, then how do you contain it and also limit the damage that it caused? Running various virus packages on one's system will perhaps limit the virus from affecting the system or causing serious damage. The adversary will always find ways to develop new viruses. Therefore, we have to be one step or many steps ahead of the enemy. We need to examine the current state of the practice in risk analysis and develop new solutions, especially to handle the new kinds of threats present in the cyber world.

B.6.2 Biometrics, Forensics, and Other Solutions

Some of the recent developments in computer security are tools for biometrics and forensic analysis. Biometrics tools include understanding handwriting and signatures and recognizing people from their features and eyes, including the pupils. Although this is a very challenging area, much progress has been made. Voice recognition tools to authenticate users are also being developed. In the future, we can expect many to use these tools.

Forensic analysis essentially carries out postmortems just as they do in medicine. Once the attacks have occurred, how do you detect these attacks? Who are the enemies and perpetrators? Although progress has been made, there are still challenges. For example, if one accesses the web pages and uses passwords that are stolen, it will be difficult to determine from the web logs who the culprit is. We still need a lot of research in the area. Digital Forensics also deals with using computer evidence for crime analysis.

Biometrics and Forensics are just some of the new developments. Other solutions being developed include smartcards, tools for detecting spoofing and jamming, as well as tools to carry out sniffing.

B.7 Summary

This appendix has provided a brief overview of the developments in trustworthy systems. We first discussed secure systems, including basic concepts in access control, as well as discretionary and mandatory policies; types of secure systems, such as secure operating systems, secure databases, secure networks, and emerging technologies; the impact of the web; and the steps to building secure systems. Next we discussed web security and building secure systems from untested components. This was followed by a discussion of dependable systems. Then we focused on risk analysis and topics such as biometrics.

Research in trustworthy systems is moving at a rapid pace. Some of the challenges include malware detection and prevention, insider threat analysis, and building secure systems from untrusted components. This book has addressed one such topic and that is malware detection with data mining tools.

References

[AFSB, 1983] Air Force Studies Board, Committee on Multilevel Data Management Security, *Multilevel Data Management Security*, National Academy Press, Washington DC, 1983.

[Atluri et al., 1997] Atluri, V., S. Jajodia, E. Bertino, Transaction Processing in Multilevel Secure Databases with Kernelized Architectures: Challenges and Solutions, *IEEE Transactions on Knowledge and Data Engineering*, Vol. 9, No. 5, 1997, pp. 697–708.

[Bell and LaPadula, 1973] Bell, D., and L. LaPadula, *Secure Computer Systems: Mathematical Foundations and Model*, M74-244, MITRE Corporation, Bedford, MA, 1973.

[Bertino et al., 2010] Bertino, E., G. Ghinita, K. Hamlen, M. Kantarcioglu, S. H. Lee, N. Li, et al., *Securing the Execution Environment Applications and Data from Multi-Trusted Components*, UT Dallas Technical Report #UTDCS-03-10, March 2010.

[Denning, 1982] Denning, D., *Cryptography and Data Security*, Addison-Wesley, 1982.

[Ferrari and Thuraisingham, 2000] Ferrari E., and B. Thuraisingham, Secure Database Systems, in *Advances in Database Management*, M. Piatini and O. Diaz, Editors, Artech House, 2000.

[Gasser, 1998] Gasser, M., *Building a Secure Computer System*, Van Nostrand Reinhold, 1988.

[Ghosh, 1998] Ghosh, A., *E-commerce Security, Weak Links and Strong Defenses*, John Wiley, 1998.

[Goguen and Meseguer, 1982] Goguen, J., and J. Meseguer, Security Policies and Security Models, *Proceedings of the IEEE Symposium on Security and Privacy*, Oakland, CA, April 1982, pp. 11–20.

[Harris, 2010] Harris, S., *CISSP All-in-One Exam Guide*, McGraw-Hill, 2010.

[Hassler, 2000] Hassler, V., *Security Fundamentals for E-Commerce*, Artech House, 2000.

[Iannella, 2001] Iannella, R., Digital Rights Management (DRM) Architectures, *D-Lib Magazine*, Vol. 7, No. 6, http://www.dlib.org/dlib/june01/iannella/06iannella.html

[IEEE, 1983] *IEEE Computer Magazine*, Special Issue on Computer Security, Vol. 16, No. 7, 1983.

[Kaufmann et al., 2002] Kaufmann, C., R. Perlman, M. Speciner, *Network Security: Private Communication in a Public World*, Pearson Publishers, 2002.

[Ning et al., 2004] Ning, P., Y. Cui, D. S. Reeves, D. Xu, Techniques and Tools for Analyzing Intrusion Alerts, *ACM Transactions on Information and Systems Security*, Vol. 7, No. 2, 2004, pp. 274–318.

[OMG, 2011] The Object Management Group, www.omg.org

[Tannenbaum, 1990] Tannenbaum, A., *Computer Networks*, Prentice Hall, 1990.

[TCSE, 1985] *Trusted Computer Systems Evaluation Criteria*, National Computer Security Center, MD, 1985.

[TDI, 1991] *Trusted Database Interpretation*, National Computer Security Center, MD, 1991.

[Thuraisingham, 1989] Thuraisingham, B., Mandatory Security in Object-Oriented Database Systems, *Proceedings of the ACM Object-Oriented Programming Systems, Language, and Applications (OOPSLA) Conference*, New Orleans, LA, October 1989, pp. 203–210.

[Thuraisingham, 1991] Thuraisingham, B., Multilevel Security for Distributed Database Systems, *Computers and Security*, Vol. 10, No. 9, 1991, pp. 727–747.

[Thuraisingham, 1994] Thuraisingham, B., Security Issues for Federated Database Systems, *Computers and Security*, Vol. 13, No. 6, 1994, pp. 509–525.

[Thuraisingham, 2003] Thuraisingham, B., *Web Data Mining Technologies and Their Applications in Business Intelligence and Counter-Terrorism*, CRC Press, 2003.

[Thuraisingham, 2005] Thuraisingham, B., *Database and Applications Security: Integrating Data Management and Information Security*, CRC Press, 2005.

[Thuraisingham et al., 1993] Thuraisingham, B., W. Ford, M. Collins, Design and Implementation of a Database Inference Controller, *Data and Knowledge Engineering Journal*, Vol. 11, No. 3, 1993, pp. 271–297.

[TNI, 1987] *Trusted Network Interpretation*, National Computer Security Center, MD, 1987.

[Yu and Winslett, 2003] Yu, T., and M. Winslett, A Unified Scheme for Resource Protection in Automated Trust Negotiation, *IEEE Symposium on Security and Privacy*, Oakland, CA, May 2003, pp. 110–122.

Appendix C: Secure Data, Information, and Knowledge Management

C.1 Introduction

In this appendix, we discuss secure data, information, and knowledge management technologies. Note that data, information, and knowledge management technologies have influenced the development of data mining. Next we discuss the security impact on these technologies since data mining for security applications falls under secure data, information, and knowledge management.

Data management technologies include database management, database integration, data warehousing, and data mining. Information management technologies include information retrieval, multimedia information management, collaborative information management, e-commerce, and digital libraries. Knowledge management is about organizations utilizing the corporate knowledge to get a business advantage.

The organization of this chapter is as follows. Secure data management will be discussed in Section C.2. Secure information management will be discussed in Section C.3. Secure knowledge management will be discussed in Section C.4. The chapter is summarized in Section C.5.

C.2 Secure Data Management

C.2.1 Introduction

Database security has evolved from database management and information security technologies. In this appendix, we will discuss secure data management. In particular, we will provide an overview of database management and then discuss the security impact.

Database systems technology has advanced a great deal during the past four decades, from the legacy systems based on network and hierarchical models to relational and object-oriented database systems based on client-server architectures. We consider a database system to include both the database management system (DBMS) and the database (see also the discussion in [Date, 1990]). The DBMS component of the database system manages the database. The database contains persistent data. That is, the data are permanent even if the application programs go away.

The organization of this section of the appendix is as follows. In Section C.2.2 we will discuss database management. Database integration will be discussed in Section C.2.3. Data warehousing and data mining will be discussed in Section C.2.4. Web data management will be discussed in Section C.2.5. Security impact of data management technologies will be discussed in Section C.2.6.

C.2.2 Database Management

We discuss data modeling, function, and distribution for a database management system.

C.2.2.1 Data Model The purpose of a data model is to capture the universe that it is representing as accurately, completely, and naturally as possible [Tsichritzis and Lochovsky, 1982]. Data models include hierarchical models, network models, relational models, entity relationship models, object models, and logic-based models. The relational data model is the most popular data model for database systems. With the relational model [Codd, 1970], the database is viewed as a collection of relations. Each relation has attributes and rows. For example, Figure C.1 illustrates a database with two relations, EMP and

EMP

SS#	Ename	Salary	D#
1	John	20 K	10
2	Paul	30 K	20
3	Mary	40 K	20

DEPT

D#	Dname	Mgr
10	Math	Smith
20	Physics	Jones

Figure C.1   Relational database.

DEPT. Various languages to manipulate the relations have been proposed. Notable among these languages is the ANSI Standard SQL (Structured Query Language). This language is used to access and manipulate data in relational databases. A detailed discussion of the relational data model is given in [Date, 1990] and [Ullman, 1988].

C.2.2.2 Functions   The functions of a DBMS carry out its operations. A DBMS essentially manages a database, and it provides support to the user by enabling him to query and update the database. Therefore, the basic functions of a DBMS are query processing and update processing. In some applications, such as banking, queries and updates are issued as part of transactions. Therefore, transaction management is also another function of a DBMS. To carry out these functions, information about the data in the database has to be maintained. This information is called the metadata. The function that is associated with managing the metadata is metadata management. Special techniques are needed to manage the data stores that actually store the data. The function that is associated with managing these techniques is storage management. To ensure that these functions are carried out properly and that the user gets accurate data, there are some additional functions. These include security management, integrity management, and fault management (i.e., fault tolerance). The functional architecture of a DBMS is illustrated in Figure C.2 (see also [Ullman, 1988]).

C.2.2.3 Data Distribution   As stated by [Ceri and Pelagatti, 1984], a distributed database system includes a distributed database management system (DDBMS), a distributed database, and a network for

Figure C.2   Database architecture.

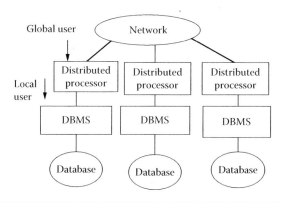

Figure C.3   Distributed data management.

interconnection (Figure C.3). The DDBMS manages the distributed database. A distributed database is data that is distributed across multiple databases. The nodes are connected via a communication subsystem, and local applications are handled by the local DBMS. In addition, each node is also involved in at least one global application, so there is no centralized control in this architecture. The DBMSs are connected through a component called the Distributed Processor (DP). Distributed database system functions include distributed query processing, distributed transaction management, distributed metadata management, and security and integrity enforcement across the multiple nodes. It has been stated that the semantic web can be considered to be a large distributed database.

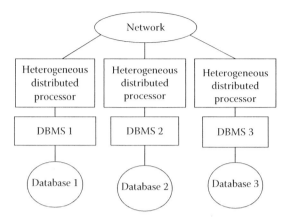

Figure C.4   Heterogeneous database integration.

C.2.3 Heterogeneous Data Integration

Figure C.4 illustrates an example of interoperability between heterogeneous database systems. The goal is to provide transparent access, both for users and application programs, for querying and executing transactions (see, e.g., [Wiederhold, 1992]). Note that in a heterogeneous environment, the local DBMSs may be heterogeneous. Furthermore, the modules of the DP have both local DBMS specific processing as well as local DBMS independent processing. We call such a DP a heterogeneous distributed processor (HDP). There are several technical issues that need to be resolved for the successful interoperation between these diverse database systems. Note that heterogeneity could exist with respect to different data models, schemas, query processing techniques, query languages, transaction management techniques, semantics, integrity, and security.

Some of the nodes in a heterogeneous database environment may form a federation. Such an environment is classified as a federated data mainsheet environment. As stated by [Sheth and Larson, 1990], a federated database system is a collection of cooperating but autonomous database systems belonging to a federation. That is, the goal is for the database management systems, which belong to a federation, to cooperate with one another and yet maintain some degree of autonomy. Figures C.5 illustrates a federated database system.

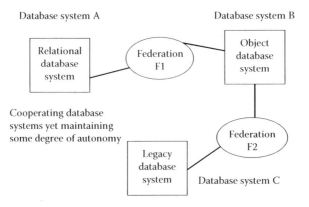

Figure C.5 Federated data management.

C.2.4 Data Warehousing and Data Mining

Data warehousing is one of the key data management technologies to support data mining and data analysis. As stated by [Inmon, 1993], data warehouses are subject oriented. Their design depends to a great extent on the application utilizing them. They integrate diverse and possibly heterogeneous data sources. They are persistent. That is, the warehouses are very much like databases. They vary with time. This is because as the data sources from which the warehouse is built get updated, the changes have to be reflected in the warehouse. Essentially, data warehouses provide support for decision support functions of an enterprise or an organization. For example, while the data sources may have the raw data, the data warehouse may have correlated data, summary reports, and aggregate functions applied to the raw data.

Figure C.6 illustrates a data warehouse. The data sources are managed by database systems A, B, and C. The information in these databases is merged and put into a warehouse. With a data warehouse, data may often be viewed differently by different applications. That is, the data is multidimensional. For example, the payroll department may want data to be in a certain format, whereas the project department may want data to be in a different format. The warehouse must provide support for such multidimensional data.

Data mining is the process of posing various queries and extracting useful information, patterns, and trends, often previously unknown, from large quantities of data possibly stored in databases. Essentially, for many organizations, the goals of data mining include improving

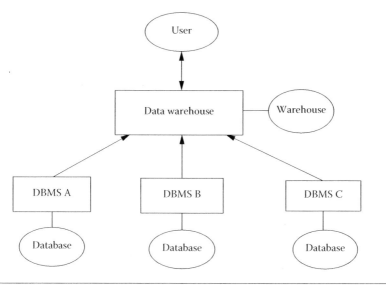

Figure C.6 Data warehouse.

marketing capabilities, detecting abnormal patterns, and predicting the future based on past experiences and current trends.

Some of the data mining techniques include those based on statistical reasoning techniques, inductive logic programming, machine learning, fuzzy sets, and neural networks, among others. The data mining outcomes include classification (finding rules to partition data into groups), association (finding rules to make associations between data), and sequencing (finding rules to order data). Essentially one arrives at some hypothesis, which is the information extracted, from examples and patterns observed. These patterns are observed from posing a series of queries; each query may depend on the responses obtained to the previous queries posed. There have been several developments in data mining. A discussion of the various tools is given in [KDN, 2011]. A good discussion of the outcomes and techniques is given in [Berry and Linoff, 1997]. Figure C.7 illustrates the data mining process.

C.2.5 Web Data Management

A major challenge for web data management researchers and practitioners is coming up with an appropriate data representation scheme. The question is, is there a need for a standard data model for web database systems? Is it at all possible to develop such a standard? If

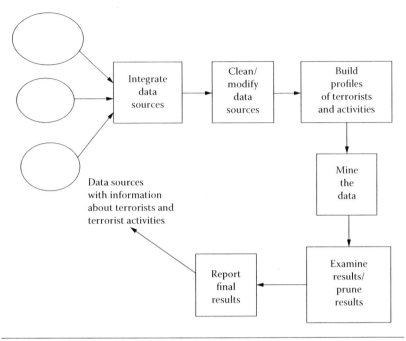

Figure C.7   Steps to data mining.

so, what are the relationships between the standard model and the individual models used by the databases on the web?

Database management functions for the web include query processing, metadata management, security, and integrity. In [Thuraisingham, 2000], we have examined various database management system functions and discussed the impact of web database access on these functions. Some of the issues are discussed here. Figure C.8 illustrates the functions. Querying and browsing are two of the key functions. First of all, an appropriate query language is needed. Because SQL is a popular language, appropriate extensions to SQL may be desired.

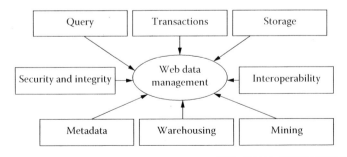

Figure C.8   Web data management.

XML-QL, which has evolved from XML (eXtensible Markup Language) and SQL, is moving in this direction. Query processing involves developing a cost model. Are there special cost models for Internet database management? With respect to browsing operation, the query processing techniques have to be integrated with techniques for following links. That is, hypermedia technology has to be integrated with database management technology.

Updating web databases could mean different things. One could create a new web site, place servers at that site, and update the data managed by the servers. The question is can a user of the library send information to update the data at a web site? An issue here is with security privileges. If the user has write privileges, then he could update the databases that he is authorized to modify. Agents and mediators could be used to locate the databases as well as to process the update.

Transaction management is essential for many applications. There may be new kinds of transactions on the web. For example, various items may be sold through the Internet. In this case, the item should not be locked immediately when a potential buyer makes a bid. It has to be left open until several bids are received and the item is sold. That is, special transaction models are needed. Appropriate concurrency control and recovery techniques have to be developed for the transaction models.

Metadata management is a major concern for web data management. The question is what is metadata? Metadata describes all of the information pertaining to the library. This could include the various web sites, the types of users, access control issues, and policies enforced. Where should the metadata be located? Should each participating site maintain its own metadata? Should the metadata be replicated, or should there be a centralized metadata repository? Metadata in such an environment could be very dynamic, especially because the users and the web sites may be changing continuously.

Storage management for web database access is a complex function. Appropriate index strategies and access methods for handling multimedia data are needed. In addition, because of the large volumes of data, techniques for integrating database management technology with mass storage technology are also needed. Other data management functions include integrating heterogeneous databases, managing multimedia data, and mining. We discussed them in [Thuraisingham, 2002-a].

C.2.6 *Security Impact*

Now that we have discussed data management technologies, we will provide an overview of the security impact. With respect to data management, we need to enforce appropriate access control techniques. Early work focused on discretionary access control; later, in the 1980s, focus was on mandatory access control. More recently, the focus has been on applying some of the novel access control techniques such as role-based access control and usage control. Extension to SQL to express security assertions, as well as extensions to the relational data model to support multilevel security, has received a lot of attention. More details can be found in [Thuraisingham, 2005].

With respect to data integration, the goal is to ensure the security of operation when heterogeneous databases are integrated. That is, the policies enforced by the individual data management systems have to be enforced at the coalition level. Data warehousing and data mining results in additional security concerns, and this includes the inference problem. When data is combined, the combined data could be at a higher security level. Specifically, inference is the process of posing queries and deducing unauthorized information from the legitimate responses received. The inference problem exists for all types of database systems and has been studied extensively within the context of multilevel databases. Figure C.9 illustrates the security impact on data management.

C.3 Secure Information Management

C.3.1 *Introduction*

In this section, we discuss various secure information management technologies. In particular, we will first discuss information retrieval, multimedia information management, collaborative information management, and e-business and digital libraries and then discuss the security impact.

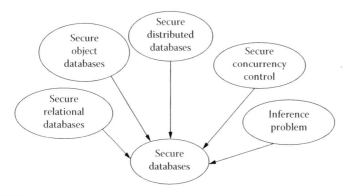

Figure C.9 Secure data management.

Note that we have tried to separate data management and information management. Data management focuses on database systems technologies such as query processing, transaction management, and storage management. Information management is much broader than data management, and we have included many topics in this category, such as information retrieval and multimedia information management.

The organization of this section is as follows. Information retrieval is discussed in Section C.3.2. Multimedia information management is the subject of Section C.3.3. Collaboration and data management are discussed in Section C.3.4. Digital libraries are discussed in Section C.3.5. E-commerce technologies will be discussed in Section C.3.6. Security impact will be discussed in Section C.3.7.

C.3.2 Information Retrieval

Information retrieval systems essentially provide support for managing documents. The functions include document retrieval, document update, and document storage management, among others. These systems are essentially database management systems for managing documents. There are various types of information retrieval systems, and they include text retrieval systems, image retrieval systems, and audio and video retrieval systems. Figure C.10 illustrates a general purpose information retrieval system that may be utilized for text retrieval, image retrieval, audio retrieval, and video retrieval. Such architecture can also be utilized for a multimedia data management system (see [Thuraisingham, 2001]).

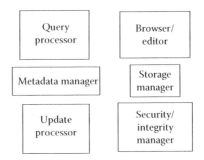

Figure C.10 Information retrieval system.

C.3.3 Multimedia Information Management

A multimedia data manager (MM-DM) provides support for storing, manipulating, and retrieving multimedia data from a multimedia database. In a sense, a multimedia database system is a type of heterogeneous database system, as it manages heterogeneous data types. Heterogeneity is due to the multiple media of the data such as text, video, and audio. Because multimedia data also convey information such as speeches, music, and video, we have grouped this under information management. One important aspect of multimedia data management is data representation. Both extended relational models and object models have been proposed.

An MM-DM must provide support for typical database management system functions. These include query processing, update processing, transaction management, storage management, metadata management, security, and integrity. In addition, in many cases, the various types of data, such as voice and video, have to be synchronized for display, and therefore, real-time processing is also a major issue in an MM-DM.

Various architectures are being examined to design and develop an MM-DM. In one approach, the data manager is used just to manage the metadata, and a multimedia file manager is used to manage the multimedia data. There is a module for integrating the data manager and the multimedia file manager. In this case, the MM-DM consists of the three modules: the data manager managing the metadata, the multimedia file manager, and the module for integrating the two. The second architecture is the tight coupling approach. In this architecture, the data manager manages both the multimedia data and the

Figure C.11   Multimedia information management system.

metadata. The tight coupling architecture has an advantage because all of the data management functions could be applied on the multimedia database. This includes query processing, transaction management, metadata management, storage management, and security and integrity management. Note that with the loose coupling approach, unless the file manager performs the DBMS functions, the DBMS only manages the metadata for the multimedia data.

There are also other aspects to architectures, as discussed in [Thuraisingham, 1997]. For example, a multimedia database system could use a commercial database system such as an object-oriented database system to manage multimedia objects. However, relationships between objects and the representation of temporal relationships may involve extensions to the database management system. That is, a DBMS together with an extension layer provide complete support to manage multimedia data. In the alternative case, both the extensions and the database management functions are integrated so that there is one database management system to manage multimedia objects as well as the relationships between the objects. Further details of these architectures as well as managing multimedia databases are discussed in [Thuraisingham, 2001]. Figure C.11 illustrates a multimedia information management system.

C.3.4 *Collaboration and Data Management*

Although the notion of computer supported cooperative work (CSCW) was first proposed in the early 1980s, it is only in the 1990s that much interest was shown on this topic. Collaborative computing enables people, groups of individuals, and organizations to work together with one another to accomplish a task or a collection of tasks. These tasks could vary from participating in conferences, solving a specific problem, or working on the design of a system (see [ACM, 1991]).

One aspect of collaborative computing that is of particular interest to the database community is workflow computing. *Workflow* is defined as the automation of a series of functions that comprise a business process, such as data entry, data review, and monitoring performed by one or more people. An example of a process that is well suited for workflow automation is the purchasing process. Some early commercial workflow system products targeted for office environments were based on a messaging architecture. This architecture supports the distributed nature of current workteams. However, the messaging architecture is usually file based and lacks many of the features supported by database management systems, such as data representation, consistency management, tracking, and monitoring. The emerging workflow systems utilize data management capabilities.

Figure C.12 illustrates an example in which teams A and B are working on a geographical problem, such as analyzing and predicting the weather in North America. The two teams must have a global

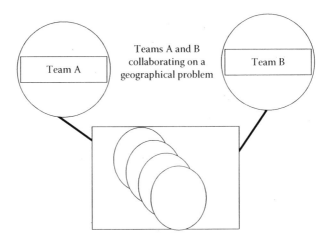

Figure C.12   Collaborative computing system.

picture of the map as well as any notes that go with it. Any changes made by one team should be instantly visible to the other team, and both teams communicate as if they are in the same room.

To enable such transparent communication, data management support is needed. One could utilize a database management system to manage the data or some type of data manager that provides some of the essential features such as data integrity, concurrent access, and retrieval capabilities. In the previously mentioned example, the database may consist of information describing the problem the teams are working on, the data that are involved, history data, and the metadata information. The data manager must provide appropriate concurrency control features so that when both teams simultaneously access the common picture and make changes, these changes are coordinated.

The web has increased the need for collaboration even further. Users now share documents on the web and work on papers and designs on the web. Corporate information infrastructures promote collaboration and sharing of information and documents. Therefore, the collaborative tools have to work effectively on the web. More details are given in [IEEE, 1999].

C.3.5 Digital Libraries

Digital libraries gained prominence with the initial efforts of the National Science Foundation (NSF), Defense Advanced Research Projects Agency (DARPA), and National Aeronautics and Space Administration (NASA). NSF continued to fund special projects in this area and as a result the field has grown very rapidly. The idea behind digital libraries is to digitize all types of documents and provide efficient access to these digitized documents.

Several technologies have to work together to make digital libraries a reality. These include web data management, markup languages, search engines, and question answering systems. In addition, multimedia information management and information retrieval systems play an important role. This section will review the various developments in some of the digital libraries technologies. Figure C.13 illustrates an example digital library system.

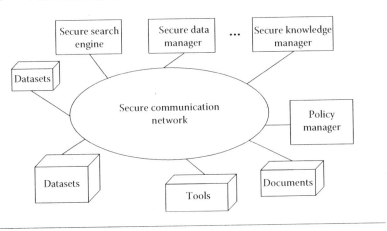

Figure C.13   Digital libraries.

C.3.6 E-Business

Various models, architectures, and technologies are being developed. Business-to-business e-commerce is all about two businesses conducting transactions on the web. We give some examples. Suppose corporation A is an automobile manufacturer and needs microprocessors to be installed in its automobiles. It will then purchase the microprocessors from corporation B, who manufactures the microprocessors. Another example is when an individual purchases some goods, such as toys from a toy manufacturer. This manufacturer then contacts a packaging company via the web to deliver the toys to the individual. The transaction between the manufacturer and the packaging company is a business-to-business transaction. Business-to-business e-commerce also involves one business purchasing a unit of another business or two businesses merging. The main point is that such transactions have to be carried out on the web. Business-to-consumer e-commerce is when a consumer makes purchases on the web. In the toy manufacturer example, the purchase between the individual and the toy manufacturer is a business-to-consumer transaction.

The modules of the e-commerce server may include modules for managing the data and web pages, mining customer information, security enforcement, and transaction management. E-commerce client functions may include presentation management, user interface, as well as caching data and hosting browsers. There could also be a middle tier, which may implement the business objects

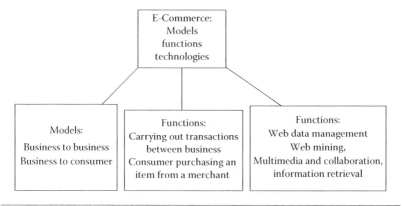

Figure C.14 E-business components.

to carry out the business functions of e-commerce. These business functions may include brokering, mediation, negotiations, purchasing, sales, marketing, and other e-commerce functions. The e-commerce server functions are impacted by the information management technologies for the web. In addition to the data management functions and the business functions, the e-commerce functions also include those for managing distribution, heterogeneity, and federations.

E-commerce also includes non-technological aspects such as policies, laws, social impacts, and psychological impacts. We are now doing business in an entirely different way and therefore we need a paradigm shift. We cannot do successful e-commerce if we still want the traditional way of buying and selling products. We have to be more efficient and rely on the technologies a lot more to gain a competitive edge. Some key points for e-commerce are illustrated in Figure C.14.

C.3.7 Security Impact

Security impact for information management technologies include developing appropriate secure data models, functions, and architectures. For example, to develop secure multimedia information management systems, we need appropriate security policies for text, audio, and video data. The next step is to develop secure multimedia data models. These could be based on relations or objects or a combination of these representations. What is the level of granularity?

Should access be controlled to the entire video of video frames? How can access be controlled based on semantics? For digital libraries there is research on developing flexible policies. Note that digital libraries may be managed by multiple administrators under different environments. Therefore, policies cannot be rigid. For collaborative information systems, we need policies for different users to collaborate with one another. How can the participants trust each other? How can truth be established? What sort of access control is appropriate? There is research on developing security models for workflow and collaboration systems [Bertino et al., 1999].

Secure e-business is receiving a lot of attention. How can the models, processes, and functions be secured? What are these security models? Closely related to e-business is supply chain management. The challenge here is ensuring security as well as timely communication between the suppliers and the customers.

C.4 Secure Knowledge Management

We first discuss knowledge management and then describe the security impact.

C.4.1 Knowledge Management

Knowledge management is the process of using knowledge as a resource to manage an organization. It could mean sharing expertise, developing a learning organization, teaching the staff, learning from experiences, or collaborating. Essentially, knowledge management will include data management and information management. However, this is not a view shared by everyone. Various definitions of knowledge management have been proposed. Knowledge management is a discipline invented mainly by business schools. The concepts have been around for a long time. But the term *knowledge management* was coined as a result of information technology and the web.

In the collection of papers on knowledge management by [Morey et al., 2001], knowledge management is divided into three areas. These are strategies such as building a knowledge company and making the staff knowledge workers; processes (such as techniques) for knowledge management, including developing a method to share documents and tools; and metrics that measure the effectiveness of knowledge management. In the *Harvard Business Review* in the area of knowledge management, there is an excellent collection of articles describing a knowledge-creating company, building a learning organization, and teaching people how to learn [Harvard, 1996]. Organizational behavior and team dynamics play major roles in knowledge management.

Knowledge management technologies include several information management technologies, including knowledge representation and knowledge-based management systems. Other knowledge management technologies include collaboration tools, tools for organizing information on the web, and tools for measuring the effectiveness of the knowledge gained, such as collecting various metrics. Knowledge management technologies essentially include data management and information management technologies as well as decision support technologies. Figure C.15 illustrates some of the knowledge management components and technologies. It also lists the aspects of the knowledge management cycle. Web technologies play a major role in knowledge management. Knowledge management and the web are closely related. Although knowledge management practices have existed for many years, it is the web that has promoted knowledge management.

Many corporations now have Intranets, and an Intranet is the single most powerful knowledge management tool. Thousands of employees are connected through the web in an organization. Large corporations have sites all over the world, and the employees are becoming

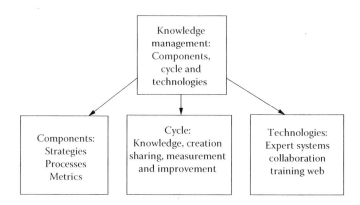

Figure C.15   Knowledge management components and technologies.

well connected with one another. Email can be regarded to be one of the early knowledge management tools. Now there are many tools, such as search engines and e-commerce tools.

With the proliferation of web data management and e-commerce tools, knowledge management will become an essential part of the web and e-commerce. A collection of papers on knowledge management experiences covers strategies, processes, and metrics [Morey et al., 2001]. Collaborative knowledge management is discussed in [Thuraisingham et al., 2002-b].

C.4.2 Security Impact

Secure knowledge management is receiving a lot of attention [SKM, 2004]. One of the major challenges here is to determine the security impact on knowledge management strategies, processes, and metrics [Bertino et al., 2006]. We will examine each of the components.

Note that an organization's knowledge management strategy must be aligned with its business strategy. That is, an organization must utilize its knowledge to enhance its business, which will ultimately include improved revenues and profits. Therefore, the security strategy has to be aligned with its business strategy. For example, an organization may need to protect its intellectual property. Patents are one aspect of intellectual property; other aspects include papers and trade secrets. Some of this intellectual property should not be widely disseminated to maintain the competitive edge. Therefore, policies are needed to ensure that sensitive intellectual property is treated as classified material.

With respect to knowledge management processes, we need to incorporate security into them. For example, consider the workflow management for purchase orders. Only authorized individuals should be able to execute the various processes. This means that security for workflow systems is an aspect of secure knowledge management. That is, the data and information management technologies will contribute to knowledge management.

With respect to metrics, security will have an impact. For example, one metric could be the number of papers published by individuals. These papers may be classified or unclassified. Furthermore, the existence of the classified documents may also be classified. This means that at the unclassified level there may be one value for the metric, whereas at the classified level there may be another value. Therefore, when evaluating the employee for his or her performance, both values have to be taken into consideration. However, if the manager does not have an appropriate clearance, then there will be an issue. The organization has to then develop appropriate mechanisms to ensure that the employee's entire contributions are taken into consideration when he or she is evaluated.

C.5 Summary

In this chapter, we have provided an overview of secure data, information, and knowledge management. In particular, we have discussed data, information, and knowledge management technologies and then examined the security impact.

As we have stated earlier, data, information, and knowledge management are supporting technologies for building trustworthy semantic webs. The agents that carry out activities on the web have to utilize the data, extract information from the data, and reuse knowledge so that machine-untreatable web pages can be developed. There are several other aspects of data, information, and knowledge management that we have not covered in this chapter, such as peer-to-peer information management and information management for virtual organizations.

References

[ACM, 1991] Special Issue on Computer Supported Cooperative Work, *Communications of the ACM*, December 1991.

[Berry and Linoff, 1997] Berry, M., and G. Linoff, *Data Mining Techniques for Marketing, Sales, and Customer Support*, John Wiley, 1997.

[Bertino et al., 1999] Bertino, E., E. Ferrari, V. Atluri, The Specification and Enforcement of Authorization Constraints in Workflow Management Systems, *ACM Transactions on Information and Systems Security*, Vol. 2, No. 1, 1999, pp. 65–105.

[Bertino et al., 2006] Bertino, E., L. Khan, R. S. Sandhu, B. M. Thuraisingham, Secure Knowledge Management: Confidentiality, Trust, and Privacy, *IEEE Transactions on Systems, Man, and Cybernetics*, Part A, Vol. 36, No. 3, 2006, pp. 429–438.

[Ceri and Pelagatti, 1984] Ceri, S., and G. Pelagatti, *Distributed Databases, Principles and Systems*, McGraw-Hill, 1984.

[Codd, 1970] Codd, E. F., A Relational Model of Data for Large Shared Data Banks, *Communications of the ACM,* Vol. 26, No. 1, 1970, pp. 64–69.

[Date, 1990] Date, C., *An Introduction to Database Systems,* Addison-Wesley, Reading, MA, 1990.

[Harvard, 1996] *Harvard Business School Articles on Knowledge Management,* Harvard University, MA, 1996.

[IEEE, 1999] Special Issue in Collaborative Computing, *IEEE Computer,* Vol. 32, No. 9, 1999.

[Inmon, 1993] Inmon, W., *Building the Data Warehouse,* John Wiley and Sons, 1993.

[KDN, 2011] Kdnuggets, www.kdn.com

[Morey et al., 2001] Morey, D., M. Maybury, B. Thuraisingham, Editors, *Knowledge Management,* MIT Press, 2001.

[Sheth and Larson, 1990] Sheth A., and J. Larson, Federated Database Systems for Managing Distributed, Heterogeneous, and Autonomous Databases, *ACM Computing Surveys,* Vol. 22, No. 3, 1990, pp. 183–236. 1990.

[SKM, 2004] *Proceedings of the Secure Knowledge Management Workshop,* Buffalo, NY, 2004.

[Thuraisingham, 1997] Thuraisingham, B., *Data Management Systems Evolution and Interoperation,* CRC Press, 1997.

[Thuraisingham, 2000] Thuraisingham, B., *Web Data Management and Electronic Commerce,* CRC Press, 2000.

[Thuraisingham, 2001] Thuraisingham, B., *Managing and Mining Multimedia Databases for the Electronic Enterprise,* CRC Press, 2001.

[Thuraisingham, 2002-a] Thuraisingham, B., *XML Databases and the Semantic Web,* CRC Press, 2002.

[Thuraisingham et al., 2002-b] Thuraisingham, B., A. Gupta, E. Bertino, E. Ferrari, Collaborative Commerce and Knowledge Management, *Journal of Knowledge and Process Management,* Vol. 9, No. 1, 2002, pp. 43–53.

[Thuraisingham, 2005] Thuraisingham, B., *Database and Applications Security,* CRC Press, 2005.

[Tsichritzis and Lochovsky, 1982] Tsichritzis, D., and F. Lochovsky, *Data Models,* Prentice Hall, 1982.

[Ullman, 1988] Ullman, J. D., *Principles of Database and Knowledge Base Management Systems,* Vols. I and II, Computer Science Press, 1988.

[Wiederhold, 1992] Wiederhold, G., Mediators in the Architecture of Future Information Systems, *IEEE Computer,* Vol. 25, Issue 3, March 1992, pp. 38–49.

[Woelk et al., 1986] Woelk, D., W. Kim, W. Luther, An Object-Oriented Approach to Multimedia Databases, *Proceedings of the ACM SIGMOD Conference,* Washington, DC, June 1986, pp. 311–325.

Appendix D: Semantic Web

D.1 Introduction

Tim Berners Lee, the father of the World Wide Web, realized the inadequacies of current web technologies and subsequently strived to make the web more intelligent. His goal was to have a web that would essentially alleviate humans from the burden of having to integrate disparate information sources as well as to carry out extensive searches. He then came to the conclusion that one needs machine-understandable web pages and the use of ontologies for information integration. This resulted in the notion of the semantic web [Lee and Hendler, 2001]. The web services that take advantage of semantic web technologies are called *semantic web services.*

A semantic web can be thought of as a web that is highly intelligent and sophisticated so that one needs little or no human intervention to carry out tasks such as scheduling appointments, coordinating activities, searching for complex documents, as well as integrating disparate databases and information systems. Although much progress has been made toward developing such an intelligent web, there is still a lot to be done. For example, technologies such as ontology matching, intelligent agents, and markup languages are contributing a lot toward developing the semantic web. Nevertheless, humans are still needed to make decisions and take actions.

Recently there have been many developments on the semantic web. The World Wide Web consortium (W3C, www.w3c.org) is specifying standards for the semantic web. These standards include specifications for XML, RDF, and Interoperability. However, it is also very important that the semantic web be secure. That is, the components that constitute the semantic web have to be secure. The components include XML, RDF, and Ontologies. In addition, we need secure information integration. We also need to examine trust issues for the semantic web. It is, therefore, important that we have standards for securing the semantic web, including specifications for secure XML, secure RDF, and secure interoperability (see [Thuraisingham, 2005]). In this appendix, we will discuss the various components of the semantic web and discuss semantic web services.

Although agents are crucial to managing the data and the activities on the semantic web, usually agents are not treated as part of semantic web technologies. Because the subject of agents is vast and there are numerous efforts to develop agents, as well as secure agents, we do not discuss agents in depth in this appendix. However, we mention agents here as it is these agents that use XML and RDF and make sense of the data and understand web pages. Agents act on behalf of the users. Agents communicate with each other using well-defined protocols. Various types of agents have been developed depending on the tasks they carry out. These include mobile agents, intelligent agents, search agents, and knowledge management agents. Agents invoke web services to carry out the operations. For details of agents we refer readers to [Hendler, 2001].

The organization of this appendix is as follows. In Section D.2, we will provide an overview of the layered architecture for the semantic web as specified by Tim Berners Lee. Components such as XML, RDF, ontologies, and web rules are discussed in Sections D.3 through D.6. Semantic web services are discussed in Section D.7. The appendix is summarized in Section D.8. Much of the discussion of the semantic web is summarized from the book by Antoniou and van Harmelan [Antoniou and Harmelan, 2003]. For an up-to-date specification we refer the reader to the World Wide Web Consortium web site (www.w3c.org).

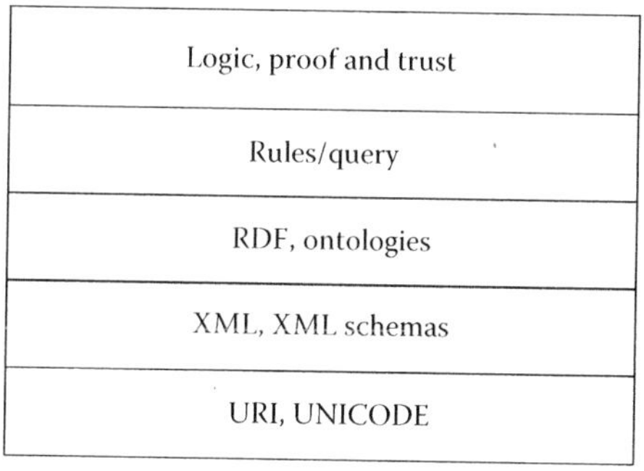

Logic, proof and trust
Rules/query
RDF, ontologies
XML, XML schemas
URI, UNICODE

Figure D.1   Layered architecture for the semantic web.

D.2 Layered Technology Stack

Figure D.1 illustrates the layered technology stack for the semantic web. This is the architecture that was developed by Tim Berners Lee. Essentially the semantic web consists of layers where each layer takes advantage of the technologies of the previous layer. The lowest layer is the protocol layer, and this is usually not included in the discussion of the semantic technologies. The next layer is the XML layer. XML is a document representation language and will be discussed in Section D.3. Whereas XML is sufficient to specify syntax, a semantic string such as "the creator of document D is John" is hard to specify in XML. Therefore, the W3C developed RDF, which uses XML syntax. The semantic web community then went further and came up with a specification of ontologies in languages such as OWL (Web Ontology Language). Note that OWL addresses the inadequacies of RDF. For example, OWL supports the notions of union and intersection of classes that RDF does not support. In order to reason about various policies, the semantic web community has come up with a web rules language such as SWRL (semantic web rules language) and RuleML (rule markup language) (e.g., the consistency of the policies or whether the policies lead to security violations).

The functional architecture is illustrated in Figure D.2. It is essentially a service-oriented architecture that hosts web services.

D.3 XML

XML is needed due to the limitations of HTML and complexities of SGML. It is an extensible markup language specified by the W3C

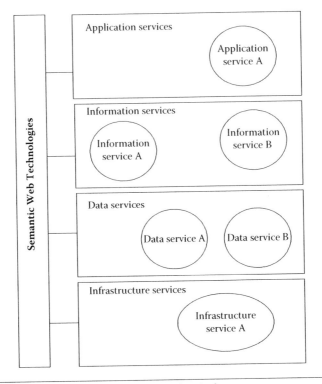

Figure D.2 Functional architecture for the semantic web.

(World Wide Web Consortium) and designed to make the interchange of structured documents over the Internet easier. An important aspect of XML used to be the notion of Document Type Definitions (DTDs) which defines the role of each element of text in a formal model. XML schemas have now become critical to specify the structure. XML schemas are also XML documents. This section will discuss various components of XML including: statements, elements, attributes, and schemas. The components of XML are illustrated in Figure D.3.

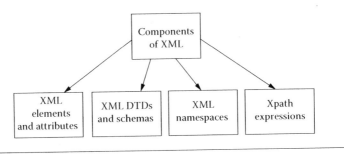

Figure D.3 Components of XML.

D.3.1 XML Statement and Elements

The following is an example of an XML statement that describes the fact that "John Smith is a Professor in Texas." The elements are name and state. The XML statement is as follows:

```
<Professor>
   <name> John Smith </name>
   <state> Texas </state>
</Professor>
```

D.3.2 XML Attributes

Suppose we want to specify that there is a professor called John Smith who makes 60K. We can use either elements or attributes to specify this. The example below shows the use of the attributes Name and Salary.

```
<Professor>
   Name = "John Smith," Access = All, Read
   Salary = "60K"
</Professor>
```

D.3.3 XML DTDs

DTDs (Document Type Definitions) essentially specify the structure of XML documents.

Consider the following DTD for Professor with elements Name and State. This will be specified as:

```
<!ELEMENT Professor Officer (Name, State)>
<!ELEMENT name (#PCDATA)>
<!ELEMENT state (#PCDATA)>
<!ELEMENT access (#PCDATA).>
```

D.3.4 XML Schemas

While DTDs were the early attempts to specify structure for XML documents, XML schemas are far more elegant to specify structures. Unlike DTDs, XML schemas essentially use the XML syntax for specification.

Consider the following example:

```
<ComplexType = name = "ProfessorType">
  <Sequence>
  <element name = "name" type = "string"/>
  <element name = "state" type = "string"/>
  <Sequence>
</ComplexType>
```

D.3.5 XML Namespaces

Namespaces are used for DISAMBIGUATION. An example is given below.

```
<CountryX: Academic-Institution
   Xmlns: CountryX = "http://www.CountryX.edu/Institution UTD"
   Xmlns: USA = "http://www.USA.edu/Institution UTD"
   Xmlns: UK = "http://www.UK.edu/Institution UTD"
<USA: Title = College
   USA: Name = "University of Texas at Dallas"
   USA: State = Texas"
<UK: Title = University
   UK: Name = "Cambridge University"
   UK: State = Cambs
</CountryX: Academic-Institution>
```

D.3.6 XML Federations/Distribution

XML data may be distributed and the databases may form federations. This is illustrated in the segment below.

Site 1 document:

```
<Professor-name>
  <ID> 111 </ID>
  <Name> John Smith </name>
  <State> Texas </state>
</Professor-name>
```

Site 2 document:

```
<Professor-salary>
   <ID> 111 </ID>
   <salary> 60K </salary>
<Professor-salary>
```

D.3.7 XML-QL, XQuery, XPath, XSLT

XML-QL and XQuery are query languages that have been proposed for XML. XPath is used to specify the queries. Essentially, Xpath expressions may be used to reach a particular element in the XML statement. In our research we have specified policy rules as Xpath expressions (see [Bertino et al., 2004]). XSLT is used to present XML documents. Details are given on the World Wide Web Consortium web site (www.w3c.org) and in [Antoniou and Harmelan, 2003]. Another useful reference is [Laurent, 2000].

D.4 RDF

Whereas XML is ideal to specify the syntax of various statements, it is difficult to use XML to specify the semantics of a statement. For example, with XML, it is difficult to specify statements such as the following:

Engineer is a subclass of Employee.
Engineer inherits all properties of Employee.

Note that the statements specify the class/subclass and inheritance relationships. RDF was developed by Tim Berners Lee and his team so that the inadequacies of XML could be handled. RDF uses XML syntax. Additional constructs are needed for RDF and we discuss some of them. Details can be found in [Antoniou and Harmelan, 2003].

Resource Description Framework (RDF) is the essence of the semantic web. It provides semantics with the use of ontologies to various statements and uses XML syntax. RDF concepts include the basic model, which consists of Resources, Properties, and Statements, and the container model, which consists of Bag, Sequence, and

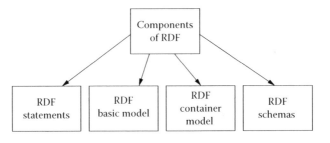

Figure D.4   Components of RDF.

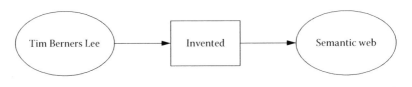

Figure D.5   RDF statement.

Alternative. We discuss some of the essential concepts. The components of RDF are illustrated in Figure D.4.

D.4.1 RDF Basics

The RDF basic model consists of resource, property, and statement. In RDF everything is a resource such as person, vehicle, and animal. Properties describe relationships between resources such as "bought," "invented," "ate." Statement is a triple of the form (Object, Property, Value). Examples of statements include the following:

Berners Lee invented the Semantic Web.
Tom ate the Apple.
Mary brought a Dress.

Figure D.5 illustrates a statement in RDF. In this statement, Berners Lee is the Object, Semantic Web is the Value, and invented is the property.

D.4.2 RDF Container Model

The RDF container model consists of bag, sequence, and alternative. As described in [Antoniou and Harmelan, 2003], these constructs are specified in RDF as follows:

Bag: Unordered container, may contain multiple occurrences
Rdf: Bag

Seq: Ordered container, may contain multiple occurrences
Rdf: Seq

Alt: a set of alternatives
Rdf: Alt

D.4.3 RDF Specification

As stated in [Antoniou and Harmelan, 2003], RDF specifications have been given for attributes, types, nesting, containers, and others. An example is the following:

"Berners Lee is the Author of the book Semantic Web."

This statement is specified as follows (see also [Antoniou and Harmelan, 2003]):

```
<rdf: RDF
    xmlns: rdf = "http://w3c.org/1999/02-22-rdf-syntax-ns#"
    xmlns: xsd = "http:// - - -
    xmlns: uni = "http:// - - - -
<rdf: Description: rdf: about = "949352"
    <uni: name = Berners Lee</uni:name>
    <uni: title> Professor < uni:title>
</rdf: Description>
<rdf: Description rdf: about: "ZZZ"
    < uni: bookname> semantic web <uni:bookname>
    < uni: authoredby: Berners Lee <uni:authoredby>
</rdf: Description>
</rdf: RDF>
```

D.4.4 RDF Schemas

Whereas XML schemas specify the structure of the XML document and can be considered to be metadata, RDF schema specifies relationships such as the class/subclass relationships. For example, we need RDF schema to specify statements such as "engineer is a subclass of employee." The following is the RDF specification for this statement.

```
<rdfs: Class rdf: ID = "engineer"
<rdfs: comment>
The class of Engineers
All engineers are employees
<rdfs: comment>
<rdfs: subClassof rdf: resource = "employee"/>
<rdfs: Class>
```

D.4.5 RDF Axiomatic Semantics

First-order logic is used to specify formulas and inferencing. The following constructs are needed:

Built in functions (First) and predicates (Type)
Modus Ponens: From A and If A then B, deduce B

The following example is taken from [Antoniou and Harmelan 2003]:

Example: All Containers are Resources; that is if X is a container, then X is a resource.
Type(?C, Container) → Type(?c, Resource)
If we have Type(A, Container) then we can infer (Type A, Resource)

D.4.6 RDF Inferencing

Unlike XML, RDF has inferencing capabilities. Although first-order logic provides a proof system, it will be computationally infeasible to develop such a system using first-order logic. As a result, Horn clause logic was developed for logic programming [Lloyd, 1987]; this is still computationally expensive. Semantic web is based on a restricted logic called Descriptive Logic; details can be found in [Antoniou and Harmelan, 2003]. RDF uses If then Rules as follows:

IF E contains the triples (?u, rdfs: subClassof, ?v)
and (?v, rdfs: subClassof ?w)
THEN
E also contains the triple (?u, rdfs: subClassof, ?w)

That is, if u is a subclass of v, and v is a subclass of w, then u is a subclass of w.

D.4.7 RDF Query

Similar to XML Query languages such as X-Query and XML-QL, query languages are also being developed for RDF. One can query RDF using XML, but this will be very difficult because RDF is much richer than XML. Thus, RQL, an SQL-like language, was developed for RDF. It is of the following form:

Select from "RDF document" where some "condition."

D.4.8 SPARQL

The RDF Data group at W3C has developed a query language for RDF called SPARQL, which is becoming the standard now for querying RDF documents. We are developing SPARQL query processing algorithms for clouds. We have also developed a query optimizer for SPARQL queries.

D.5 Ontologies

Ontologies are common definitions for any entity, person, or thing. Ontologies are needed to clarify various terms, and therefore, they are crucial for machine-understandable web pages. Several ontologies have been defined and are available for use. Defining a common ontology for an entity is a challenge, as different groups may come up with different definitions. Therefore, we need mappings for multiple ontologies. That is, these mappings map one ontology to another. Specific languages have been developed for ontologies. Note that RDF was developed because XML is not sufficient to specify semantics such as class/subclass relationship. RDF is also limited, as one cannot express several other properties such as Union and Intersection. Therefore, we need a richer language. Ontology languages were developed by the semantic web community for this purpose.

OWL (Web Ontology Language) is a popular ontology specification language. It's a language for ontologies and relies on RDF. DARPA

(Defense Advanced Research Projects Agency) developed early language DAML (DARPA Agent Markup Language). Europeans developed OIL (Ontology Interface Language). DAML+OIL is a combination of the two and was the starting point for OWL. OWL was developed by W3C. OWL is based on a subset of first-order logic and that is descriptive logic.

OWL features include Subclass relationship, Class membership, Equivalence of classes, Classification and Consistency (e.g., x is an instance of A, A is a subclass of B, x is not an instance of B).

There are three types of OWL: OWL-Full, OWL-DL, OWL-Lite. Automated tools for managing ontologies are called ontology engineering.

Below is an example of OWL specification:

Textbooks and Coursebooks are the same.
EnglishBook is not a FrenchBook
EnglishBook is not a GermanBook
< owl: Class rdf: about = "#EnglishBook">
<owl: disjointWith rdf: resource "#FrenchBook"/>
<owl: disjointWith rdf: resource = "#GermanBook"/>
</owl:Class>
<owl: Class rdf: ID = "TextBook">
<owl: equivalentClass rdf: resource = "CourseBook"/>
</owl: Class>

Below is an OWL specification for Property:

Englishbooks are read by Students
< owl: ObjectProperty rdf: about = "#readBy">
<rdfs domain rdf: resource = "#EnglishBook"/>
<rdfs: range rdf: resource = "#student"/>
<rdfs: subPropertyOf rdf: resource = "#involves"/>
</owl: ObjectProperty>

Below is an OWL specification for property restriction:

All Frenchbooks are read only by Frenchstudents.
< owl: Class rdf: about = "#"FrenchBook">
<rdfs: subClassOf>
<owl: Restriction>

<owl: onProperty rdf: resource = "#readBy">
<owl: allValuesFrom rdf: resource = "#FrenchStudent"/>
</rdfs: subClassOf>
</owl: Class>

D.6 Web Rules and SWRL

D.6.1 *Web Rules*

RDF is built on XML and OWL is built on RDF. We can express subclass relationships in RDF and additional relationships in OWL. However, reasoning power is still limited in OWL. Therefore, we need to specify rules, and subsequently a markup language for rules, so that machines can understand and make inferences.

Below are some examples as given in [ANTI03]:

Studies(X,Y), Lives(X,Z), Loc(Y,U), Loc(Z,U) →
  DomesticStudent(X)
    i.e. if John Studies at UTDallas and John lives on Campbell
      Road and the location of Campbell Road and UTDallas
      are Richardson then John is a Domestic student.

Note that Person (X) → Man(X) or Woman(X) is not a rule in predicate logic.

That is if X is a person then X is either a man or a woman cannot be expressed in first order predicate logic. Therefore, in predicate logic we express the above as if X is a person and X is not a man then X is a woman and similarly if X is a person and X is not a woman then X is a man. That is, in predicate logic, we can have a rule of the form

Person(X) and Not Man(X) → Woman(X)

However, in OWL we can specify the rule if X is a person then X is a man or X is a woman.

Rules can be monotonic or nonmonotonic.

Below is an example of a monotonic rule:

→ Mother(X,Y)
Mother(X,Y) → Parent(X,Y)
If Mary is the mother of John, then Mary is the parent of John

Rule is of the form:

B1, B2, ---- Bn → A

That is, if B1, B2, ---Bn hold then A holds.

In the case of nonmonotonic reasoning, if we have X and NOT X, we do not treat them as inconsistent as in the case of monotonic reasoning. For example, as discussed in [Antoniou and Harmelan, 2003], consider the example of an apartment that is acceptable to John. That is, in general, John is prepared to rent an apartment unless the apartment has fewer than two bedrooms and does not allow pets. This can be expressed as follows:

→ Acceptable(X)
Bedroom(X,Y), Y<2 → NOT Acceptable(X)
NOT Pets(X) → NOT Acceptable(X)

The first rule states that an apartment is, in general, acceptable to John. The second rule states that if the apartment has fewer than two bedrooms, it is not acceptable to John. The third rule states that if pets are not allowed, then the apartment is not acceptable to John. Note that there could be a contradiction. With nonmonotonic reasoning this is allowed, whereas it is not allowed in monotonic reasoning.

We need rule markup languages for the machine to understand the rules. The various components of logic are expressed in the Rule Markup Language called RuleML, developed for the semantic web. Both monotonic and nonmonotonic rules can be represented in RuleML.

An example representation of the Fact Parent(A), which means "A is a parent" is expressed as follows:

```
<fact>
    <atom>
    <predicate>Parent</predicate>
        <term>
            <const>A</const>
        </term>
    </atom>
</fact>
```

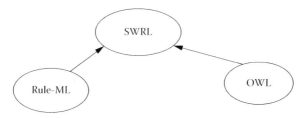

Figure D.6 SWRL components.

D.6.2 *SWRL*

W3C has come up with a new rules language that integrates both OWL and Web Rules and this is SWRL (semantic web rules language). The authors of SWRL state that SWRL extends the set of OWL axioms to include Horn-like rules. This way, Horn-like rules can be combined with an OWL knowledge base. Such a language will have the representational power of OWL and the reasoning power of logic programming. We illustrate SWRL components in Figure D.6.

The authors of SWRL (Horrocks et al.) also state that the proposed rules are in the form of an implication between an antecedent (body) and consequent (head). The intended meaning can be read as: whenever the conditions specified in the antecedent hold, then the conditions specified in the consequent must also hold. An XML syntax is also given for these rules based on RuleML and the OWL XML presentation syntax. Furthermore, an RDF concrete syntax based on the OWL RDF/XML exchange syntax is presented. The rule syntaxes are illustrated with several running examples. Finally, we give usage suggestions and cautions.

The following is a SWRL example that we have taken from the W3C specification of SWTL [Horrocks et al., 2004]. It states that if x1 is the child of x2 and x3 is the brother of x2, then x3 is the uncle of x1. For more details of SWRL, we refer the reader to the W3C specification [Horrocks et al., 2004]. The example uses XML syntax.

```
<ruleml:imp>
  <ruleml:_rlab ruleml:href="#example1"/>
  <ruleml:_body>
```

```
            <swrlx:individualPropertyAtom swrlx:property=
               "hasParent">
               <ruleml:var>x1</ruleml:var>
               <ruleml:var>x2</ruleml:var>
            </swrlx:individualPropertyAtom>
            <swrlx:individualPropertyAtom swrlx:property=
               "hasBrother">
               <ruleml:var>x2</ruleml:var>
               <ruleml:var>x3</ruleml:var>
            </swrlx:individualPropertyAtom>
         </ruleml:_body>
         <ruleml:_head>
            <swrlx:individualPropertyAtom swrlx:property=
               "hasUncle">
               <ruleml:var>x1</ruleml:var>
               <ruleml:var>x3</ruleml:var>
            </swrlx:individualPropertyAtom>
         </ruleml:_head>
      </ruleml:imp>
```

D.7 Semantic Web Services

Semantic web services utilize semantic web technologies. Web services utilize WSDL and SOAP messages, which are based on XML. With semantic web technologies, one could utilize RDF to express semantics in the messages as well as with web services description languages. Ontologies could be utilized for handling heterogeneity. For example, if the words in the messages or service descriptions are ambiguous, then ontologies could resolve these ambiguities. Finally, rule languages such as SWRL could be used for reasoning power for the messages as well as the service descriptions.

As stated in [SWS], the mainstream XML standards for interoperation of web services specify only syntactic interoperability, not the semantic meaning of messages. For example, WSDL can specify the operations available through a web service and the structure of data sent and received, but it cannot specify semantic meaning of the data or semantic constraints on the data. This requires programmers to

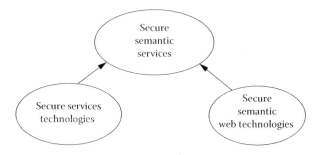

Figure D.7 Semantic web services.

reach specific agreements on the interaction of web services and makes automatic web service composition difficult.

Semantic web services are built around semantic web standards for the interchange of semantic data, which makes it easy for programmers to combine data from different sources and services without losing meaning. Web services can be activated "behind the scenes" when a web browser makes a request to a web server, which then uses various web services to construct a more sophisticated reply than it would have been able to do on its own. Semantic web services can also be used by automatic programs that run without any connection to a web browser. Figure D.7 illustrates the components of semantic web services.

D.8 Summary

This appendix has provided an overview of semantic web technologies and the notion of semantic web services. In particular, we have discussed Tim Berners Lee's technology stack as well as a functional architecture for the semantic web. Then we discussed XML, RDF, and ontologies, as well as web rules for the semantic web. Finally, we discussed semantic web services and how they can make use of semantic web technologies.

There is still a lot of work to be carried out on semantic web services. Much of the development of web services focused on XML technologies. We need to develop standards for using RDF for web services. For example, we need to develop RDF-like languages for web services descriptions. Security has to be integrated into semantic web technologies. Finally, we need to develop semantic web technologies for applications such as multimedia geospatial technologies and video processing. Some of the directions are discussed in [Thuraisingham, 2007] and [Thuraisingham, 2010].

References

[Antoniou and Harmelan, 2003] Antoniou, G., and F. van Harmelan, *A Semantic Web Primer,* MIT Press, 2003.

[Bertino et al., 2004] Bertino, E., B. Carminati, E. Ferrari, B. Thuraisingham, A. Gupta, Selective and Authentic Third-Party Distribution of XML Documents, *IEEE Transactions on Knowledge and Data Engineering,* Vol. 16, No. 10, 2004, pp. 1263–1278.

[Hendler, 2001] Hendler, J., Agents and the Semantic Web, *IEEE Intelligent Systems Journal,* Vol. 16, No. 2, 2001, pp. 30–37.

[Horrocks et al., 2004] Horrocks, I., P. F. Patel-Schneider, H. Boley, S. Tabet, B. Grosof, M. Dean, *A Semantic Web Rule Language Combining OWL and RuleML,* National Research Council of Canada, Network Inference, and Stanford University, http://www.w3.org/Submission/SWRL/#1

[Laurent, 2000] Laurent, S. S., *XML: A Primer,* Power Books Publishing, 2000.

[Lee and Hendler, 2001] Lee, T. B., and J. Hendler, The Semantic Web, *Scientific American,* May 2001, pp. 35–43.

[Lloyd, 1987] Lloyd, J., *Logic Programming,* Springer, 1987.

[SWS] http://en.wikipedia.org/wiki/Semantic_Web_Services

[Thuraisingham, 2005] Thuraisingham, B., *Database and Applications Security: Integrating Data Management and Information Security,* CRC Press, 2005.

[Thuraisingham, 2007] Thuraisingham, B., *Building Trustworthy Semantic Webs,* CRC Press, 2007.

[Thuraisingham, 2010] Thuraisingham, B., *Secure Semantic Service-Oriented Systems,* CRC Press, 2010.

Index

A